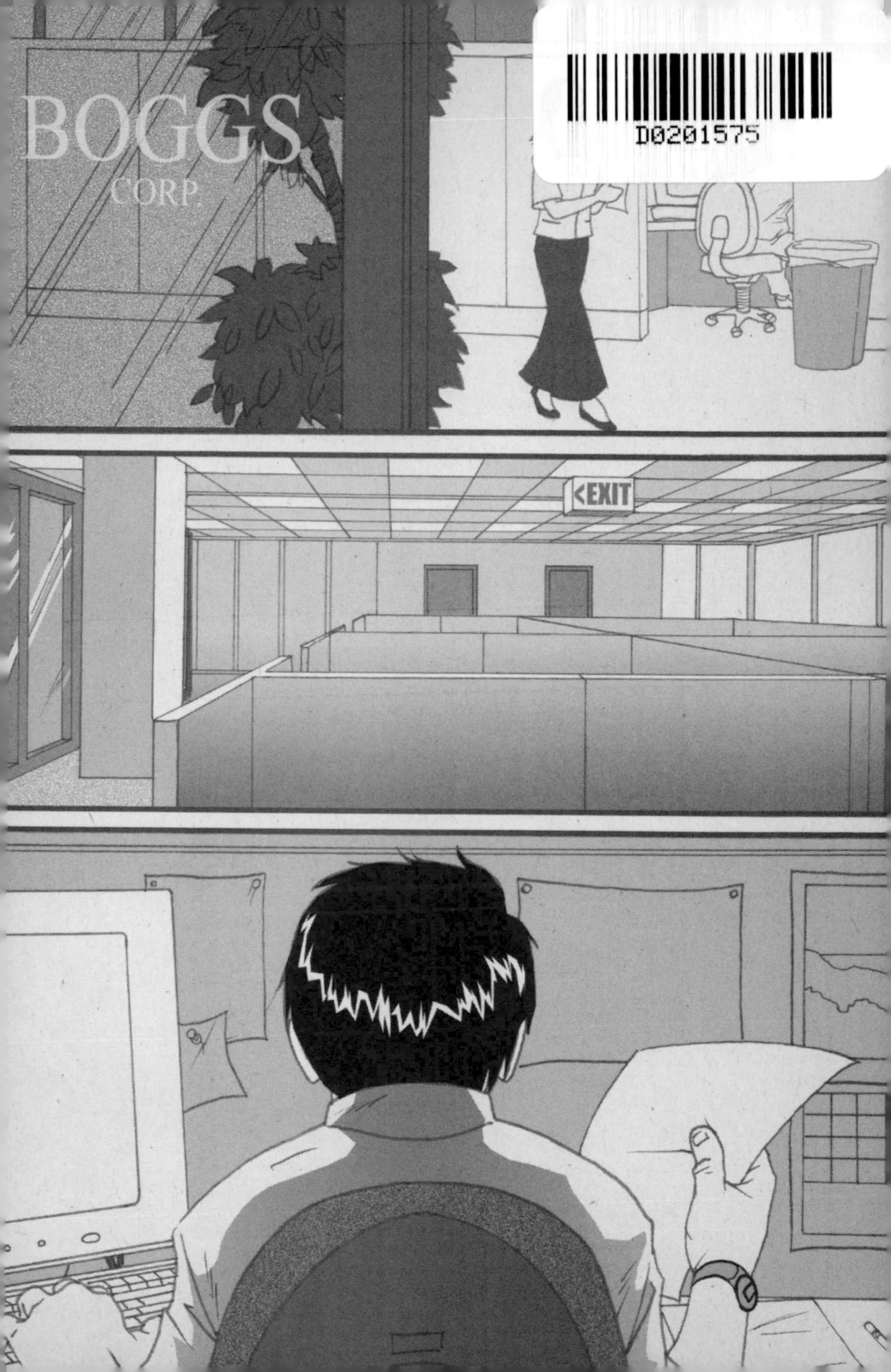
BOGGS
CORP.
EXIT

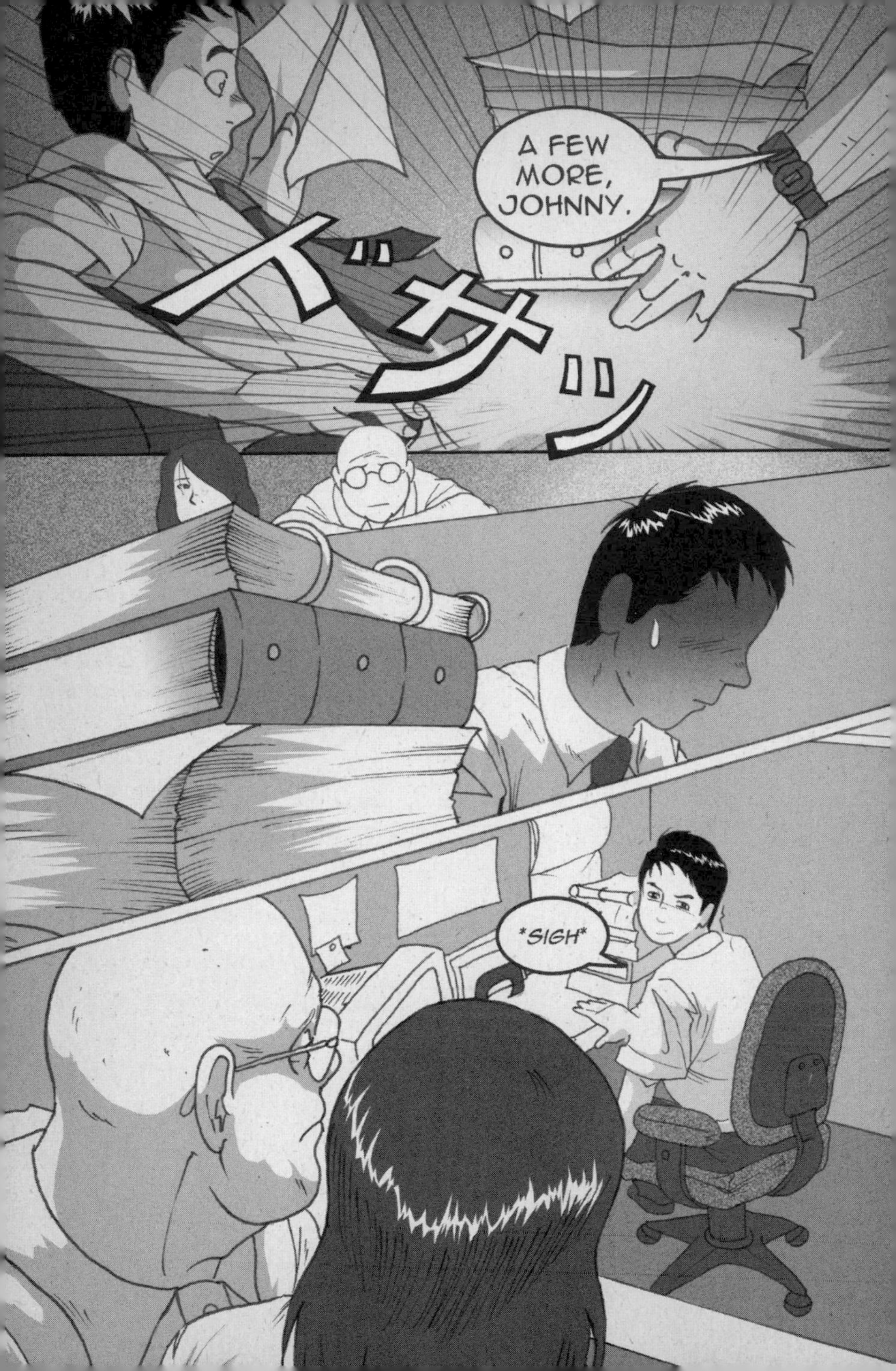
A FEW MORE, JOHNNY.
ドサッ
SIGH

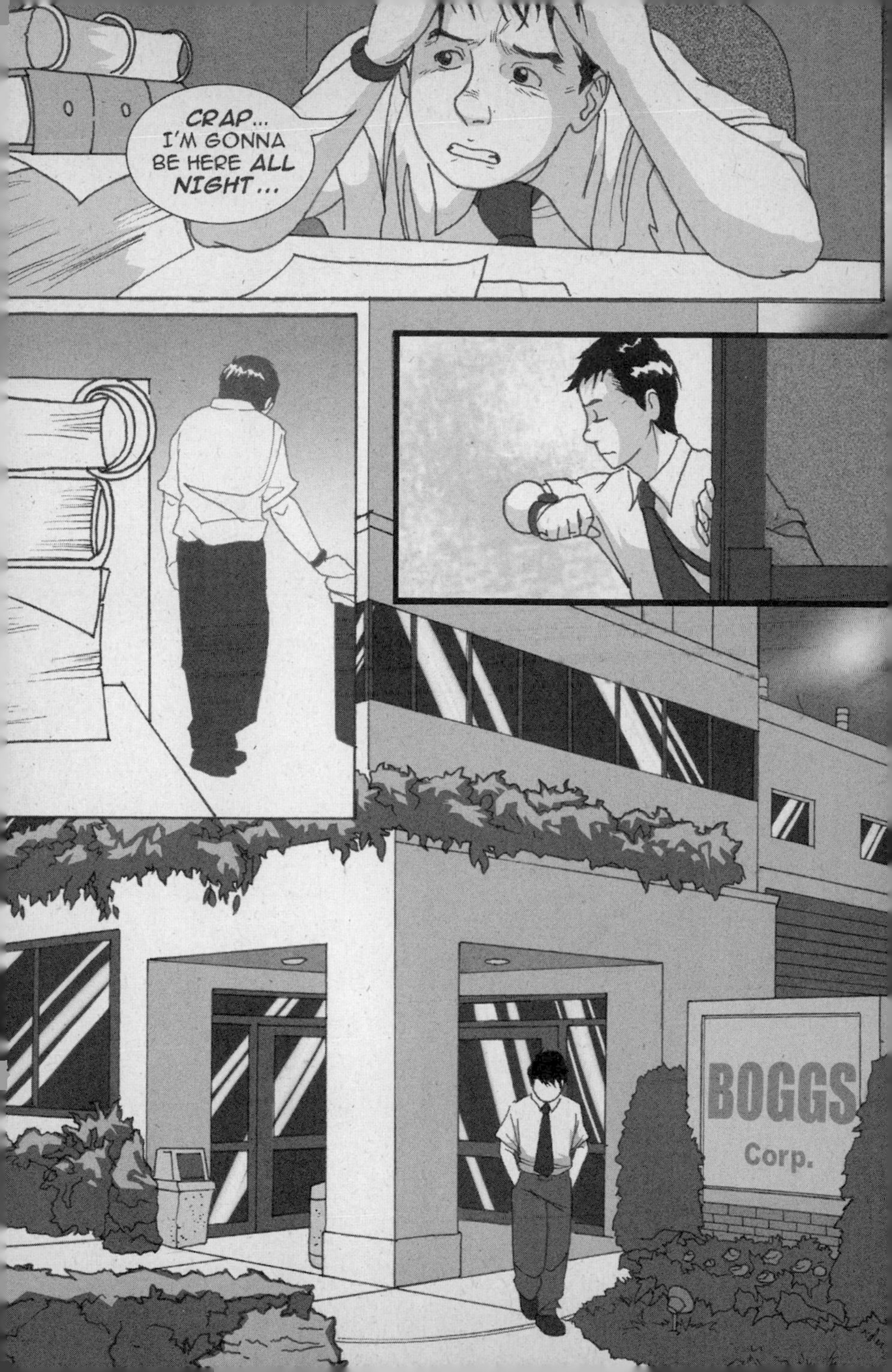
CRAP... I'M GONNA BE HERE ALL NIGHT...
BOGGS Corp.

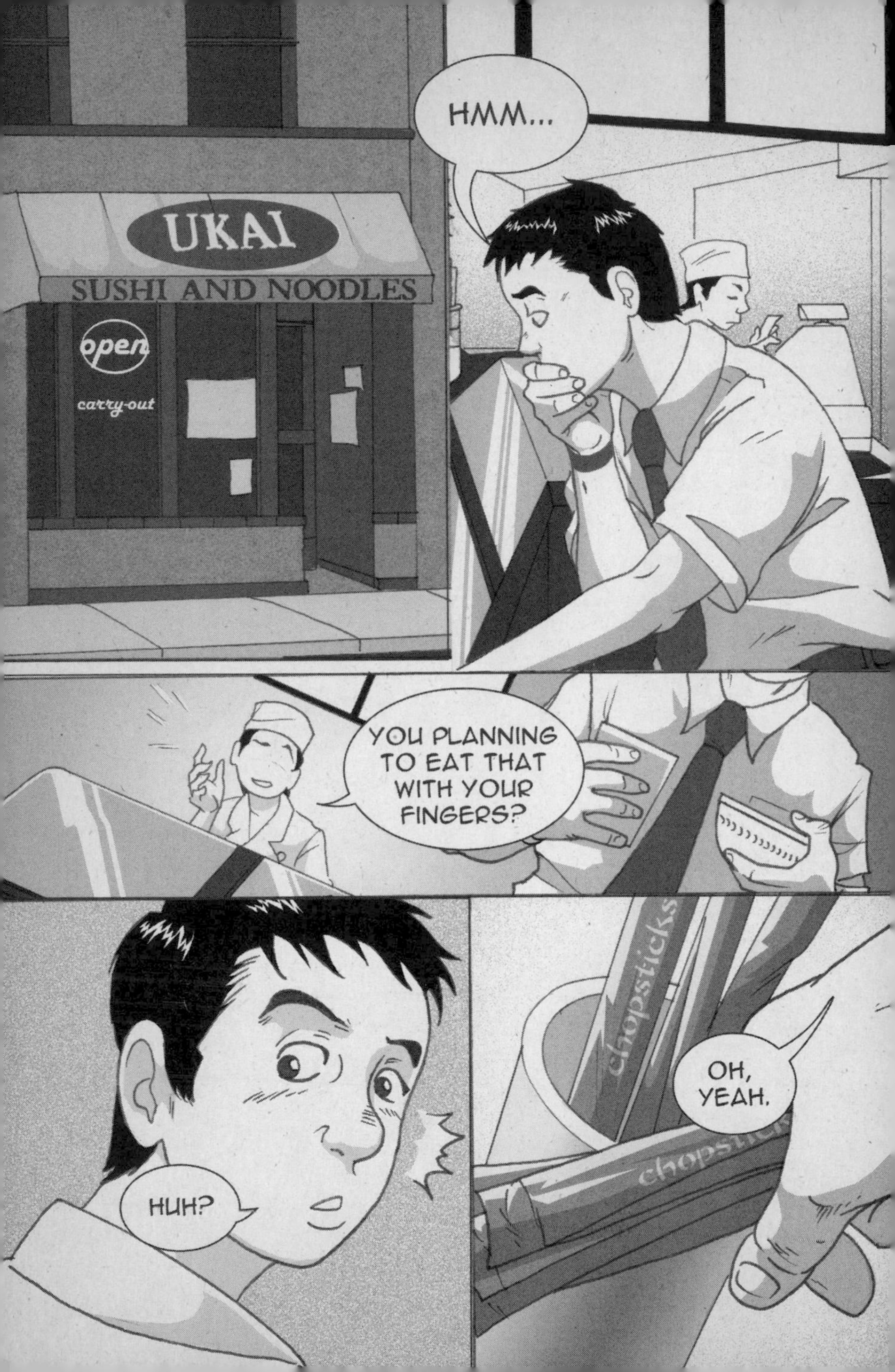
UKAI
SUSHI AND NOODLES
open
carry-out
HMM...
YOU PLANNING TO EAT THAT WITH YOUR FINGERS?
HUH?
chopsticks
OH, YEAH.
chopsticks

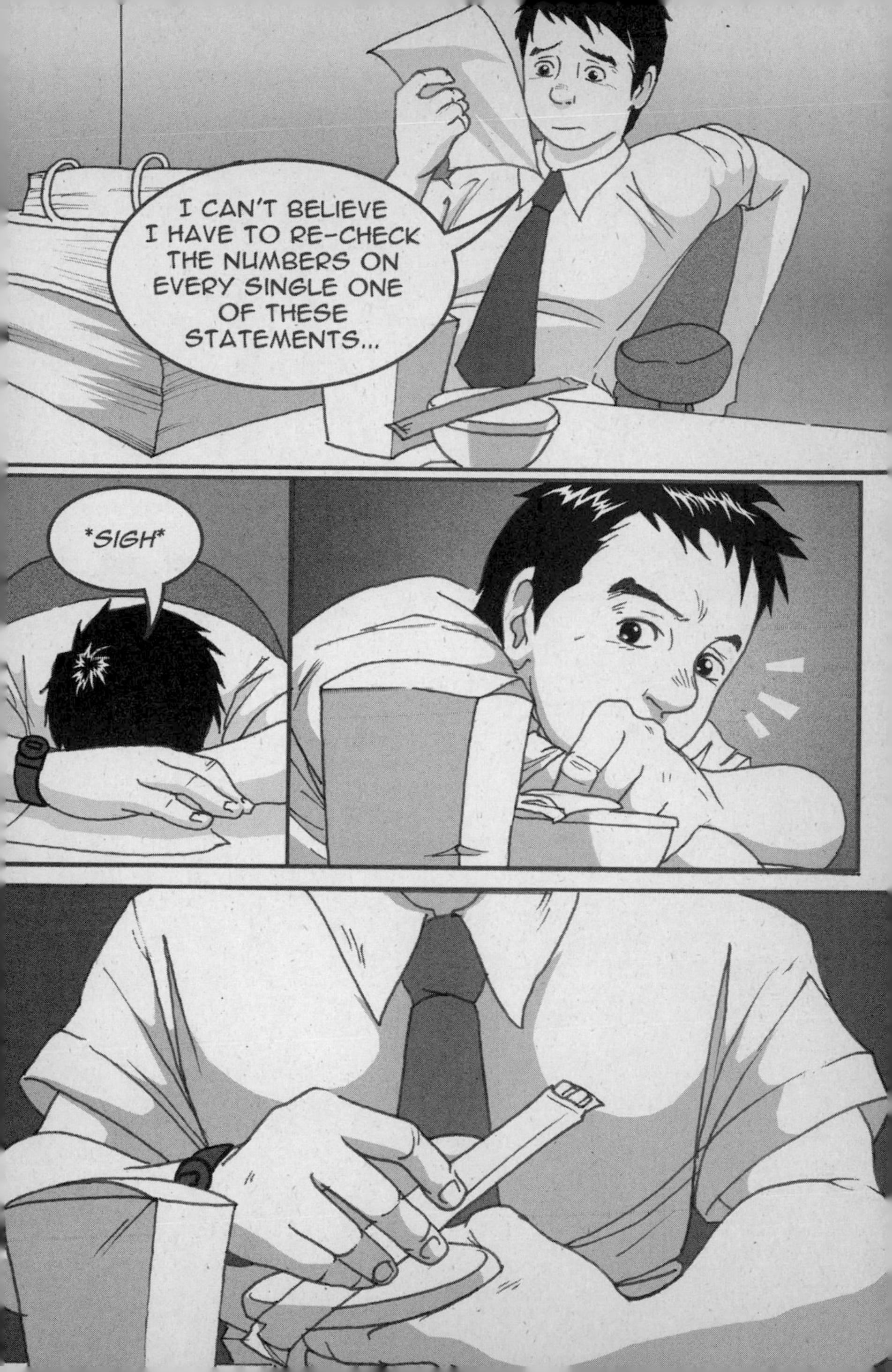
I CAN'T BELIEVE I HAVE TO RE-CHECK THE NUMBERS ON EVERY SINGLE ONE OF THESE STATEMENTS...
SIGH

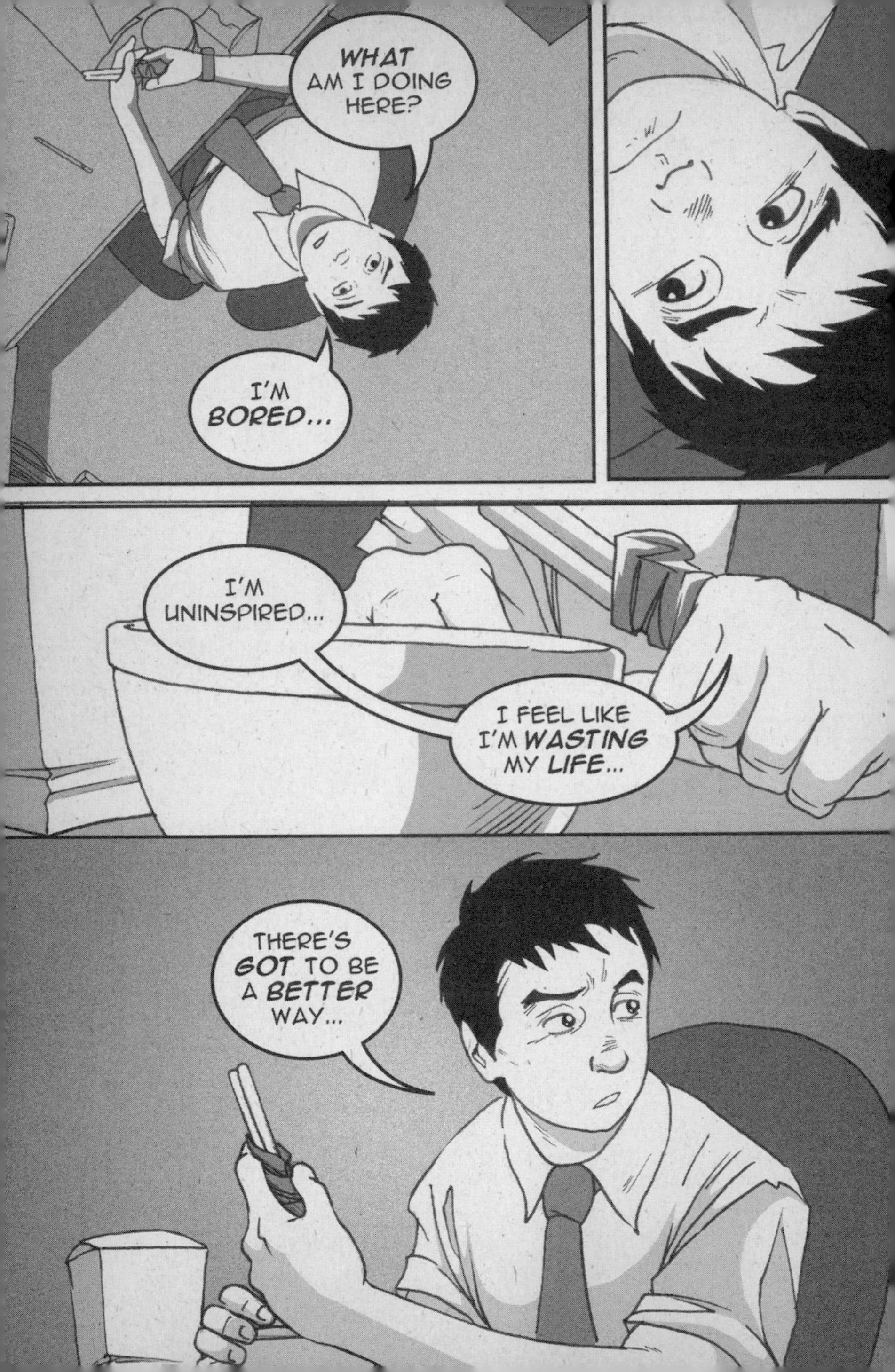
WHAT AM I DOING HERE?
I'M BORED...
I'M UNINSPIRED...
I FEEL LIKE I'M WASTING MY LIFE...
THERE'S GOT TO BE A BETTER WAY...

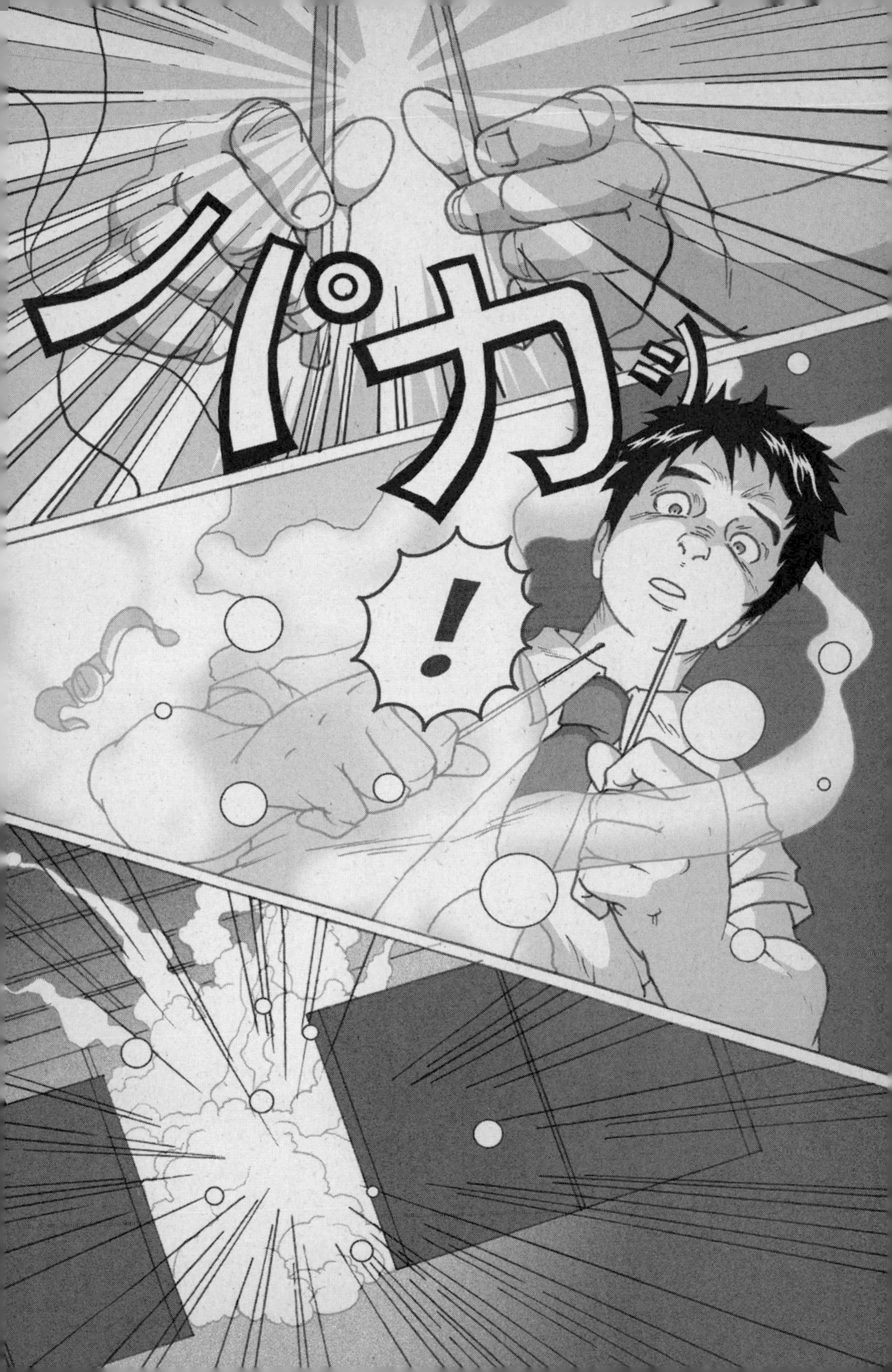
パカッ
!

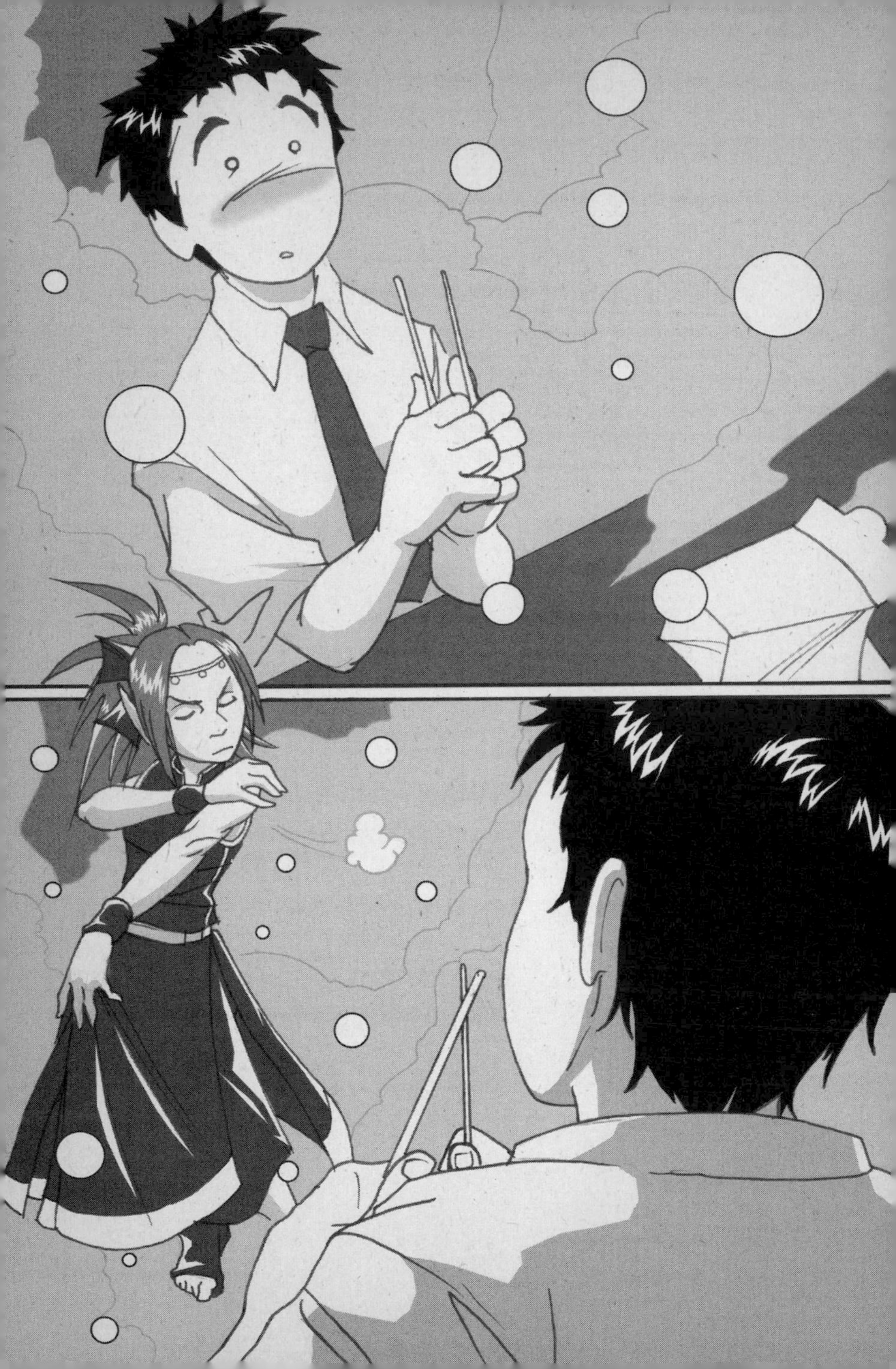

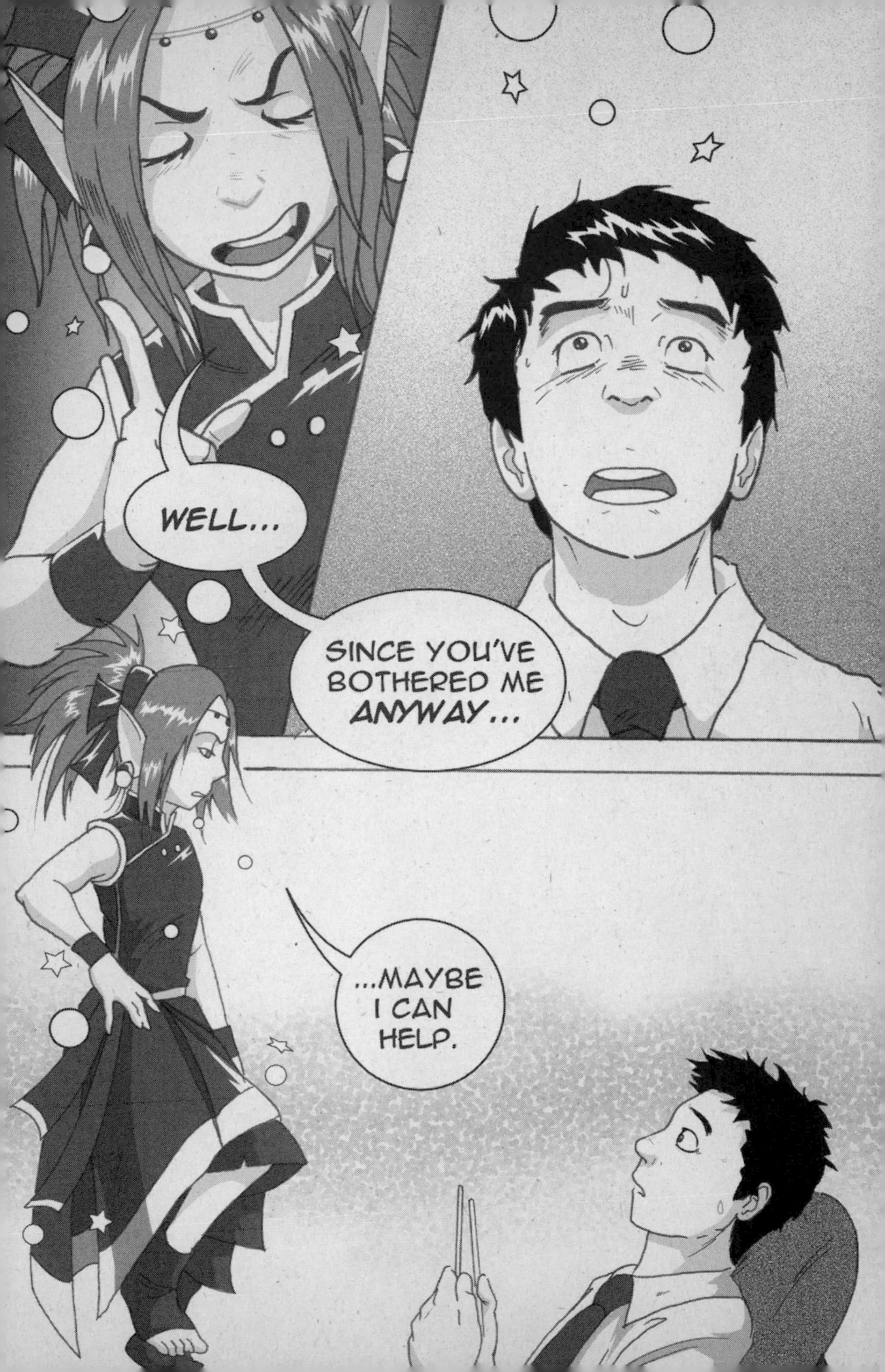
WELL...
SINCE YOU'VE BOTHERED ME ANYWAY...
...MAYBE I CAN HELP.

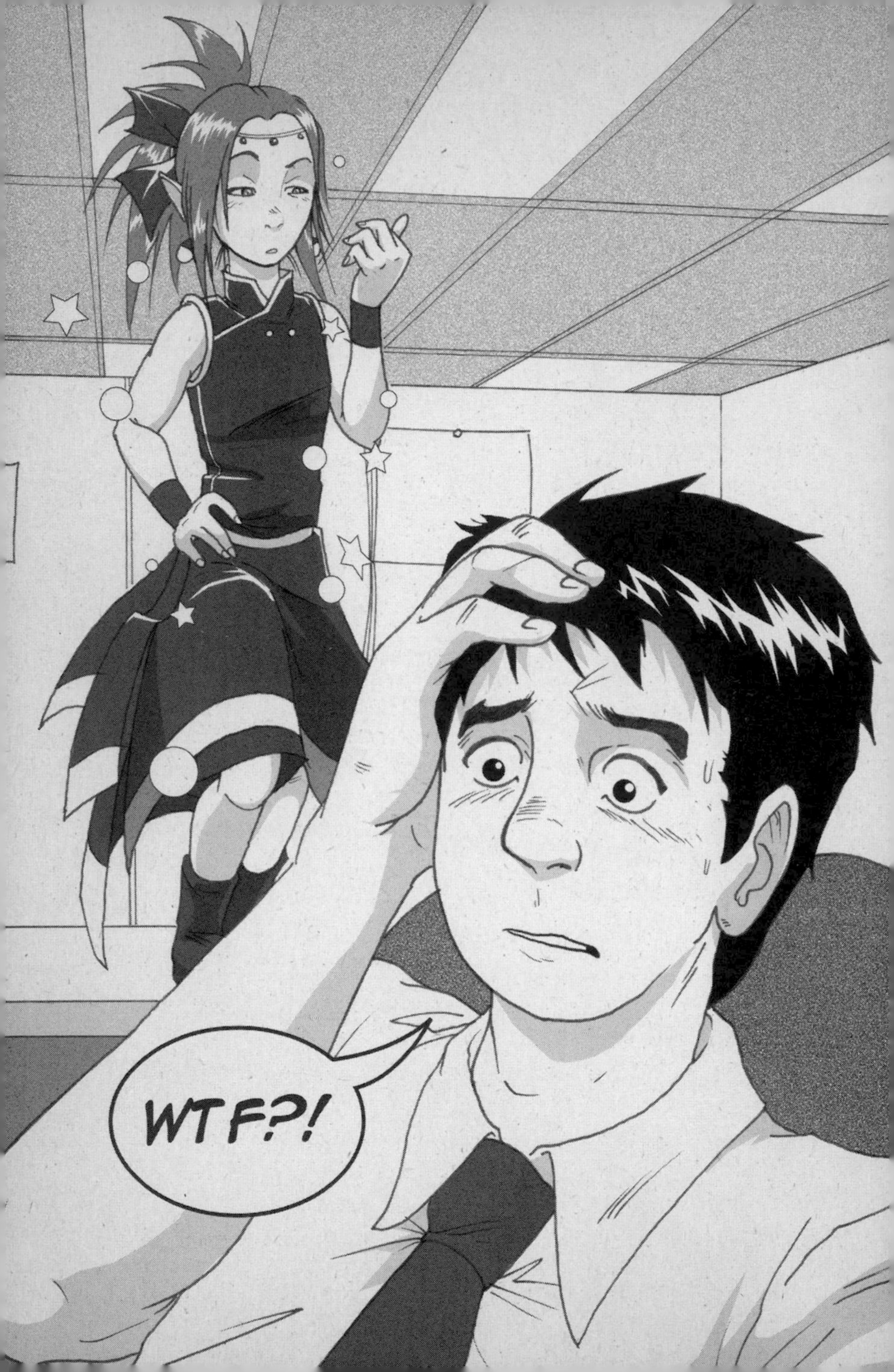
WTF?!

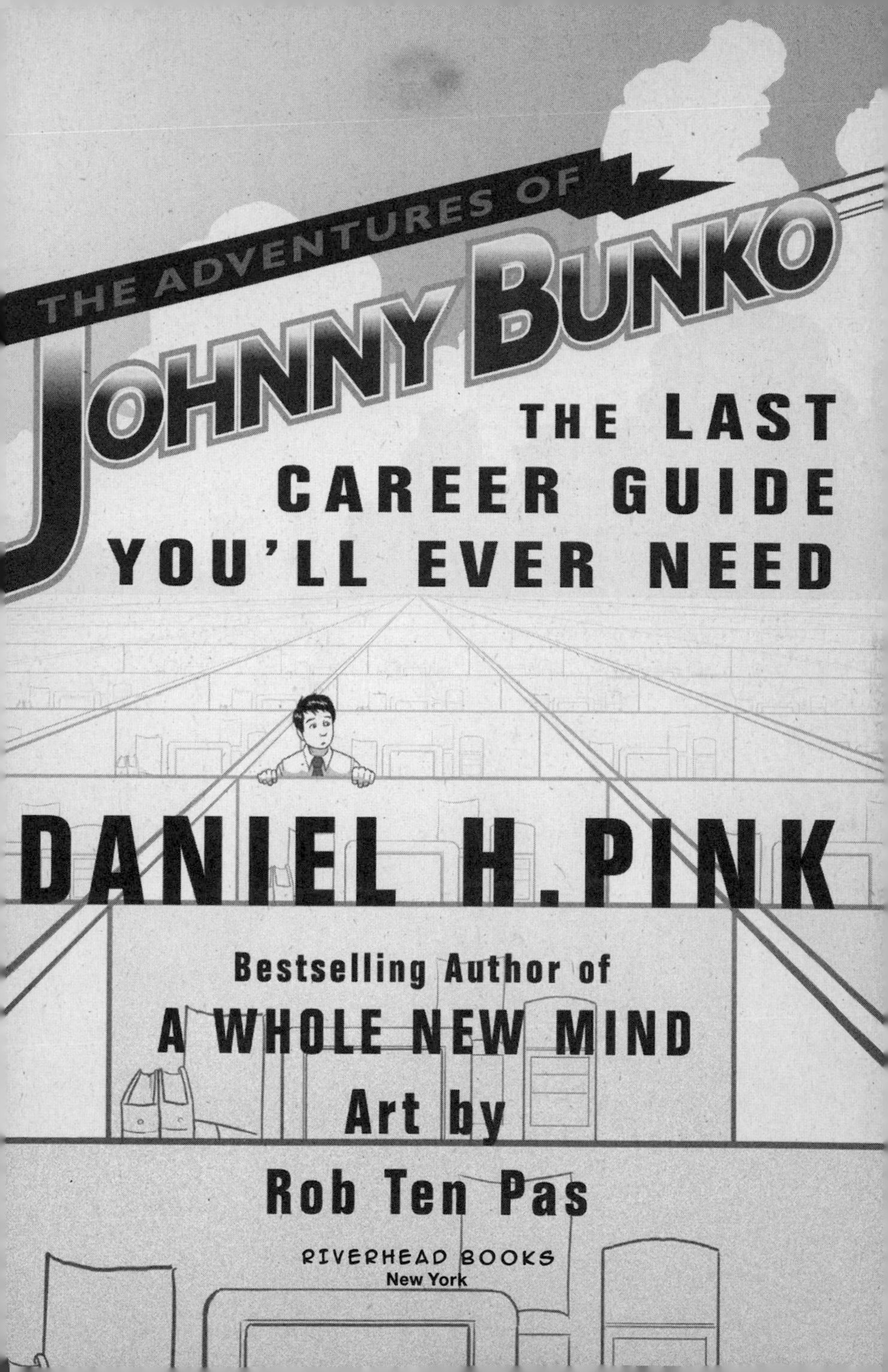

The Adventures of Johnny Bunko

The Last Career Guide You'll Ever Need

Daniel H. Pink

Bestselling Author of
A Whole New Mind

Art by
Rob Ten Pas

RIVERHEAD BOOKS
New York

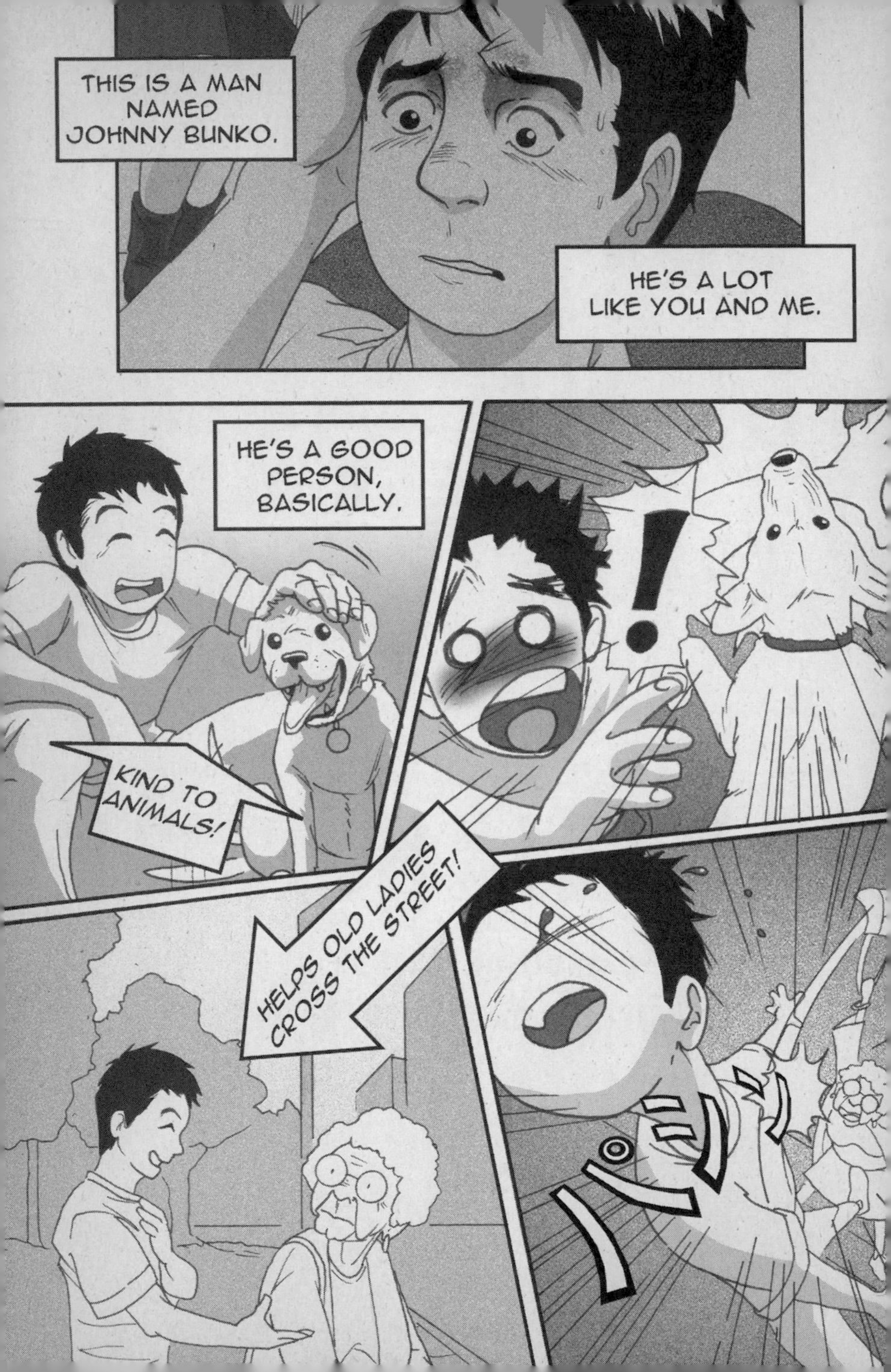
THIS IS A MAN NAMED JOHNNY BUNKO.
HE'S A LOT LIKE YOU AND ME.
HE'S A GOOD PERSON, BASICALLY.
KIND TO ANIMALS!
HELPS OLD LADIES CROSS THE STREET!

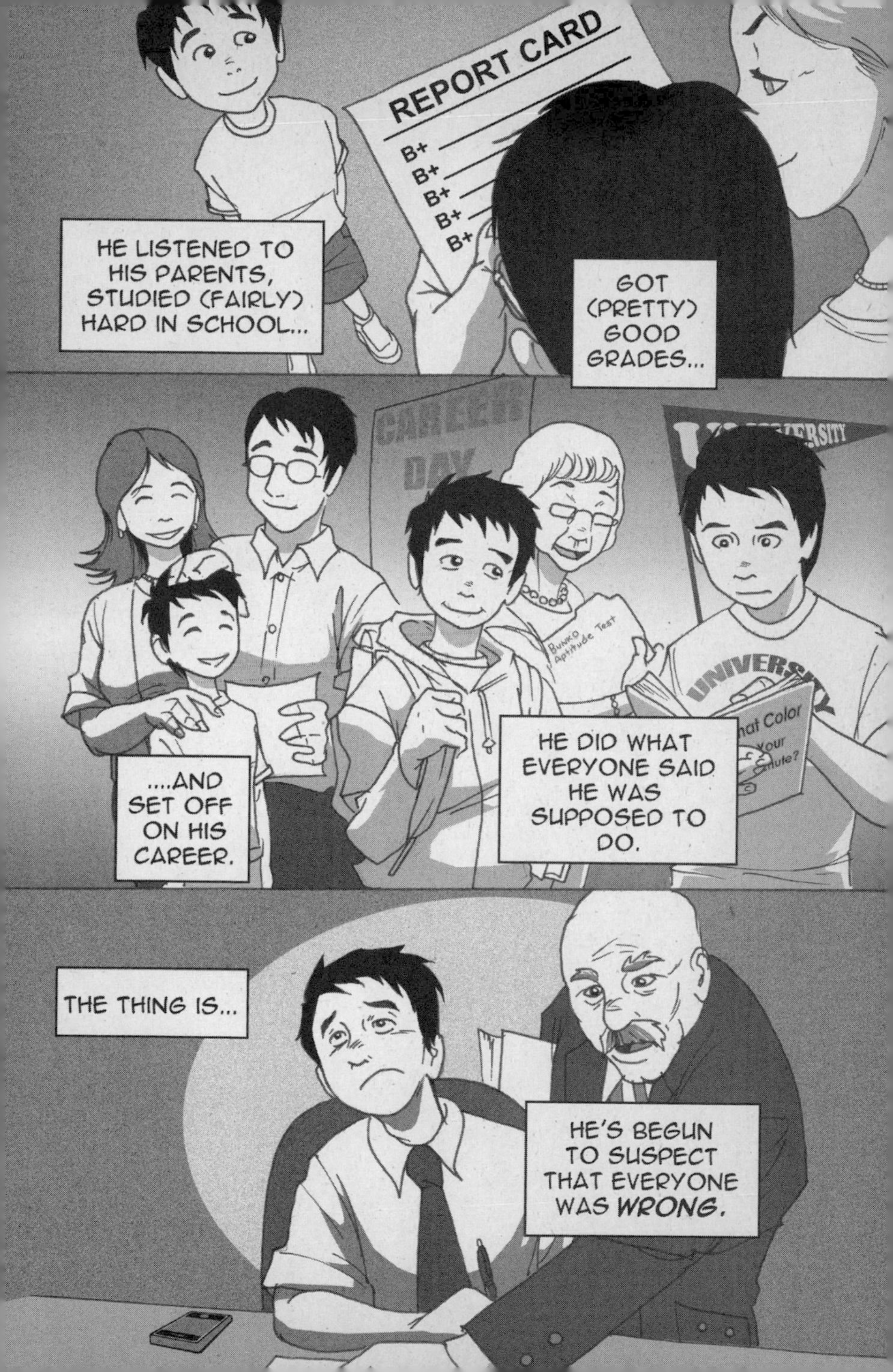

REPORT CARD
B+
B+
B+
B+
B+
HE LISTENED TO HIS PARENTS, STUDIED (FAIRLY) HARD IN SCHOOL...
GOT (PRETTY) GOOD GRADES...
Bunko Aptitude Test
....AND SET OFF ON HIS CAREER.
HE DID WHAT EVERYONE SAID HE WAS SUPPOSED TO DO.
THE THING IS...
HE'S BEGUN TO SUSPECT THAT EVERYONE WAS *WRONG*.

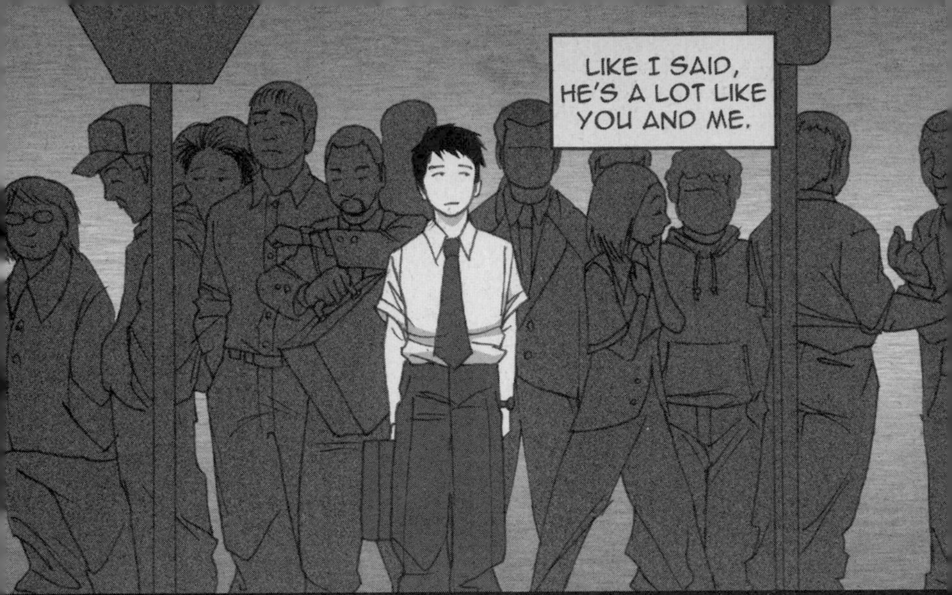
LIKE I SAID, HE'S A LOT LIKE YOU AND ME.

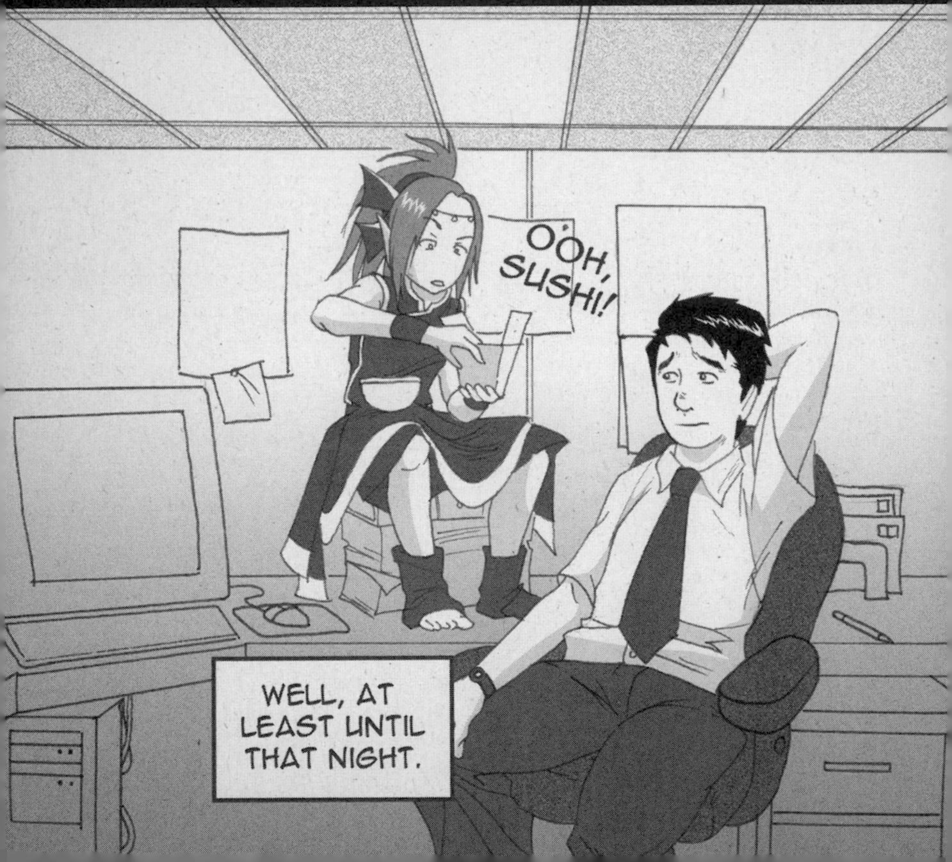
OOH, SUSHI!
WELL, AT LEAST UNTIL THAT NIGHT.

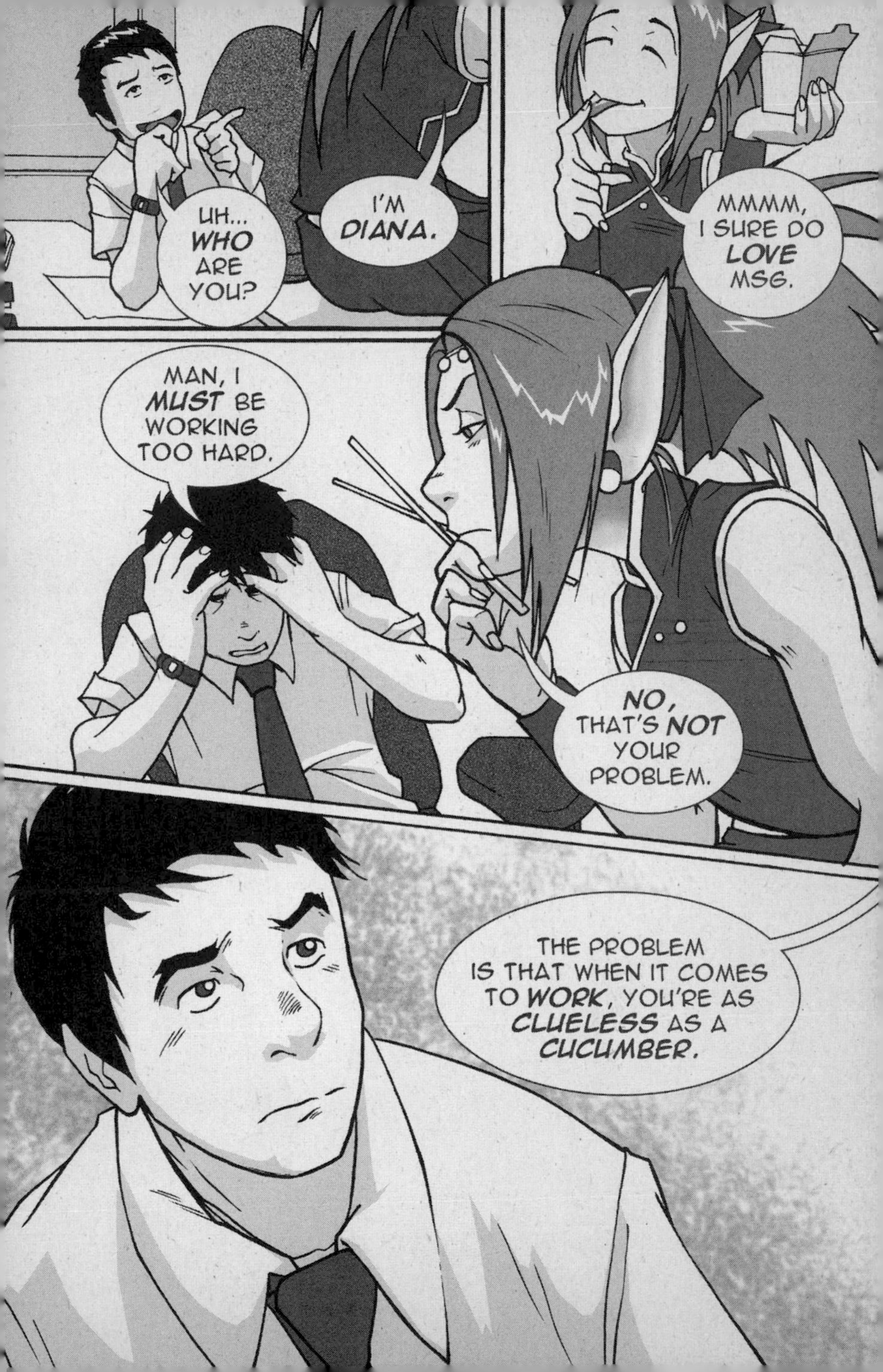
UH... WHO ARE YOU?
I'M DIANA.
MMMM, I SURE DO LOVE MSG.
MAN, I MUST BE WORKING TOO HARD.
NO, THAT'S NOT YOUR PROBLEM.
THE PROBLEM IS THAT WHEN IT COMES TO WORK, YOU'RE AS CLUELESS AS A CUCUMBER.

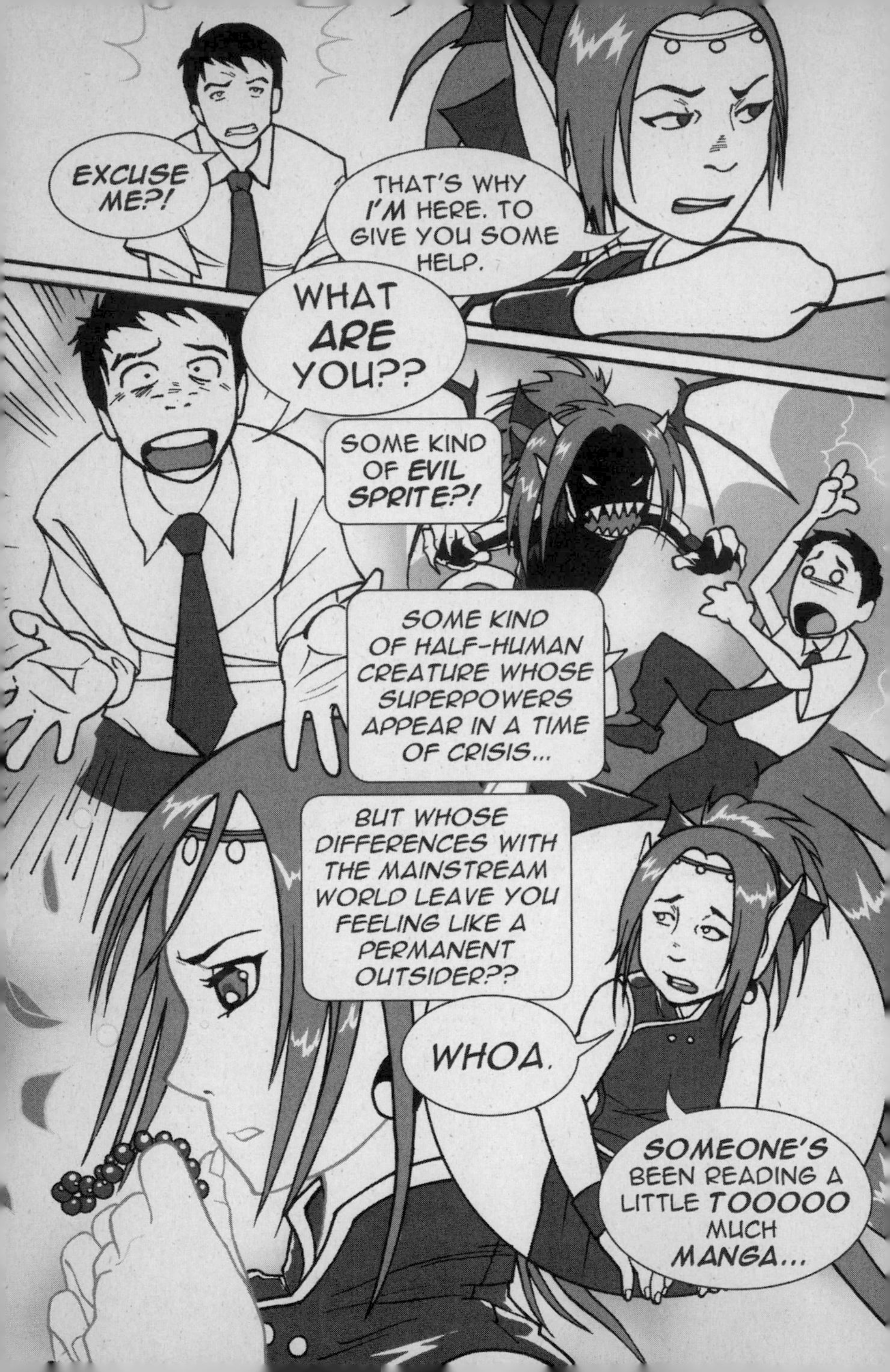
EXCUSE ME?!
THAT'S WHY I'M HERE. TO GIVE YOU SOME HELP.
WHAT ARE YOU??
SOME KIND OF EVIL SPRITE?!
SOME KIND OF HALF-HUMAN CREATURE WHOSE SUPERPOWERS APPEAR IN A TIME OF CRISIS...
BUT WHOSE DIFFERENCES WITH THE MAINSTREAM WORLD LEAVE YOU FEELING LIKE A PERMANENT OUTSIDER??
WHOA.
SOMEONE'S BEEN READING A LITTLE TOOOOO MUCH MANGA...

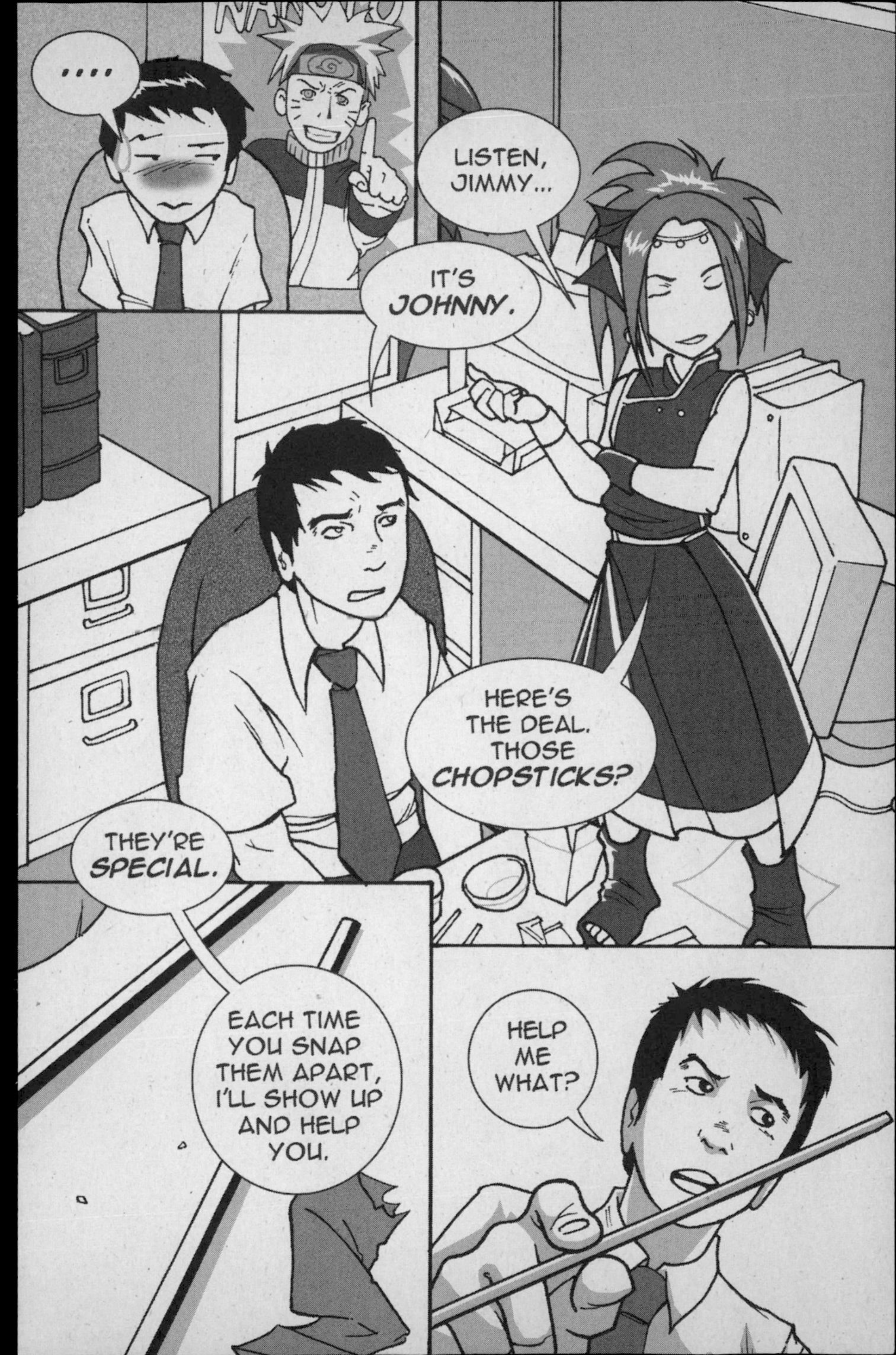

NARUTO
....
LISTEN, JIMMY...
IT'S JOHNNY.
HERE'S THE DEAL. THOSE CHOPSTICKS?
THEY'RE SPECIAL.
EACH TIME YOU SNAP THEM APART, I'LL SHOW UP AND HELP YOU.
HELP ME WHAT?

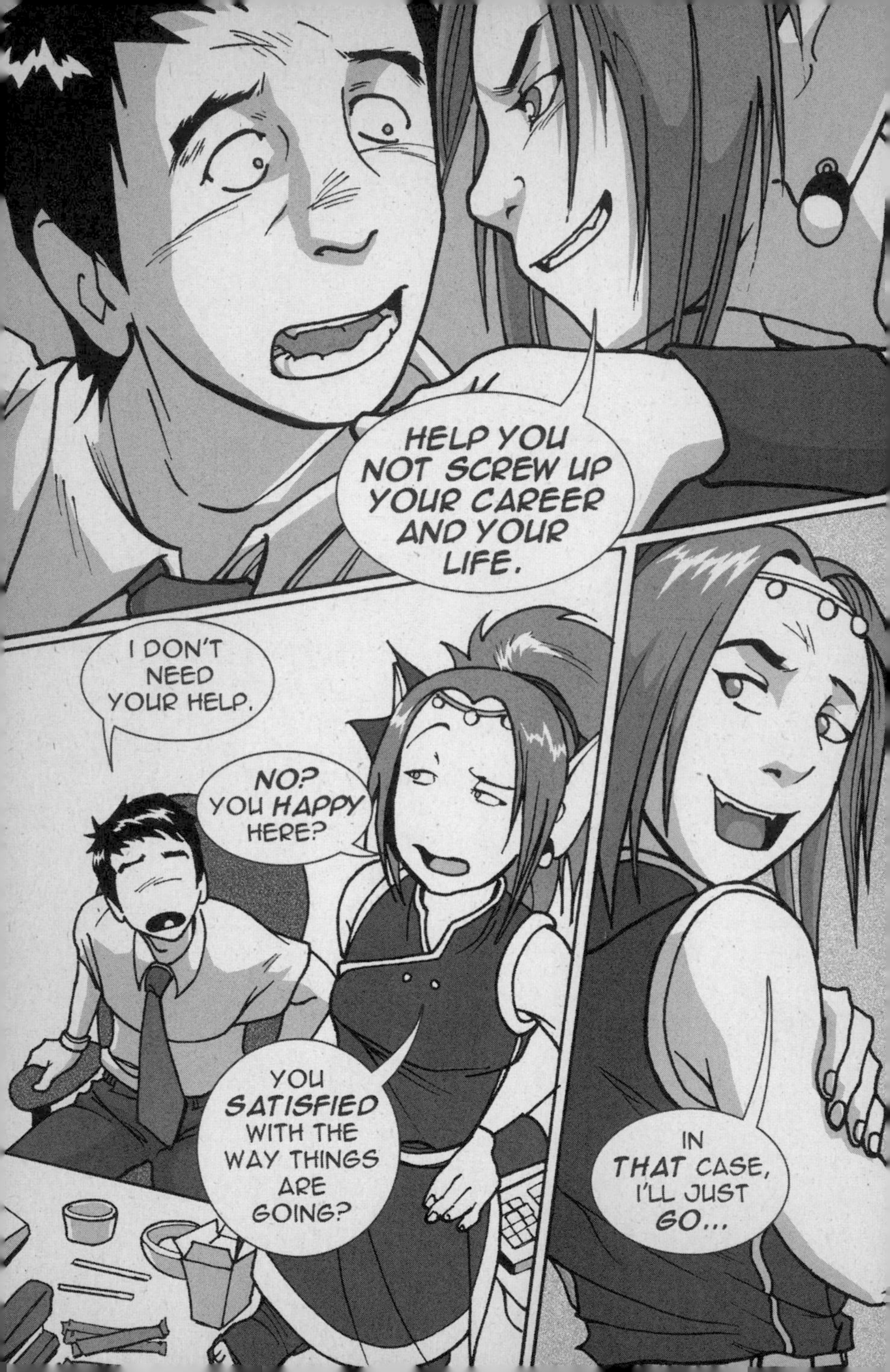
HELP YOU NOT SCREW UP YOUR CAREER AND YOUR LIFE.
I DON'T NEED YOUR HELP.
NO? YOU HAPPY HERE?
YOU SATISFIED WITH THE WAY THINGS ARE GOING?
IN THAT CASE, I'LL JUST GO...

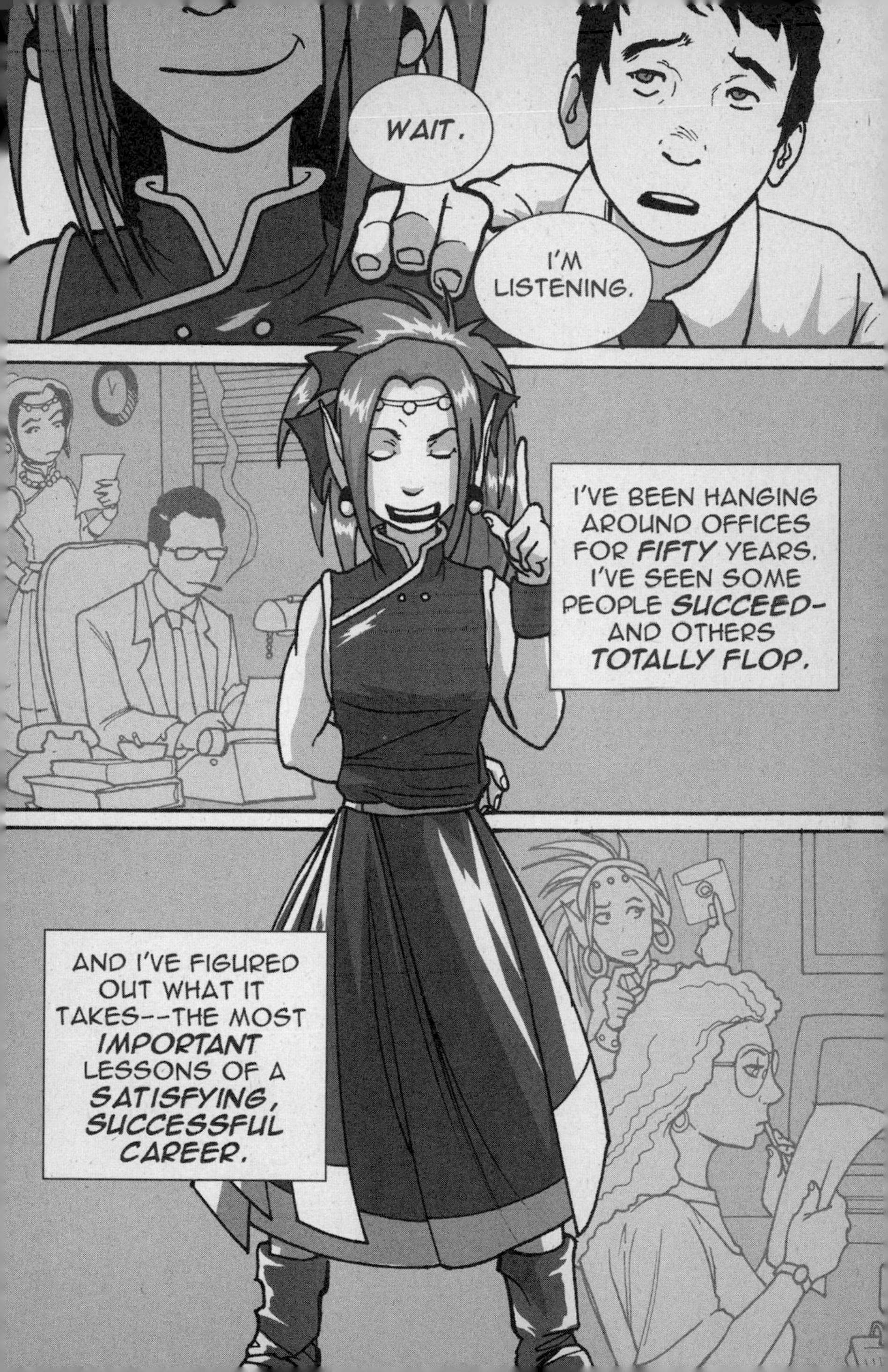
WAIT.
I'M LISTENING.
I'VE BEEN HANGING AROUND OFFICES FOR FIFTY YEARS. I'VE SEEN SOME PEOPLE SUCCEED-AND OTHERS TOTALLY FLOP.
AND I'VE FIGURED OUT WHAT IT TAKES--THE MOST IMPORTANT LESSONS OF A SATISFYING, SUCCESSFUL CAREER.

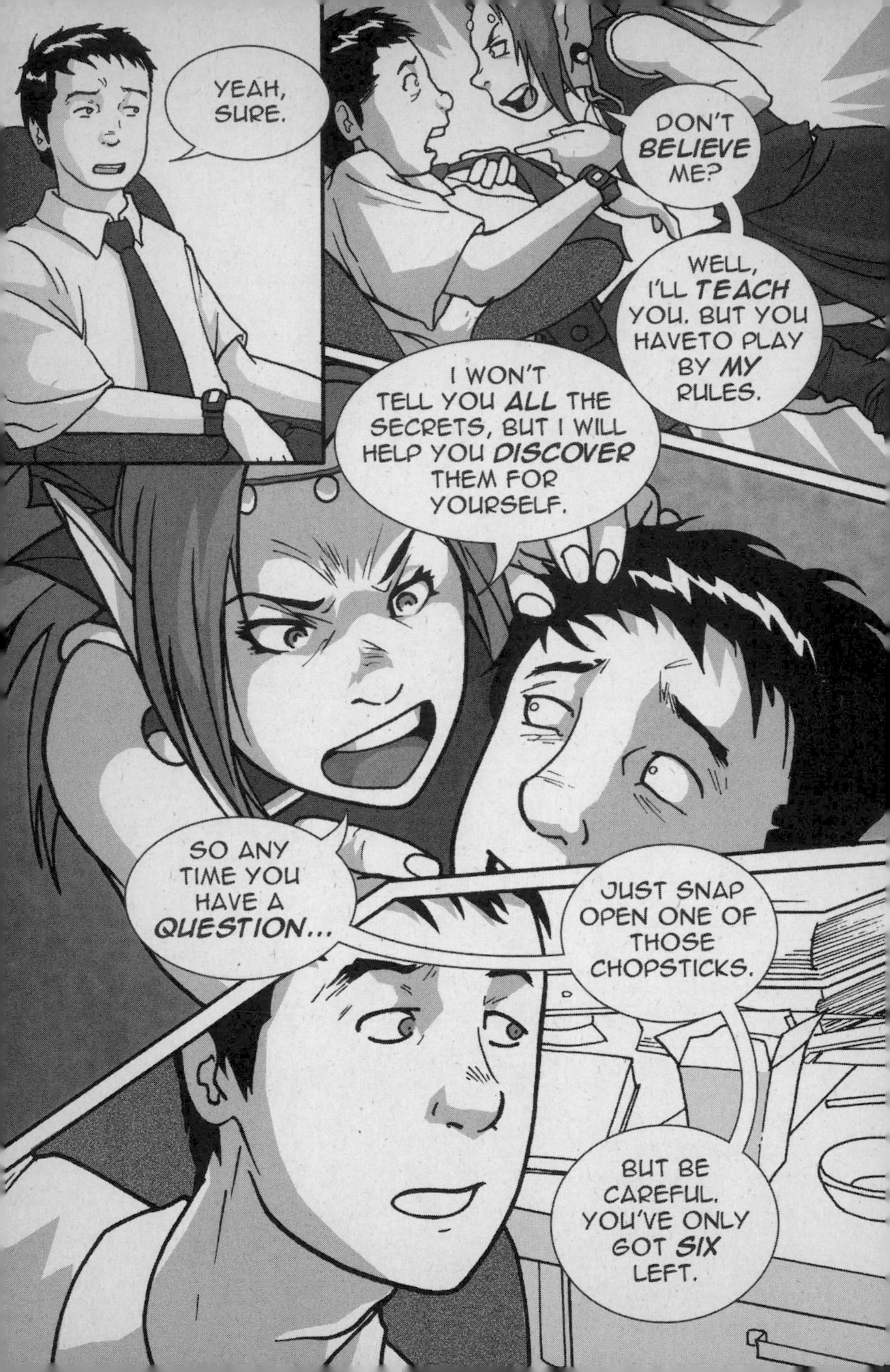
YEAH, SURE.
DON'T BELIEVE ME?
WELL, I'LL TEACH YOU. BUT YOU HAVETO PLAY BY MY RULES.
I WON'T TELL YOU ALL THE SECRETS, BUT I WILL HELP YOU DISCOVER THEM FOR YOURSELF.
SO ANY TIME YOU HAVE A QUESTION...
JUST SNAP OPEN ONE OF THOSE CHOPSTICKS.
BUT BE CAREFUL. YOU'VE ONLY GOT SIX LEFT.

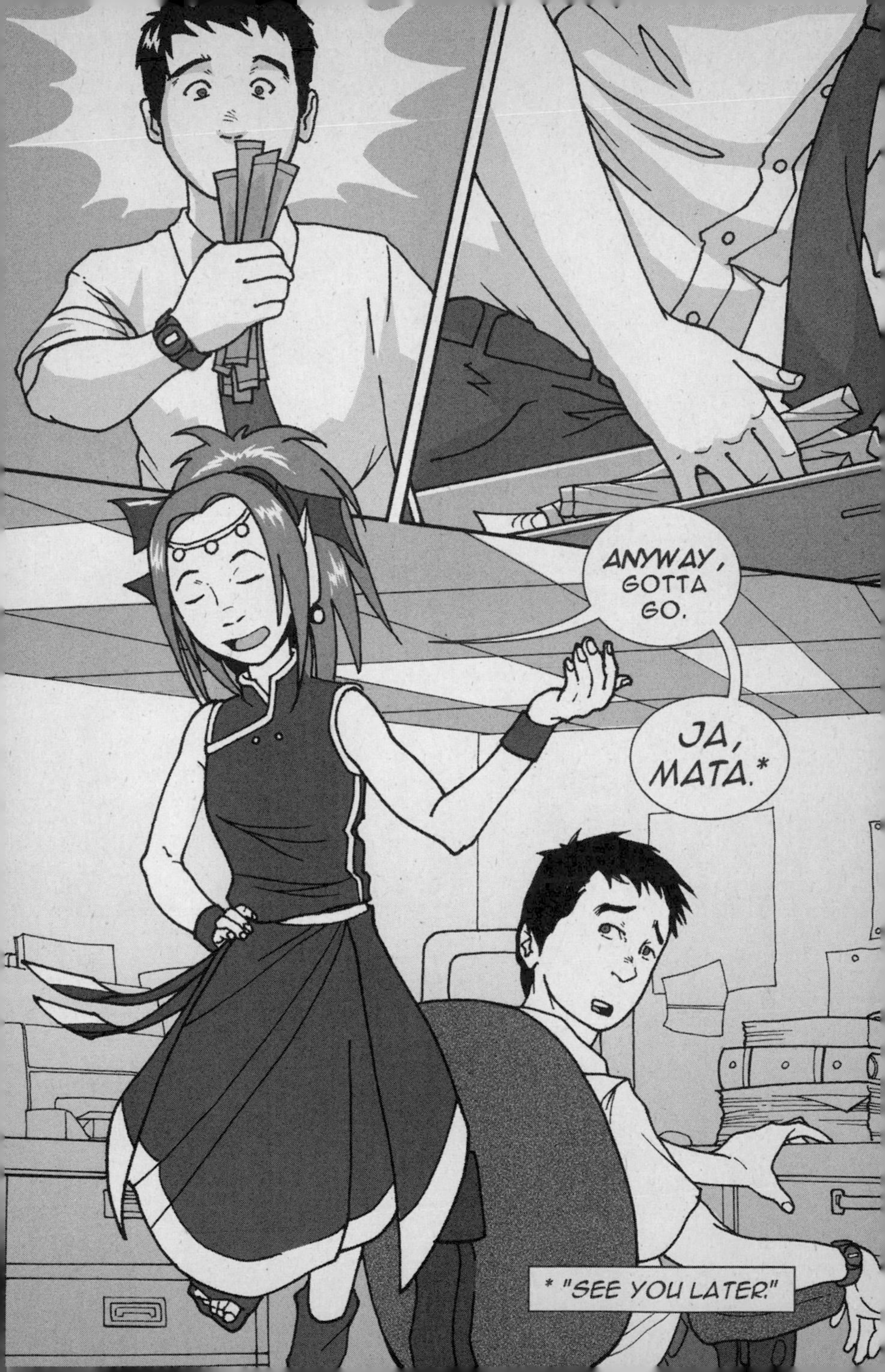
ANYWAY, GOTTA GO.
JA, MATA.*
* "SEE YOU LATER."

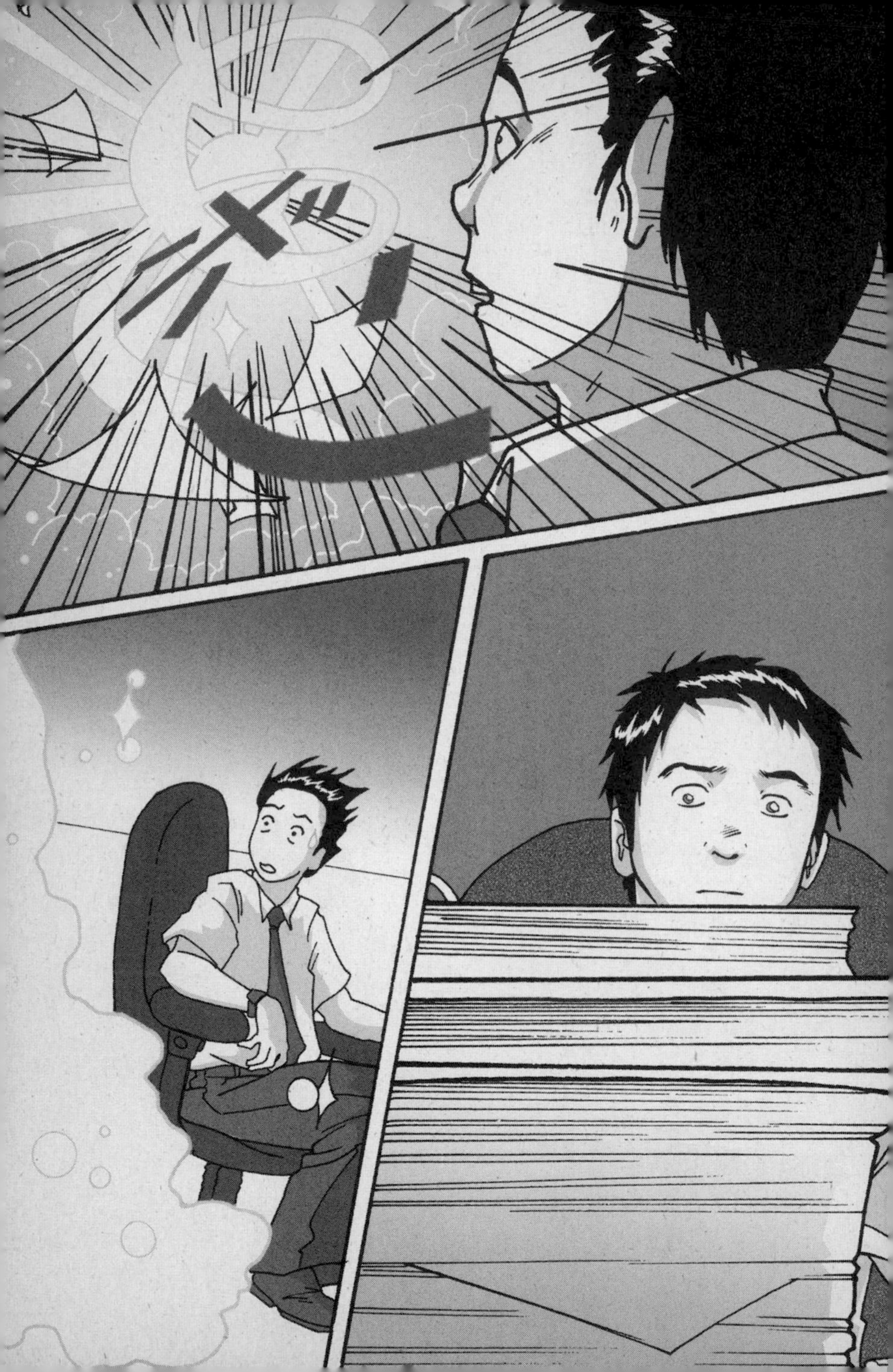

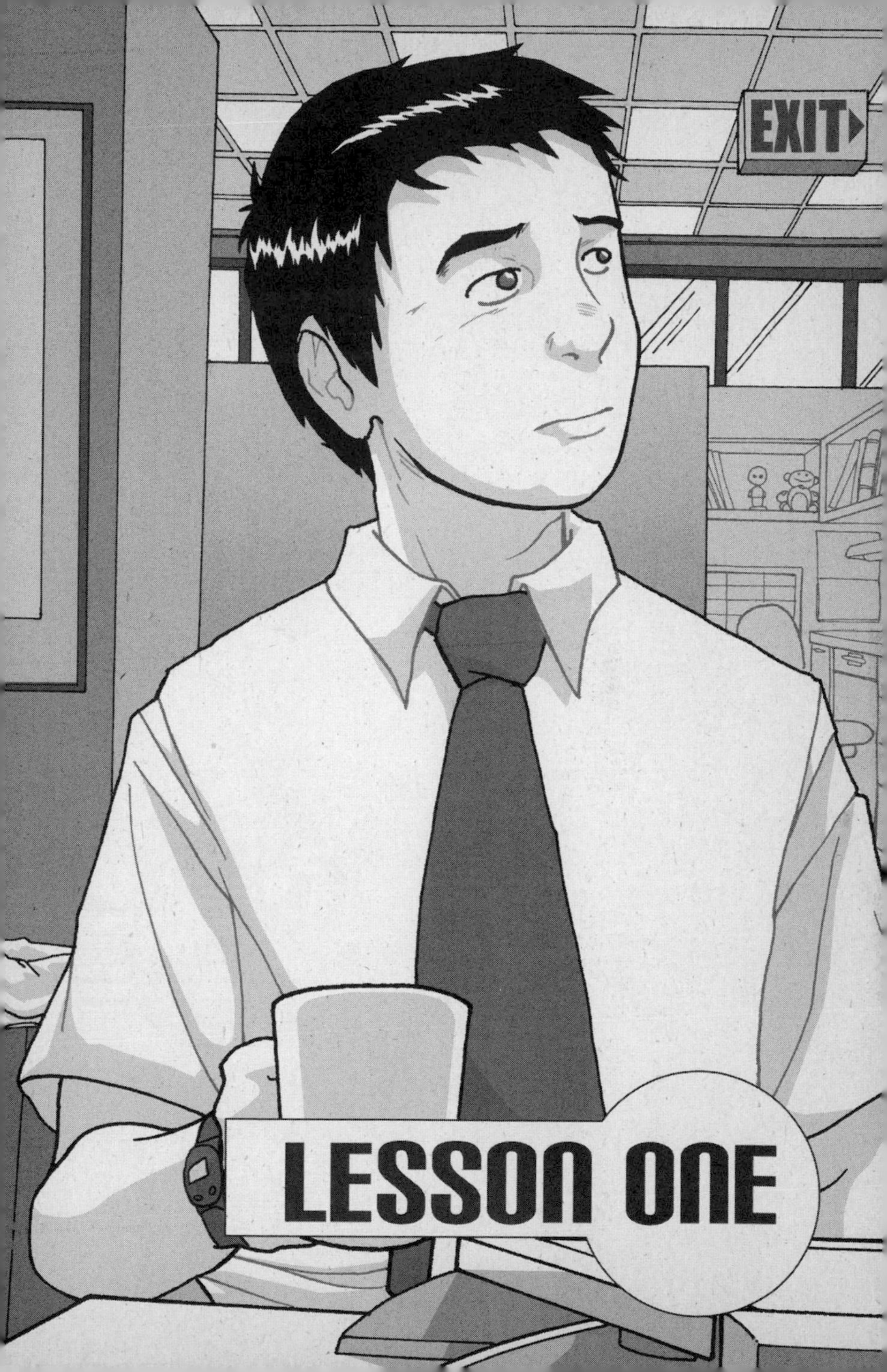
EXIT
LESSON ONE

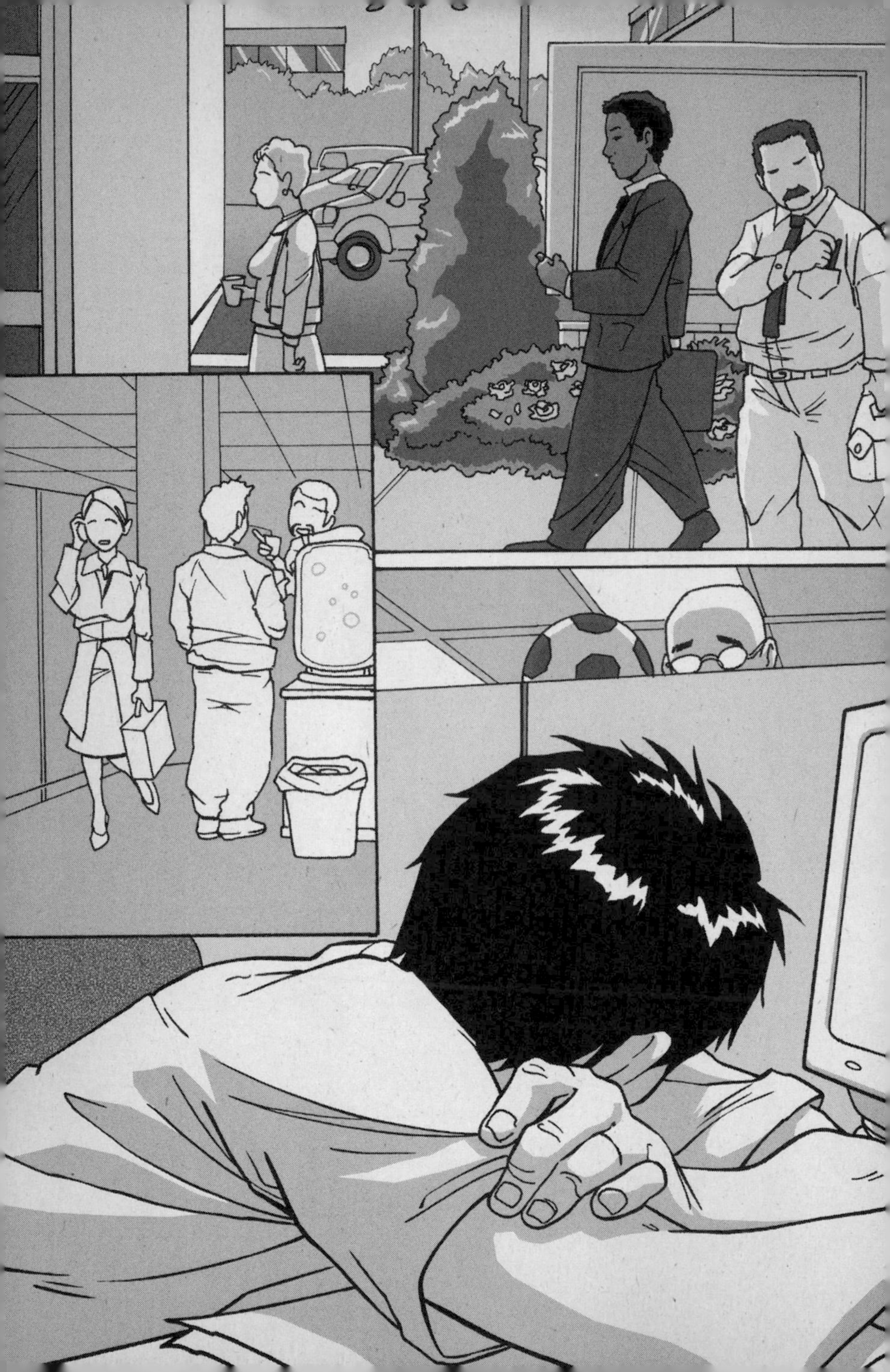

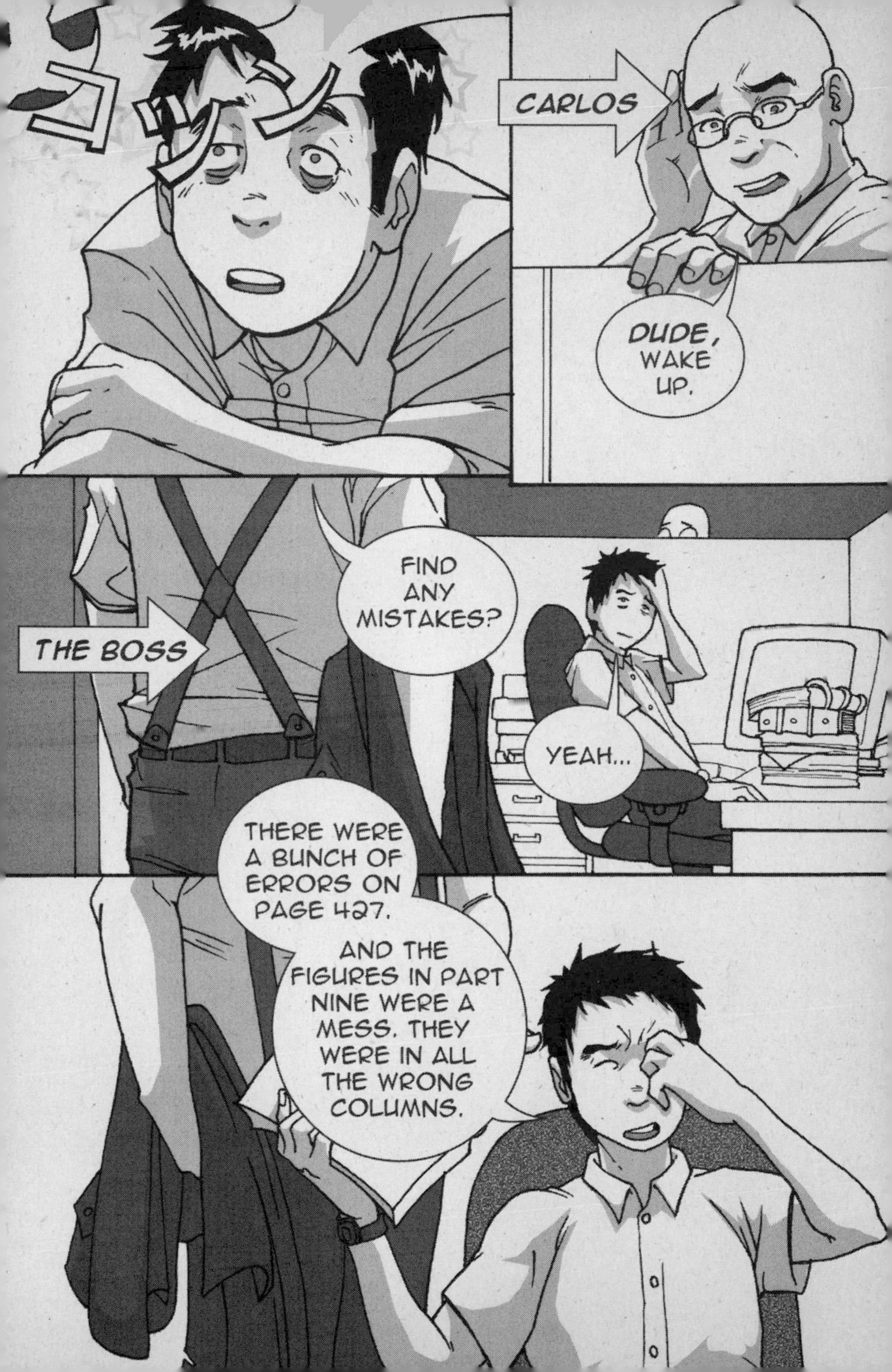
CARLOS
DUDE, WAKE UP.
FIND ANY MISTAKES?
THE BOSS
YEAH...
THERE WERE A BUNCH OF ERRORS ON PAGE 427.
AND THE FIGURES IN PART NINE WERE A MESS. THEY WERE IN ALL THE WRONG COLUMNS.

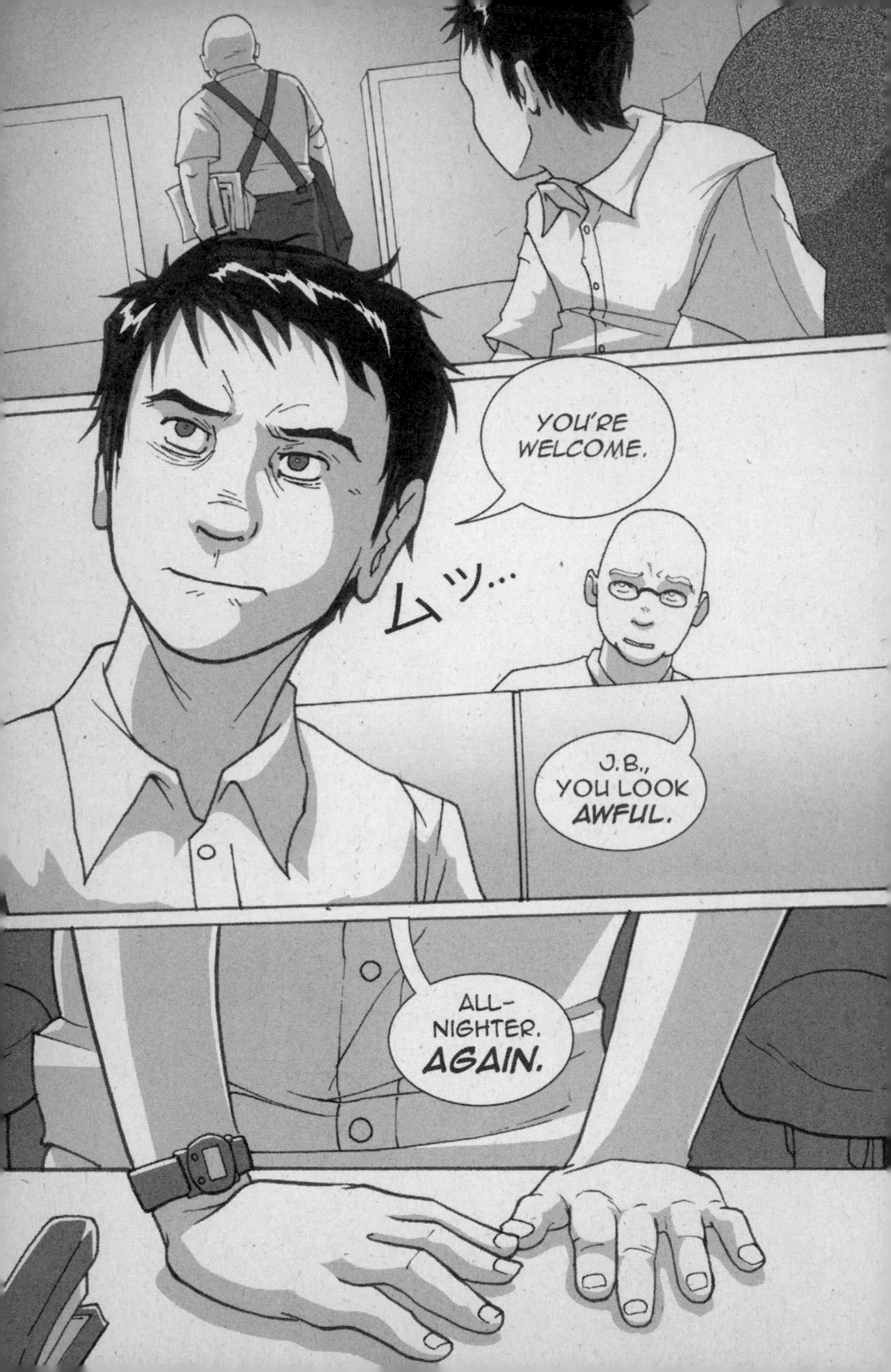
YOU'RE WELCOME.
ムッ...
J.B., YOU LOOK AWFUL.
ALL-NIGHTER. AGAIN.

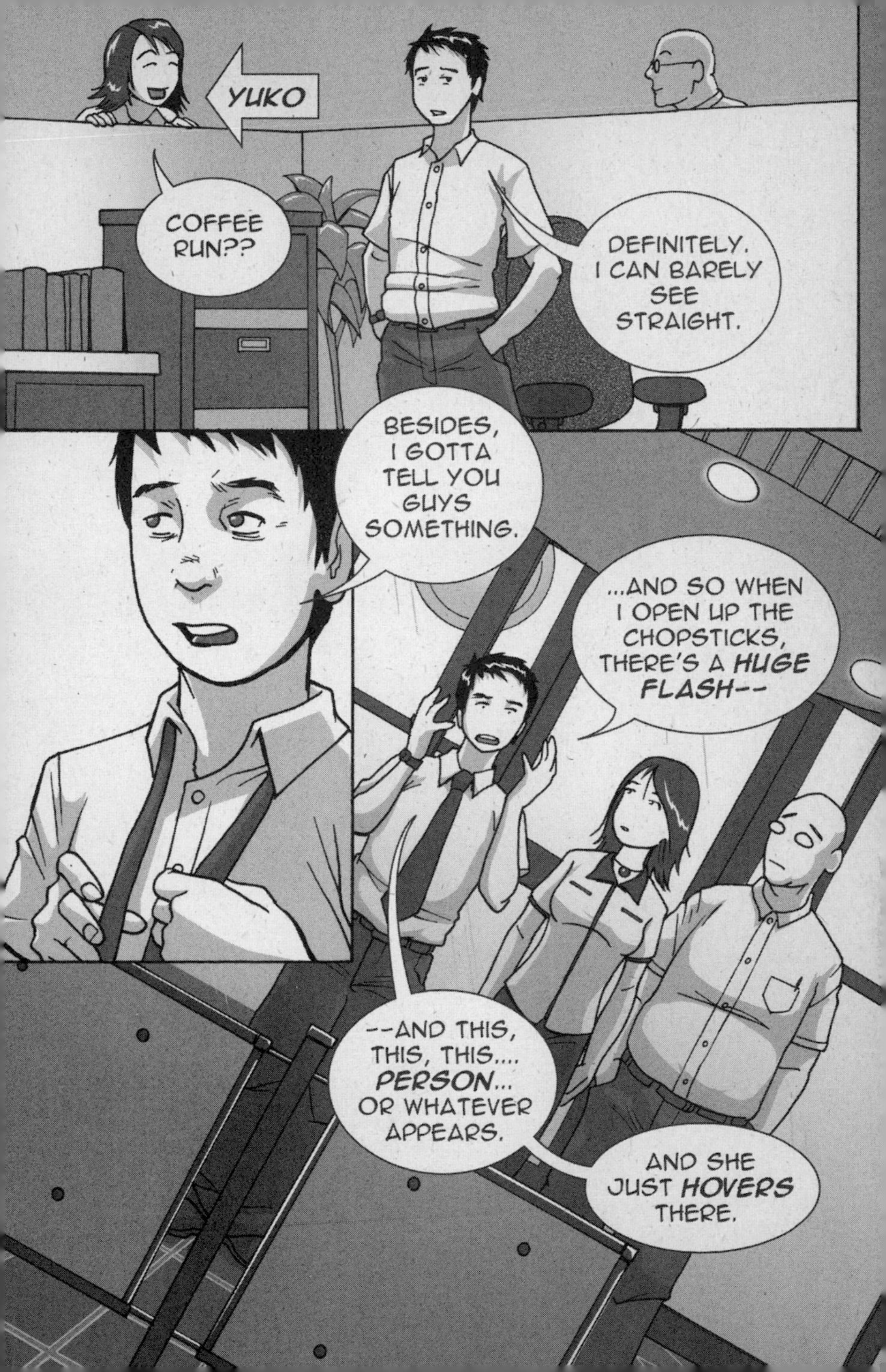
YUKO
COFFEE RUN??
DEFINITELY. I CAN BARELY SEE STRAIGHT.
BESIDES, I GOTTA TELL YOU GUYS SOMETHING.
...AND SO WHEN I OPEN UP THE CHOPSTICKS, THERE'S A HUGE FLASH--
--AND THIS, THIS, THIS.... PERSON... OR WHATEVER APPEARS.
AND SHE JUST HOVERS THERE.

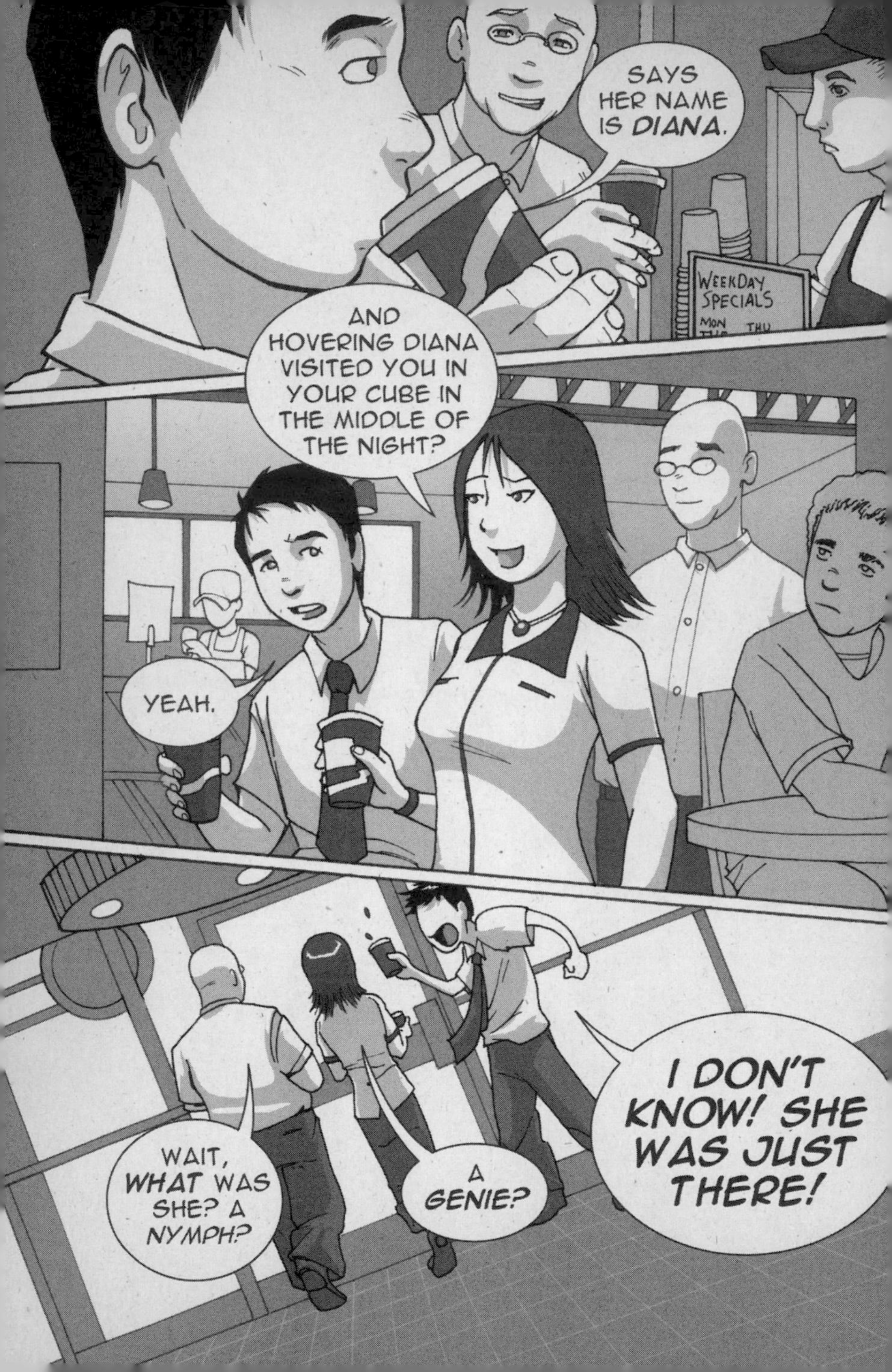
SAYS HER NAME IS DIANA.
AND HOVERING DIANA VISITED YOU IN YOUR CUBE IN THE MIDDLE OF THE NIGHT?
YEAH.
WEEKDAY SPECIALS
MON THU
I DON'T KNOW! SHE WAS JUST THERE!
A GENIE?
WAIT, WHAT WAS SHE? A NYMPH?

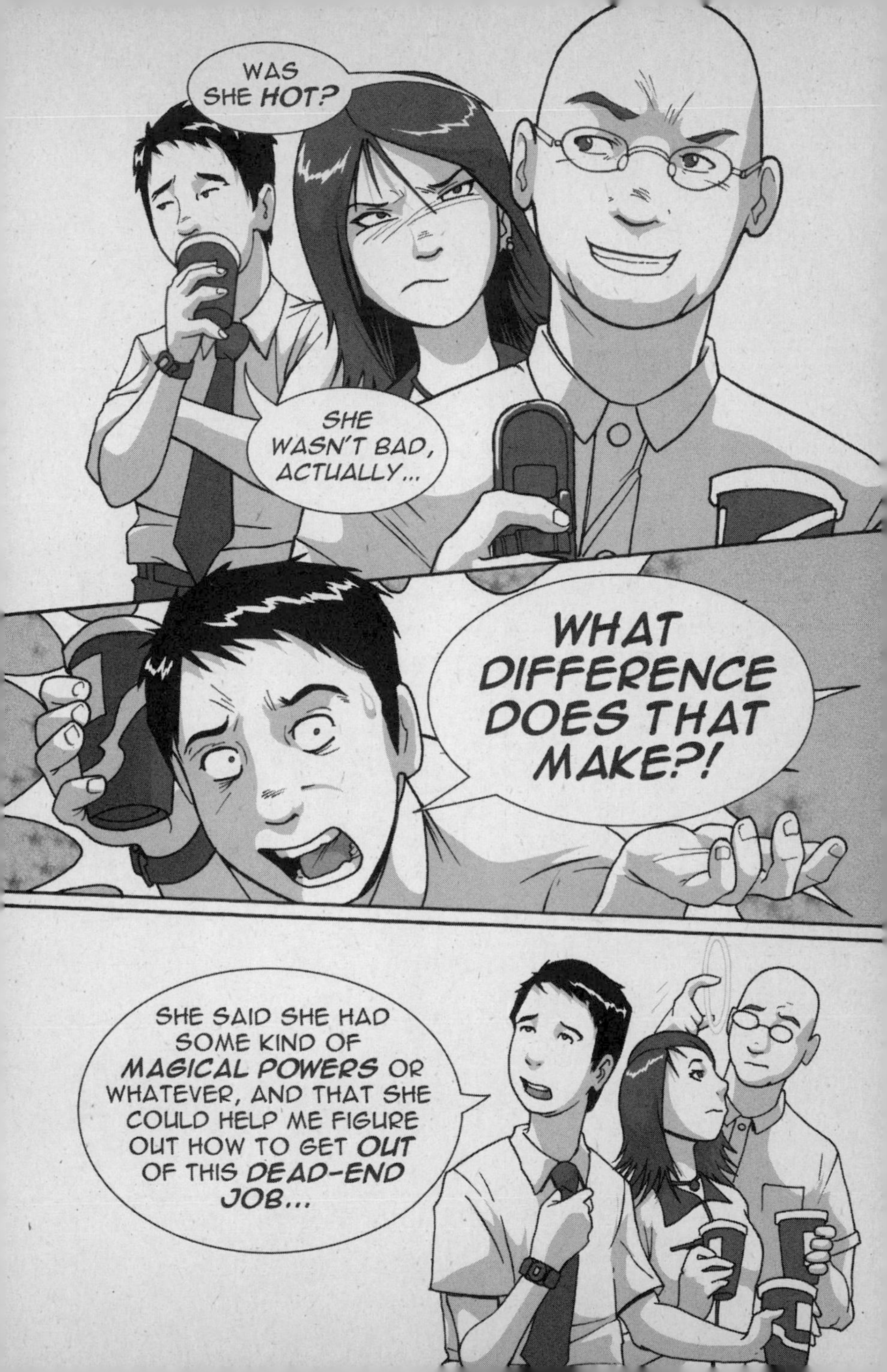
WAS SHE HOT?
SHE WASN'T BAD, ACTUALLY...
WHAT DIFFERENCE DOES THAT MAKE?!
SHE SAID SHE HAD SOME KIND OF MAGICAL POWERS OR WHATEVER, AND THAT SHE COULD HELP ME FIGURE OUT HOW TO GET OUT OF THIS DEAD-END JOB...

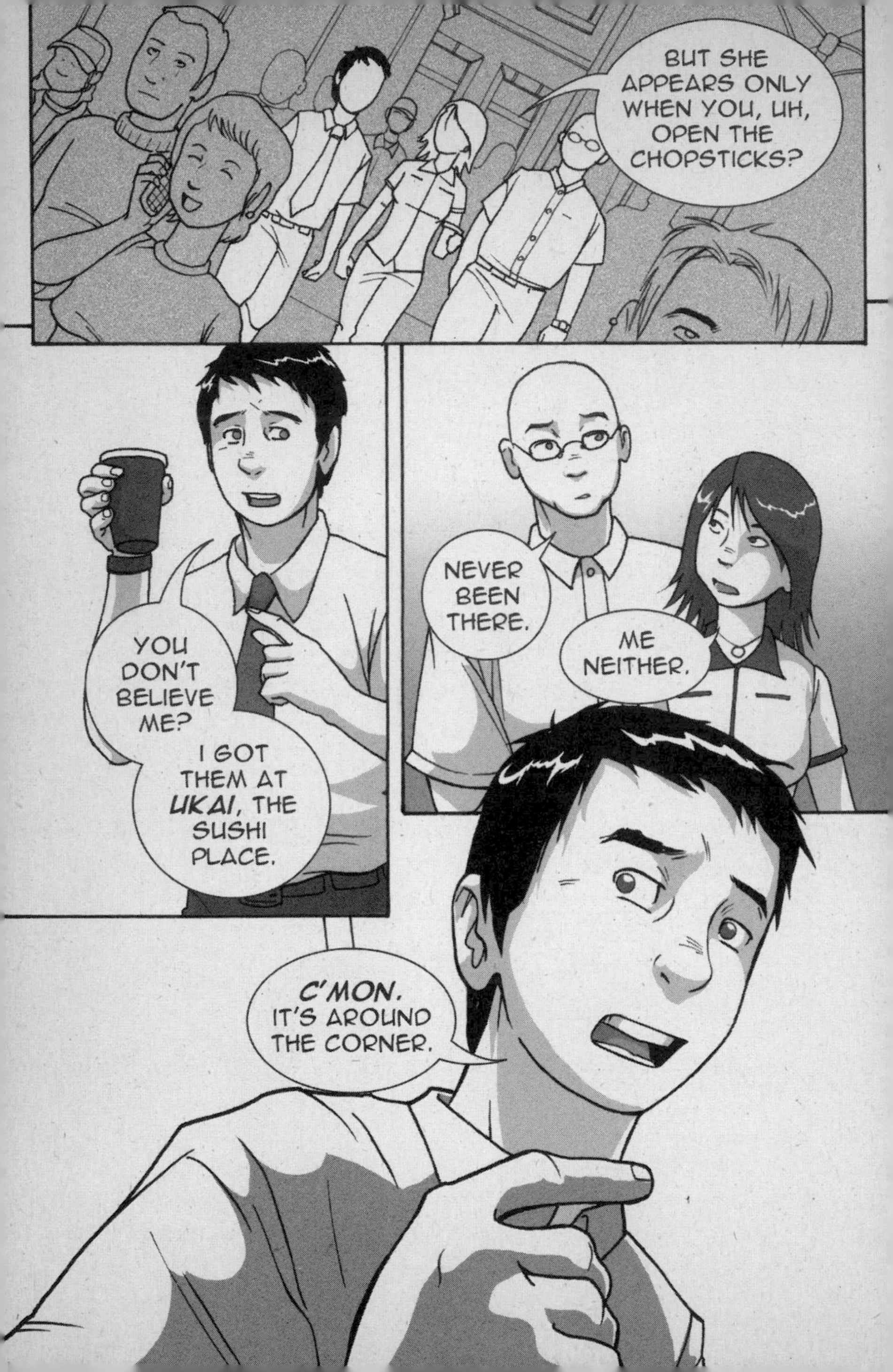
BUT SHE APPEARS ONLY WHEN YOU, UH, OPEN THE CHOPSTICKS?
YOU DON'T BELIEVE ME?
I GOT THEM AT *UKAI*, THE SUSHI PLACE.
NEVER BEEN THERE.
ME NEITHER.
C'MON. IT'S AROUND THE CORNER.

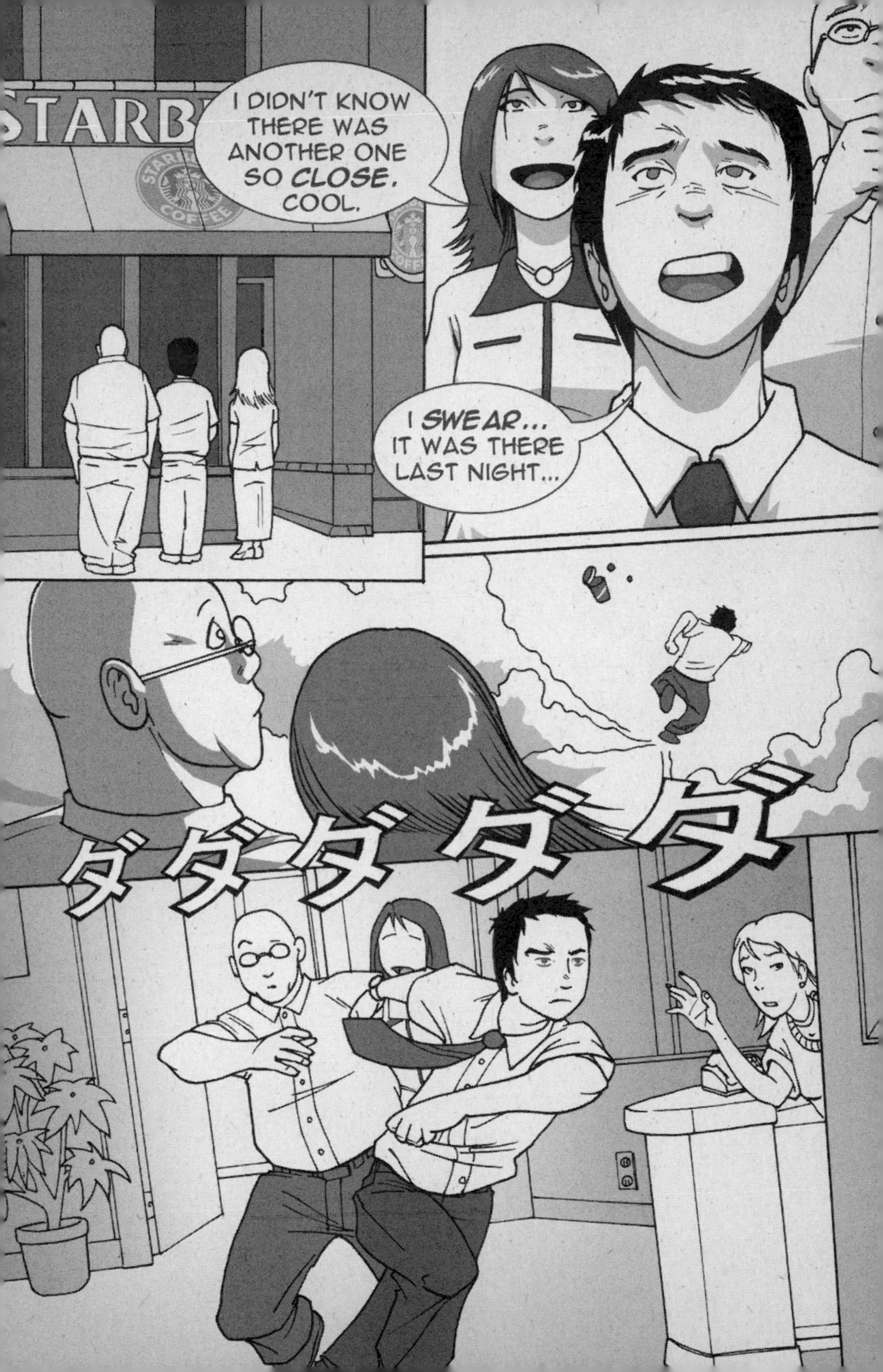
I DIDN'T KNOW THERE WAS ANOTHER ONE SO *CLOSE*. COOL.
I *SWEAR...* IT WAS THERE LAST NIGHT...
ダダダダ

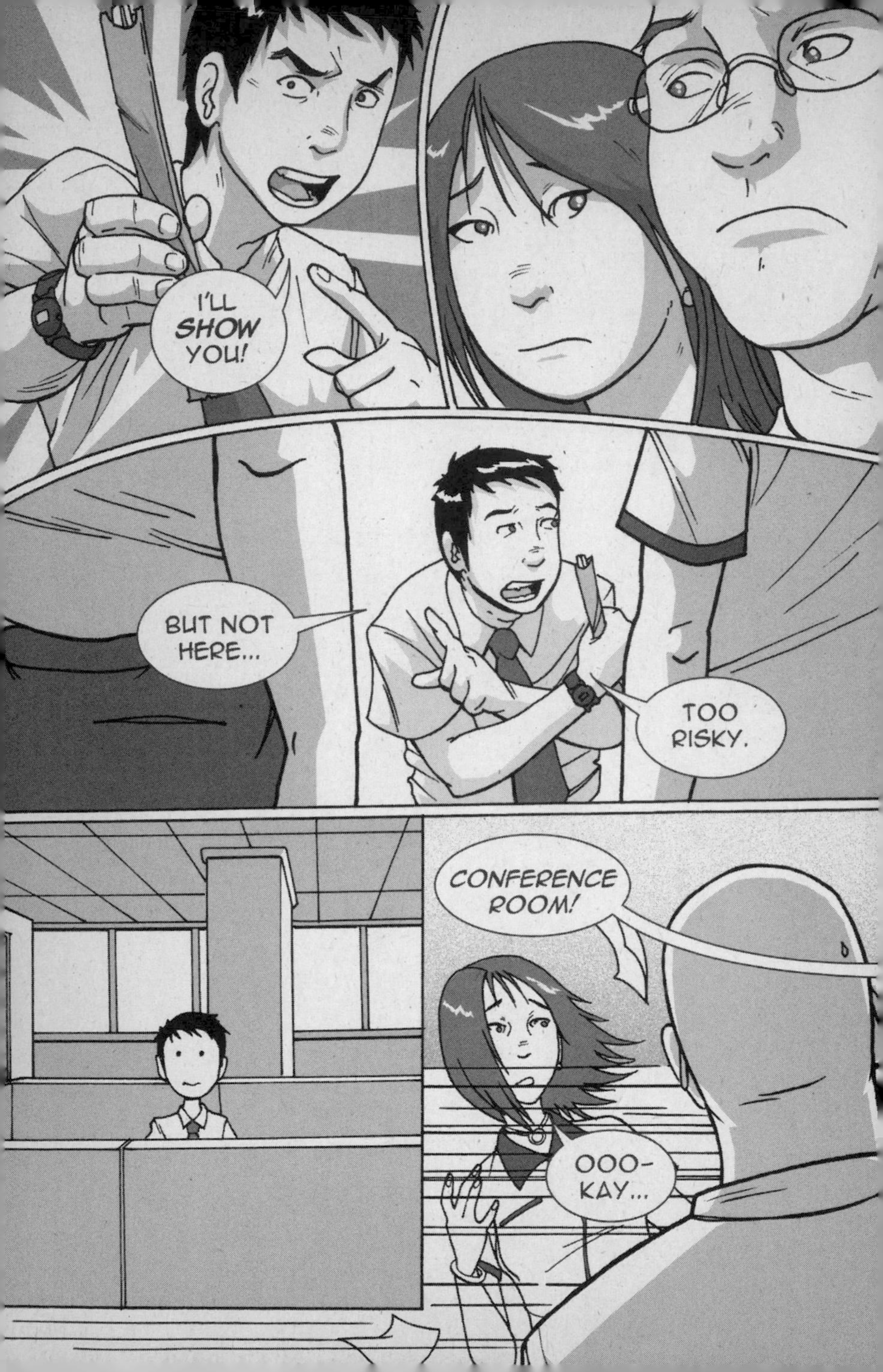
I'LL SHOW YOU!
BUT NOT HERE...
TOO RISKY.
CONFERENCE ROOM!
OOO-KAY...

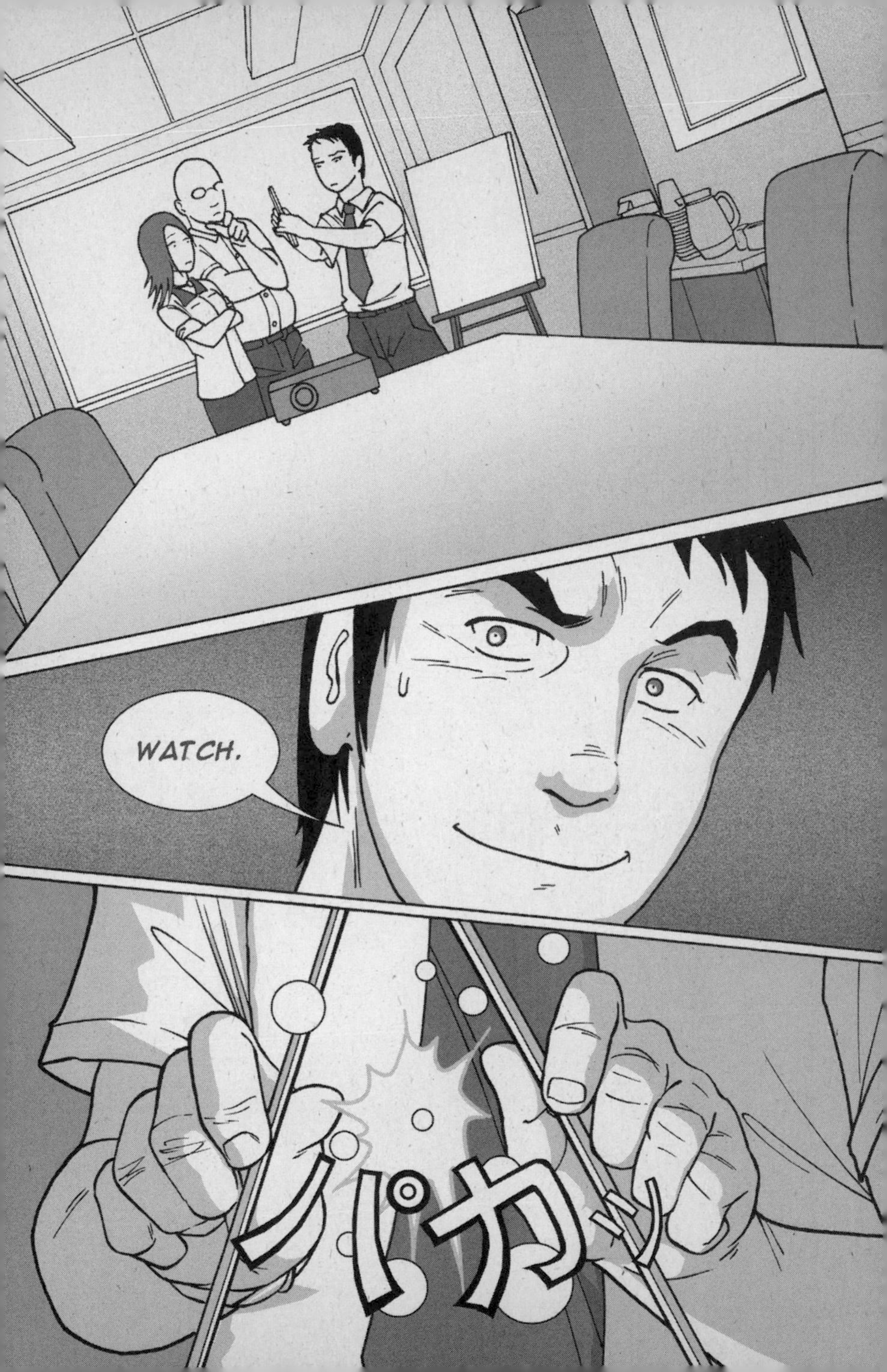
WATCH.
パカッ

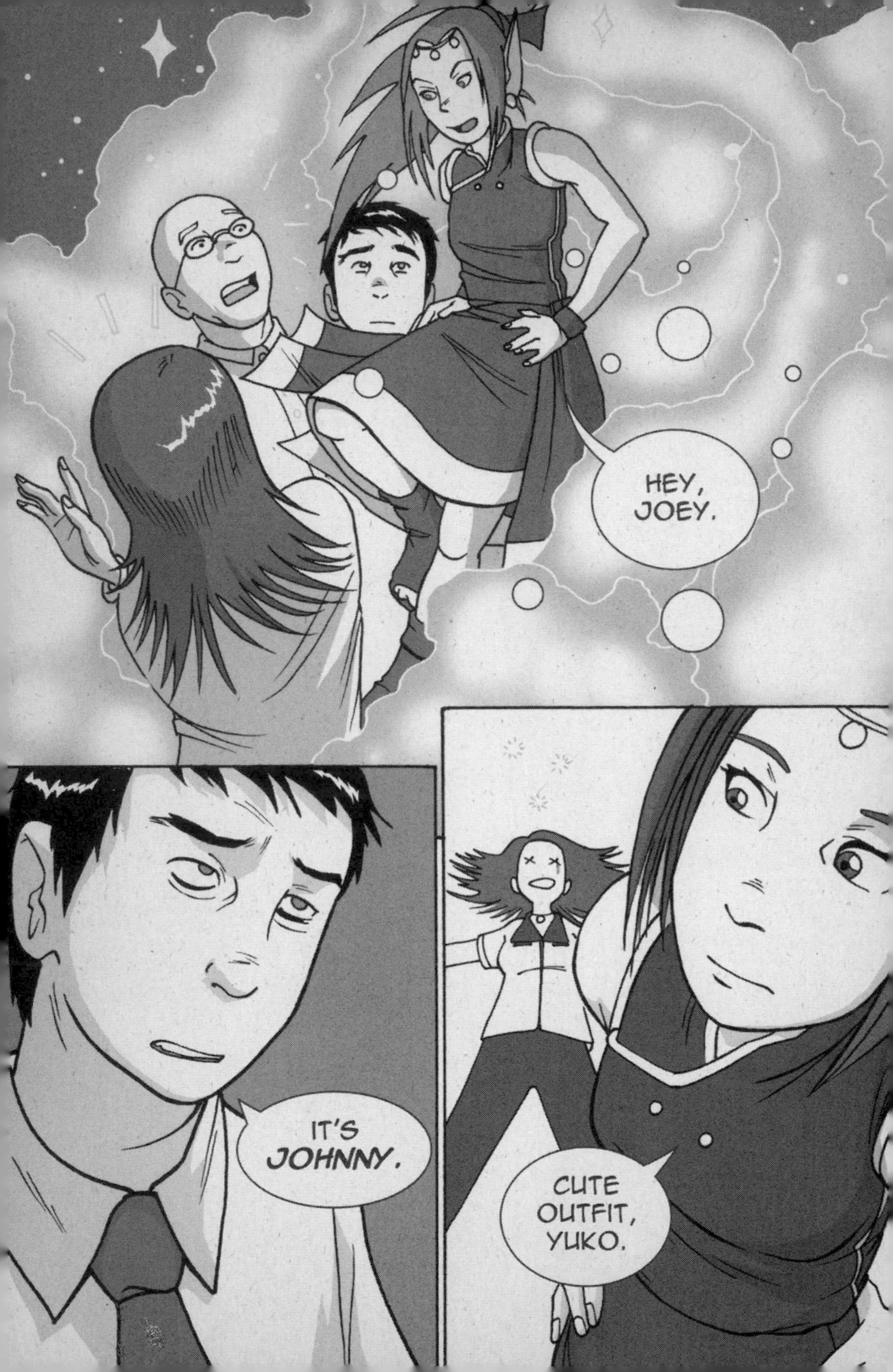
HEY, JOEY.
IT'S JOHNNY.
CUTE OUTFIT, YUKO.

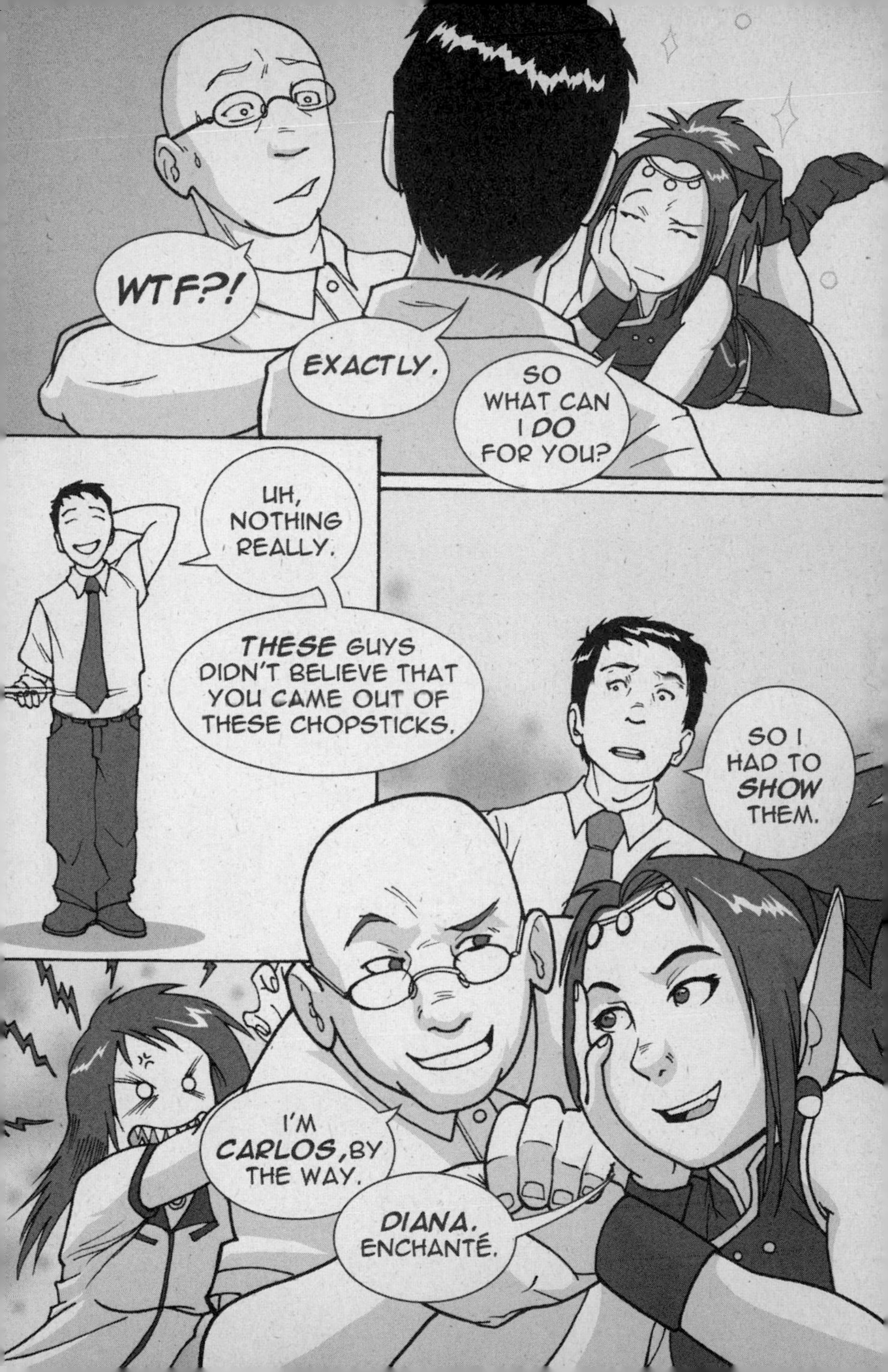
WTF?!
EXACTLY.
SO WHAT CAN I DO FOR YOU?
UH, NOTHING REALLY.
THESE GUYS DIDN'T BELIEVE THAT YOU CAME OUT OF THESE CHOPSTICKS.
SO I HAD TO SHOW THEM.
I'M CARLOS, BY THE WAY.
DIANA. ENCHANTÉ.

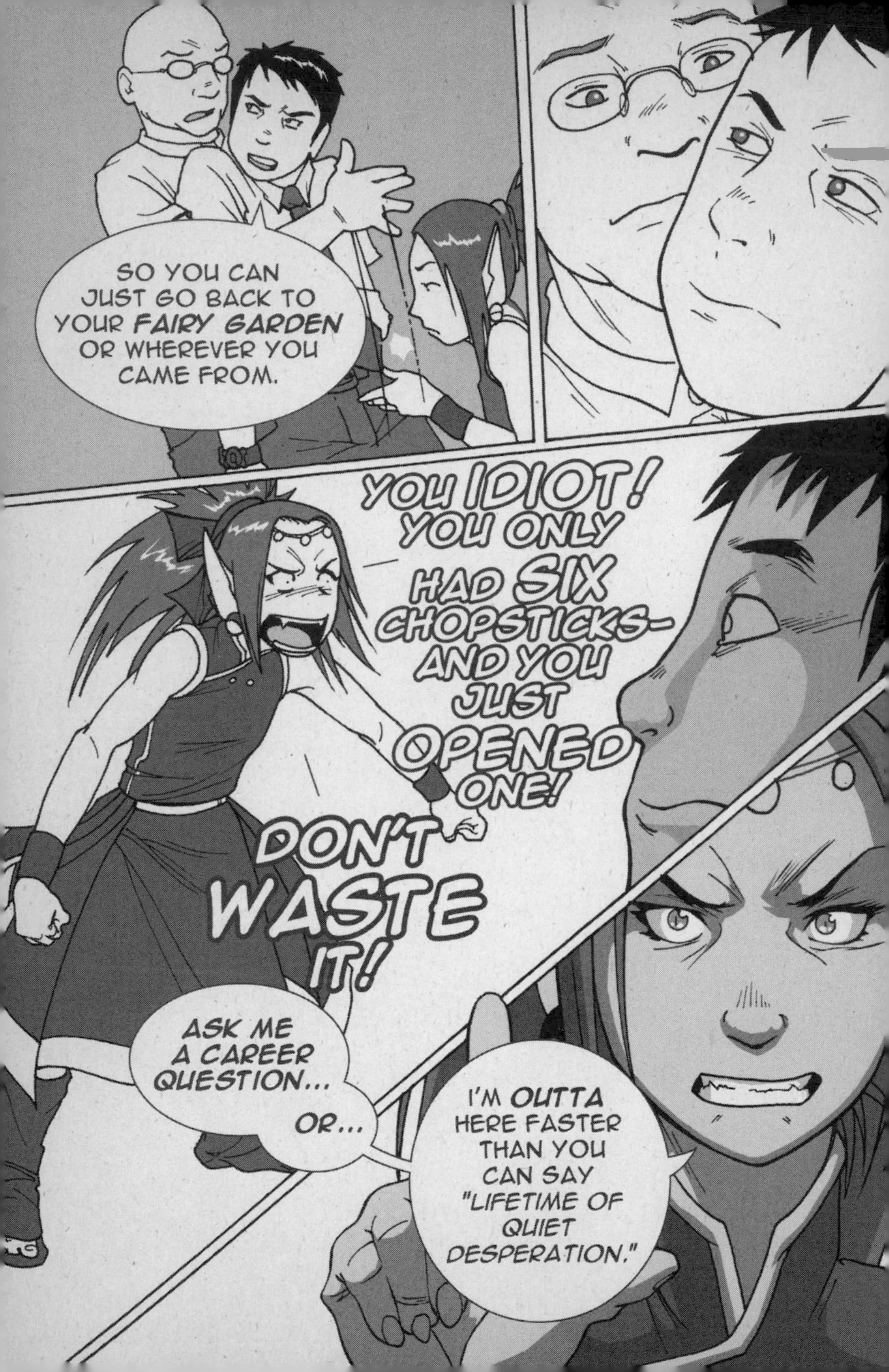
SO YOU CAN JUST GO BACK TO YOUR FAIRY GARDEN OR WHEREVER YOU CAME FROM.
YOU IDIOT! YOU ONLY HAD SIX CHOPSTICKS- AND YOU JUST OPENED ONE!
DON'T WASTE IT!
ASK ME A CAREER QUESTION...
OR...
I'M OUTTA HERE FASTER THAN YOU CAN SAY "LIFETIME OF QUIET DESPERATION."

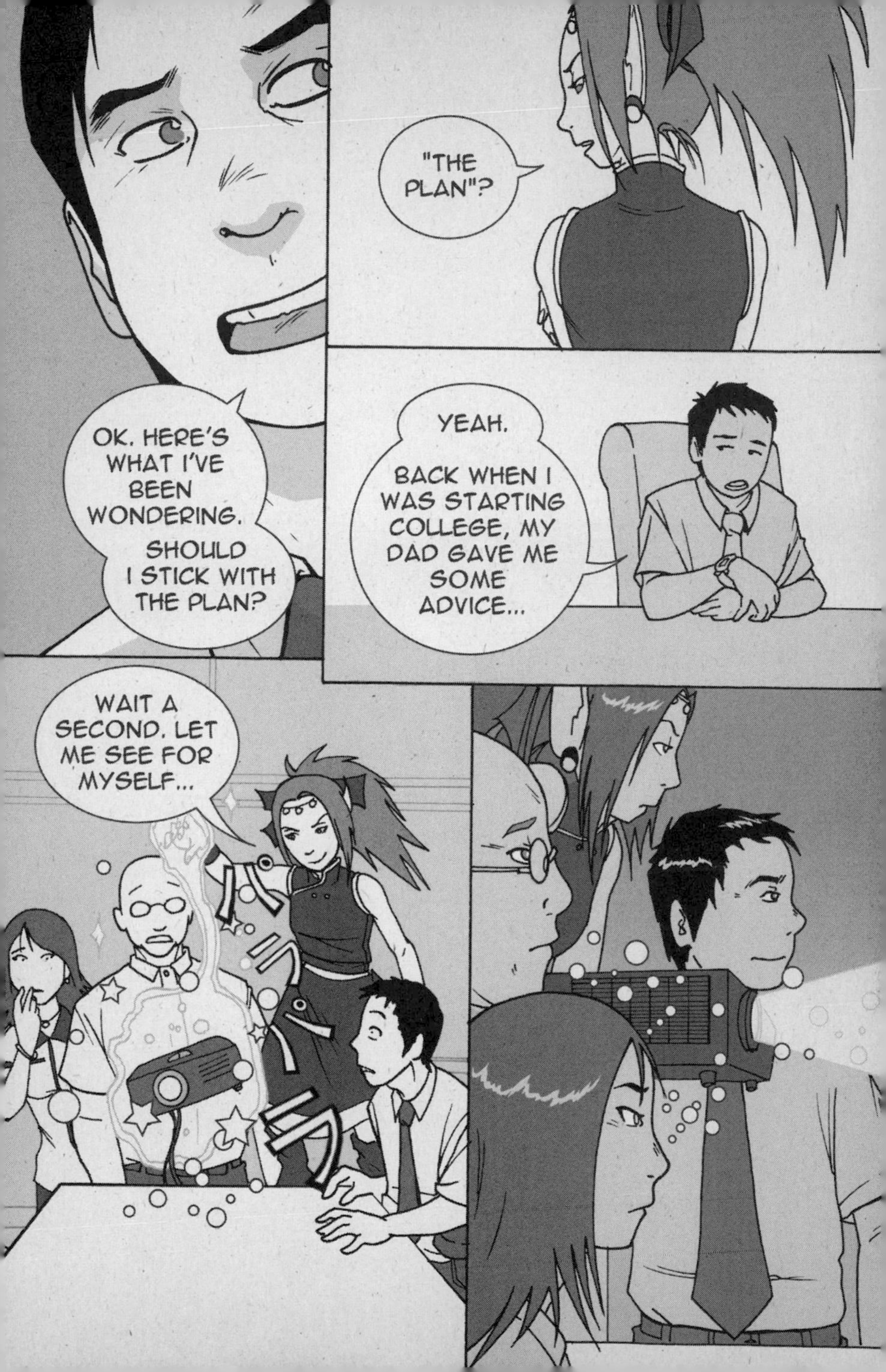

"THE PLAN"?
OK. HERE'S WHAT I'VE BEEN WONDERING.
SHOULD I STICK WITH THE PLAN?
YEAH.
BACK WHEN I WAS STARTING COLLEGE, MY DAD GAVE ME SOME ADVICE...
WAIT A SECOND. LET ME SEE FOR MYSELF...

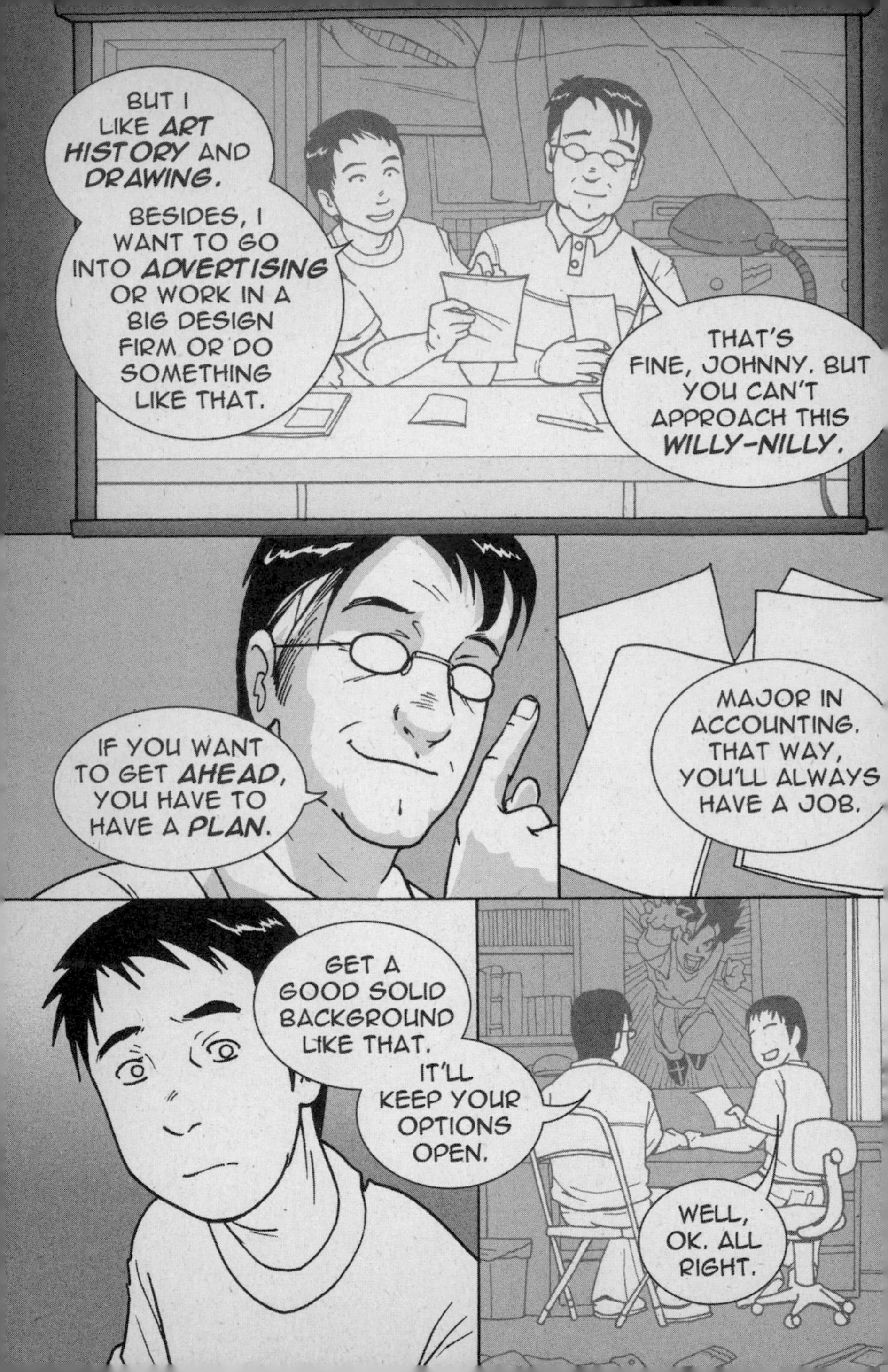
BUT I LIKE ART HISTORY AND DRAWING.
BESIDES, I WANT TO GO INTO ADVERTISING OR WORK IN A BIG DESIGN FIRM OR DO SOMETHING LIKE THAT.
THAT'S FINE, JOHNNY. BUT YOU CAN'T APPROACH THIS WILLY-NILLY.
IF YOU WANT TO GET AHEAD, YOU HAVE TO HAVE A PLAN.
MAJOR IN ACCOUNTING. THAT WAY, YOU'LL ALWAYS HAVE A JOB.
GET A GOOD SOLID BACKGROUND LIKE THAT.
IT'LL KEEP YOUR OPTIONS OPEN.
WELL, OK. ALL RIGHT.

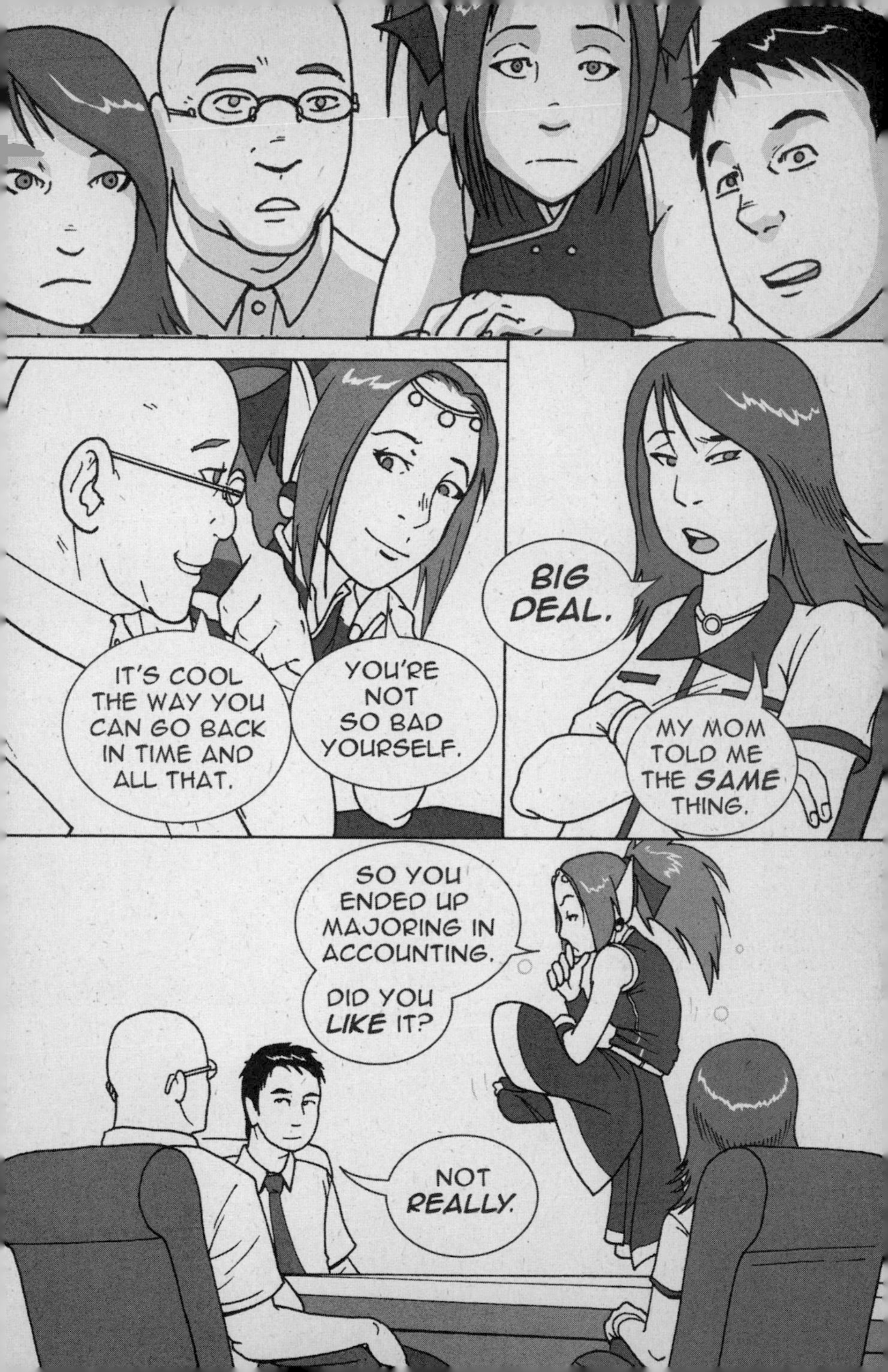
IT'S COOL THE WAY YOU CAN GO BACK IN TIME AND ALL THAT.
YOU'RE NOT SO BAD YOURSELF.
BIG DEAL.
MY MOM TOLD ME THE SAME THING.
SO YOU ENDED UP MAJORING IN ACCOUNTING.
DID YOU LIKE IT?
NOT REALLY.

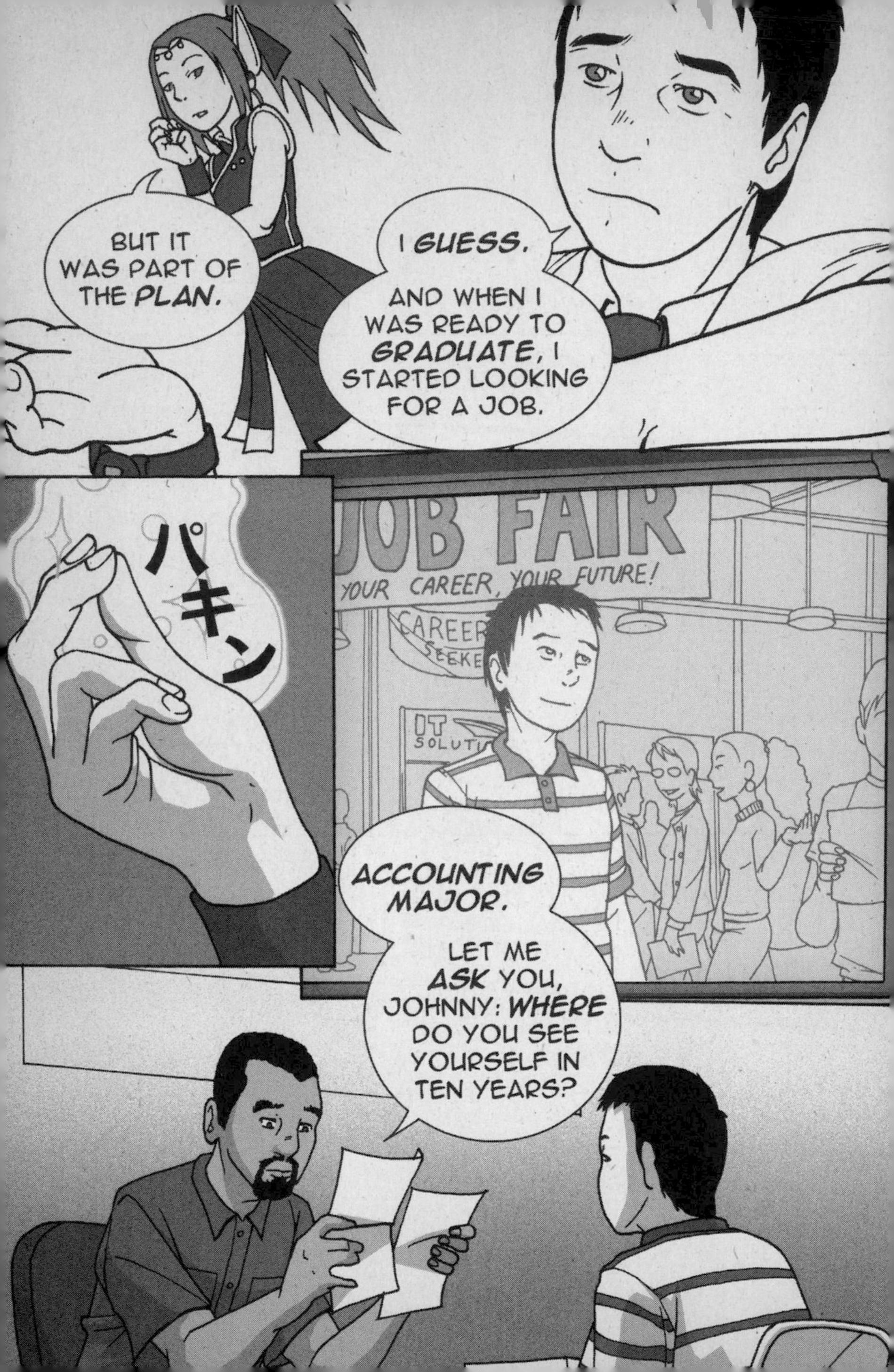
BUT IT WAS PART OF THE PLAN.
I GUESS.
AND WHEN I WAS READY TO GRADUATE, I STARTED LOOKING FOR A JOB.
パキン
JOB FAIR
YOUR CAREER, YOUR FUTURE!
ACCOUNTING MAJOR.
LET ME ASK YOU, JOHNNY: WHERE DO YOU SEE YOURSELF IN TEN YEARS?

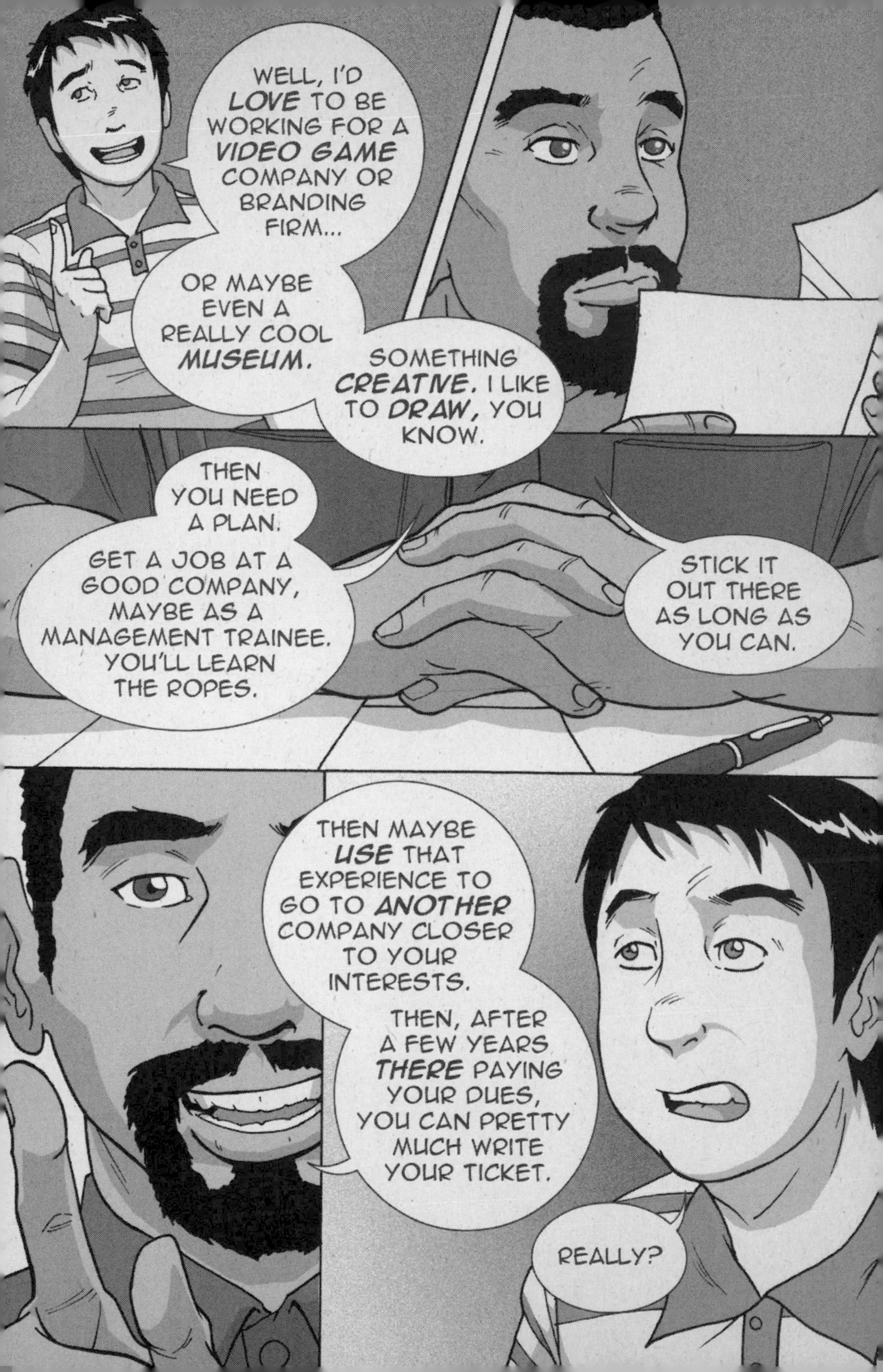
WELL, I'D LOVE TO BE WORKING FOR A VIDEO GAME COMPANY OR BRANDING FIRM...
OR MAYBE EVEN A REALLY COOL MUSEUM.
SOMETHING CREATIVE. I LIKE TO DRAW, YOU KNOW.
THEN YOU NEED A PLAN.
GET A JOB AT A GOOD COMPANY, MAYBE AS A MANAGEMENT TRAINEE. YOU'LL LEARN THE ROPES.
STICK IT OUT THERE AS LONG AS YOU CAN.
THEN MAYBE USE THAT EXPERIENCE TO GO TO ANOTHER COMPANY CLOSER TO YOUR INTERESTS.
THEN, AFTER A FEW YEARS THERE PAYING YOUR DUES, YOU CAN PRETTY MUCH WRITE YOUR TICKET.
REALLY?

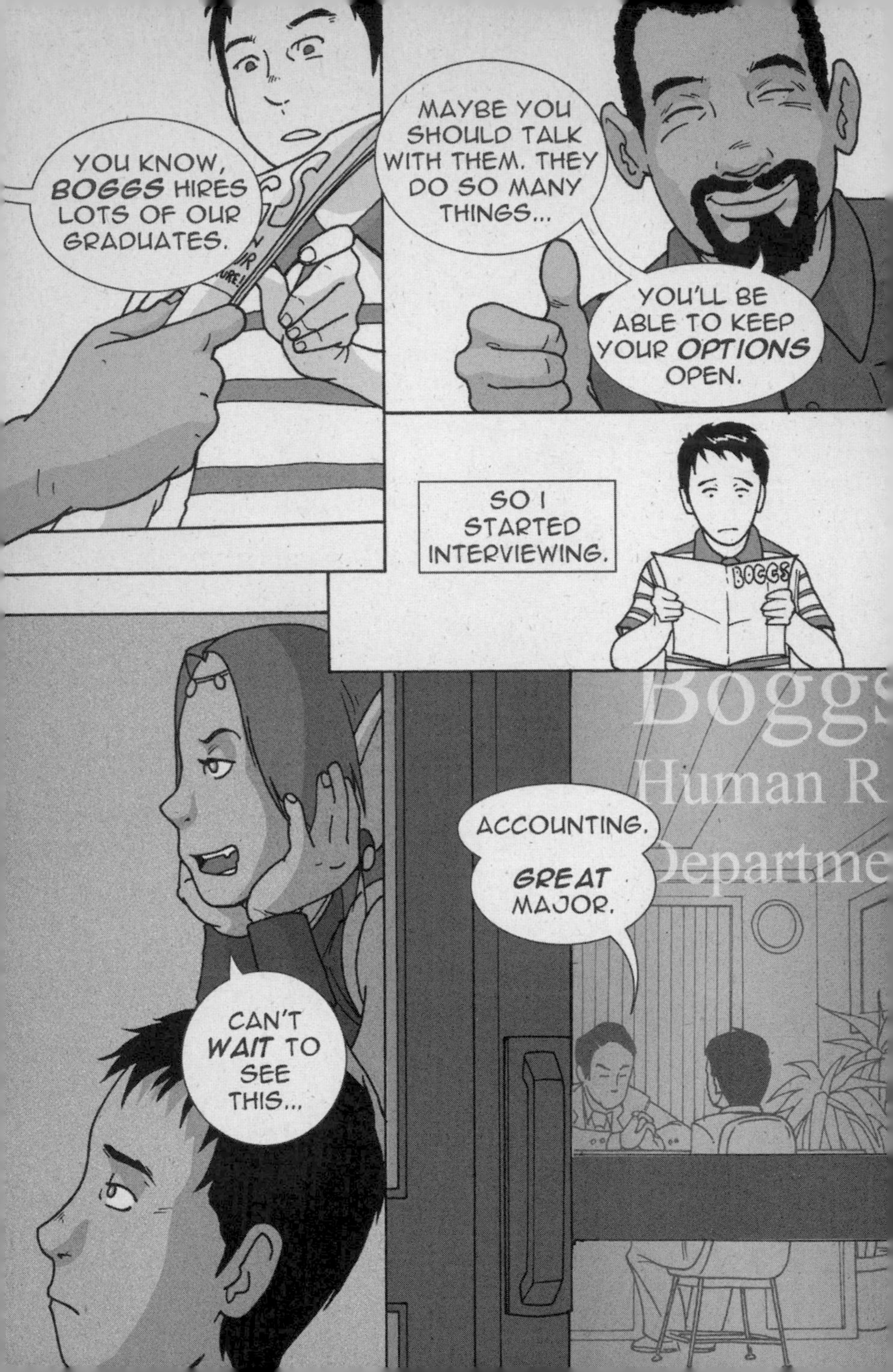
YOU KNOW, BOGGS HIRES LOTS OF OUR GRADUATES.
MAYBE YOU SHOULD TALK WITH THEM. THEY DO SO MANY THINGS...
YOU'LL BE ABLE TO KEEP YOUR OPTIONS OPEN.
SO I STARTED INTERVIEWING.
BOGGS
Boggs
Human R
Departme
ACCOUNTING.
GREAT MAJOR.
CAN'T WAIT TO SEE THIS...

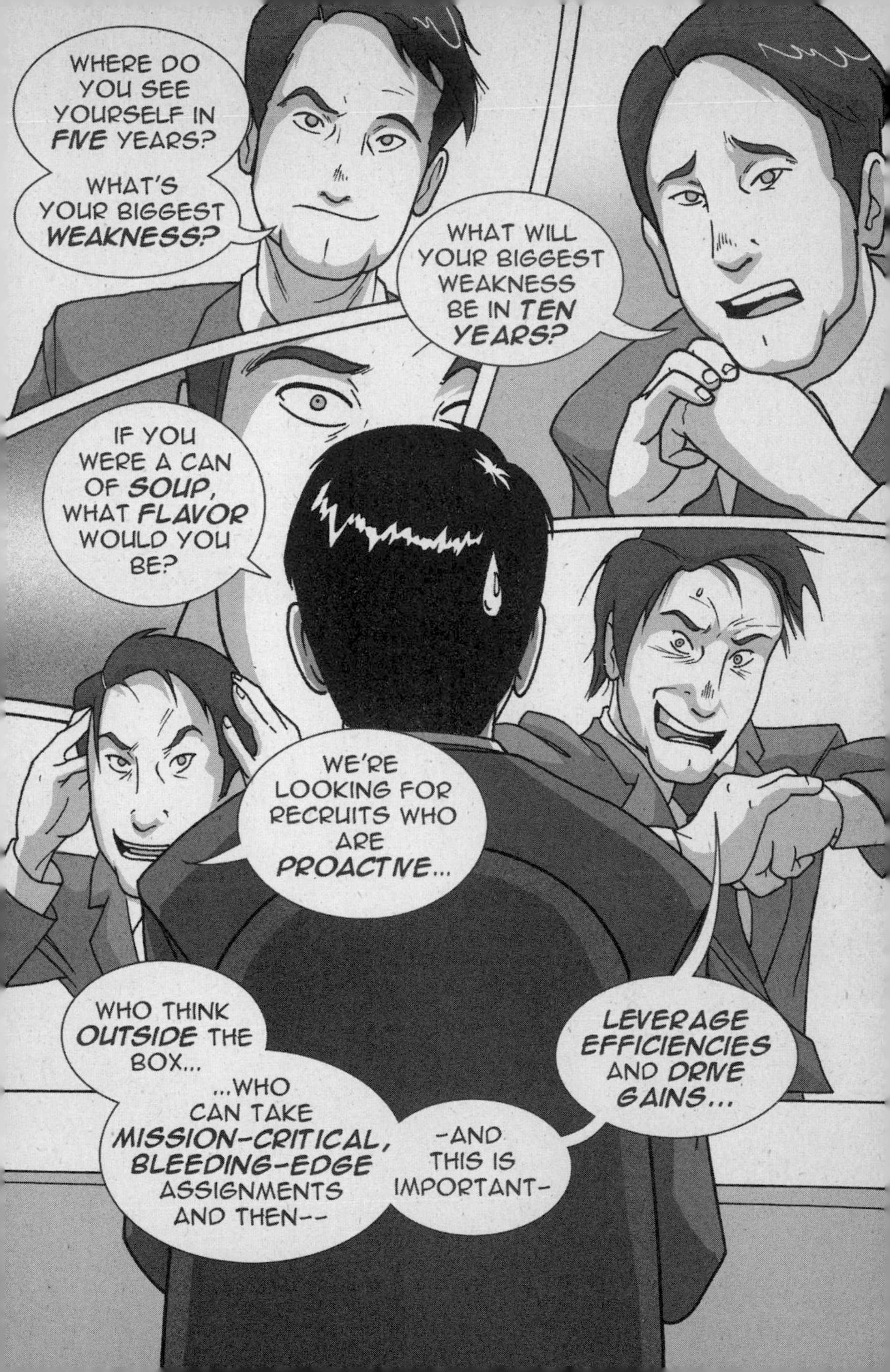
WHERE DO YOU SEE YOURSELF IN FIVE YEARS?
WHAT'S YOUR BIGGEST WEAKNESS?
WHAT WILL YOUR BIGGEST WEAKNESS BE IN TEN YEARS?
IF YOU WERE A CAN OF SOUP, WHAT FLAVOR WOULD YOU BE?
WE'RE LOOKING FOR RECRUITS WHO ARE PROACTIVE...
WHO THINK OUTSIDE THE BOX...
...WHO CAN TAKE MISSION-CRITICAL, BLEEDING-EDGE ASSIGNMENTS AND THEN--
-AND THIS IS IMPORTANT-
LEVERAGE EFFICIENCIES AND DRIVE GAINS...

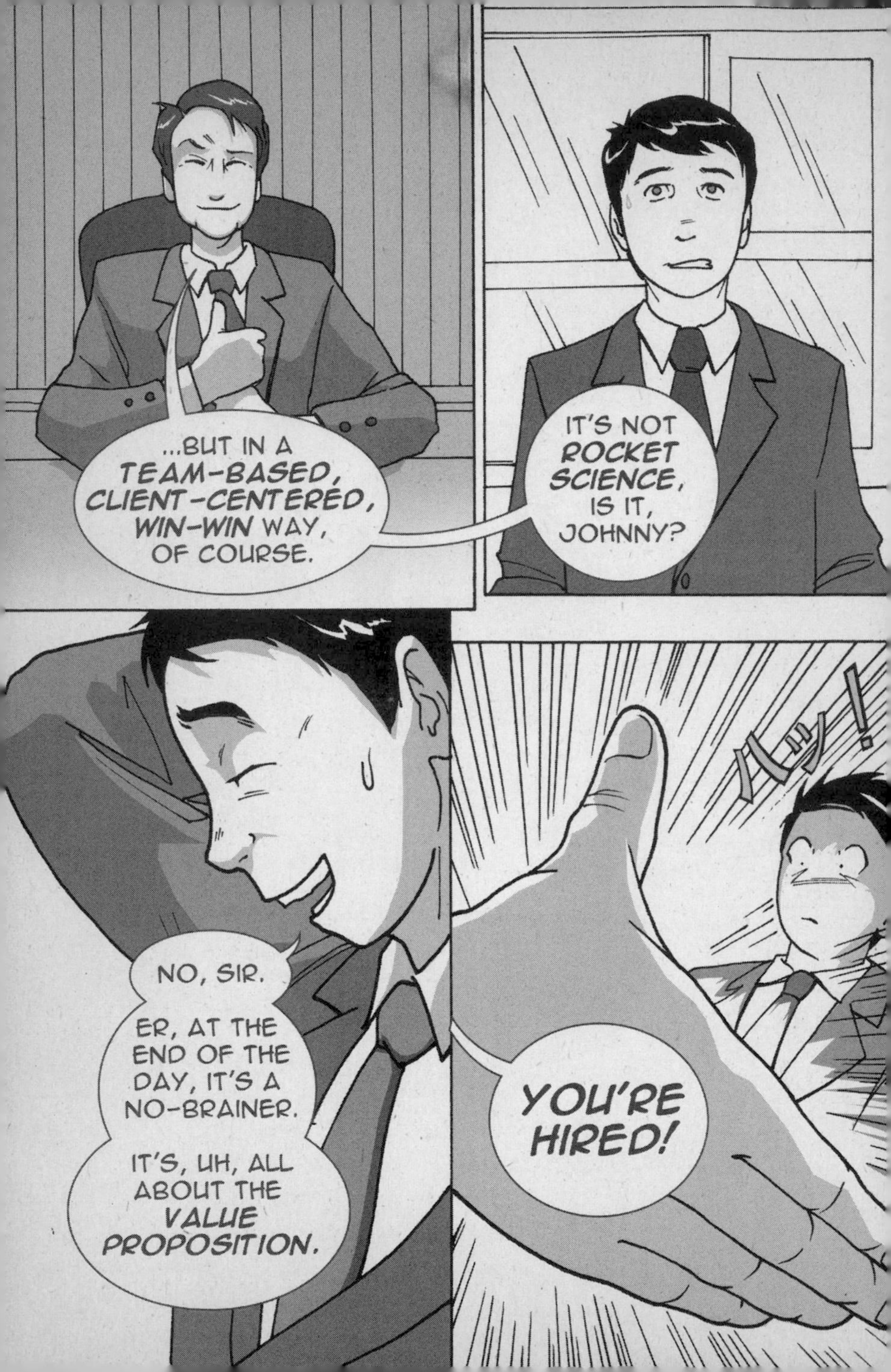
...BUT IN A TEAM-BASED, CLIENT-CENTERED, WIN-WIN WAY, OF COURSE.
IT'S NOT ROCKET SCIENCE, IS IT, JOHNNY?
NO, SIR.
ER, AT THE END OF THE DAY, IT'S A NO-BRAINER.
IT'S, UH, ALL ABOUT THE VALUE PROPOSITION.
ハッ!
YOU'RE HIRED!

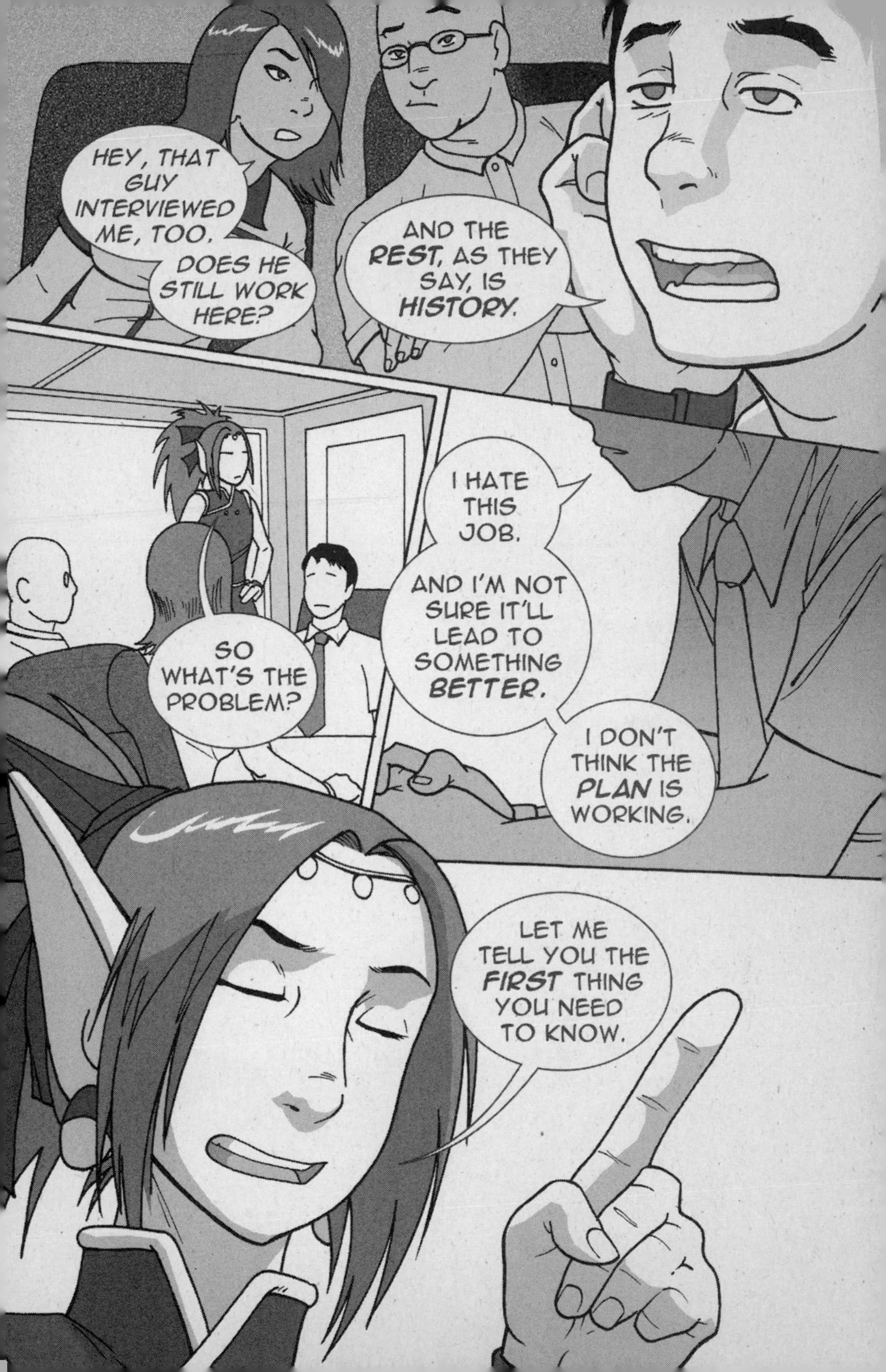
HEY, THAT GUY INTERVIEWED ME, TOO.
DOES HE STILL WORK HERE?
AND THE REST, AS THEY SAY, IS HISTORY.
I HATE THIS JOB.
AND I'M NOT SURE IT'LL LEAD TO SOMETHING BETTER.
SO WHAT'S THE PROBLEM?
I DON'T THINK THE PLAN IS WORKING.
LET ME TELL YOU THE FIRST THING YOU NEED TO KNOW.

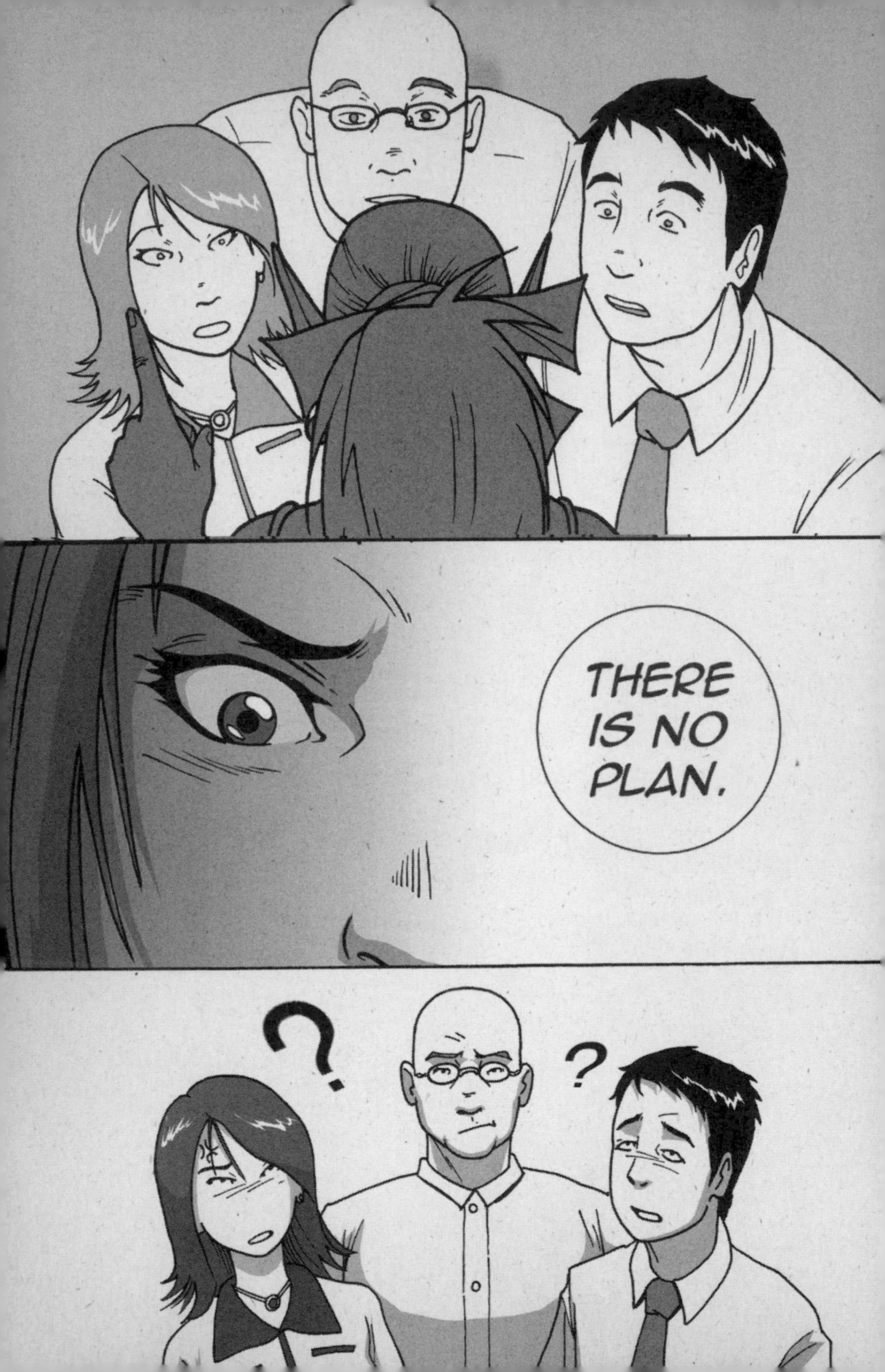
THERE IS NO PLAN.
?
?

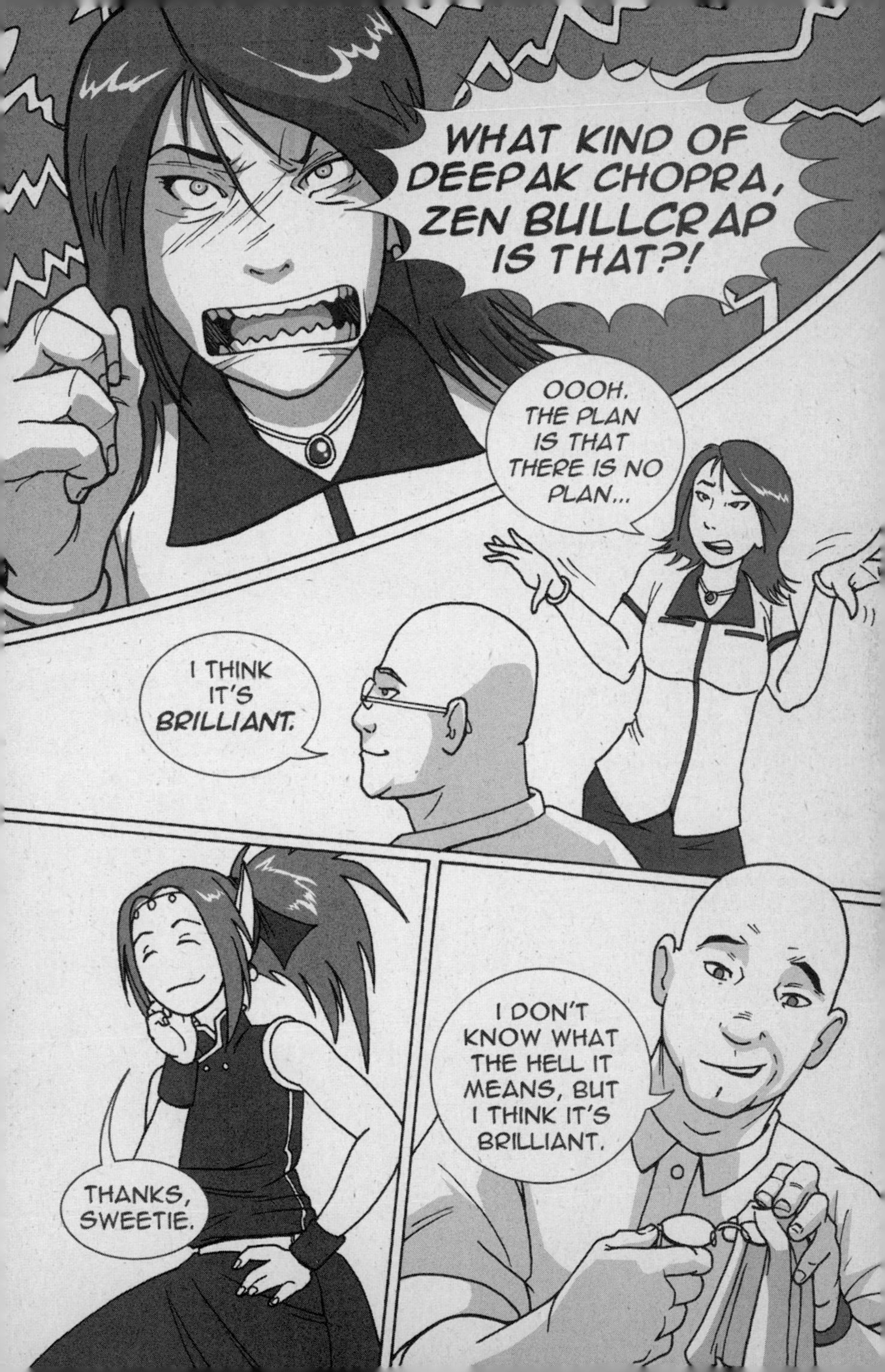
WHAT KIND OF DEEPAK CHOPRA, ZEN BULLCRAP IS THAT?!
OOOH. THE PLAN IS THAT THERE IS NO PLAN...
I THINK IT'S BRILLIANT.
THANKS, SWEETIE.
I DON'T KNOW WHAT THE HELL IT MEANS, BUT I THINK IT'S BRILLIANT.

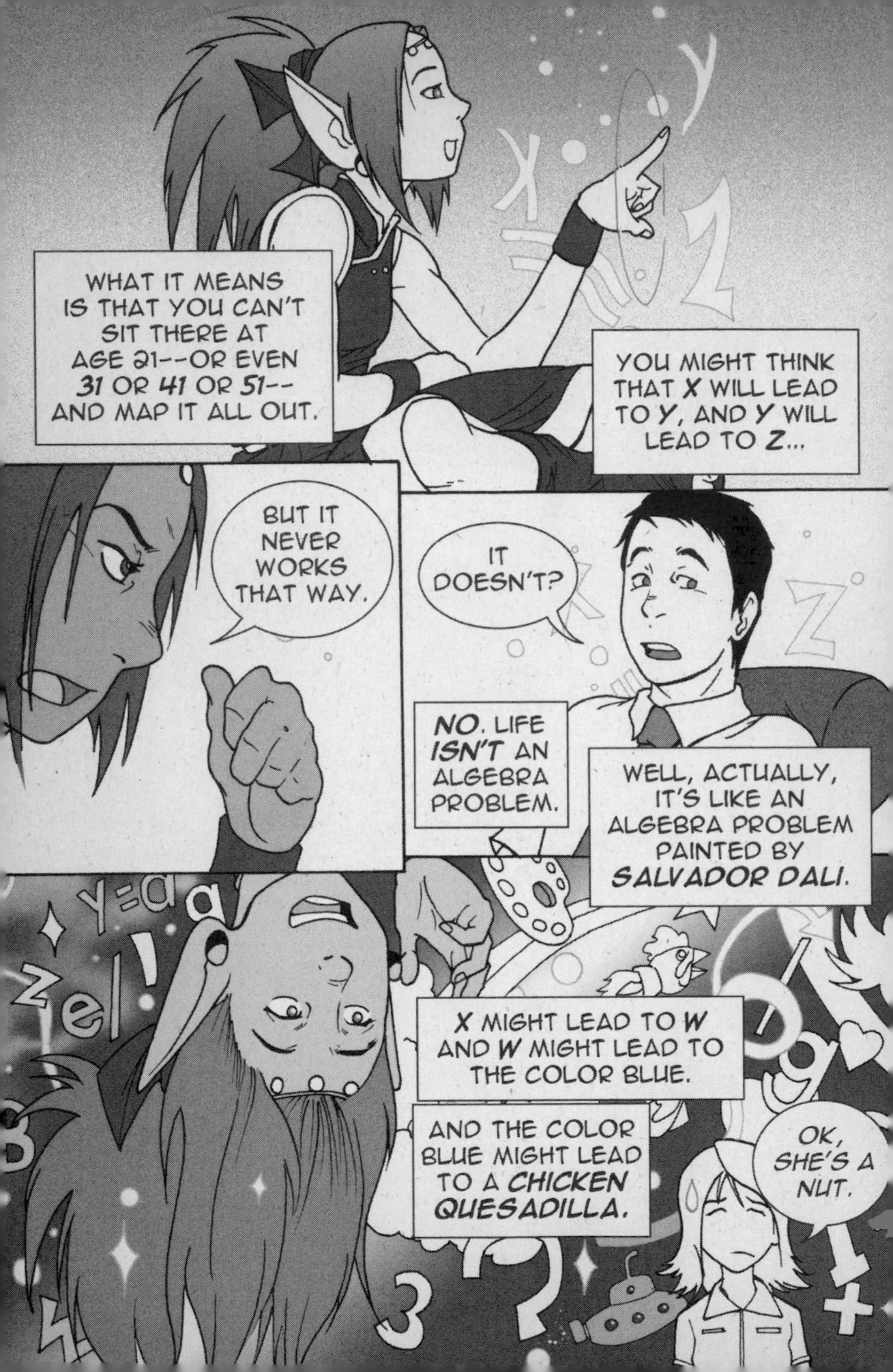
WHAT IT MEANS IS THAT YOU CAN'T SIT THERE AT AGE 21--OR EVEN 31 OR 41 OR 51--AND MAP IT ALL OUT.
YOU MIGHT THINK THAT X WILL LEAD TO Y, AND Y WILL LEAD TO Z...
BUT IT NEVER WORKS THAT WAY.
IT DOESN'T?
NO. LIFE ISN'T AN ALGEBRA PROBLEM.
WELL, ACTUALLY, IT'S LIKE AN ALGEBRA PROBLEM PAINTED BY SALVADOR DALI.
X MIGHT LEAD TO W AND W MIGHT LEAD TO THE COLOR BLUE.
AND THE COLOR BLUE MIGHT LEAD TO A CHICKEN QUESADILLA.
OK, SHE'S A NUT.

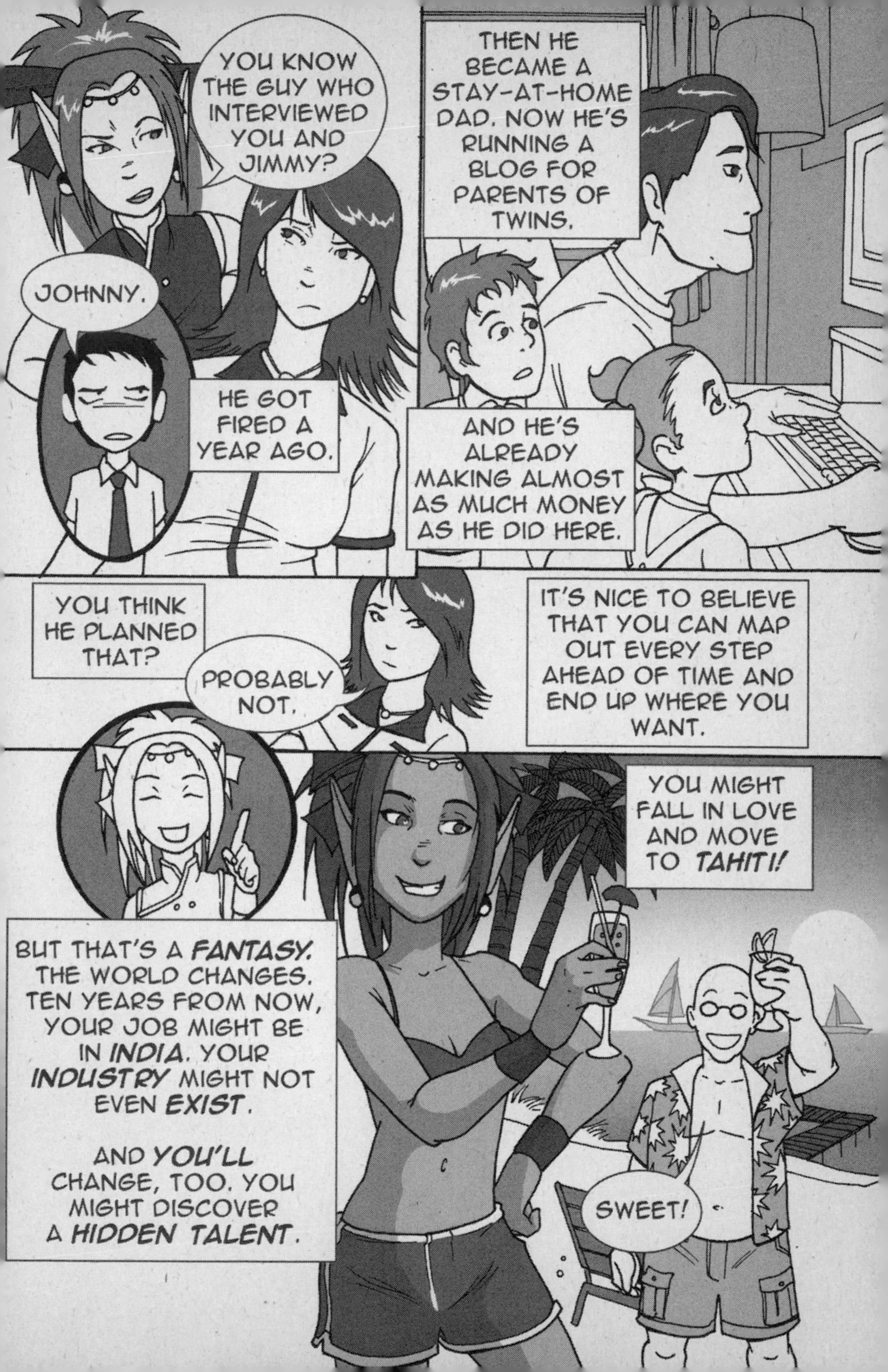
YOU KNOW THE GUY WHO INTERVIEWED YOU AND JIMMY?
JOHNNY.
HE GOT FIRED A YEAR AGO.
THEN HE BECAME A STAY-AT-HOME DAD. NOW HE'S RUNNING A BLOG FOR PARENTS OF TWINS.
AND HE'S ALREADY MAKING ALMOST AS MUCH MONEY AS HE DID HERE.
YOU THINK HE PLANNED THAT?
PROBABLY NOT.
IT'S NICE TO BELIEVE THAT YOU CAN MAP OUT EVERY STEP AHEAD OF TIME AND END UP WHERE YOU WANT.
BUT THAT'S A *FANTASY.* THE WORLD CHANGES. TEN YEARS FROM NOW, YOUR JOB MIGHT BE IN *INDIA*. YOUR *INDUSTRY* MIGHT NOT EVEN *EXIST*.
AND *YOU'LL* CHANGE, TOO. YOU MIGHT DISCOVER A *HIDDEN TALENT*.
YOU MIGHT FALL IN LOVE AND MOVE TO *TAHITI!*
SWEET!

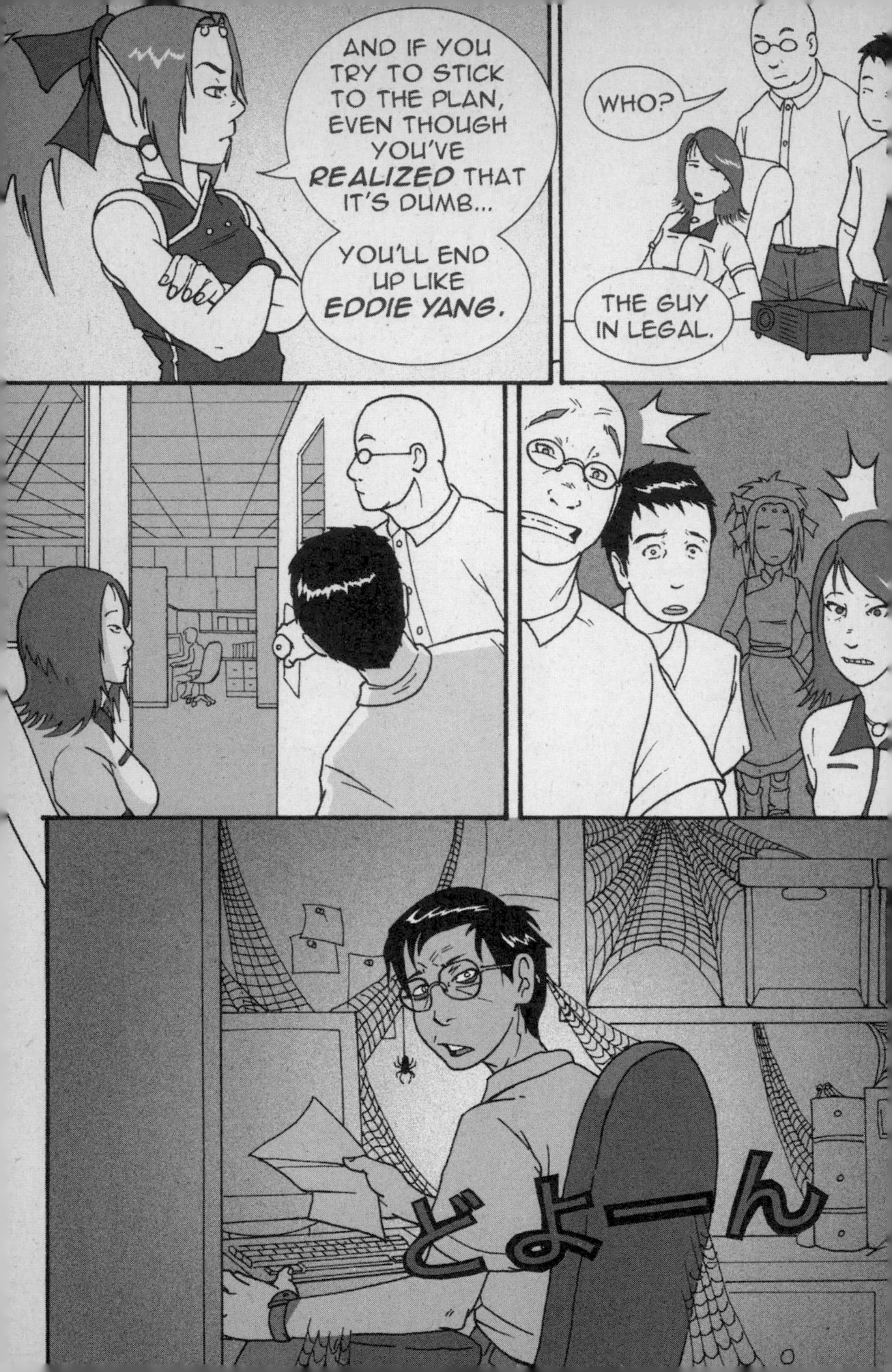
AND IF YOU TRY TO STICK TO THE PLAN, EVEN THOUGH YOU'VE REALIZED THAT IT'S DUMB...
YOU'LL END UP LIKE EDDIE YANG.
WHO?
THE GUY IN LEGAL.
どよーーん

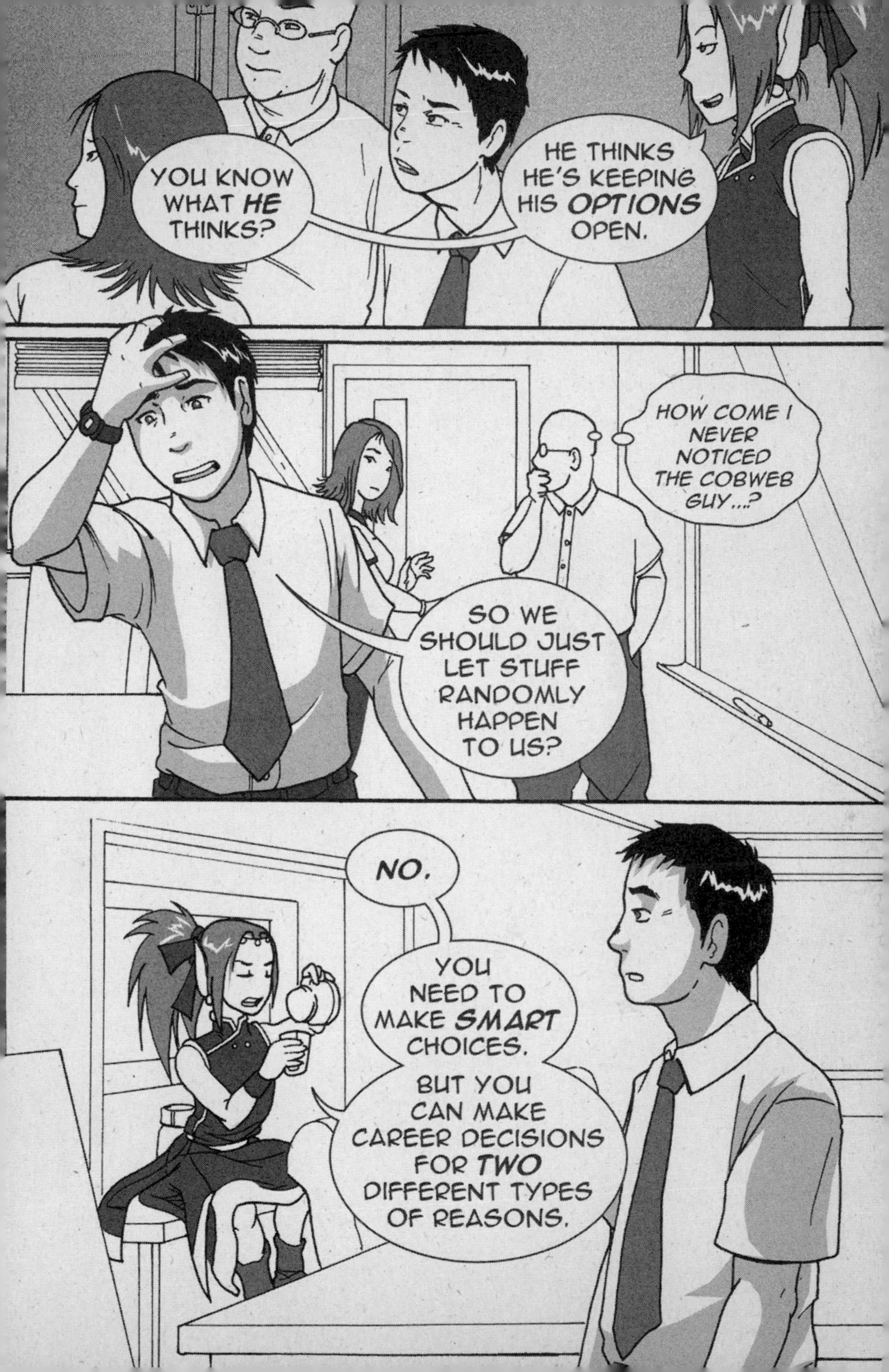
YOU KNOW WHAT HE THINKS?
HE THINKS HE'S KEEPING HIS OPTIONS OPEN.
HOW COME I NEVER NOTICED THE COBWEB GUY...?
SO WE SHOULD JUST LET STUFF RANDOMLY HAPPEN TO US?
NO.
YOU NEED TO MAKE SMART CHOICES.
BUT YOU CAN MAKE CAREER DECISIONS FOR TWO DIFFERENT TYPES OF REASONS.

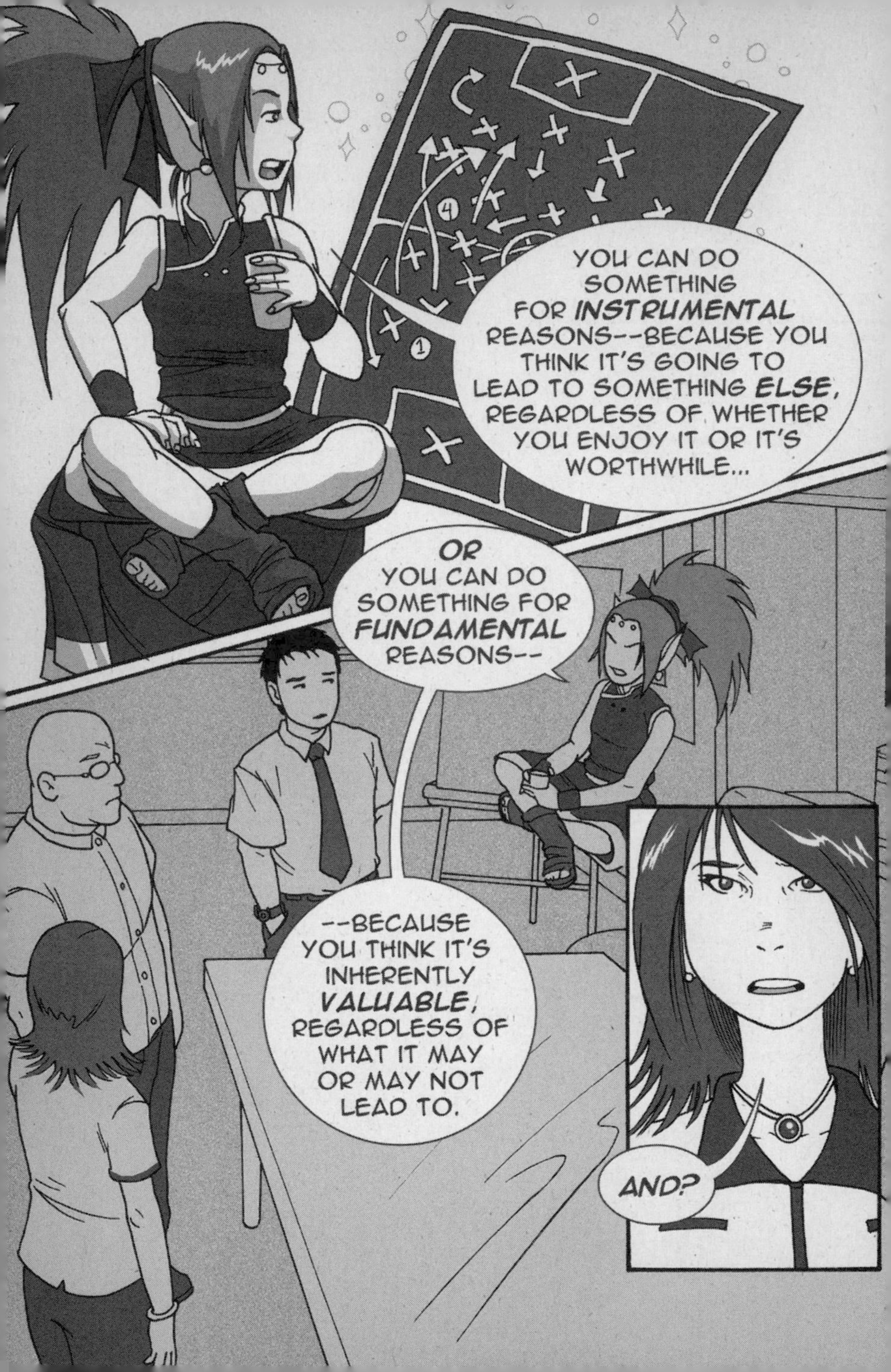
YOU CAN DO SOMETHING FOR **INSTRUMENTAL** REASONS--BECAUSE YOU THINK IT'S GOING TO LEAD TO SOMETHING **ELSE**, REGARDLESS OF WHETHER YOU ENJOY IT OR IT'S WORTHWHILE...
OR YOU CAN DO SOMETHING FOR **FUNDAMENTAL** REASONS--
--BECAUSE YOU THINK IT'S INHERENTLY **VALUABLE**, REGARDLESS OF WHAT IT MAY OR MAY NOT LEAD TO.
AND?

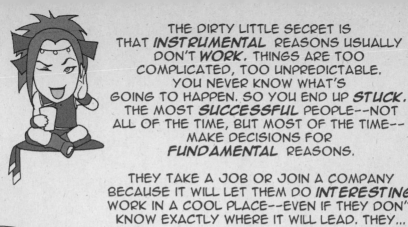

THE DIRTY LITTLE SECRET IS THAT *INSTRUMENTAL* REASONS USUALLY DON'T *WORK*. THINGS ARE TOO COMPLICATED, TOO UNPREDICTABLE. YOU NEVER KNOW WHAT'S GOING TO HAPPEN. SO YOU END UP *STUCK*. THE MOST *SUCCESSFUL* PEOPLE--NOT ALL OF THE TIME, BUT MOST OF THE TIME-- MAKE DECISIONS FOR *FUNDAMENTAL* REASONS.

THEY TAKE A JOB OR JOIN A COMPANY BECAUSE IT WILL LET THEM DO *INTERESTING* WORK IN A COOL PLACE--EVEN IF THEY DON'T KNOW EXACTLY WHERE IT WILL LEAD. THEY...

THEY STUDY *ART HISTORY* INSTEAD OF *ACCOUNTING* BECAUSE THAT'S WHAT *REALLY* TURNS THEM ON.

THEY'RE NOT *FOOLS*. THEY'RE *ENLIGHTENED PRAGMATISTS*.

THEY *UNDERSTAND* WHAT YOU AND YOUR DAD AND YOUR COLLEGE ADVISOR *DIDN'T*.

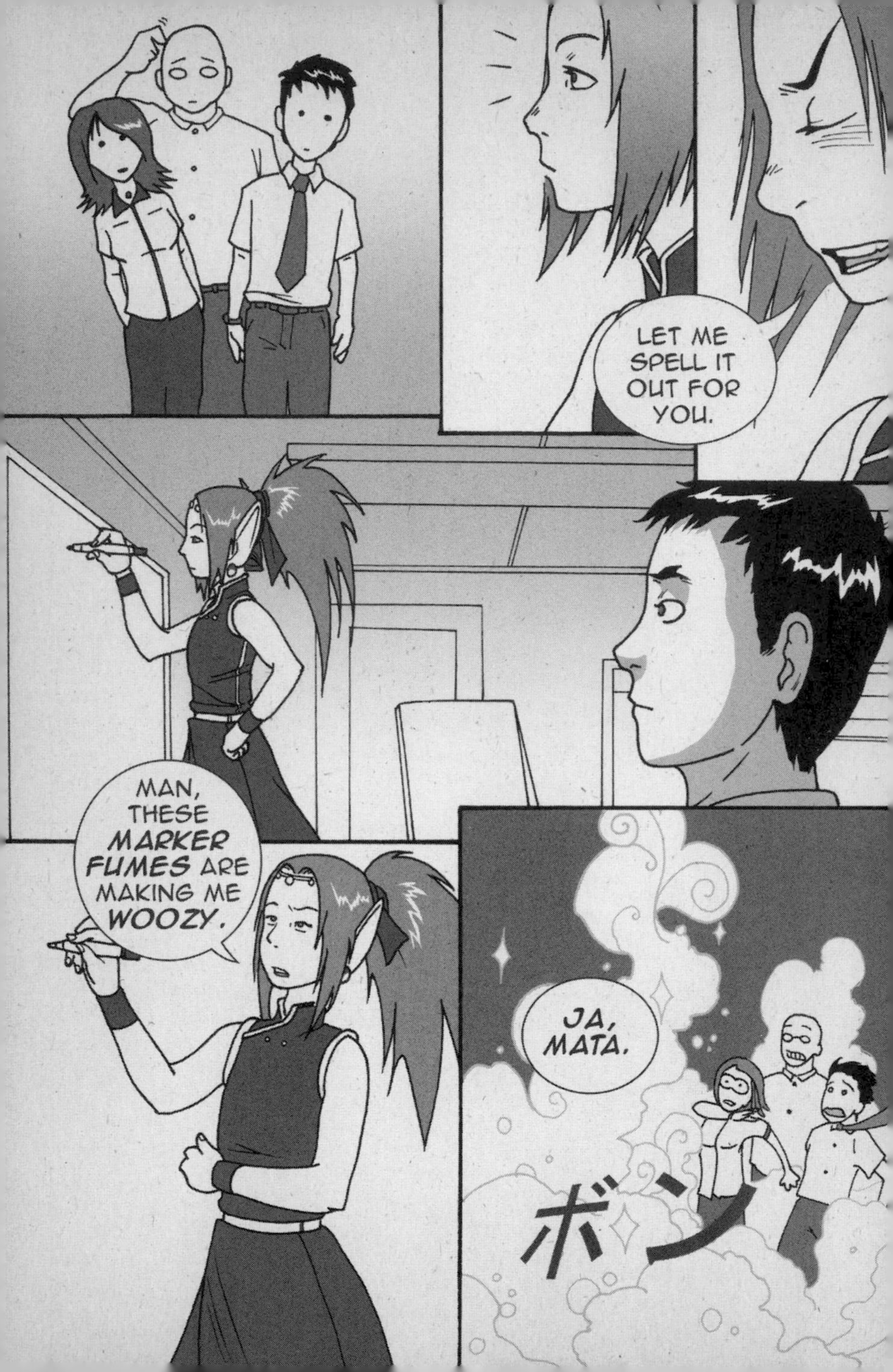
LET ME SPELL IT OUT FOR YOU.
MAN, THESE MARKER FUMES ARE MAKING ME WOOZY.
JA, MATA.
ボン

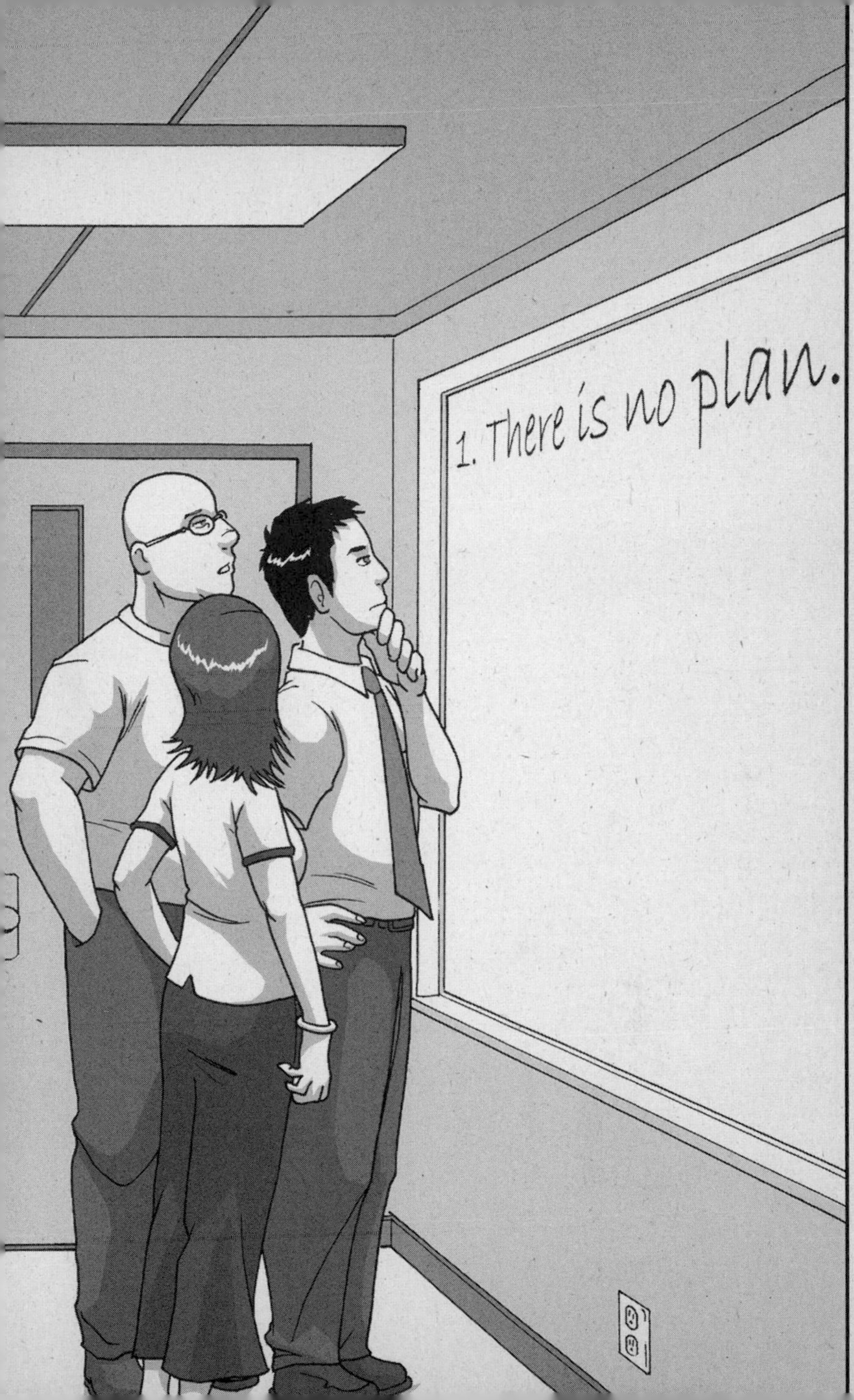
1. There is no plan.

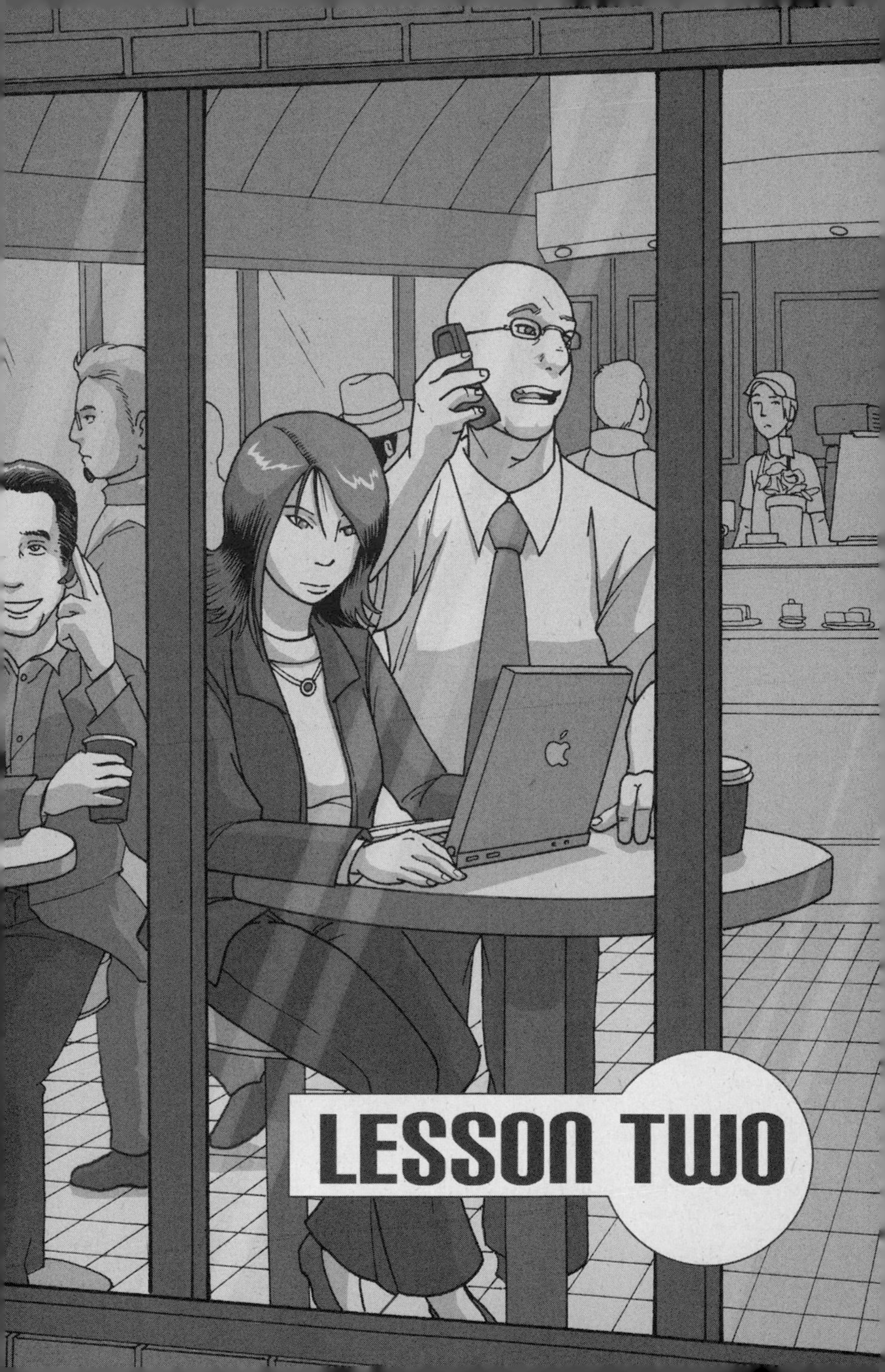
LESSON TWO

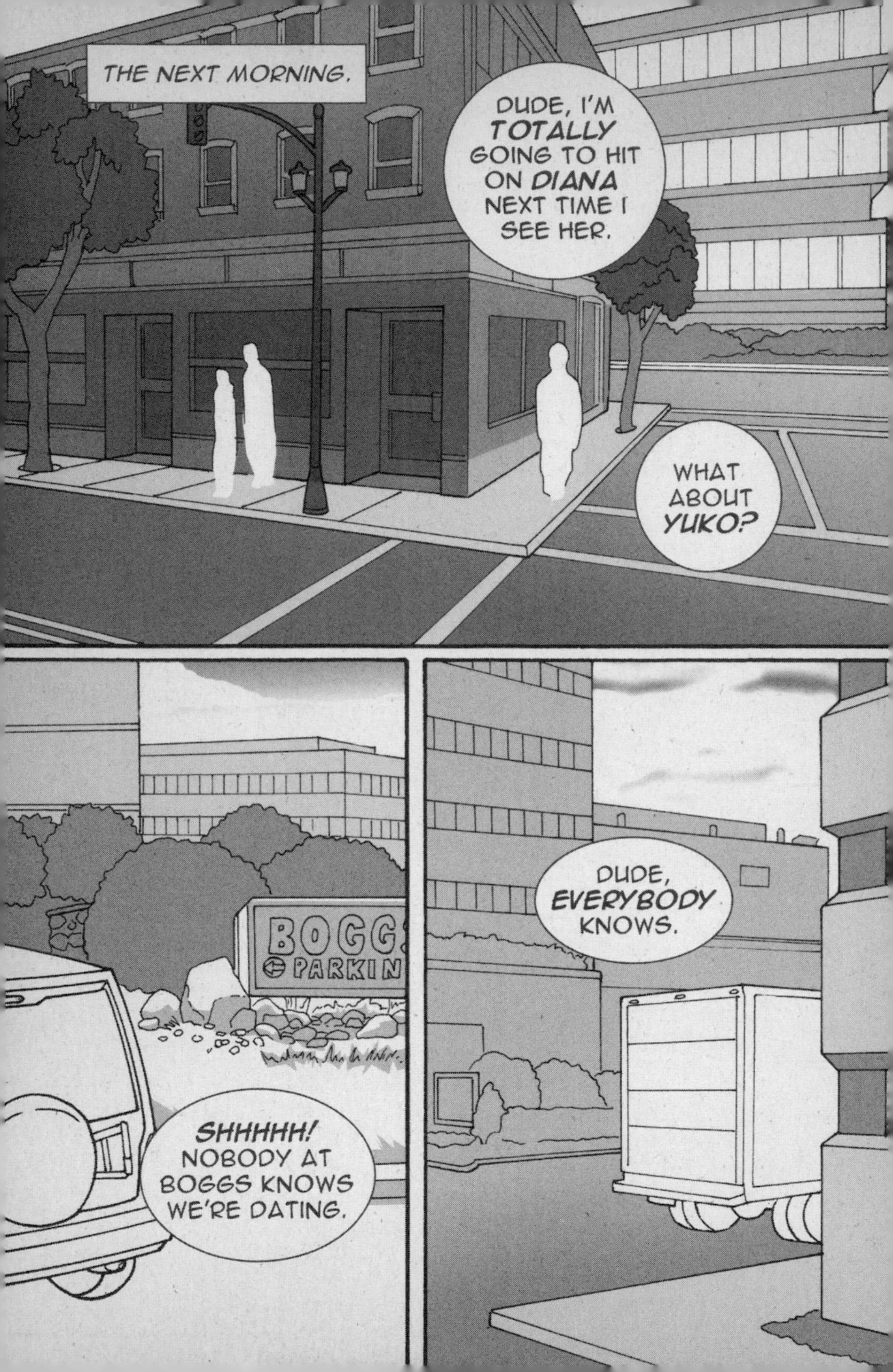
THE NEXT MORNING.
DUDE, I'M TOTALLY GOING TO HIT ON DIANA NEXT TIME I SEE HER.
WHAT ABOUT YUKO?
BOGGS PARKIN
SHHHHH! NOBODY AT BOGGS KNOWS WE'RE DATING.
DUDE, EVERYBODY KNOWS.

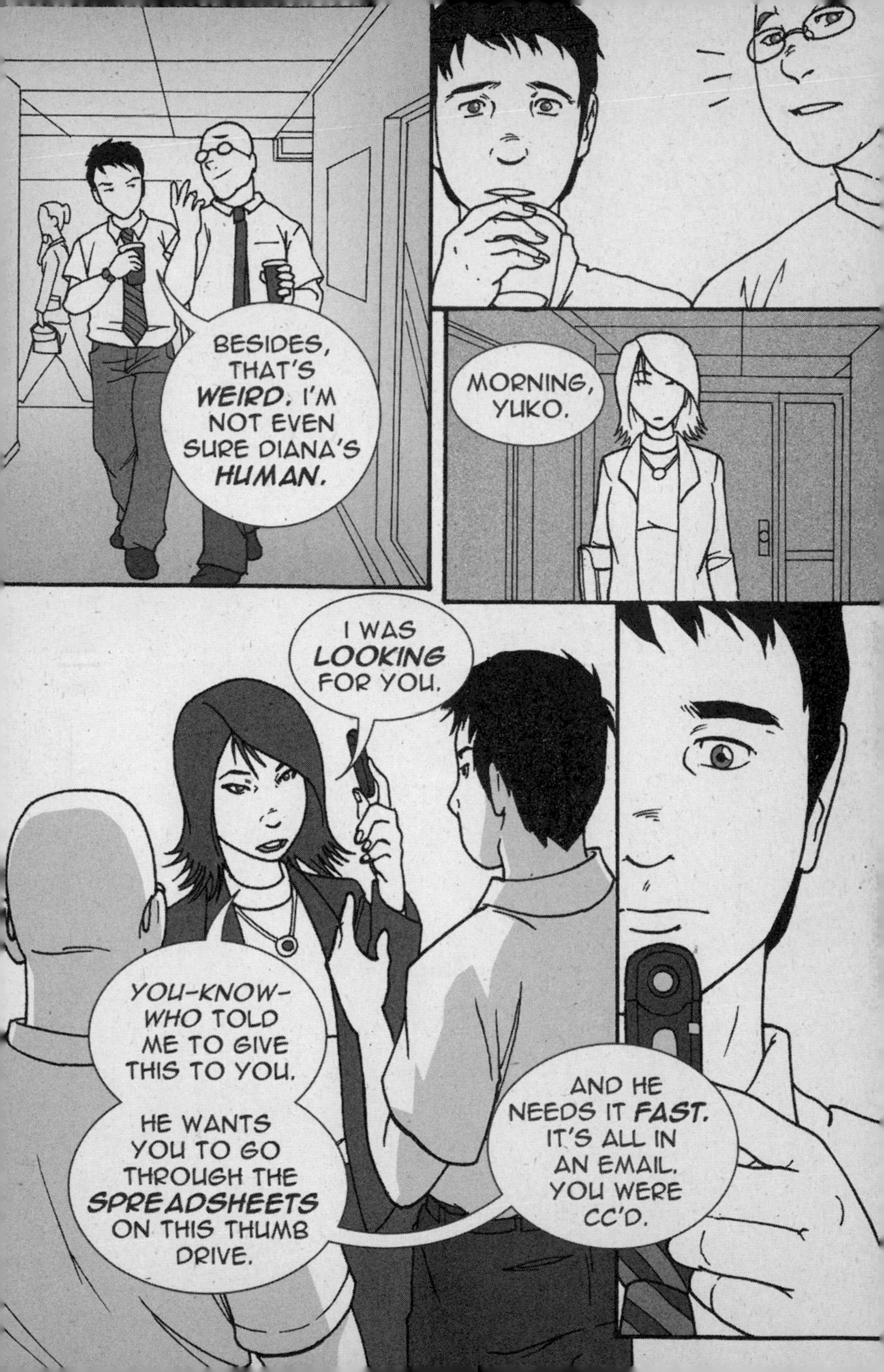
BESIDES, THAT'S WEIRD. I'M NOT EVEN SURE DIANA'S HUMAN.
MORNING, YUKO.
I WAS LOOKING FOR YOU.
YOU-KNOW-WHO TOLD ME TO GIVE THIS TO YOU.
HE WANTS YOU TO GO THROUGH THE SPREADSHEETS ON THIS THUMB DRIVE.
AND HE NEEDS IT FAST. IT'S ALL IN AN EMAIL. YOU WERE CC'D.

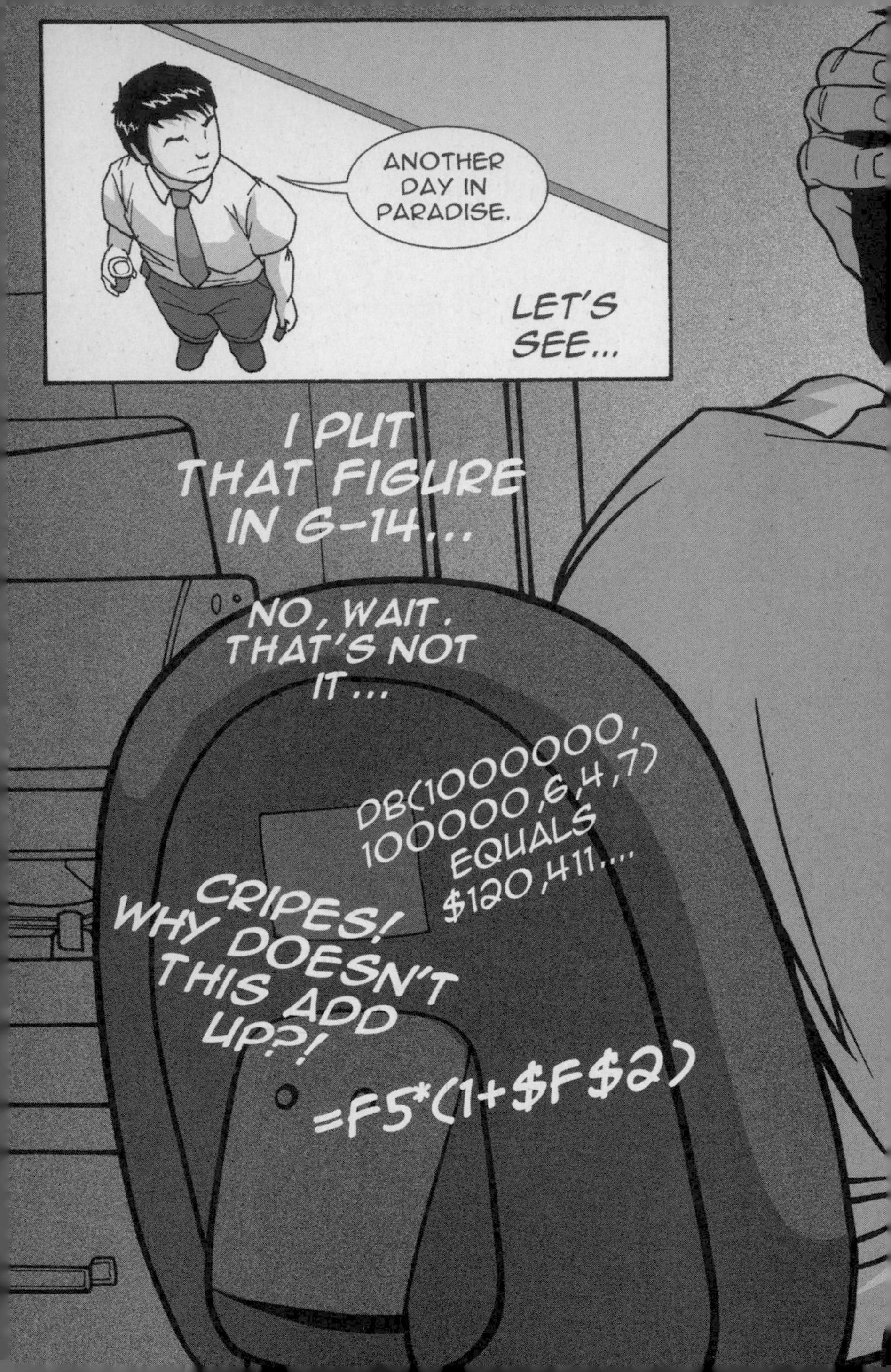
ANOTHER DAY IN PARADISE.
LET'S SEE...
I PUT THAT FIGURE IN G-14...
NO, WAIT. THAT'S NOT IT...
DB(1000000, 100000,6,4,7) EQUALS $120,411....
CRIPES! WHY DOESN'T THIS ADD UP?!
=F5*(1+F2)

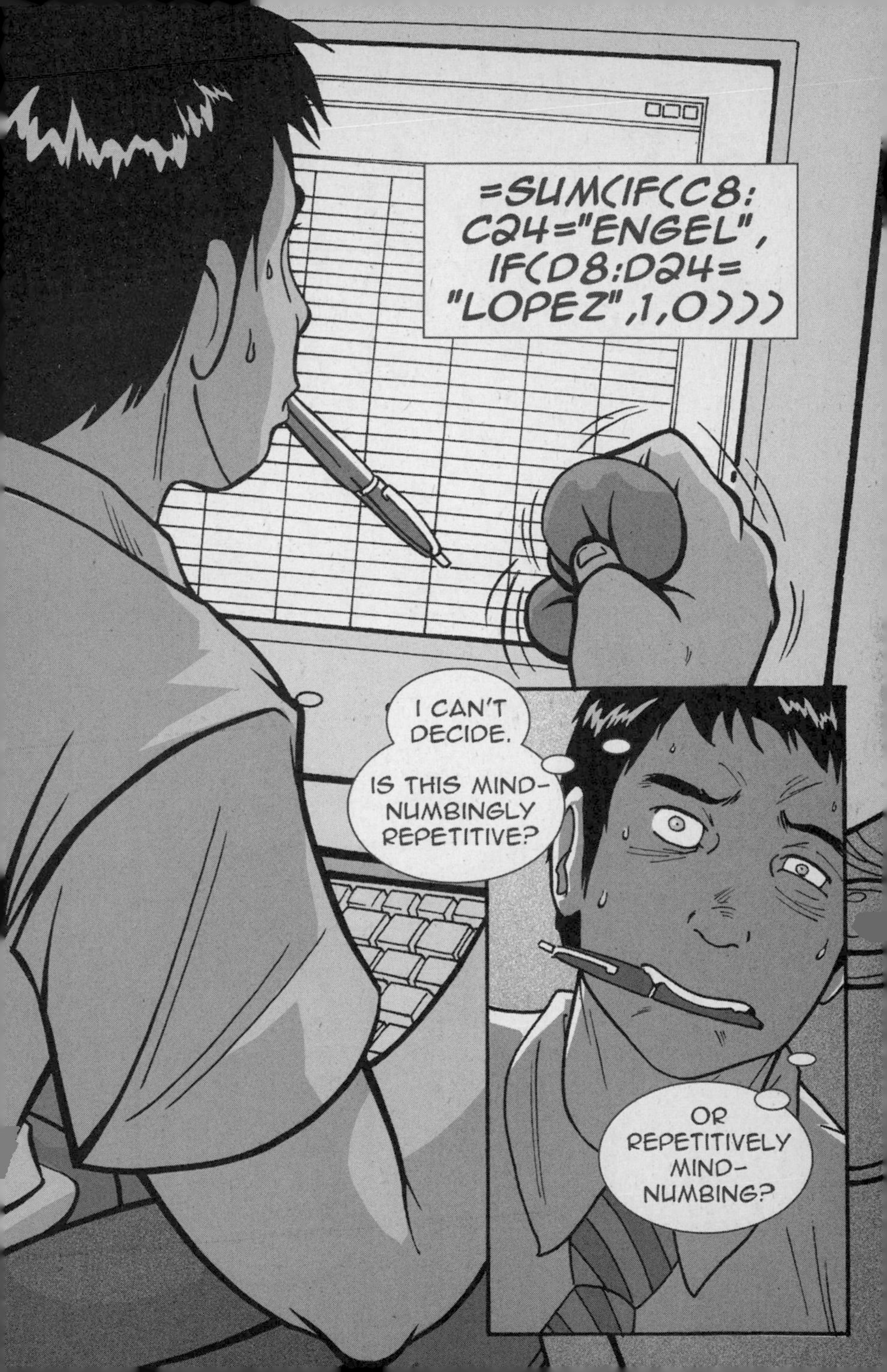
=SUM(IF(C8:C24="ENGEL", IF(D8:D24="LOPEZ",1,0)))
I CAN'T DECIDE.
IS THIS MIND-NUMBINGLY REPETITIVE?
OR REPETITIVELY MIND-NUMBING?

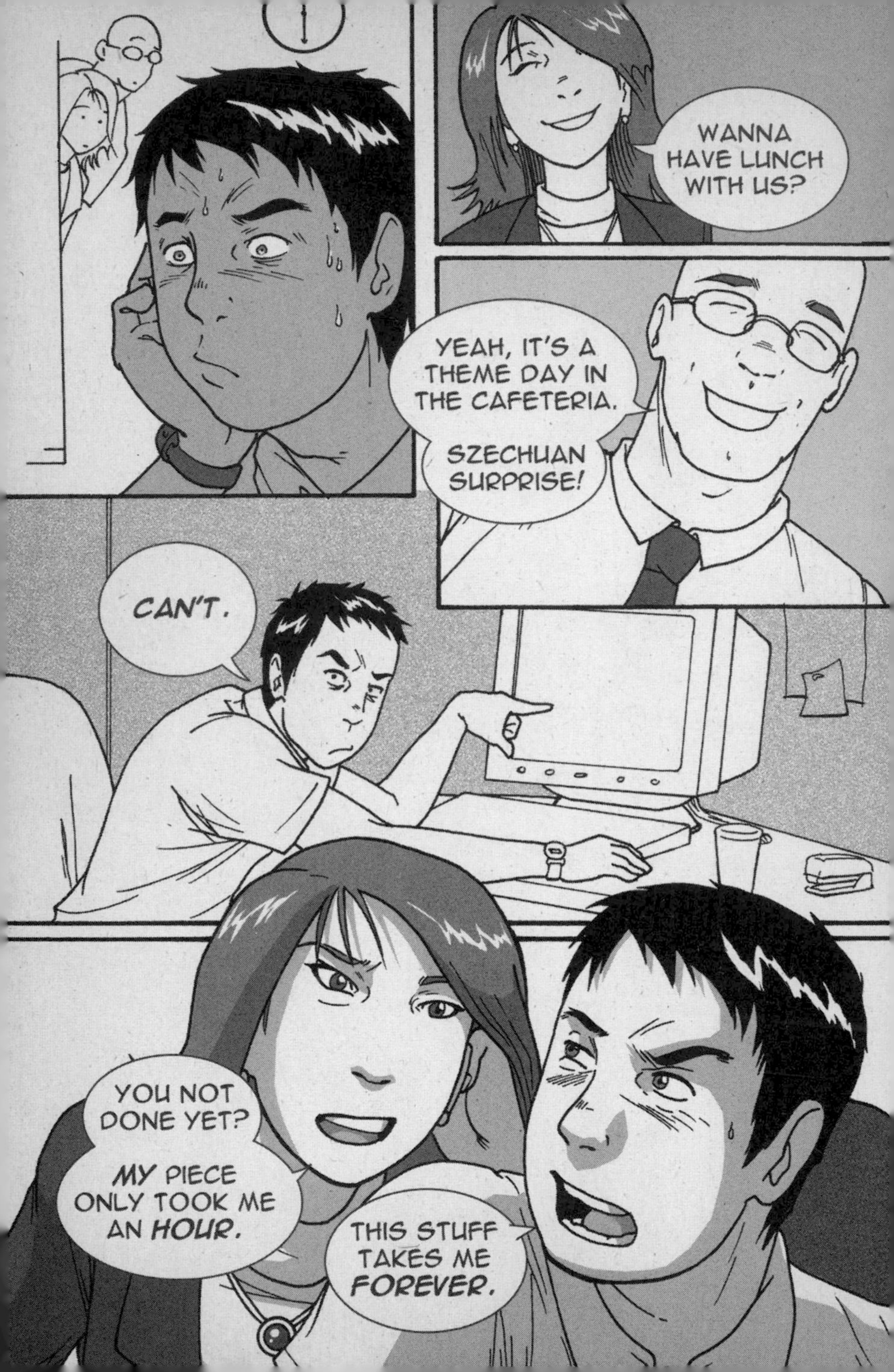
WANNA HAVE LUNCH WITH US?
YEAH, IT'S A THEME DAY IN THE CAFETERIA.
SZECHUAN SURPRISE!
CAN'T.
YOU NOT DONE YET?
MY PIECE ONLY TOOK ME AN HOUR.
THIS STUFF TAKES ME FOREVER.

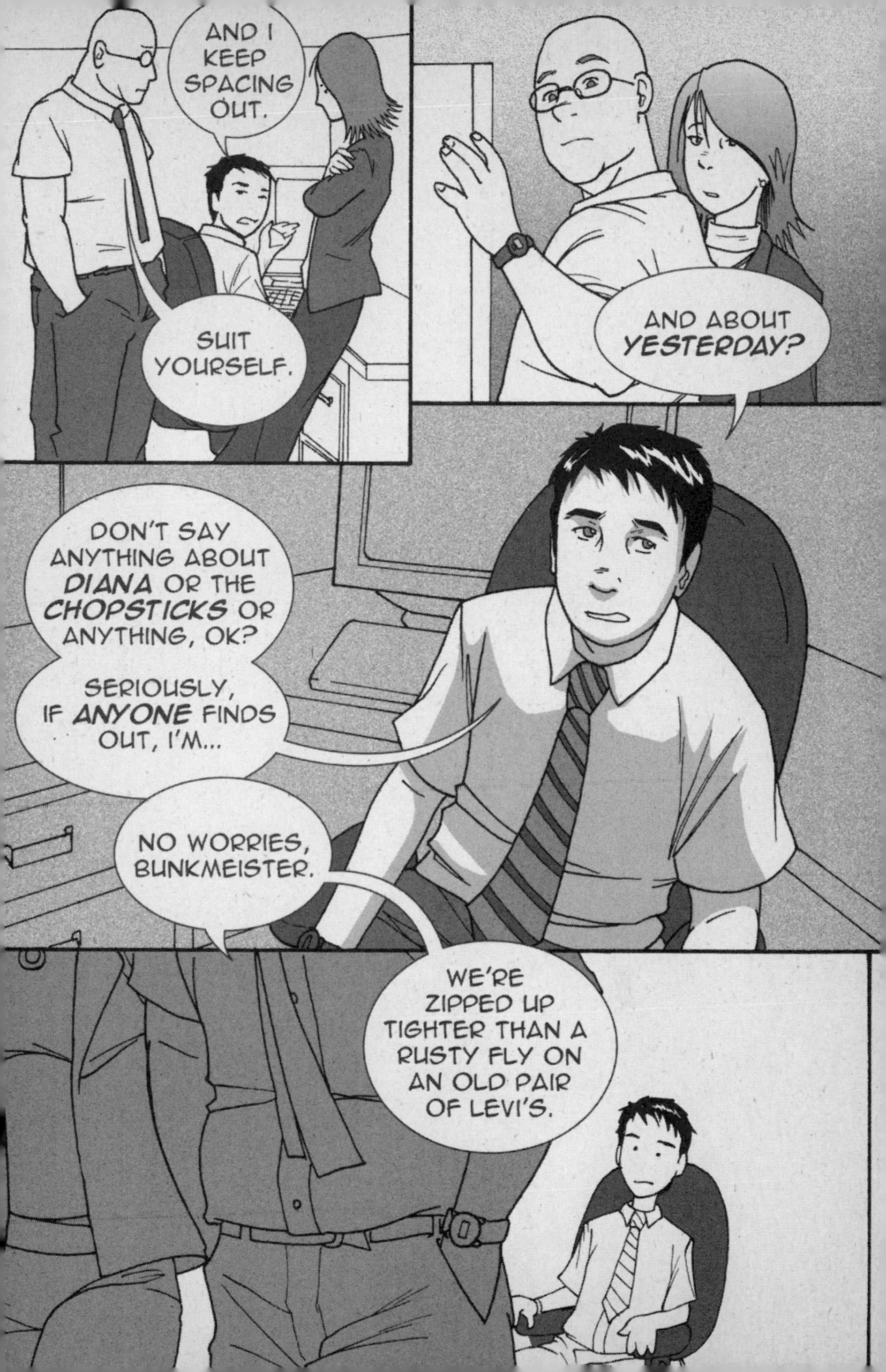
AND I KEEP SPACING OUT.
SUIT YOURSELF.
AND ABOUT *YESTERDAY?*
DON'T SAY ANYTHING ABOUT *DIANA* OR THE *CHOPSTICKS* OR ANYTHING, OK?
SERIOUSLY, IF *ANYONE* FINDS OUT, I'M...
NO WORRIES, BUNKMEISTER.
WE'RE ZIPPED UP TIGHTER THAN A RUSTY FLY ON AN OLD PAIR OF LEVI'S.

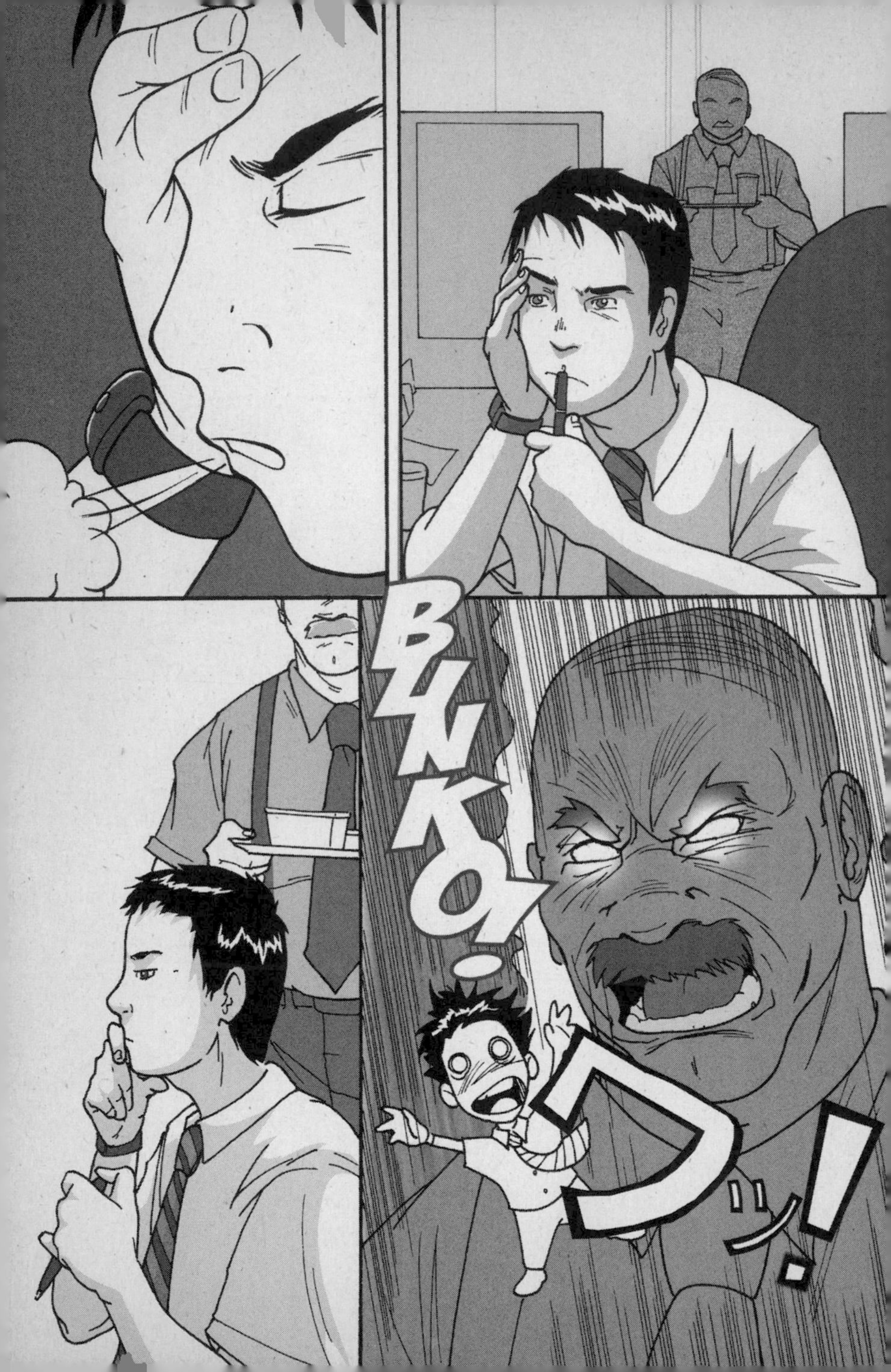

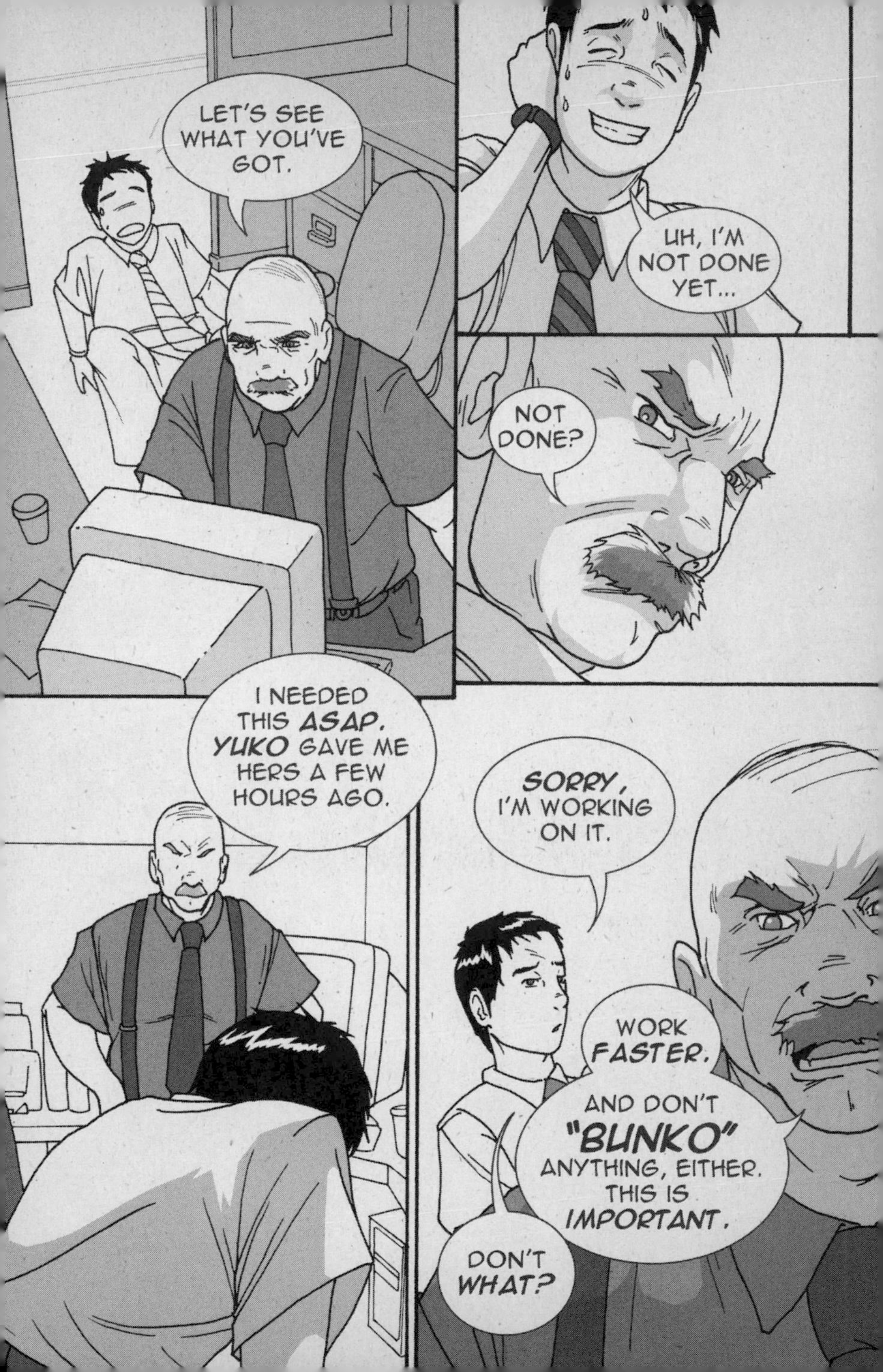
LET'S SEE WHAT YOU'VE GOT.
UH, I'M NOT DONE YET...
NOT DONE?
I NEEDED THIS ASAP. YUKO GAVE ME HERS A FEW HOURS AGO.
SORRY, I'M WORKING ON IT.
WORK FASTER.
AND DON'T "BUNKO" ANYTHING, EITHER. THIS IS IMPORTANT.
DON'T WHAT?

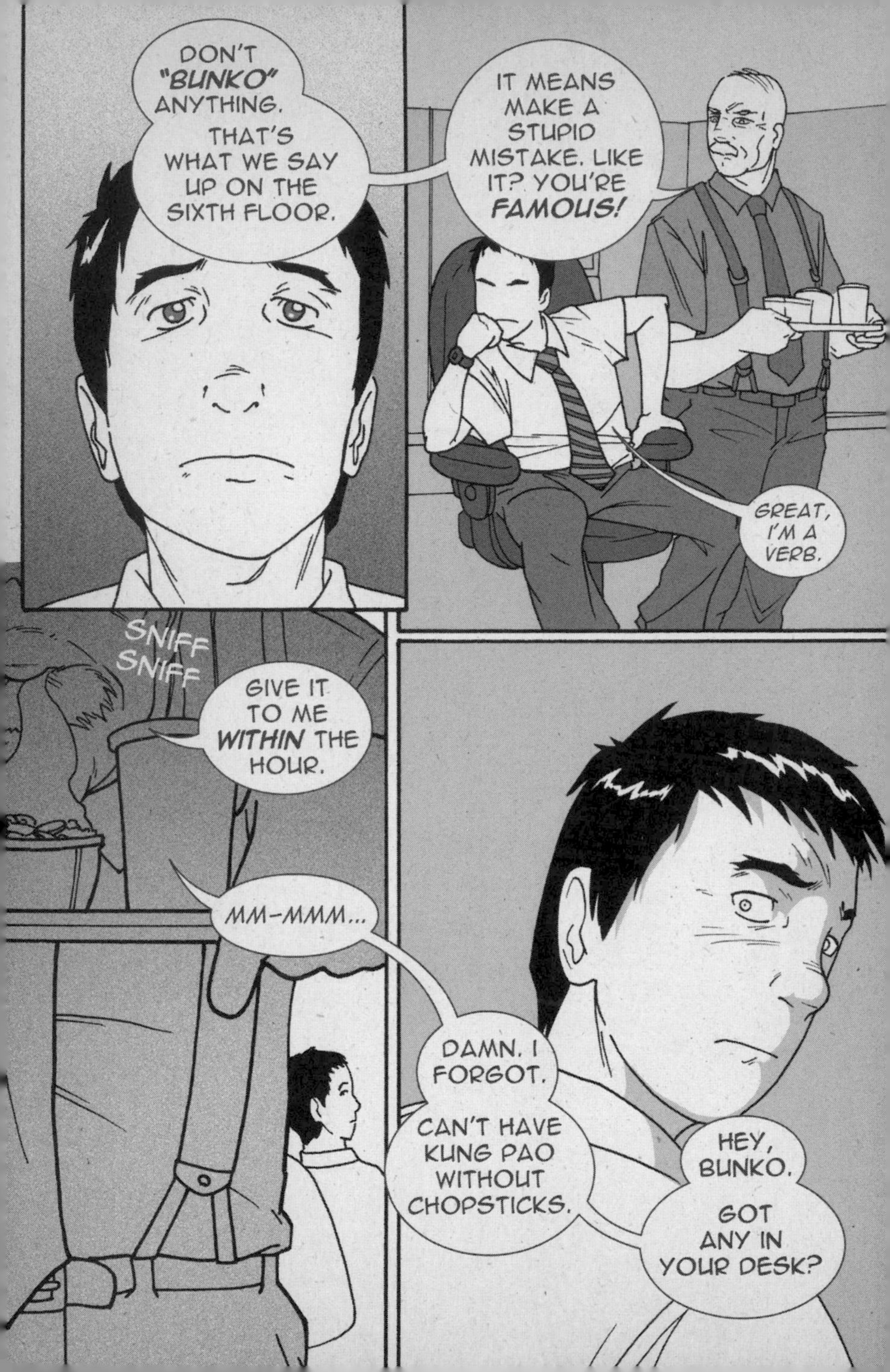
DON'T "BUNKO" ANYTHING.
THAT'S WHAT WE SAY UP ON THE SIXTH FLOOR.
IT MEANS MAKE A STUPID MISTAKE. LIKE IT? YOU'RE FAMOUS!
GREAT, I'M A VERB.
SNIFF SNIFF
GIVE IT TO ME WITHIN THE HOUR.
MM-MMM...
DAMN. I FORGOT.
CAN'T HAVE KUNG PAO WITHOUT CHOPSTICKS.
HEY, BUNKO.
GOT ANY IN YOUR DESK?

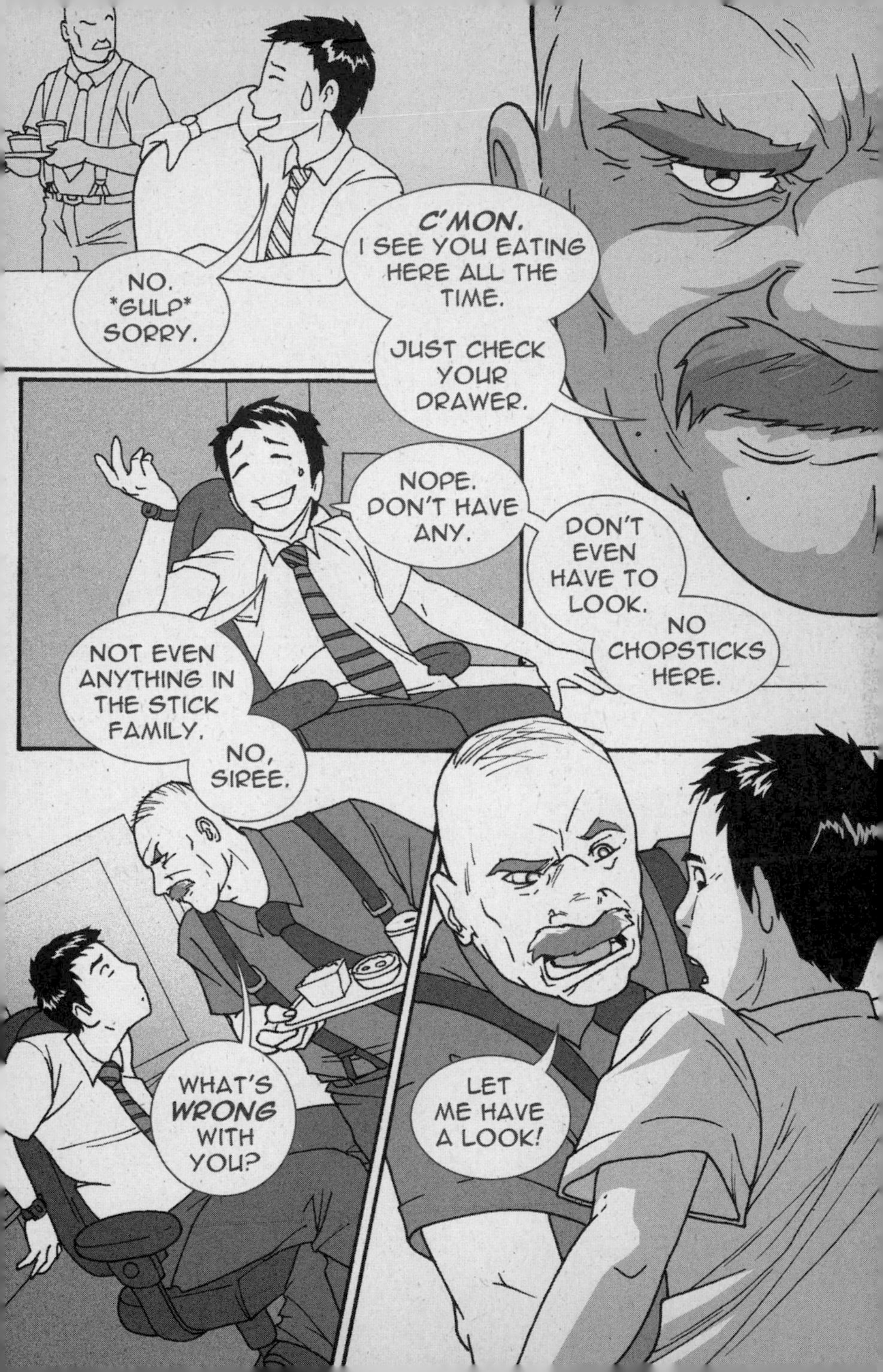
NO. *GULP* SORRY.
C'MON. I SEE YOU EATING HERE ALL THE TIME.
JUST CHECK YOUR DRAWER.
NOPE. DON'T HAVE ANY.
DON'T EVEN HAVE TO LOOK.
NO CHOPSTICKS HERE.
NOT EVEN ANYTHING IN THE STICK FAMILY.
NO, SIREE.
WHAT'S WRONG WITH YOU?
LET ME HAVE A LOOK!

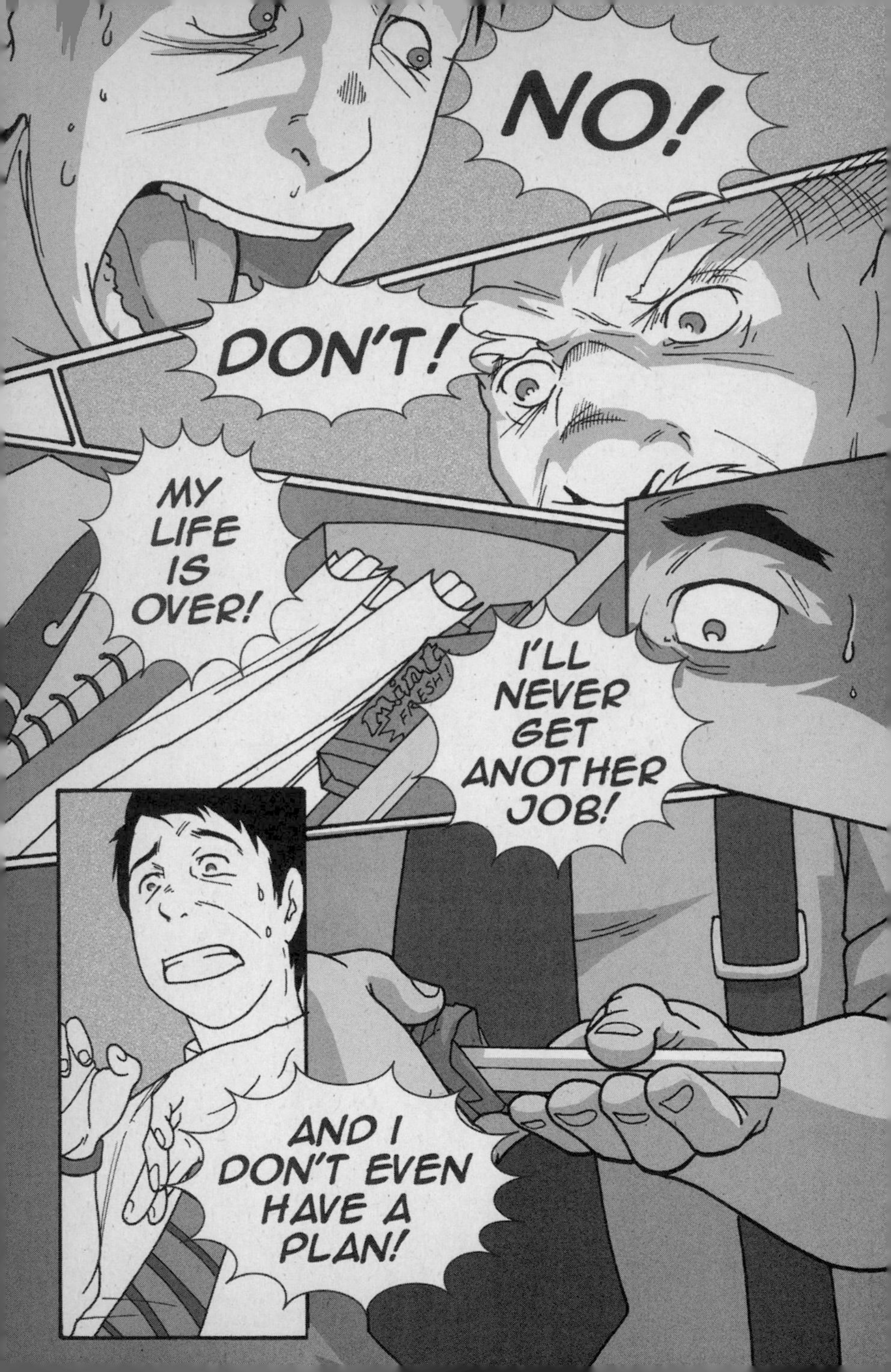
NO!
DON'T!
MY LIFE IS OVER!
I'LL NEVER GET ANOTHER JOB!
AND I DON'T EVEN HAVE A PLAN!

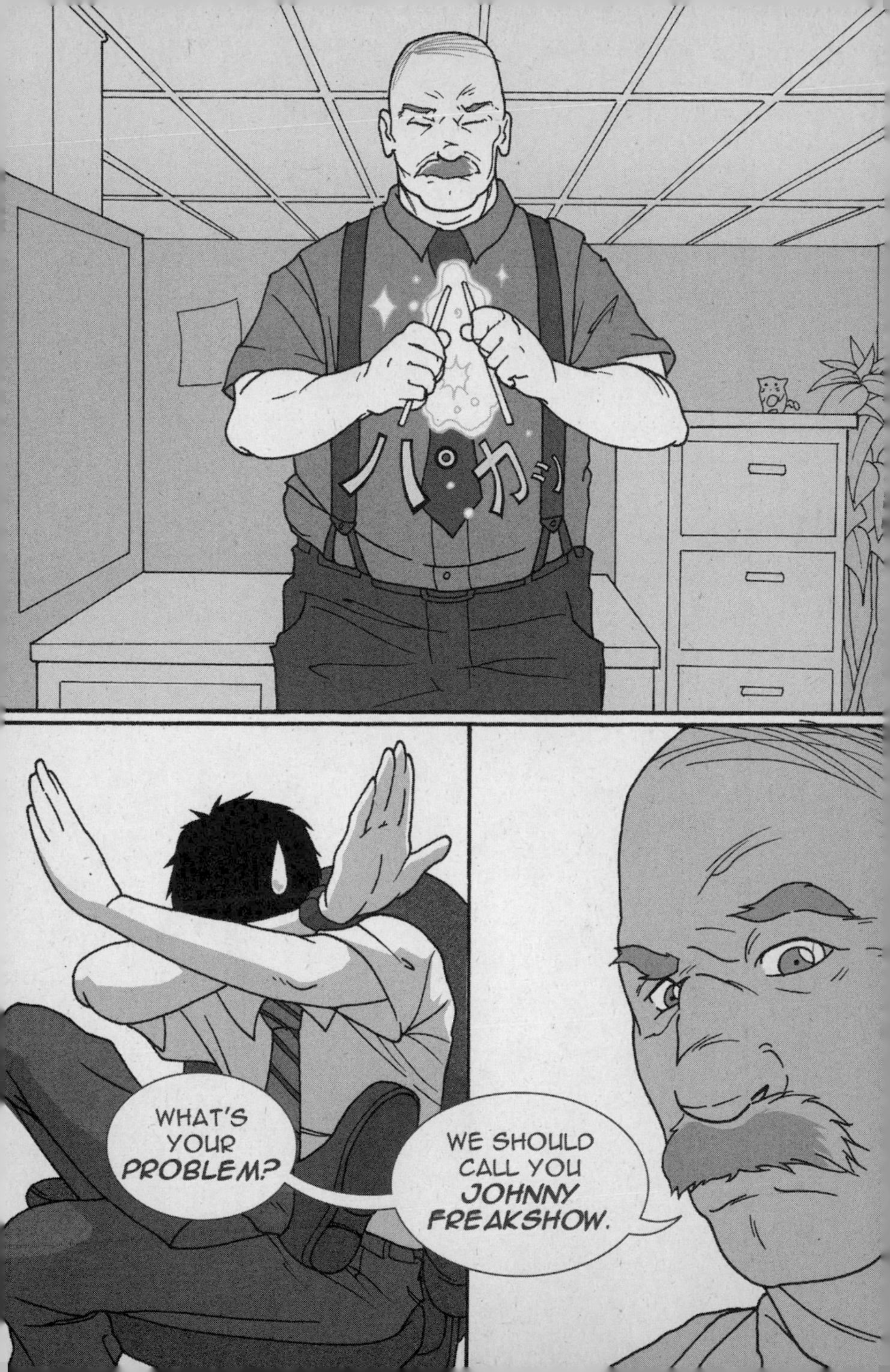
WHAT'S YOUR PROBLEM?
WE SHOULD CALL YOU JOHNNY FREAKSHOW.

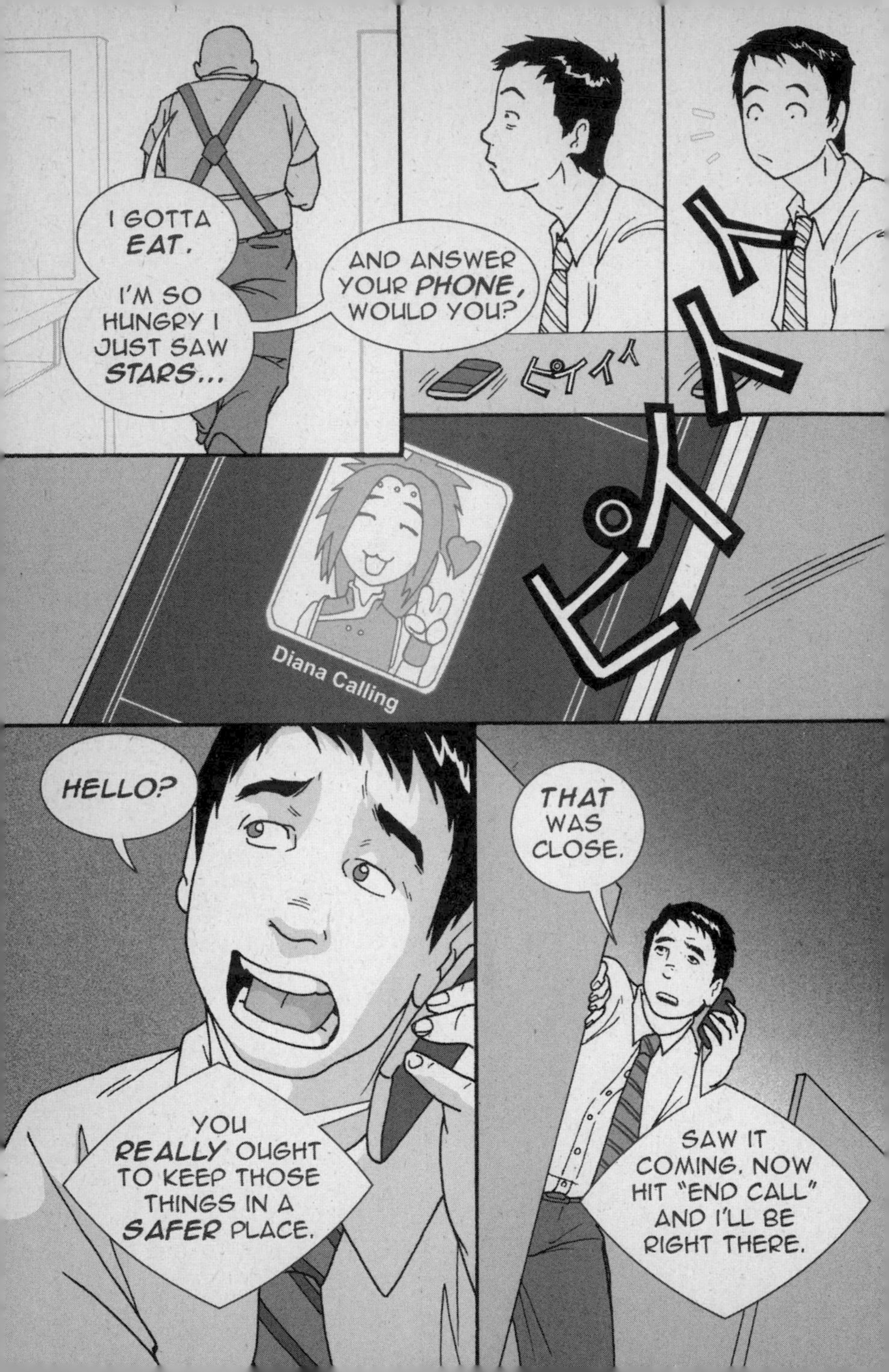
I GOTTA EAT.
I'M SO HUNGRY I JUST SAW STARS...
AND ANSWER YOUR PHONE, WOULD YOU?
ピイイ
ピイイ
Diana Calling
HELLO?
YOU REALLY OUGHT TO KEEP THOSE THINGS IN A SAFER PLACE.
THAT WAS CLOSE.
SAW IT COMING. NOW HIT "END CALL" AND I'LL BE RIGHT THERE.

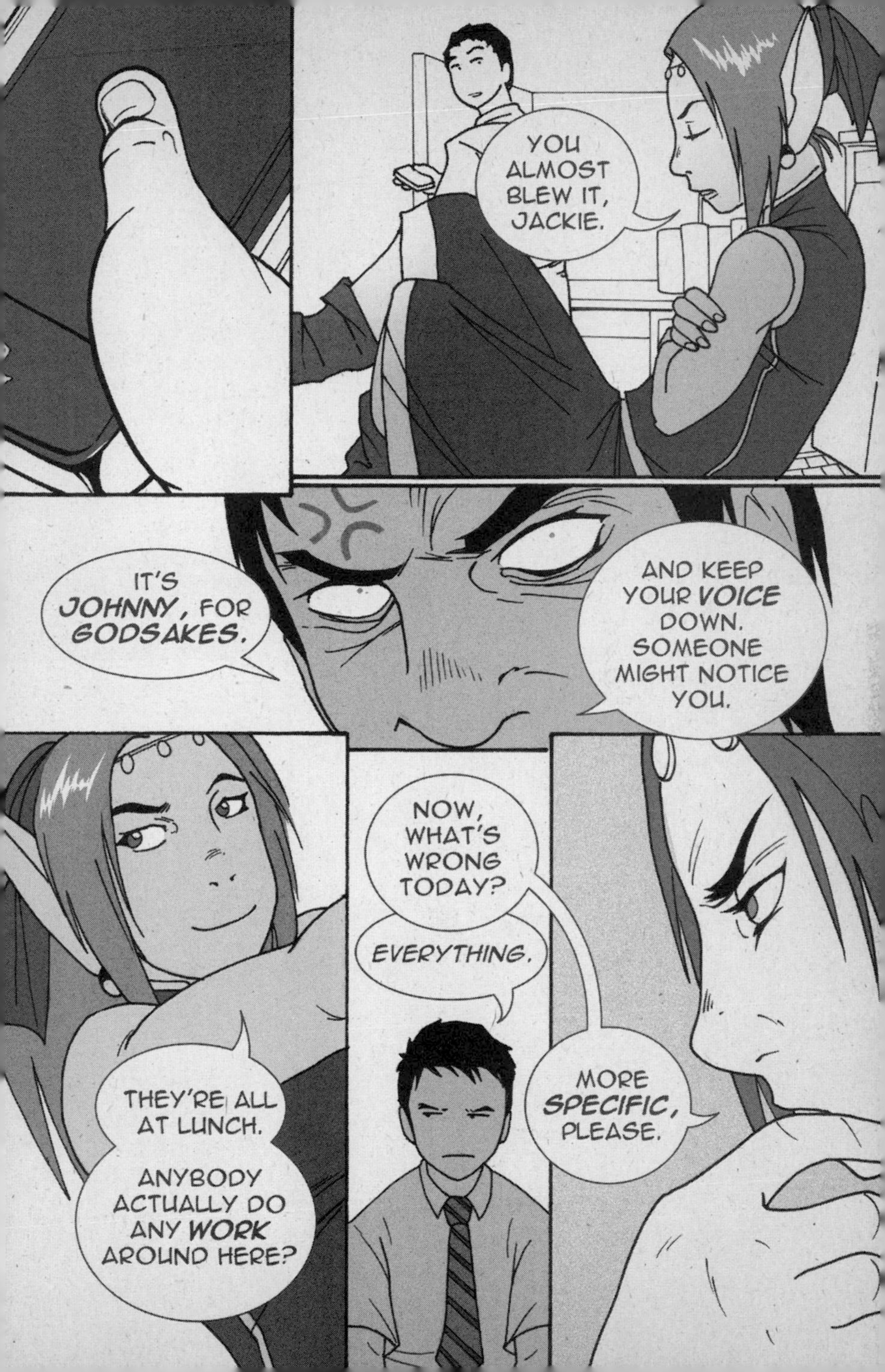
YOU ALMOST BLEW IT, JACKIE.
IT'S JOHNNY, FOR GODSAKES.
AND KEEP YOUR VOICE DOWN. SOMEONE MIGHT NOTICE YOU.
THEY'RE ALL AT LUNCH.
ANYBODY ACTUALLY DO ANY WORK AROUND HERE?
NOW, WHAT'S WRONG TODAY?
EVERYTHING.
MORE SPECIFIC, PLEASE.

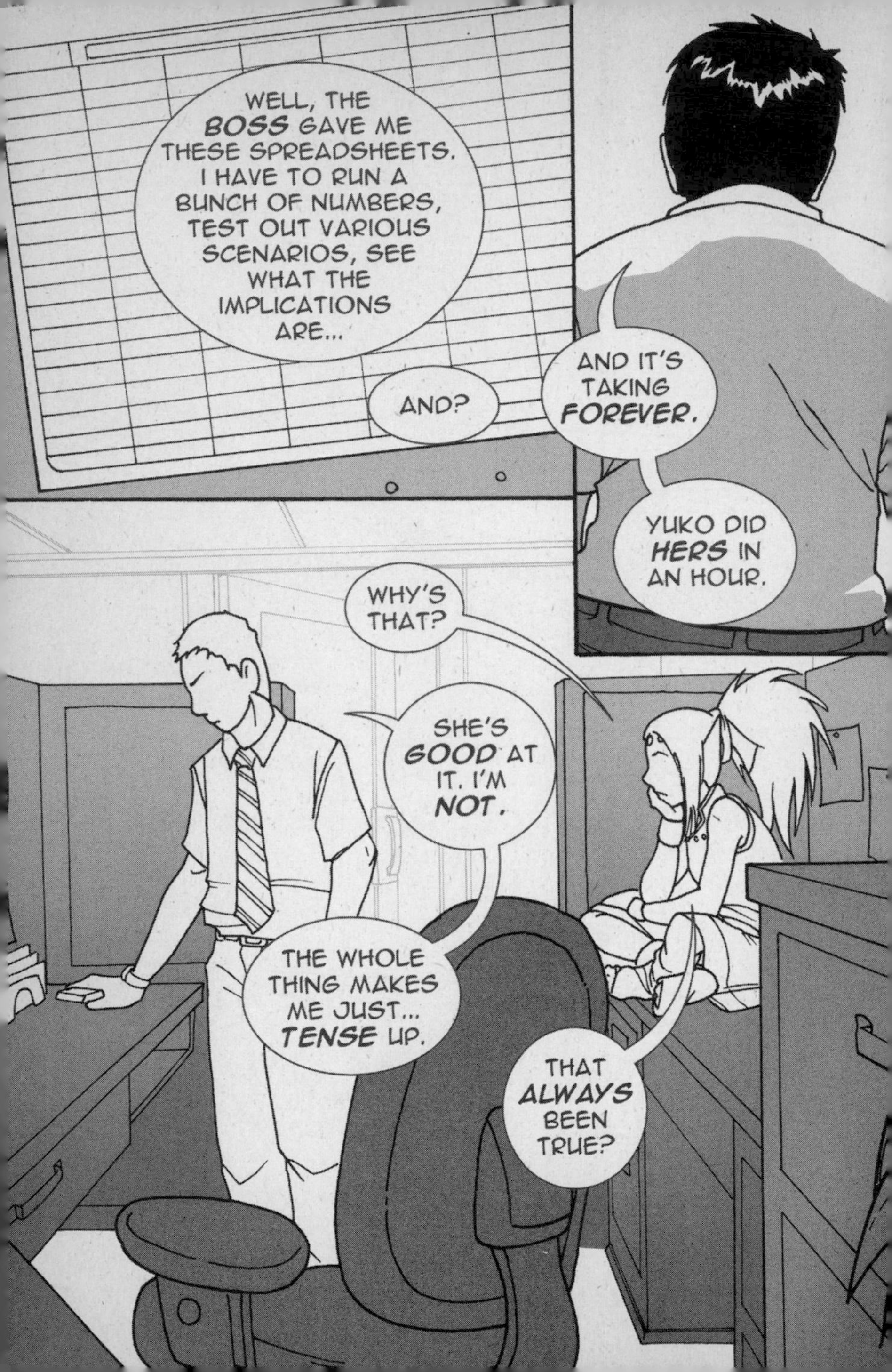
WELL, THE BOSS GAVE ME THESE SPREADSHEETS. I HAVE TO RUN A BUNCH OF NUMBERS, TEST OUT VARIOUS SCENARIOS, SEE WHAT THE IMPLICATIONS ARE...
AND?
AND IT'S TAKING FOREVER.
YUKO DID HERS IN AN HOUR.
WHY'S THAT?
SHE'S GOOD AT IT. I'M NOT.
THE WHOLE THING MAKES ME JUST... TENSE UP.
THAT ALWAYS BEEN TRUE?

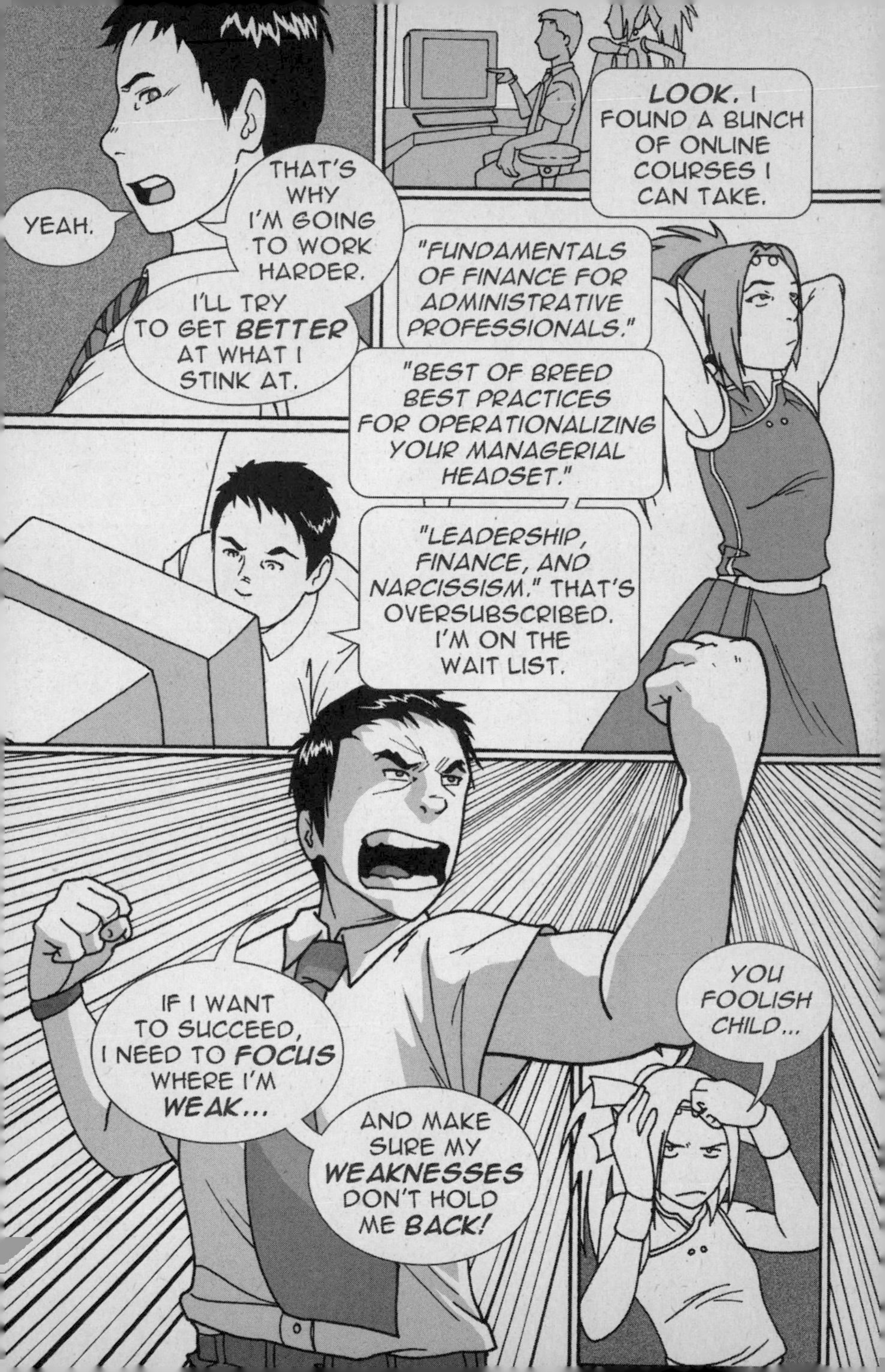
YEAH.
THAT'S WHY I'M GOING TO WORK HARDER.
I'LL TRY TO GET BETTER AT WHAT I STINK AT.
LOOK. I FOUND A BUNCH OF ONLINE COURSES I CAN TAKE.
"FUNDAMENTALS OF FINANCE FOR ADMINISTRATIVE PROFESSIONALS."
"BEST OF BREED BEST PRACTICES FOR OPERATIONALIZING YOUR MANAGERIAL HEADSET."
"LEADERSHIP, FINANCE, AND NARCISSISM." THAT'S OVERSUBSCRIBED. I'M ON THE WAIT LIST.
IF I WANT TO SUCCEED, I NEED TO FOCUS WHERE I'M WEAK...
AND MAKE SURE MY WEAKNESSES DON'T HOLD ME BACK!
YOU FOOLISH CHILD...

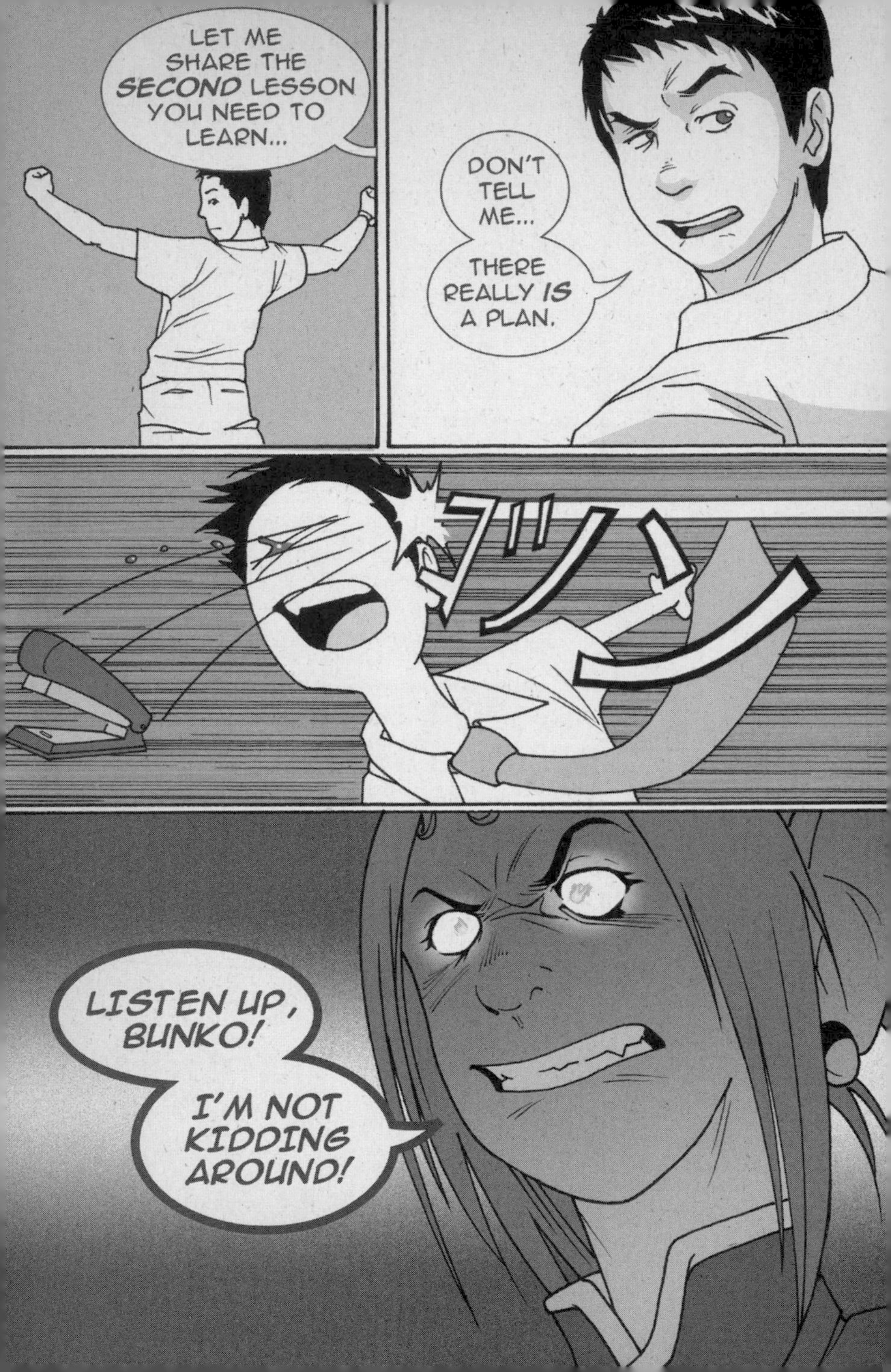
LET ME SHARE THE SECOND LESSON YOU NEED TO LEARN...
DON'T TELL ME...
THERE REALLY IS A PLAN.
ブツン
LISTEN UP, BUNKO!
I'M NOT KIDDING AROUND!

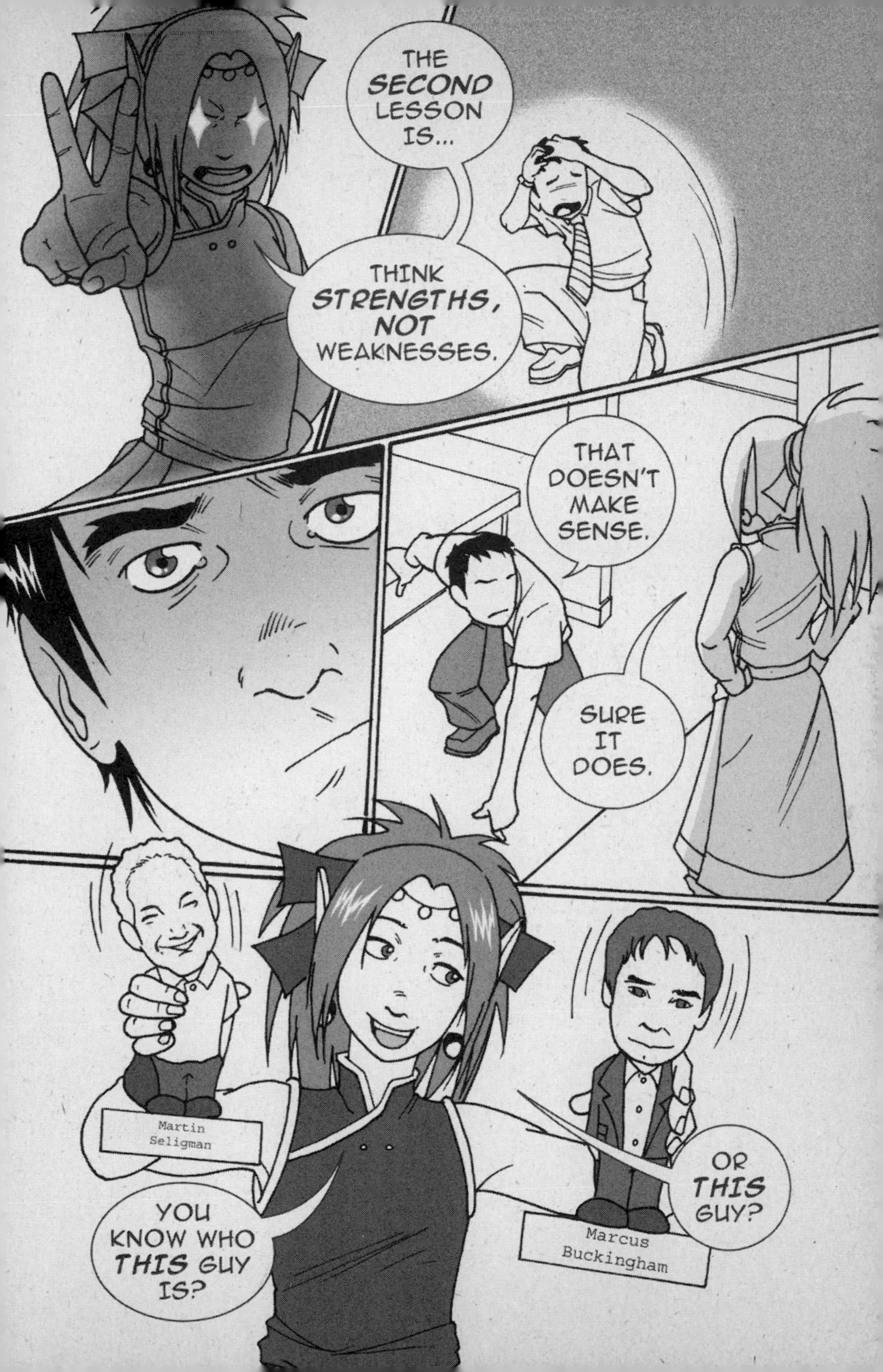
THE SECOND LESSON IS...
THINK STRENGTHS, NOT WEAKNESSES.
THAT DOESN'T MAKE SENSE.
SURE IT DOES.
Martin Seligman
YOU KNOW WHO THIS GUY IS?
Marcus Buckingham
OR THIS GUY?

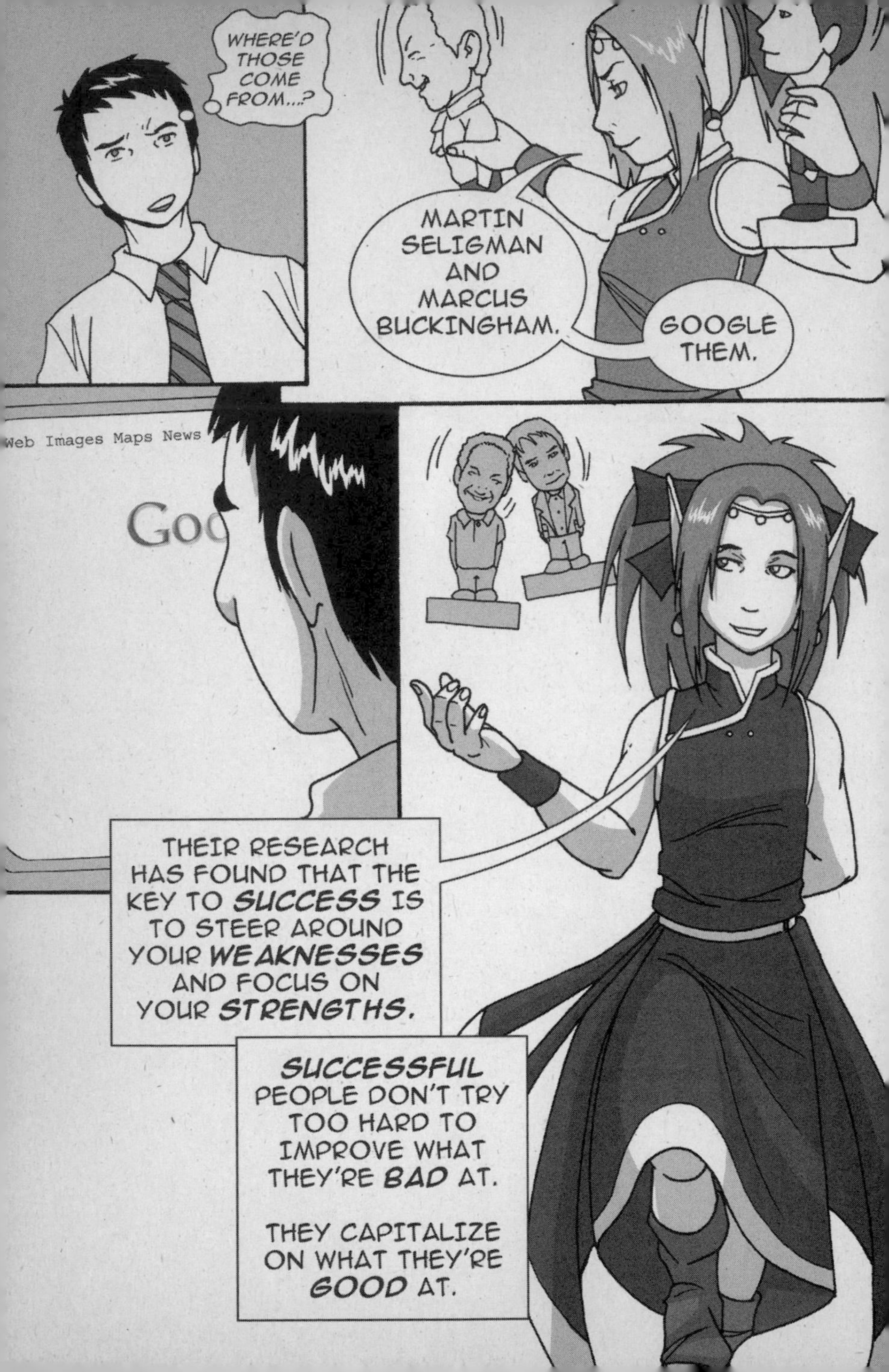
WHERE'D THOSE COME FROM...?
MARTIN SELIGMAN AND MARCUS BUCKINGHAM.
GOOGLE THEM.
Web Images Maps News
THEIR RESEARCH HAS FOUND THAT THE KEY TO SUCCESS IS TO STEER AROUND YOUR WEAKNESSES AND FOCUS ON YOUR STRENGTHS.
SUCCESSFUL PEOPLE DON'T TRY TOO HARD TO IMPROVE WHAT THEY'RE BAD AT.
THEY CAPITALIZE ON WHAT THEY'RE GOOD AT.

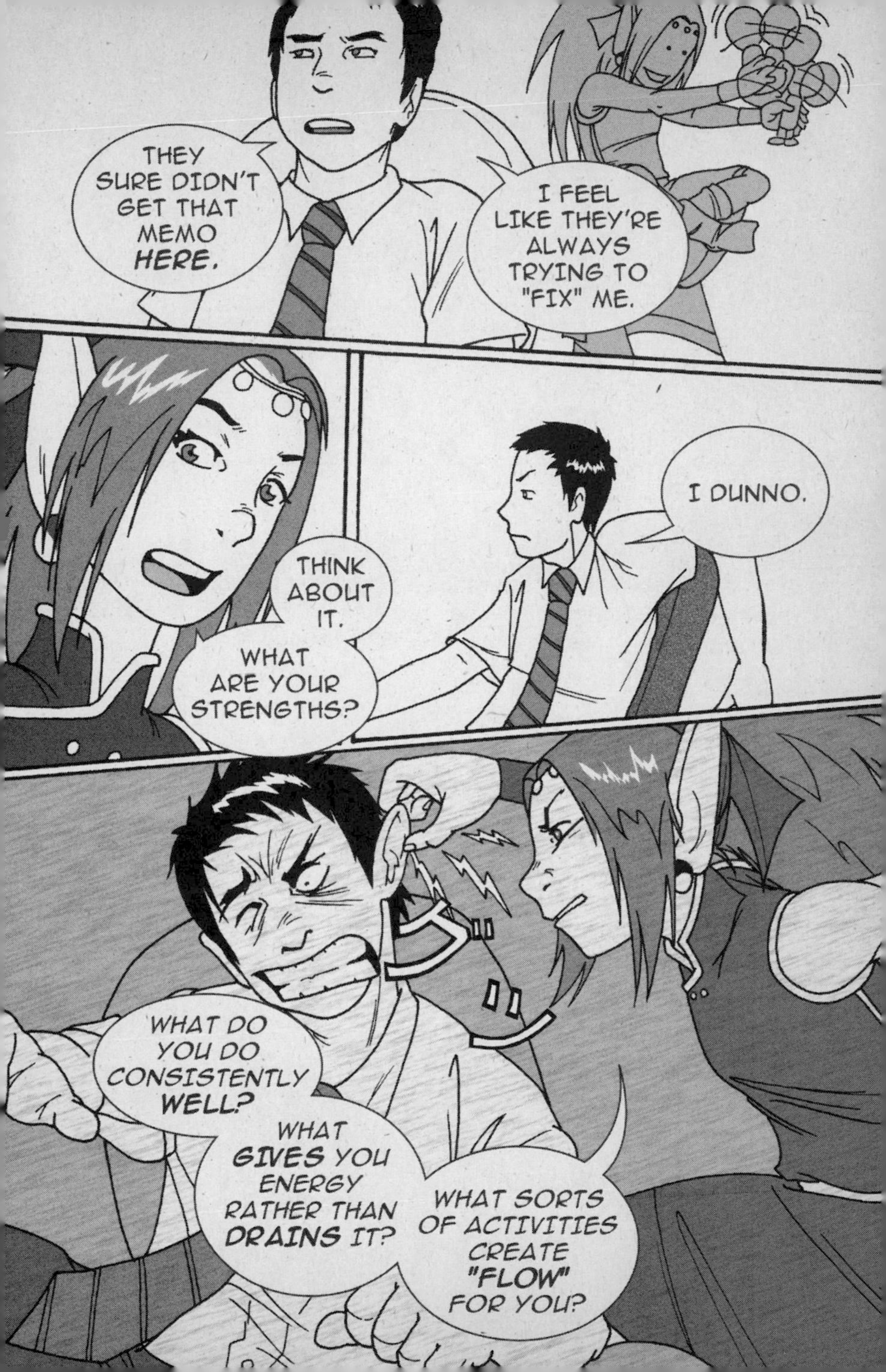
THEY SURE DIDN'T GET THAT MEMO **HERE.**
I FEEL LIKE THEY'RE ALWAYS TRYING TO "FIX" ME.
I DUNNO.
THINK ABOUT IT.
WHAT ARE YOUR STRENGTHS?
WHAT DO YOU DO CONSISTENTLY **WELL?**
WHAT **GIVES** YOU ENERGY RATHER THAN **DRAINS** IT?
WHAT SORTS OF ACTIVITIES CREATE **"FLOW"** FOR YOU?

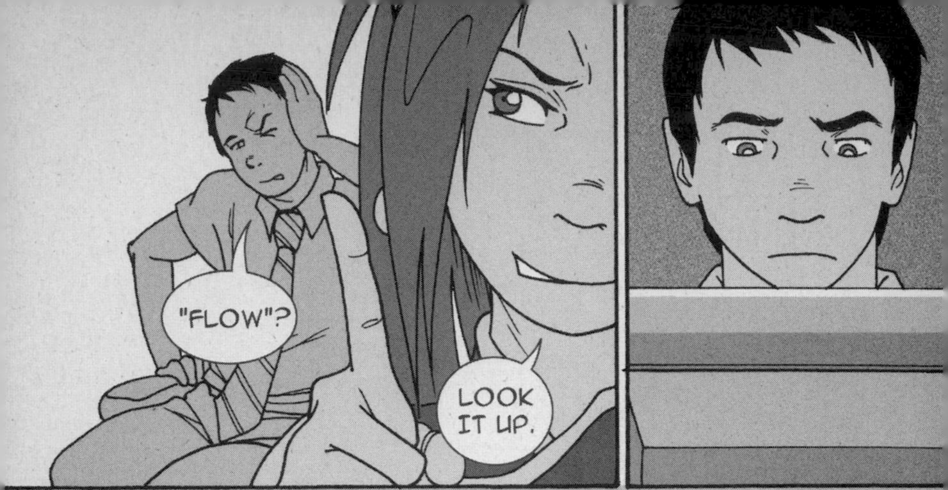
"FLOW"?
LOOK IT UP.

FLOW is the mental state of operation in which the person is fully immersed in what he or she is doing, characterized by a feeling of energized focus, full involvement, and success in the process of the activity.

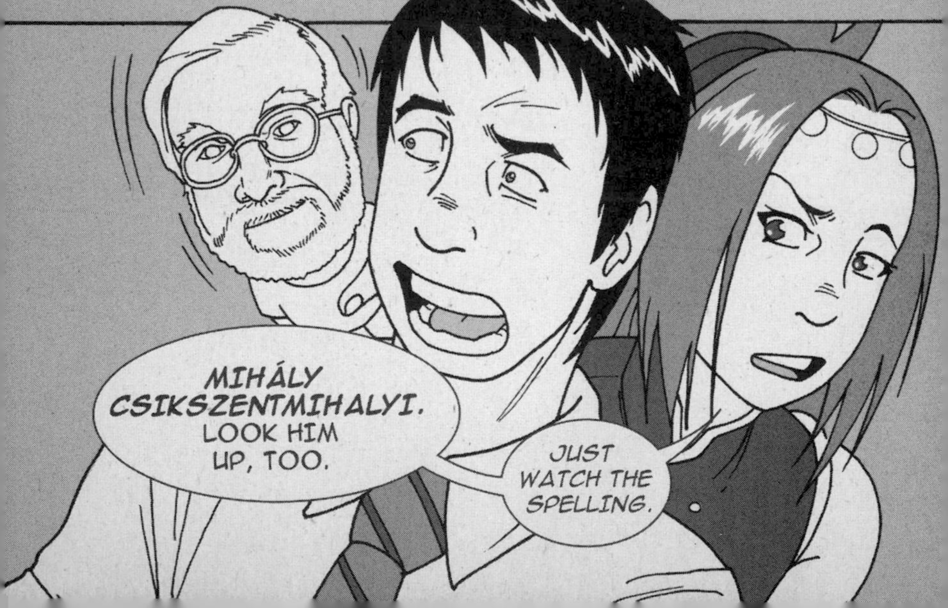
MIHÁLY CSIKSZENTMIHALYI. LOOK HIM UP, TOO.
JUST WATCH THE SPELLING.

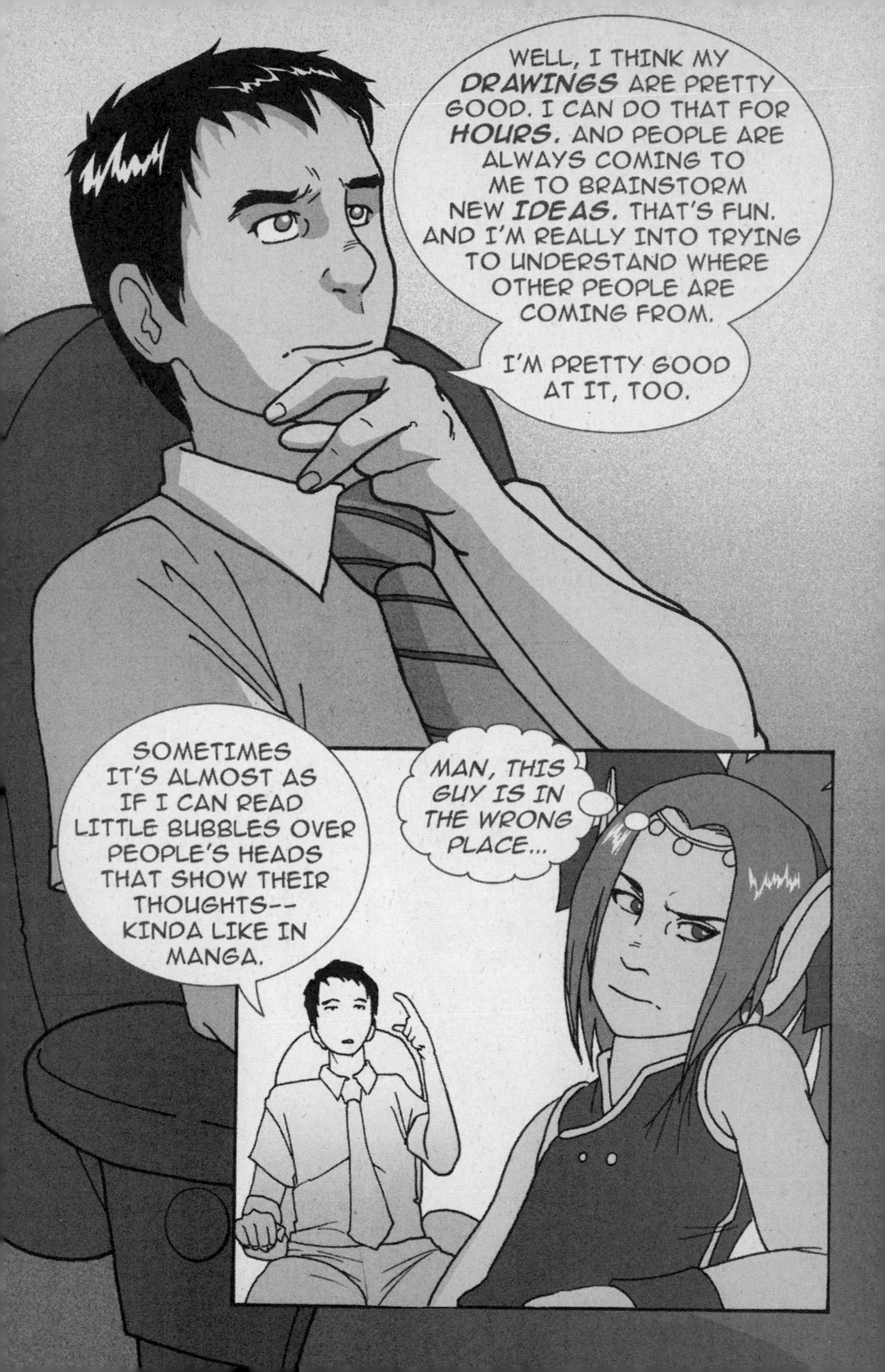
WELL, I THINK MY *DRAWINGS* ARE PRETTY GOOD. I CAN DO THAT FOR *HOURS.* AND PEOPLE ARE ALWAYS COMING TO ME TO BRAINSTORM NEW *IDEAS.* THAT'S FUN. AND I'M REALLY INTO TRYING TO UNDERSTAND WHERE OTHER PEOPLE ARE COMING FROM.
I'M PRETTY GOOD AT IT, TOO.
SOMETIMES IT'S ALMOST AS IF I CAN READ LITTLE BUBBLES OVER PEOPLE'S HEADS THAT SHOW THEIR THOUGHTS-- KINDA LIKE IN MANGA.
MAN, THIS GUY IS IN THE WRONG PLACE...

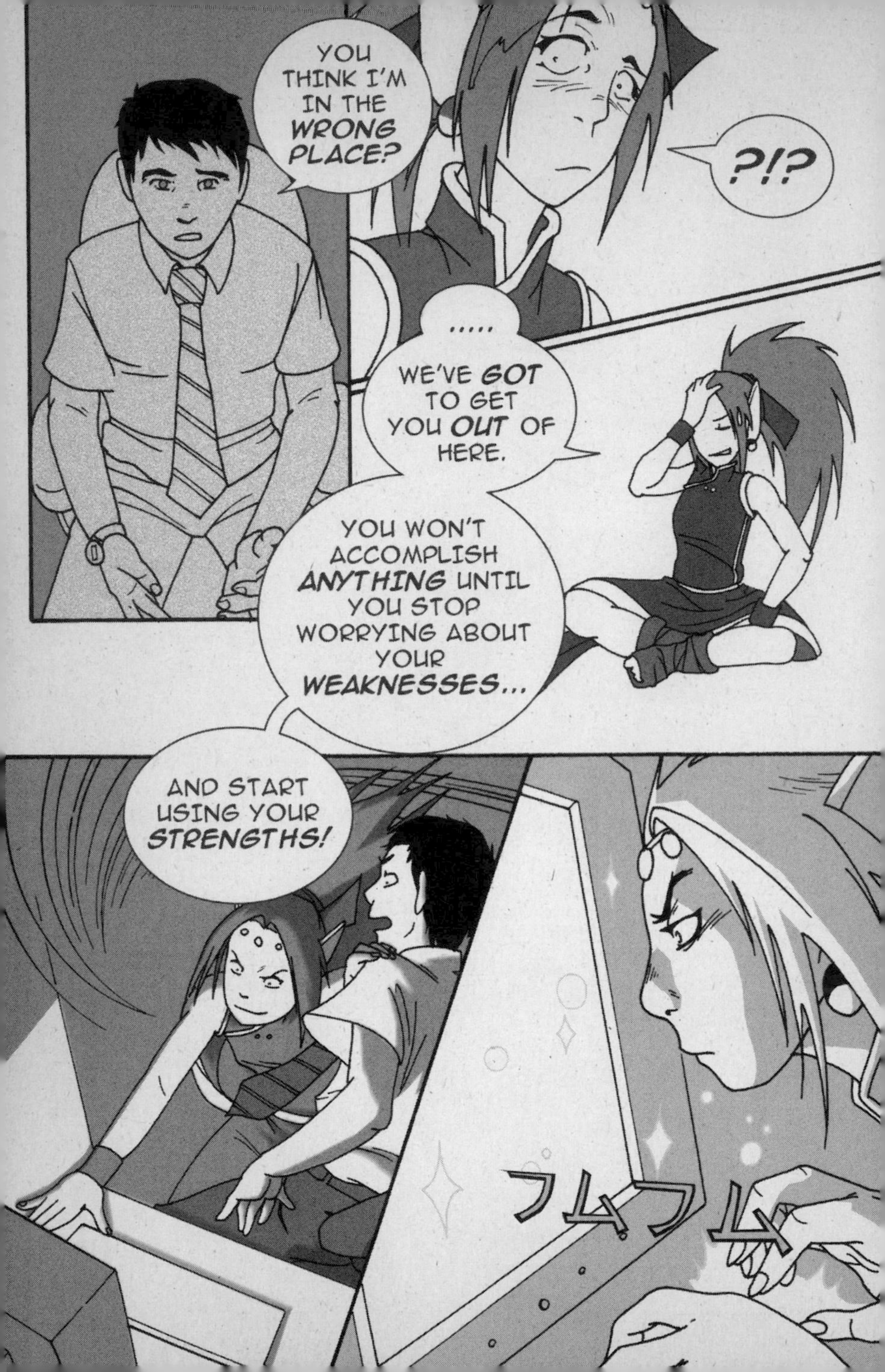
YOU THINK I'M IN THE WRONG PLACE?
?!?
.....
WE'VE GOT TO GET YOU OUT OF HERE.
YOU WON'T ACCOMPLISH ANYTHING UNTIL YOU STOP WORRYING ABOUT YOUR WEAKNESSES...
AND START USING YOUR STRENGTHS!
フムフム

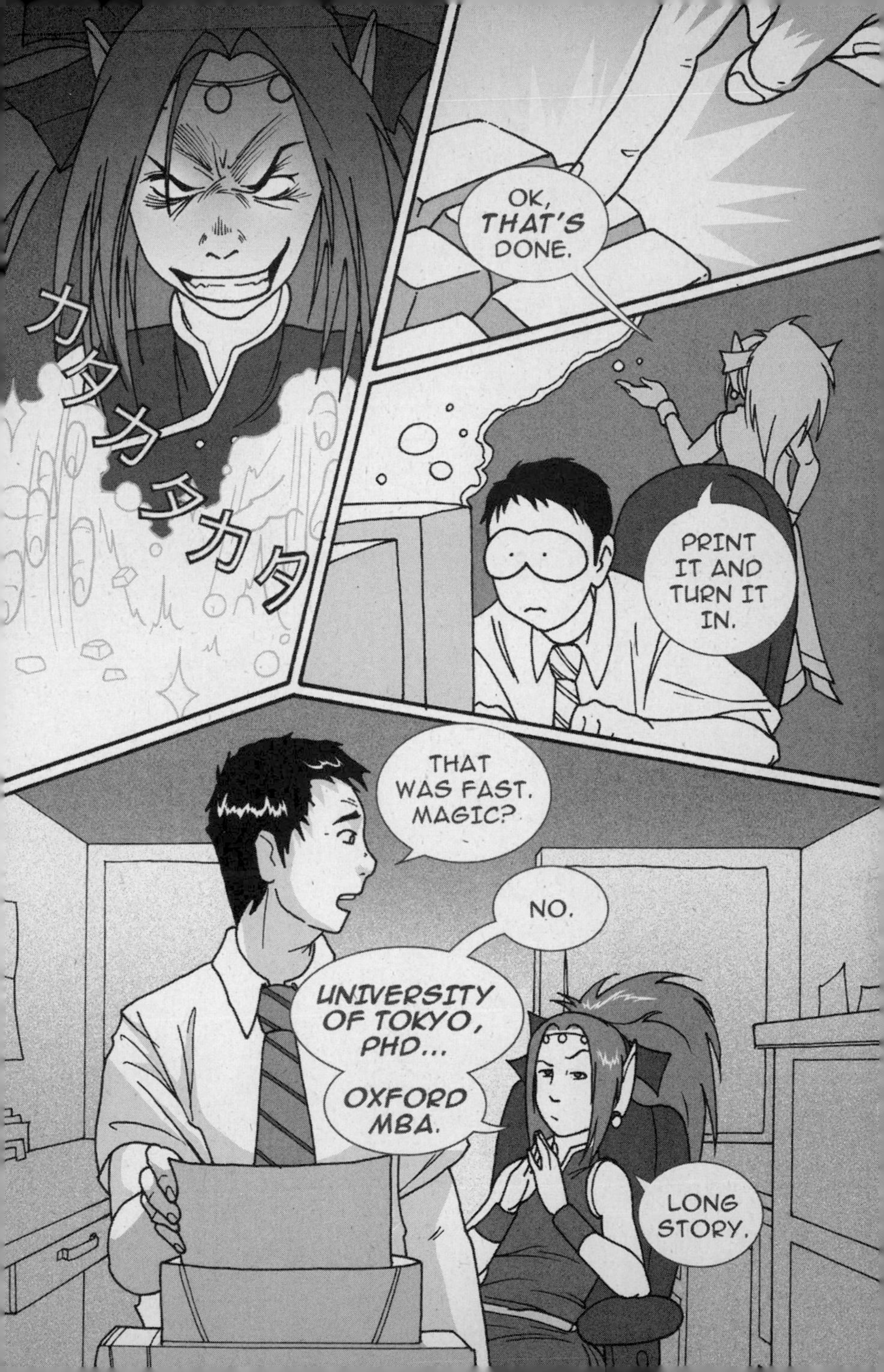
カタカタカタカタ
OK, THAT'S DONE.
PRINT IT AND TURN IT IN.
THAT WAS FAST. MAGIC?
NO.
UNIVERSITY OF TOKYO, PHD...
OXFORD MBA.
LONG STORY.

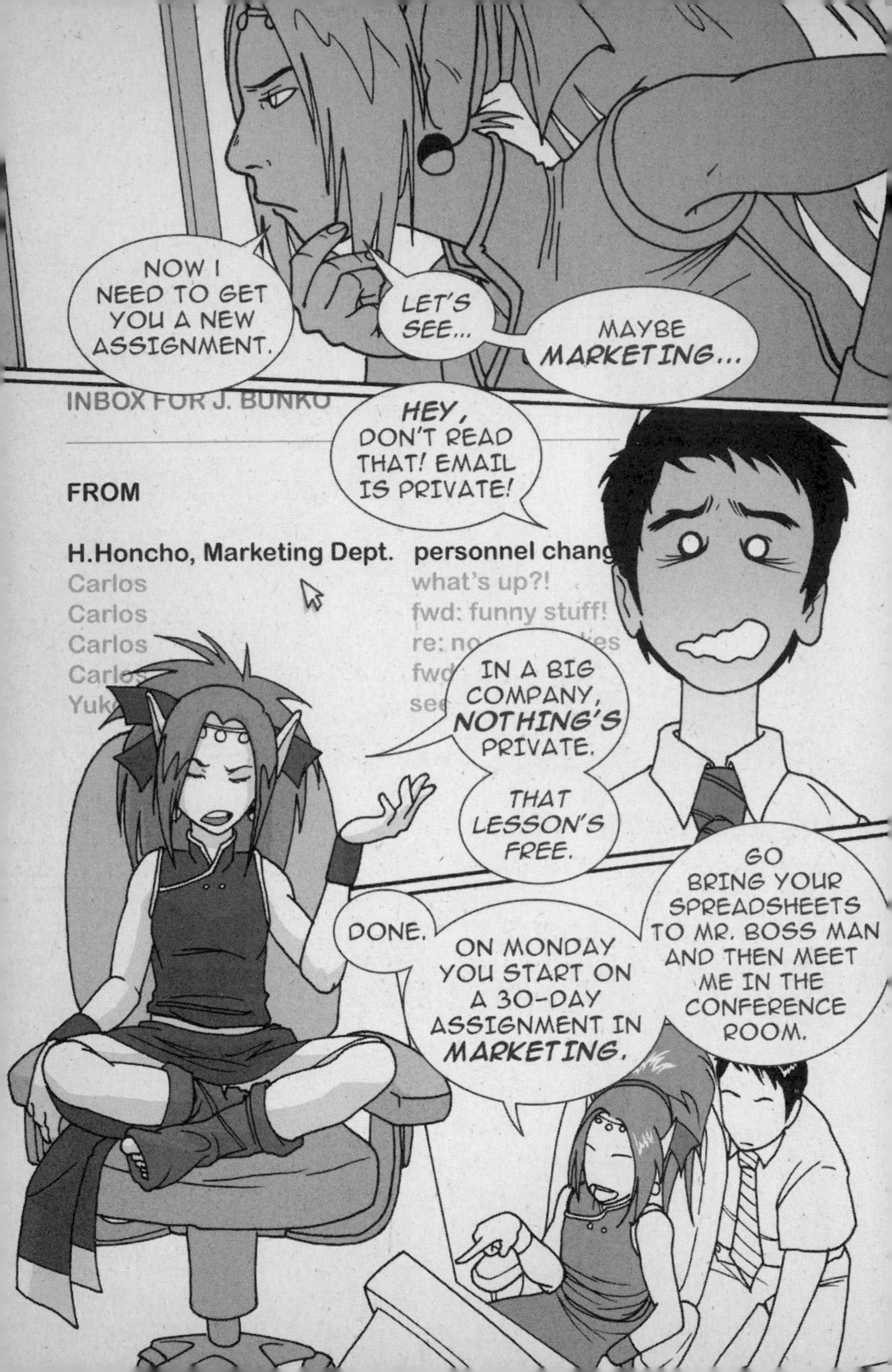
NOW I NEED TO GET YOU A NEW ASSIGNMENT.
LET'S SEE...
MAYBE MARKETING...
INBOX FOR J. BUNKO
FROM
H.Honcho, Marketing Dept. personnel chang
Carlos what's up?!
Carlos fwd: funny stuff!
Carlos
Carlos
HEY, DON'T READ THAT! EMAIL IS PRIVATE!
IN A BIG COMPANY, NOTHING'S PRIVATE.
THAT LESSON'S FREE.
DONE.
ON MONDAY YOU START ON A 30-DAY ASSIGNMENT IN MARKETING.
GO BRING YOUR SPREADSHEETS TO MR. BOSS MAN AND THEN MEET ME IN THE CONFERENCE ROOM.

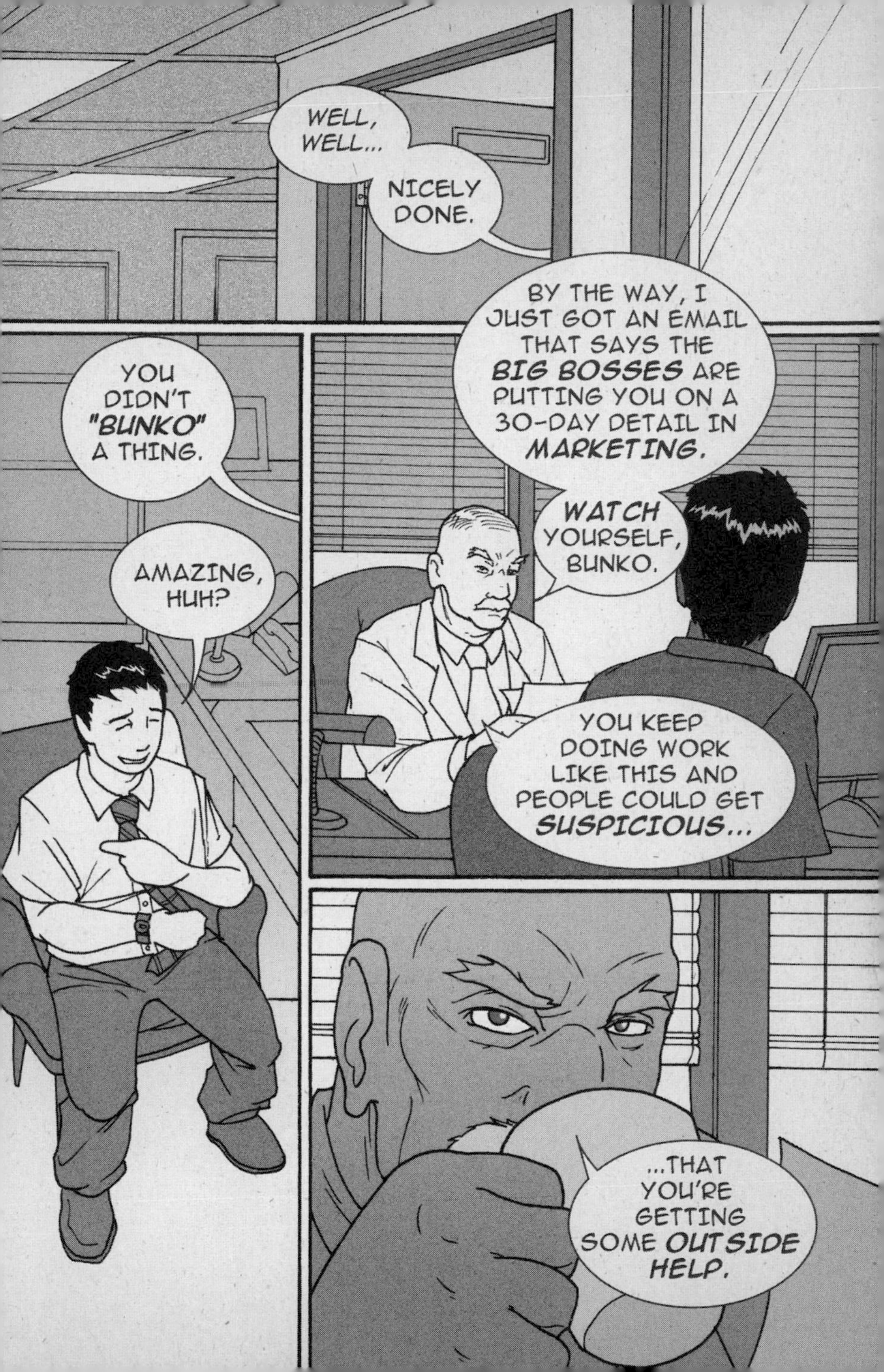
WELL, WELL...
NICELY DONE.
YOU DIDN'T "BUNKO" A THING.
AMAZING, HUH?
BY THE WAY, I JUST GOT AN EMAIL THAT SAYS THE BIG BOSSES ARE PUTTING YOU ON A 30-DAY DETAIL IN MARKETING.
WATCH YOURSELF, BUNKO.
YOU KEEP DOING WORK LIKE THIS AND PEOPLE COULD GET SUSPICIOUS...
...THAT YOU'RE GETTING SOME OUTSIDE HELP.

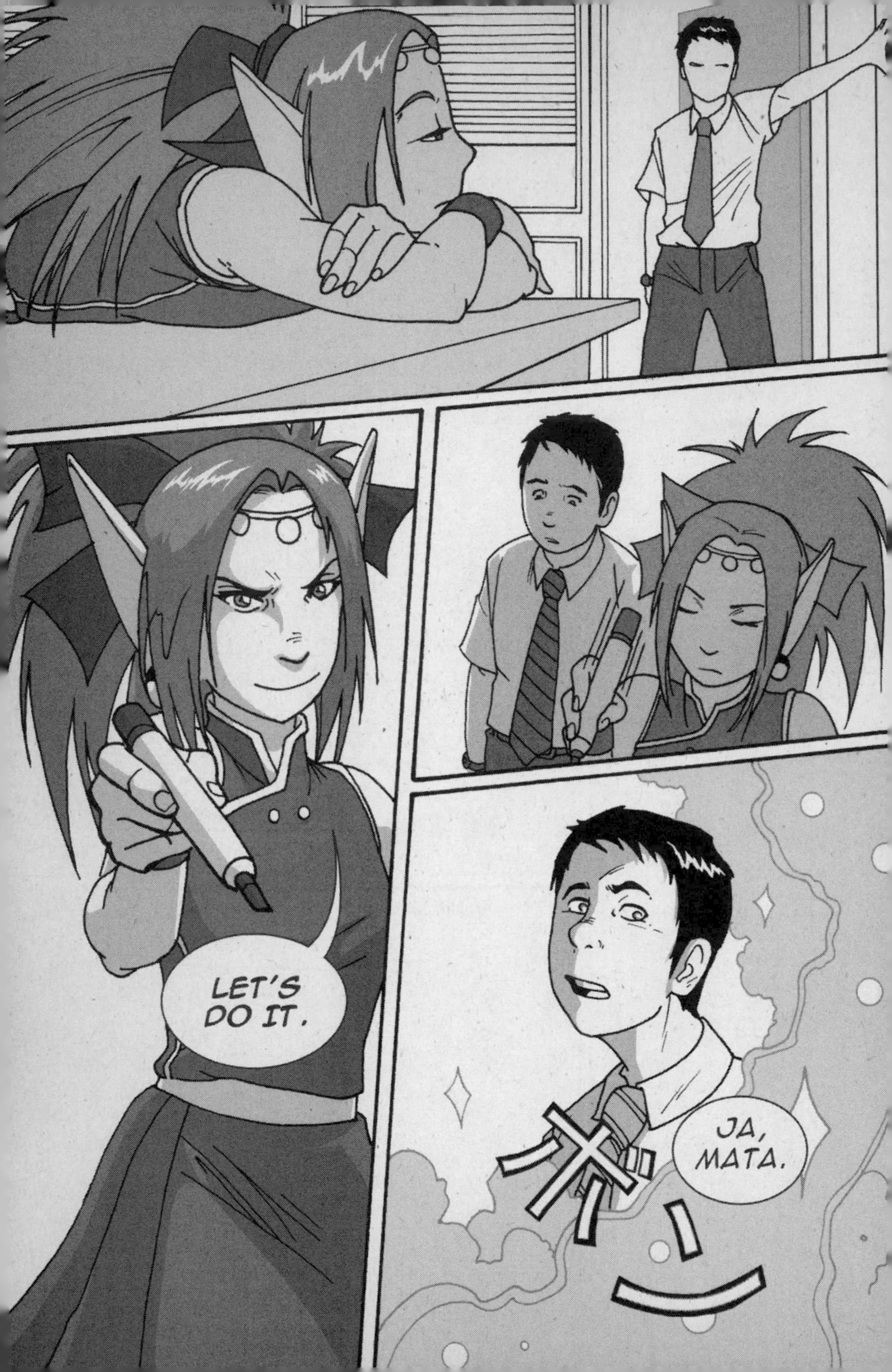
LET'S DO IT.
JA, MATA.

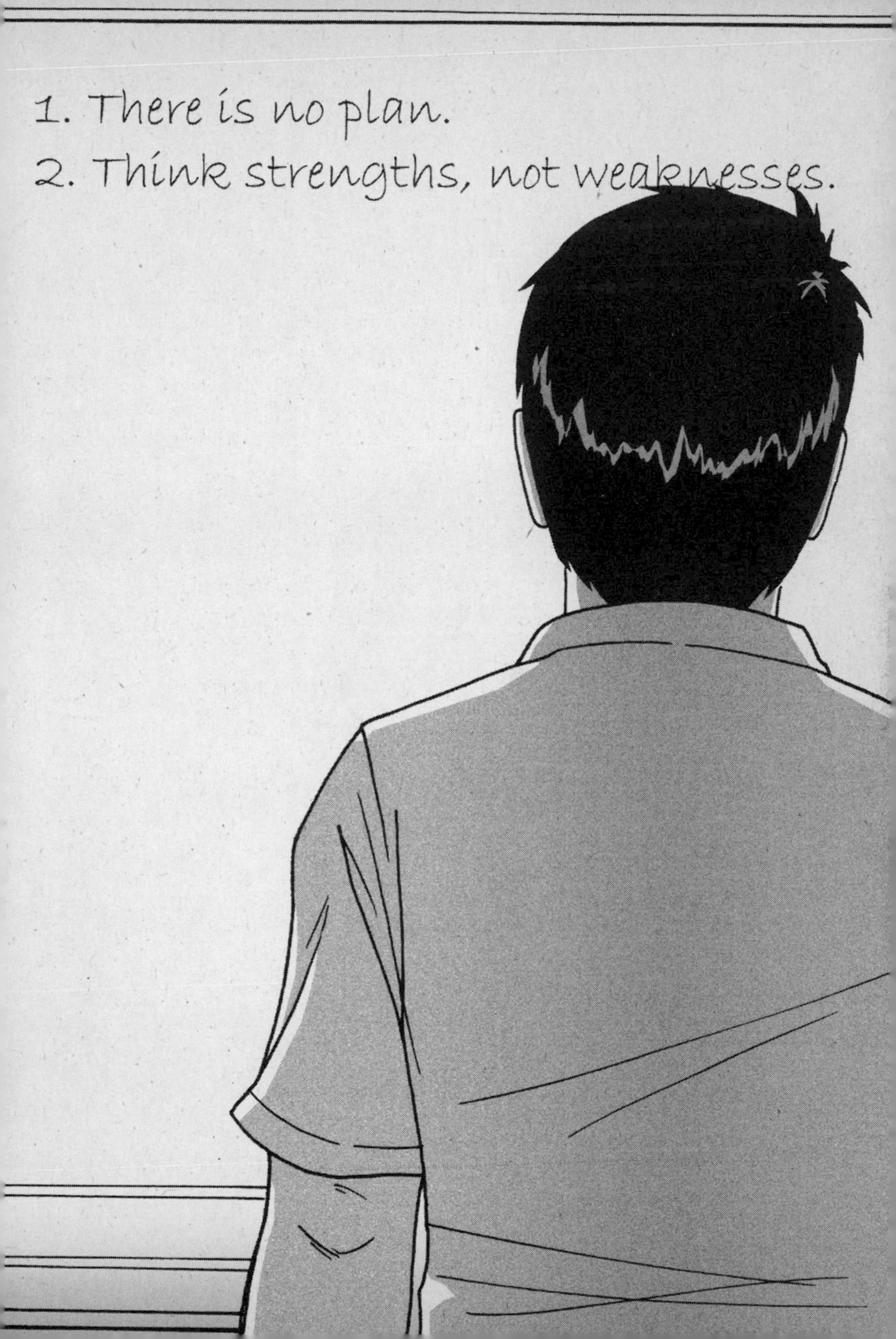
1. There is no plan.
2. Think strengths, not weaknesses.

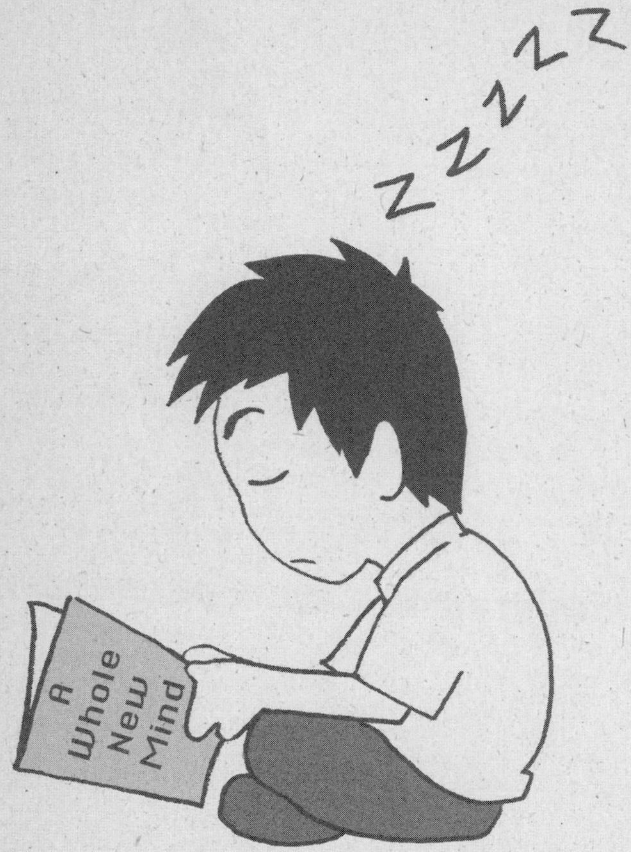
ZZZZZZ
A Whole New Mind

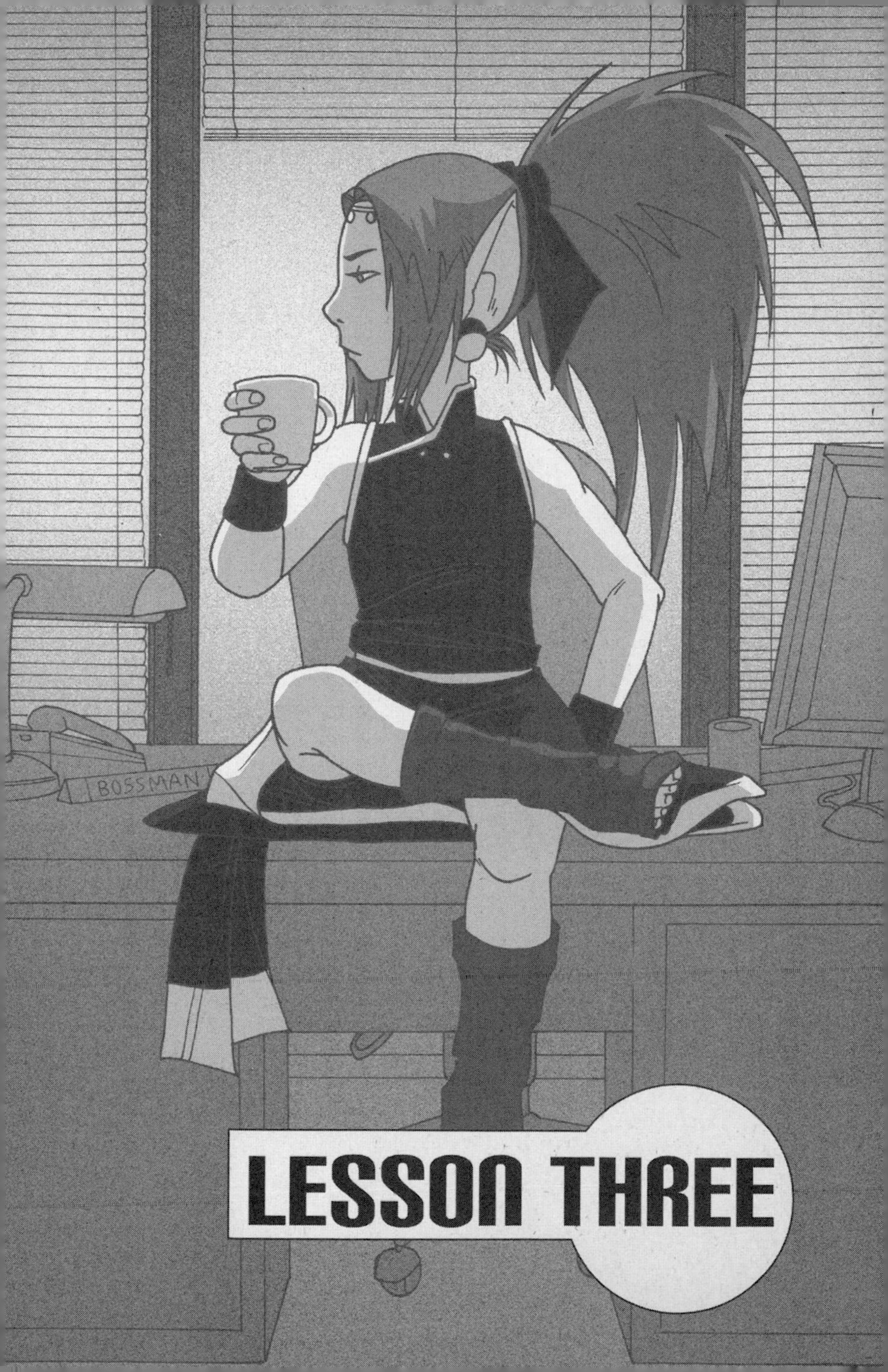
BOSSMAN
LESSON THREE

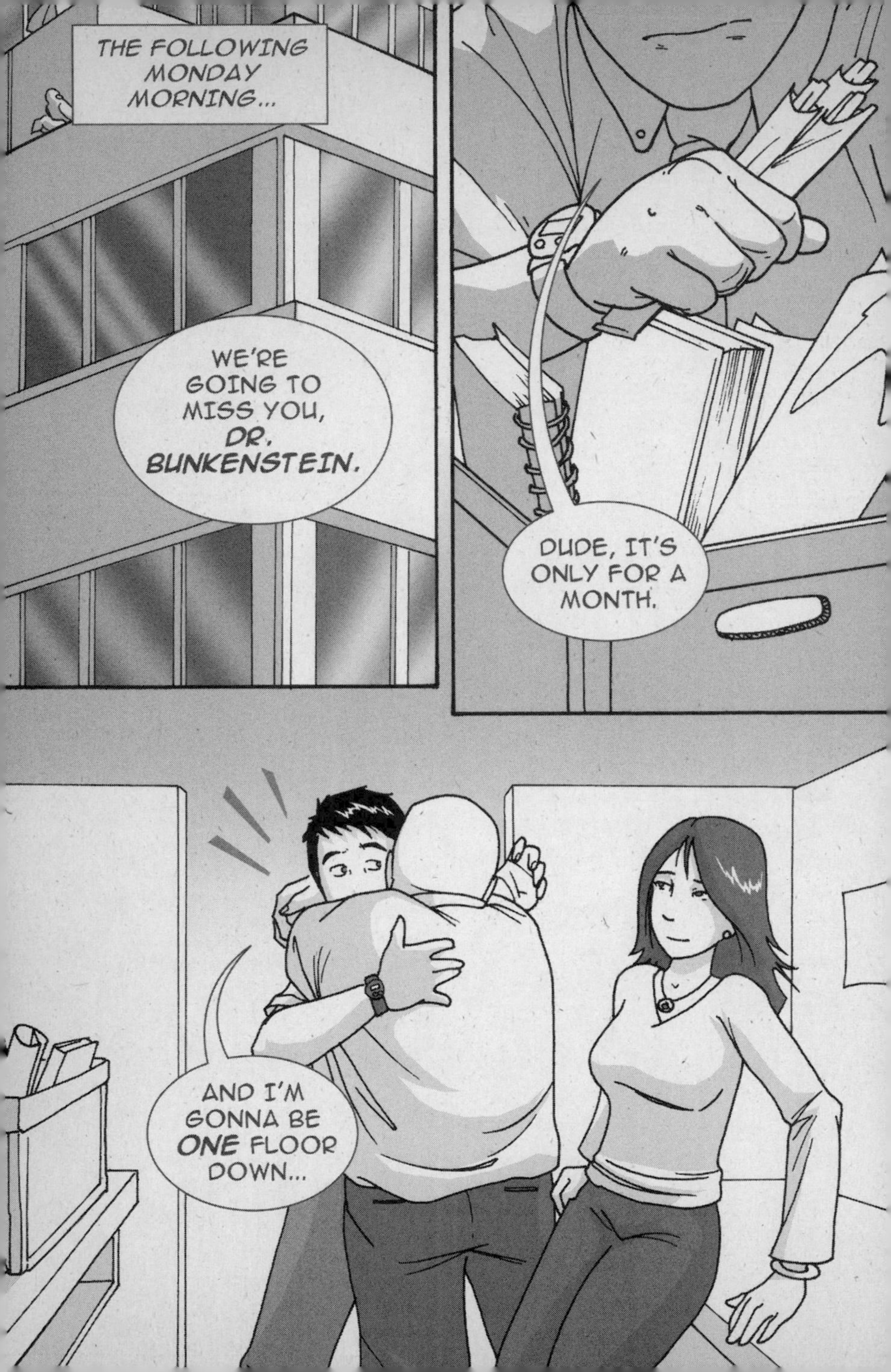
THE FOLLOWING MONDAY MORNING...
WE'RE GOING TO MISS YOU, DR. BUNKENSTEIN.
DUDE, IT'S ONLY FOR A MONTH.
AND I'M GONNA BE ONE FLOOR DOWN...

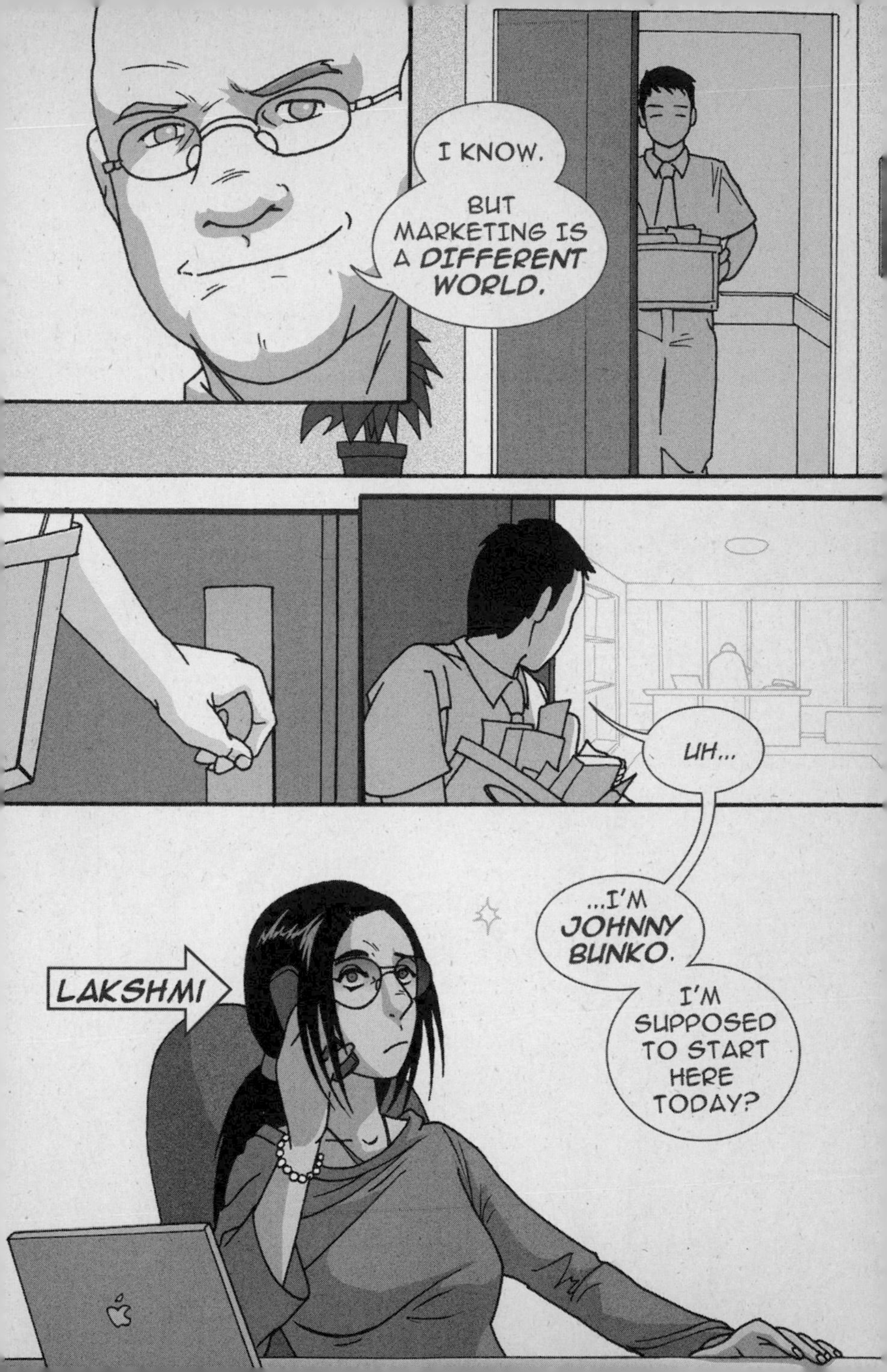
I KNOW.
BUT MARKETING IS A DIFFERENT WORLD.
UH...
...I'M JOHNNY BUNKO.
I'M SUPPOSED TO START HERE TODAY?
LAKSHMI

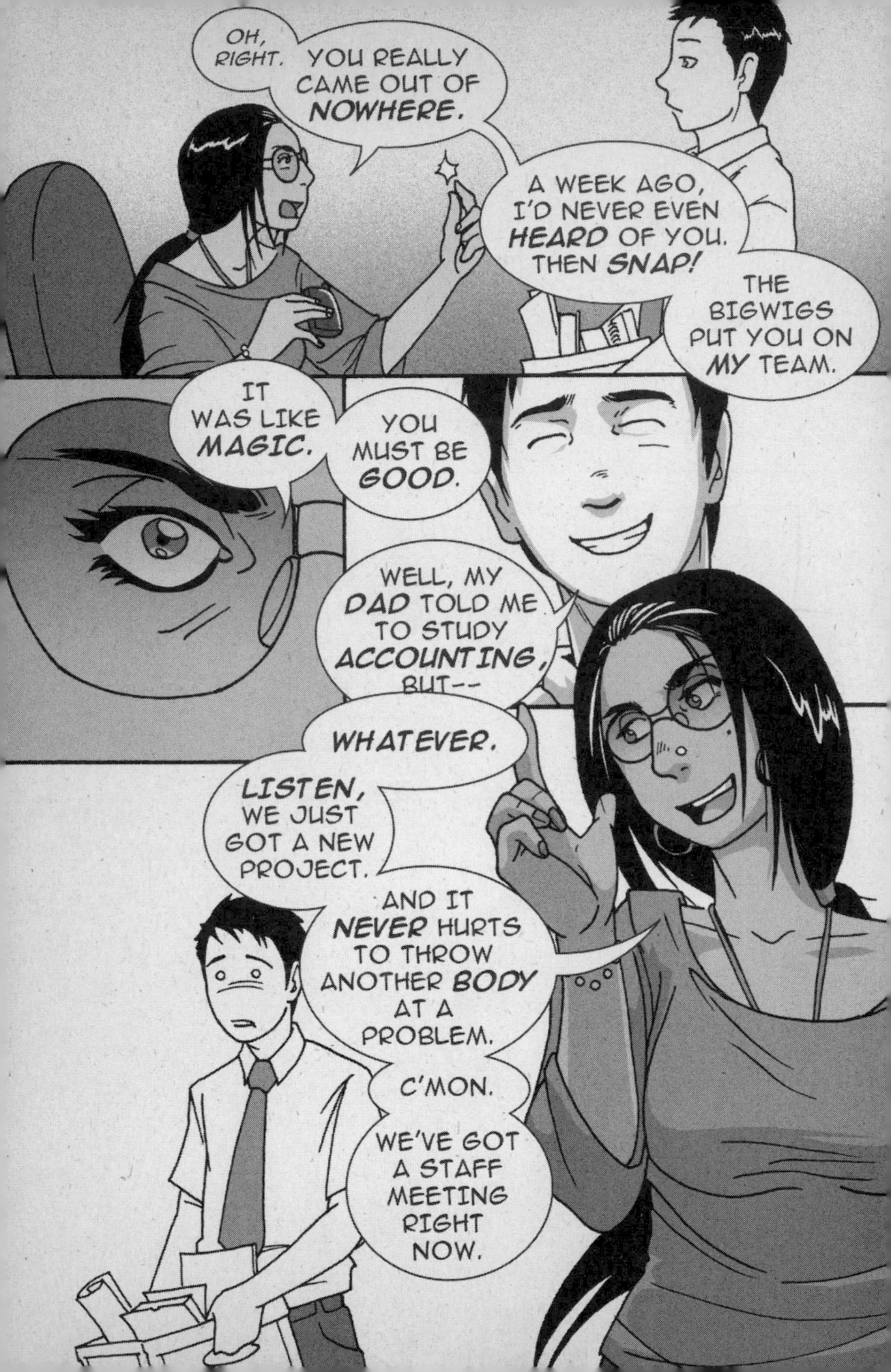
OH, RIGHT.
YOU REALLY CAME OUT OF NOWHERE.
A WEEK AGO, I'D NEVER EVEN HEARD OF YOU. THEN SNAP!
THE BIGWIGS PUT YOU ON MY TEAM.
IT WAS LIKE MAGIC.
YOU MUST BE GOOD.
WELL, MY DAD TOLD ME TO STUDY ACCOUNTING, BUT--
WHATEVER.
LISTEN, WE JUST GOT A NEW PROJECT.
AND IT NEVER HURTS TO THROW ANOTHER BODY AT A PROBLEM.
C'MON.
WE'VE GOT A STAFF MEETING RIGHT NOW.

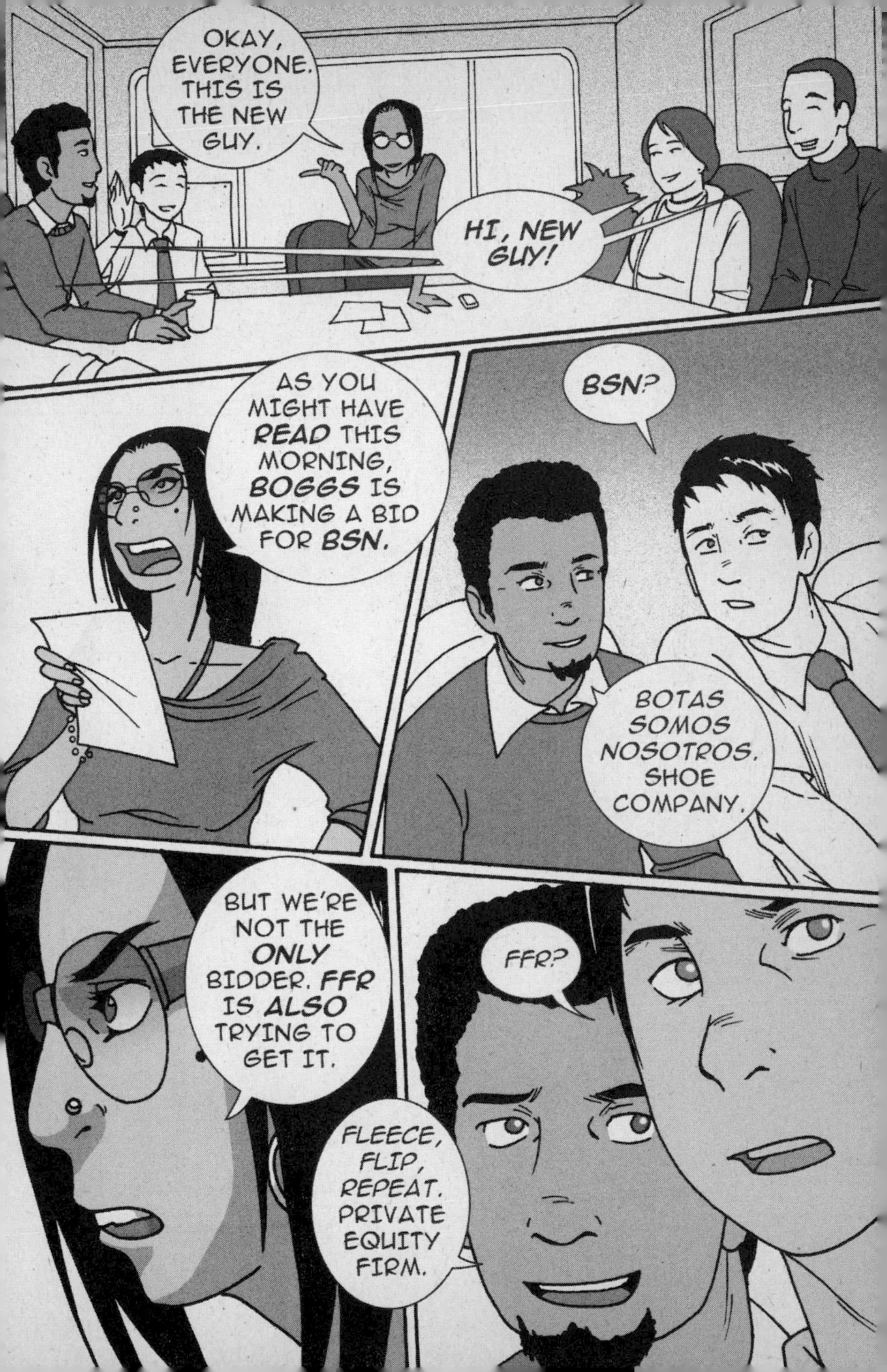
OKAY, EVERYONE. THIS IS THE NEW GUY.
HI, NEW GUY!
AS YOU MIGHT HAVE READ THIS MORNING, BOGGS IS MAKING A BID FOR BSN.
BSN?
BOTAS SOMOS NOSOTROS. SHOE COMPANY.
BUT WE'RE NOT THE ONLY BIDDER. FFR IS ALSO TRYING TO GET IT.
FFR?
FLEECE, FLIP, REPEAT. PRIVATE EQUITY FIRM.

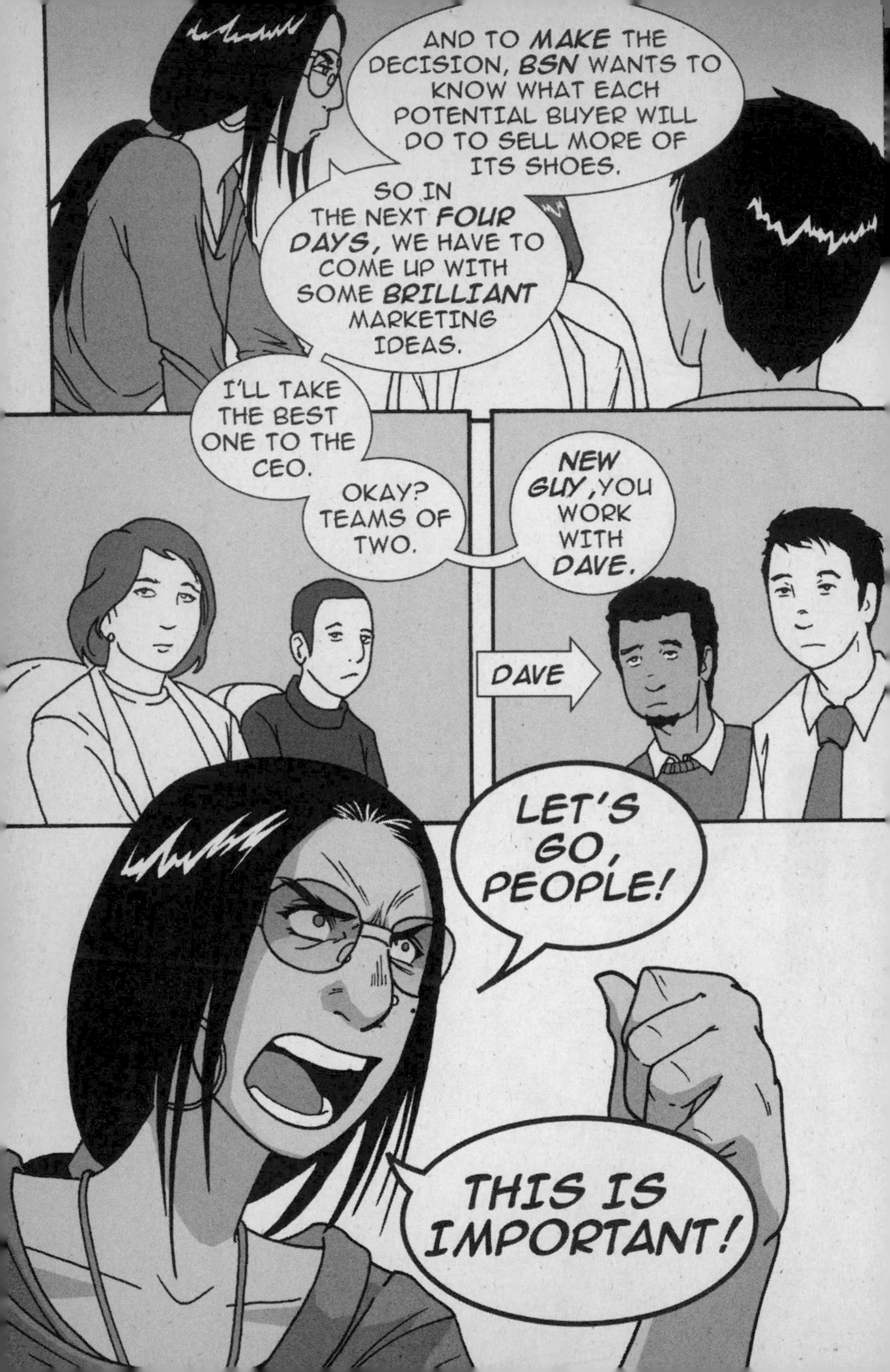
AND TO MAKE THE DECISION, BSN WANTS TO KNOW WHAT EACH POTENTIAL BUYER WILL DO TO SELL MORE OF ITS SHOES.
SO IN THE NEXT FOUR DAYS, WE HAVE TO COME UP WITH SOME BRILLIANT MARKETING IDEAS.
I'LL TAKE THE BEST ONE TO THE CEO.
OKAY? TEAMS OF TWO.
NEW GUY, YOU WORK WITH DAVE.
DAVE
LET'S GO, PEOPLE!
THIS IS IMPORTANT!

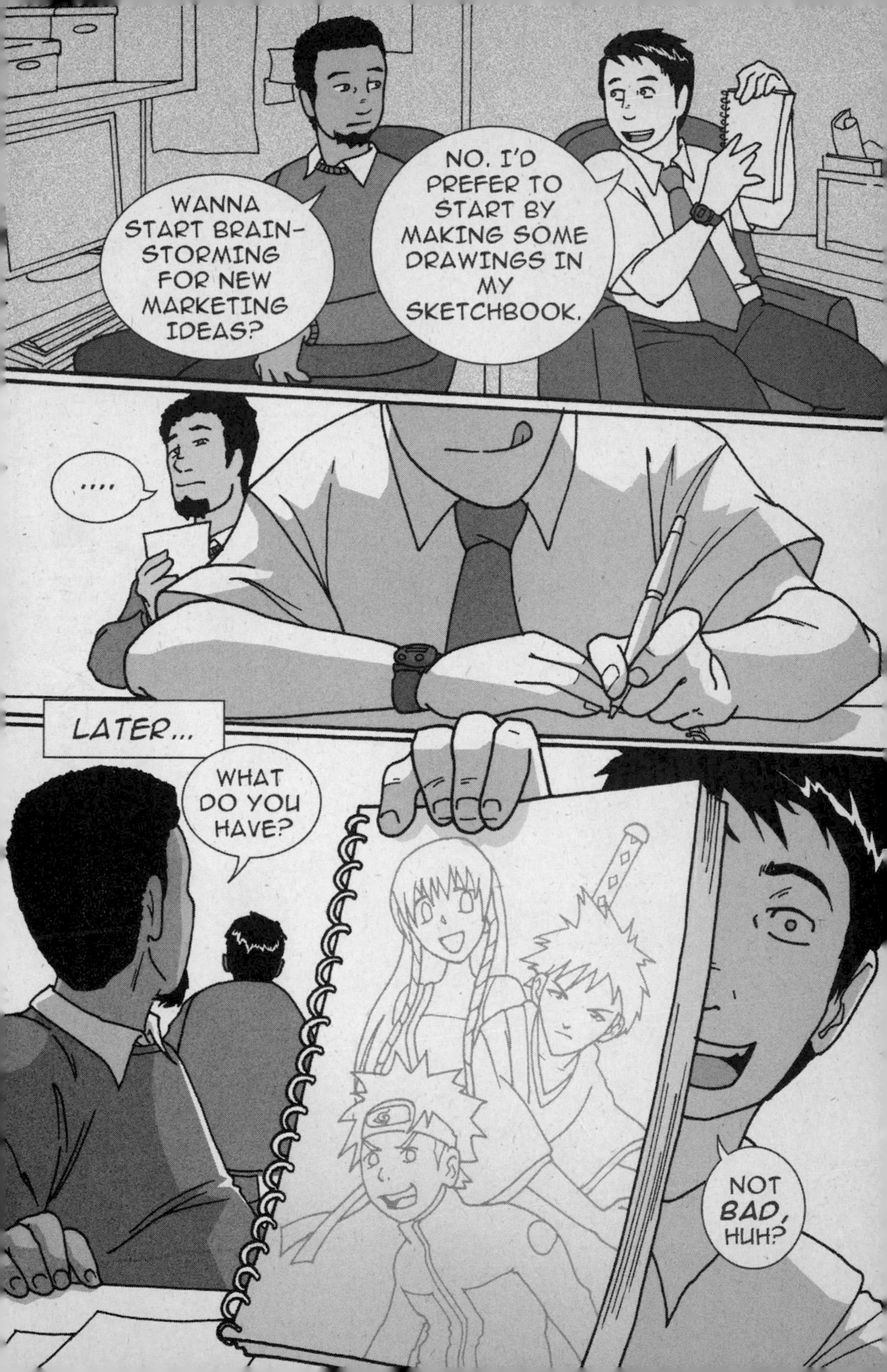
WANNA START BRAIN-STORMING FOR NEW MARKETING IDEAS?
NO. I'D PREFER TO START BY MAKING SOME DRAWINGS IN MY SKETCHBOOK.
....
LATER...
WHAT DO YOU HAVE?
NOT BAD, HUH?

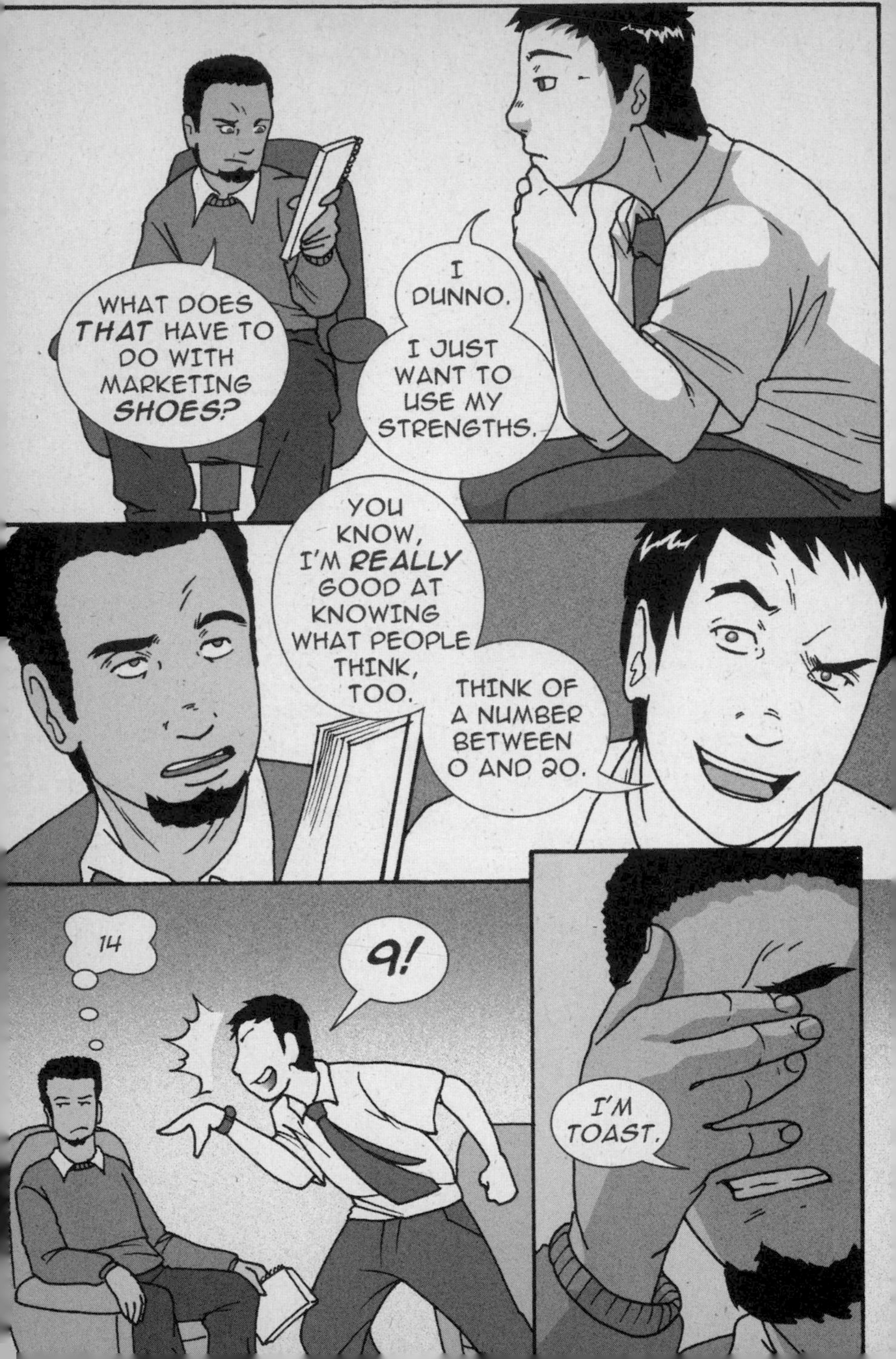
WHAT DOES *THAT* HAVE TO DO WITH MARKETING *SHOES?*
I DUNNO.
I JUST WANT TO USE MY STRENGTHS.
YOU KNOW, I'M *REALLY* GOOD AT KNOWING WHAT PEOPLE THINK, TOO.
THINK OF A NUMBER BETWEEN 0 AND 20.
14
9!
I'M TOAST.

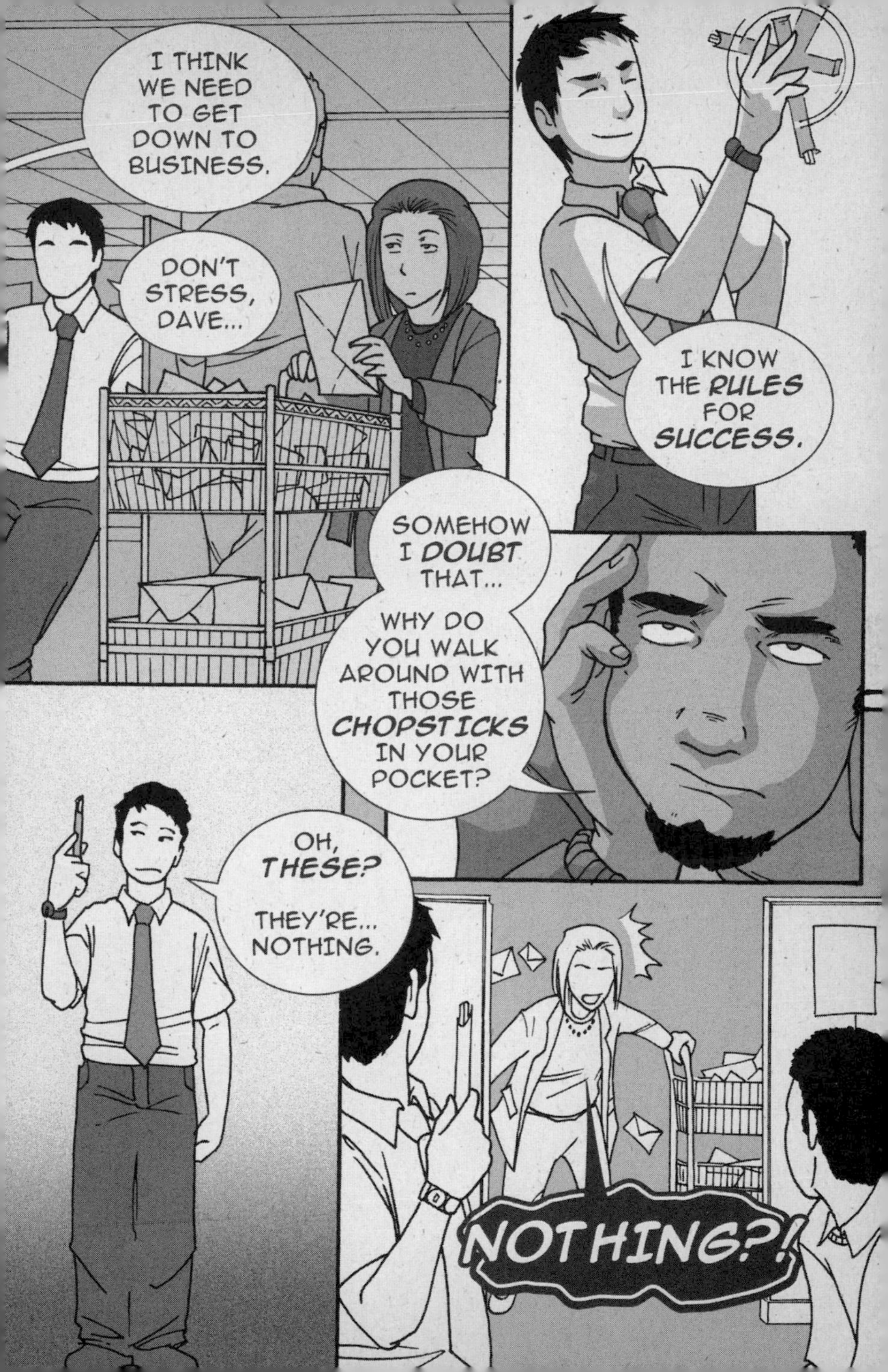
I THINK WE NEED TO GET DOWN TO BUSINESS.
DON'T STRESS, DAVE...
I KNOW THE RULES FOR SUCCESS.
SOMEHOW I DOUBT THAT...
WHY DO YOU WALK AROUND WITH THOSE CHOPSTICKS IN YOUR POCKET?
OH, THESE?
THEY'RE... NOTHING.
NOTHING?!

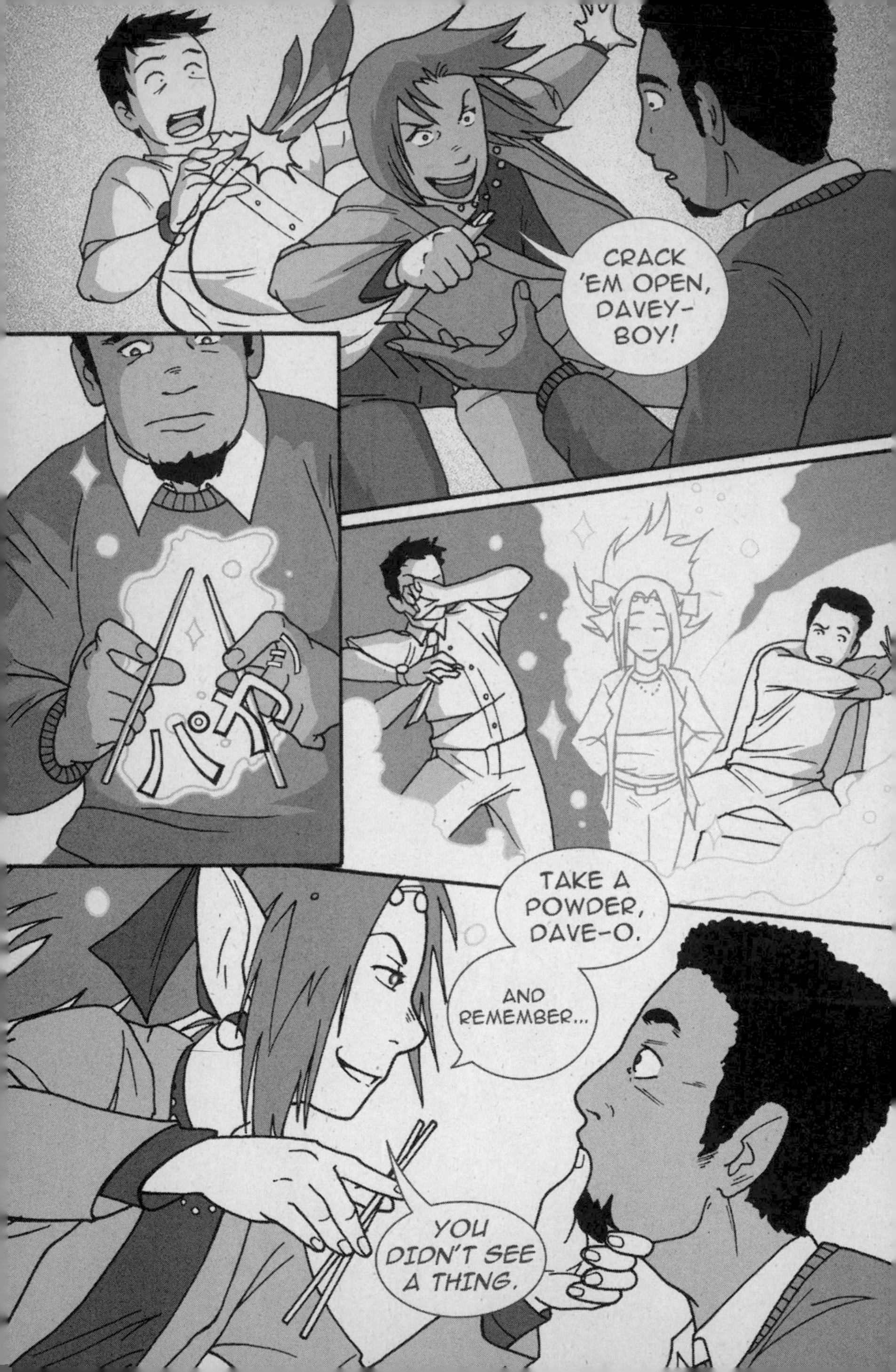
CRACK 'EM OPEN, DAVEY-BOY!
TAKE A POWDER, DAVE-O.
AND REMEMBER...
YOU DIDN'T SEE A THING.

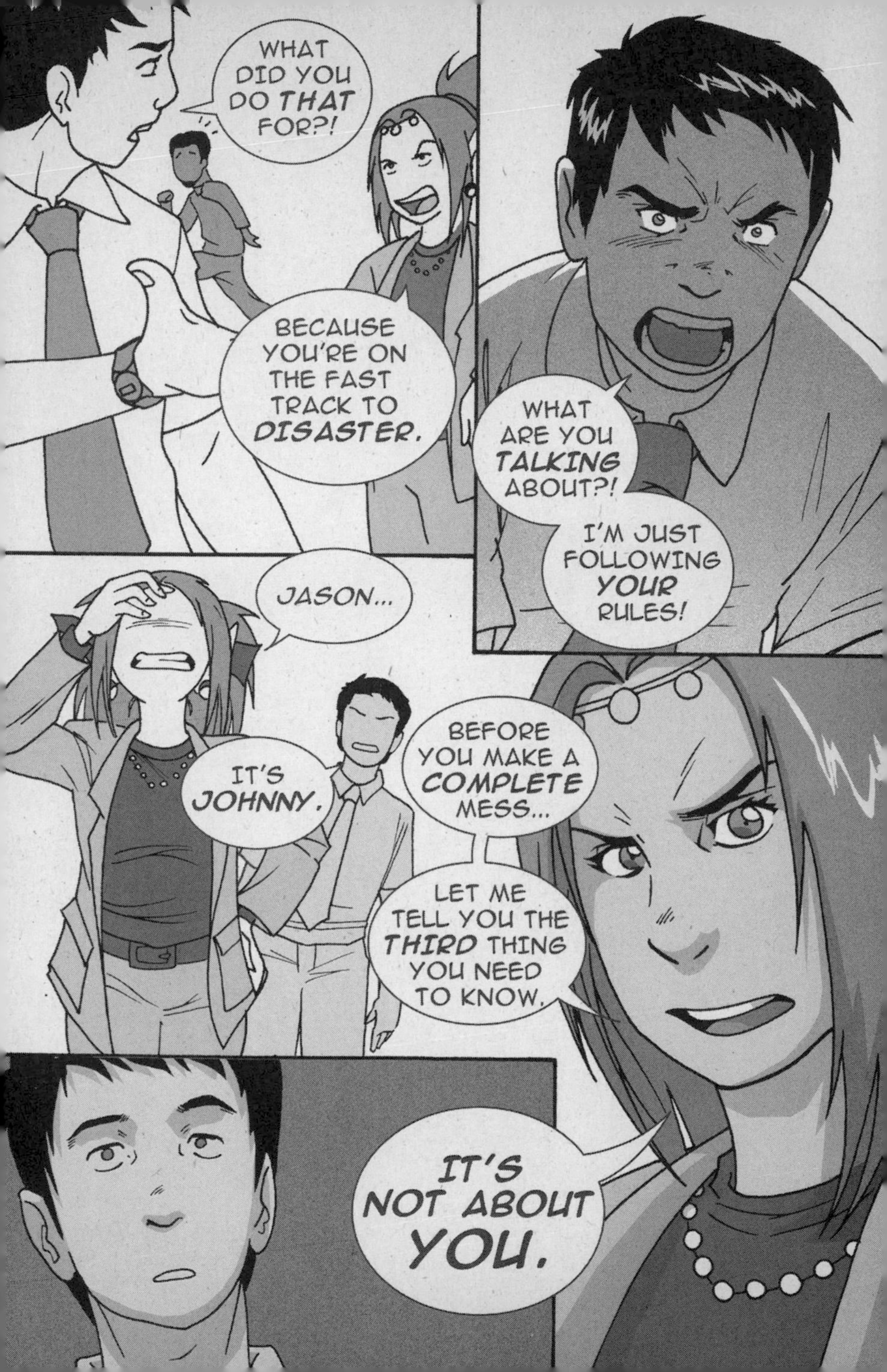
WHAT DID YOU DO THAT FOR?!
BECAUSE YOU'RE ON THE FAST TRACK TO DISASTER.
WHAT ARE YOU TALKING ABOUT?!
I'M JUST FOLLOWING YOUR RULES!
JASON...
IT'S JOHNNY.
BEFORE YOU MAKE A COMPLETE MESS...
LET ME TELL YOU THE THIRD THING YOU NEED TO KNOW.
IT'S NOT ABOUT YOU.

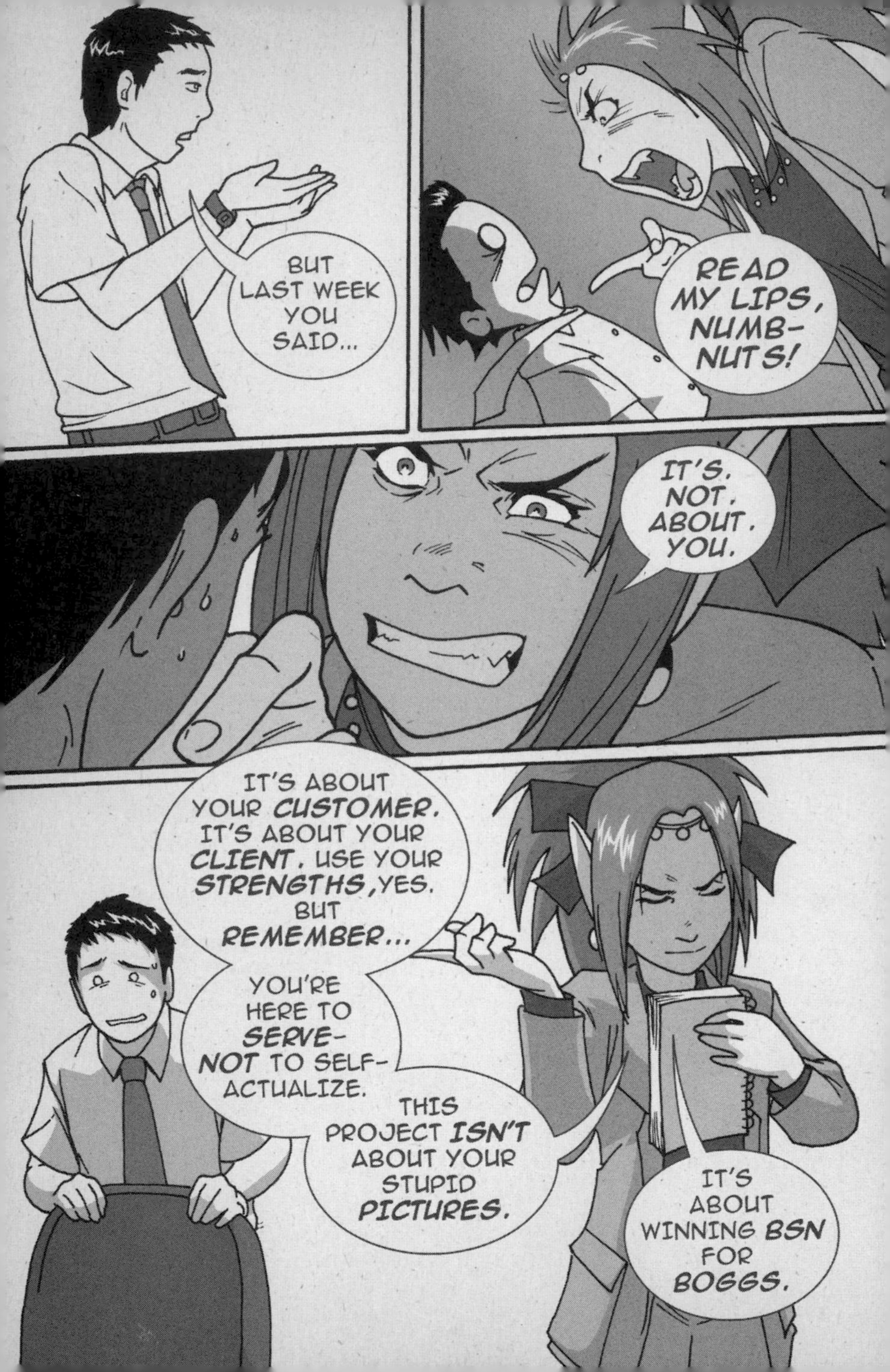
BUT LAST WEEK YOU SAID...
READ MY LIPS, NUMB-NUTS!
IT'S. NOT. ABOUT. YOU.
IT'S ABOUT YOUR CUSTOMER. IT'S ABOUT YOUR CLIENT. USE YOUR STRENGTHS, YES. BUT REMEMBER...
YOU'RE HERE TO SERVE- NOT TO SELF-ACTUALIZE.
THIS PROJECT ISN'T ABOUT YOUR STUPID PICTURES.
IT'S ABOUT WINNING BSN FOR BOGGS.

SO I DON'T MATTER AT ALL?

OF *COURSE* YOU MATTER. BUT THE MOST SUCCESSFUL PEOPLE IMPROVE THEIR OWN LIVES BY IMPROVING *OTHERS'* LIVES.

THEY HELP THEIR CUSTOMER SOLVE ITS PROBLEM. THEY GIVE THEIR CLIENT SOMETHING IT DIDN'T KNOW IT WAS MISSING. THAT'S WHERE THEY FOCUS THEIR ENERGY, TALENT, AND BRAINPOWER.

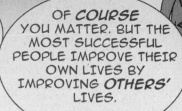

OUTWARD, NOT INWARD.

EXACTLY. AND YOU'RE NOT IN THIS ALONE. THINK ABOUT *LAKSHMI* AND *DAVE*. OR *CARLOS* AND *YUKO*.

THE MOST VALUABLE PEOPLE IN ANY JOB BRING OUT THE BEST IN OTHERS. THEY MAKE THEIR BOSS LOOK GOOD. THEY HELP THEIR TEAMMATES SUCCEED.

SO PULL YOUR HEAD OUT OF YOUR... *EGO*. THEN SIT DOWN WITH DAVE AND GET BACK TO *WORK*.

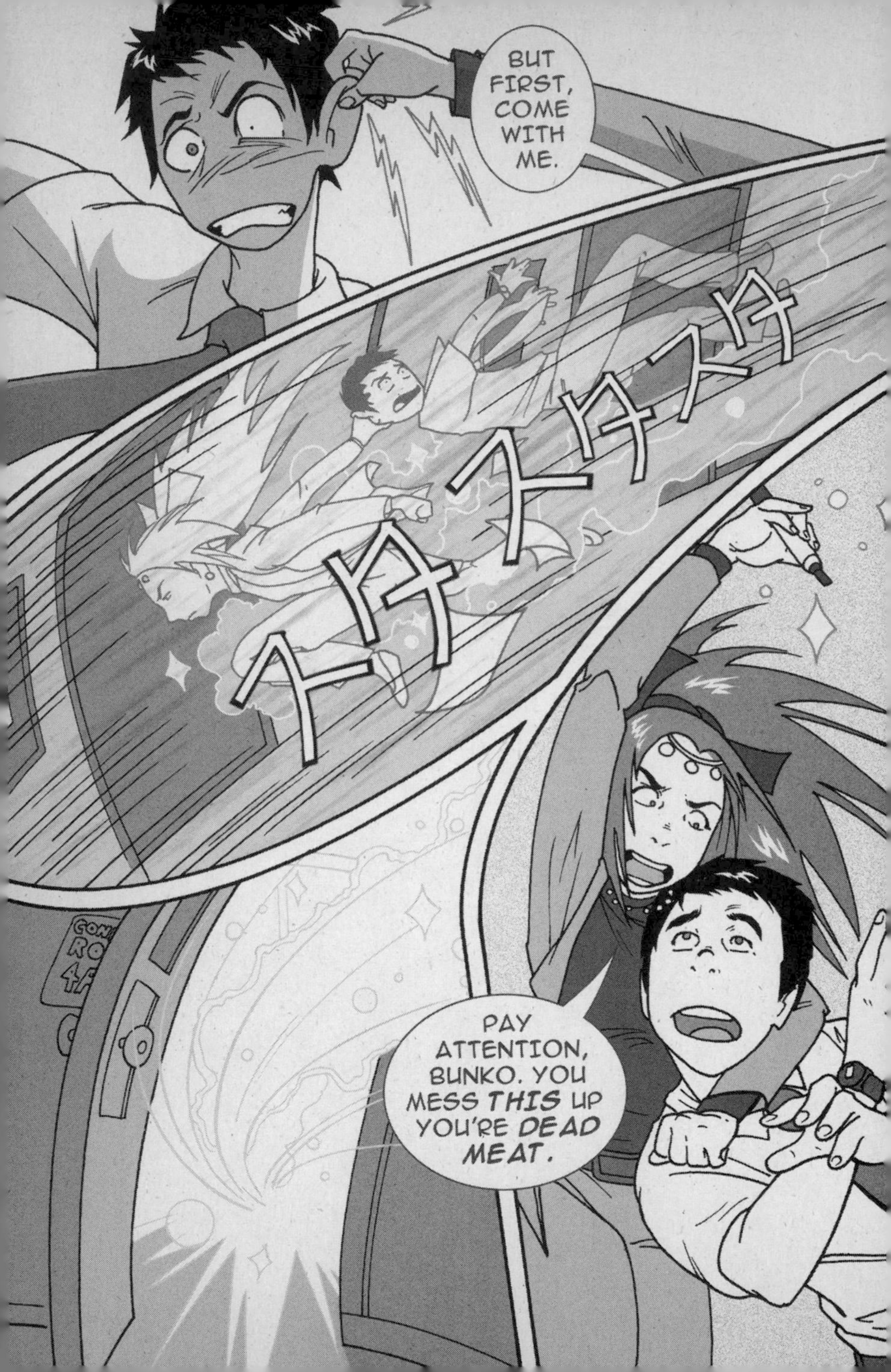
BUT FIRST, COME WITH ME.
PAY ATTENTION, BUNKO. YOU MESS THIS UP YOU'RE DEAD MEAT.

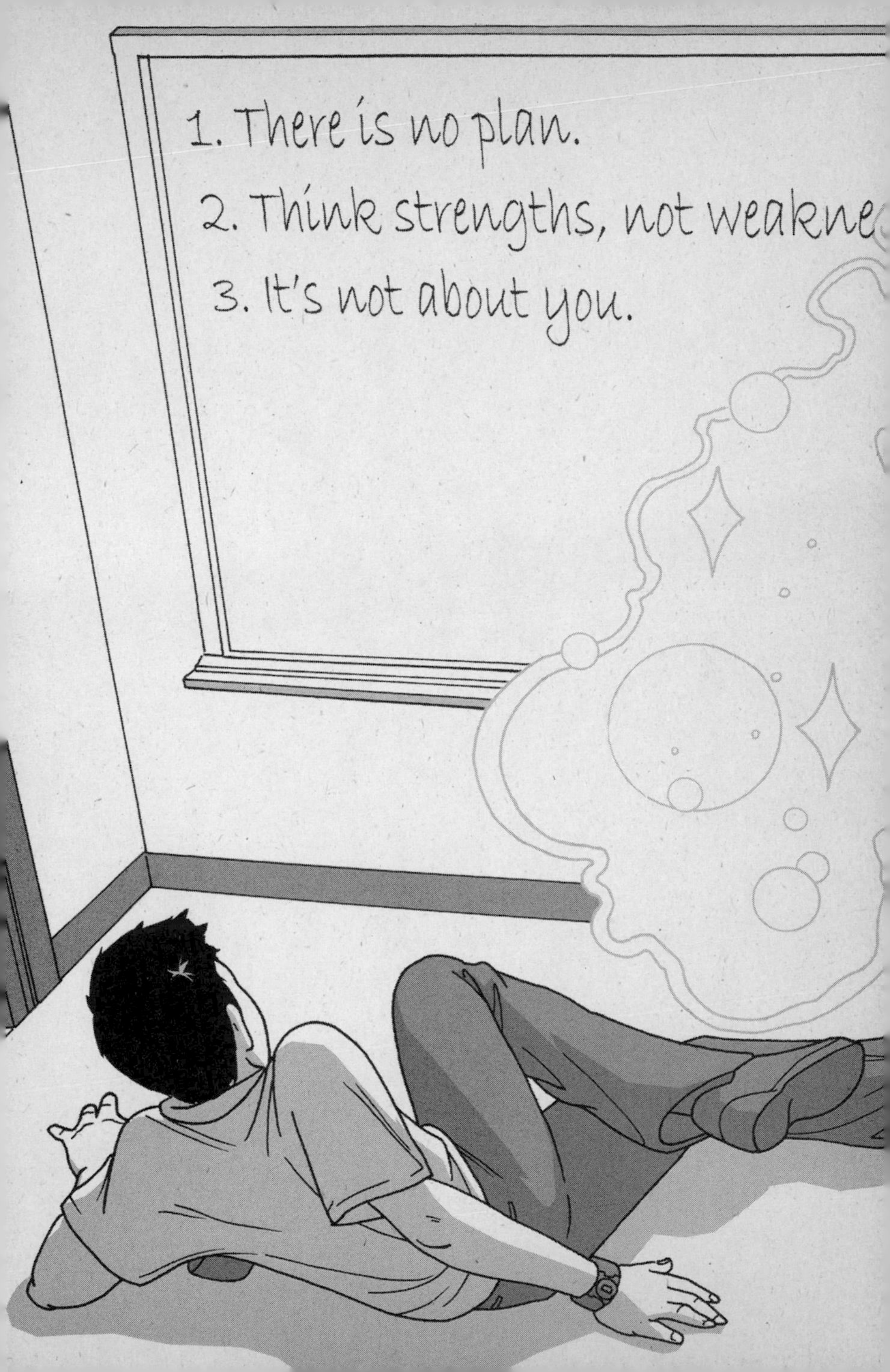
1. There is no plan.
2. Think strengths, not weakne
3. It's not about you.

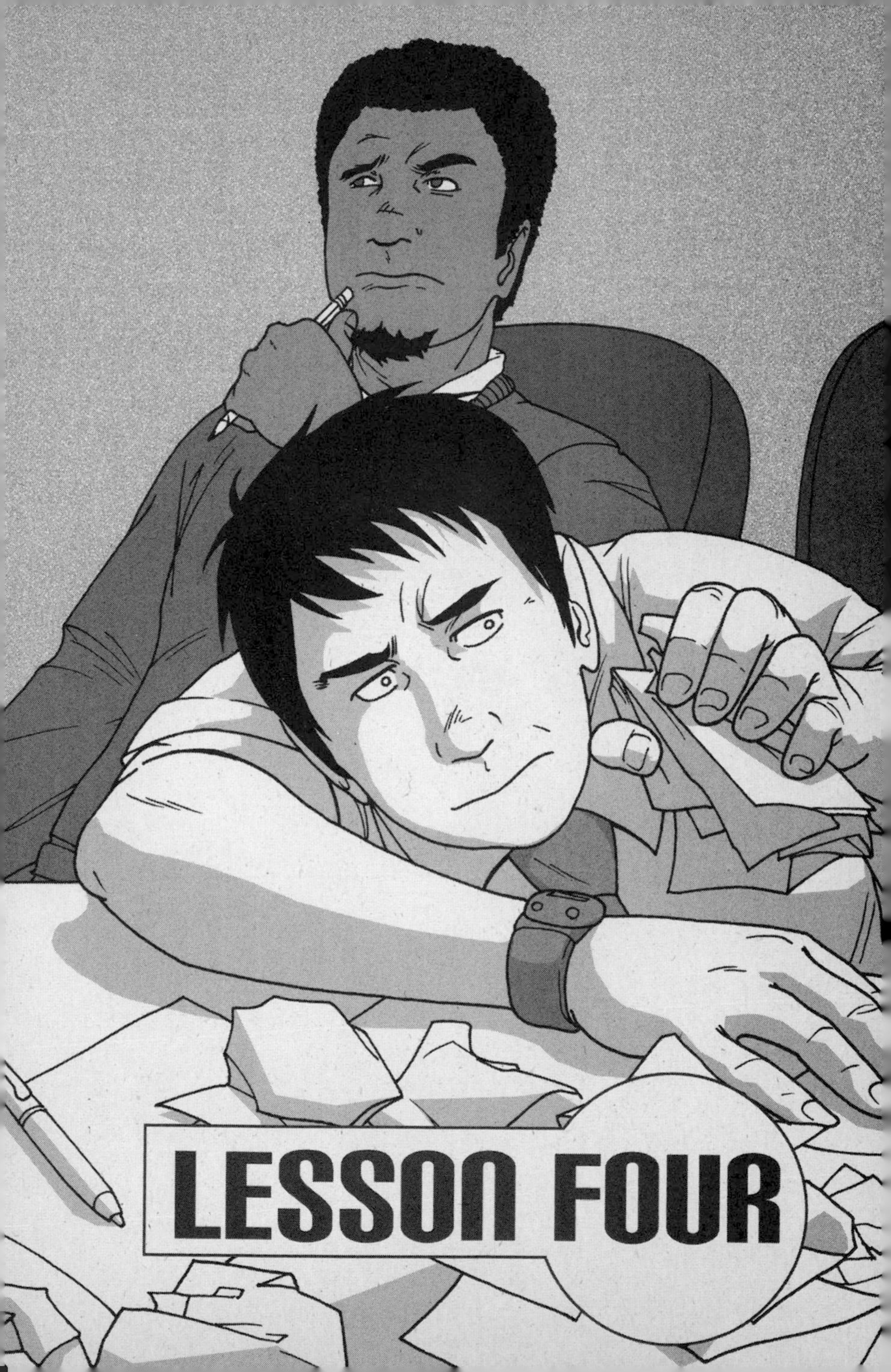
LESSON FOUR

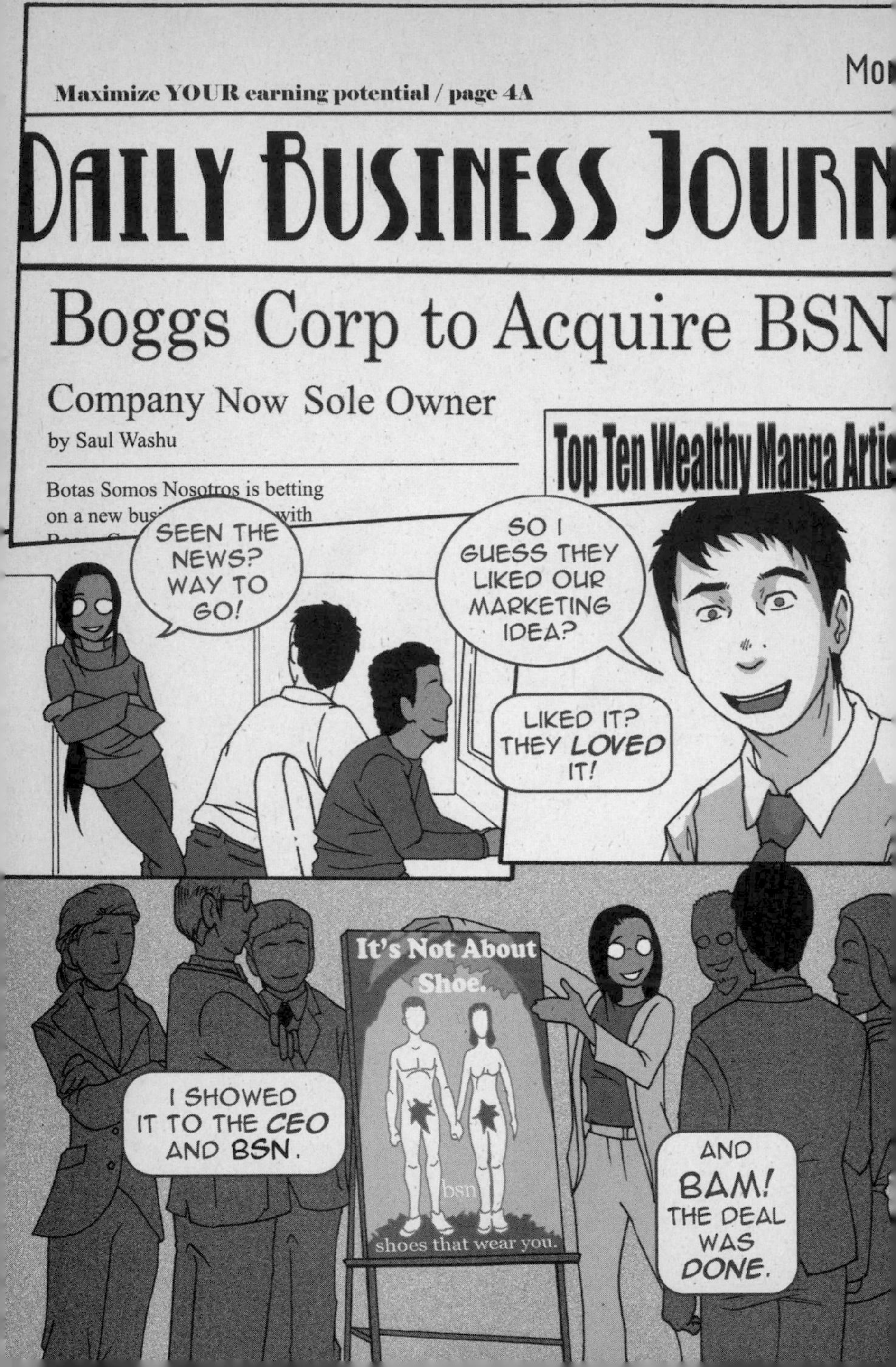
Mo
Maximize YOUR earning potential / page 4A
DAILY BUSINESS JOURN
Boggs Corp to Acquire BSN
Company Now Sole Owner
by Saul Washu
Botas Somos Nosotros is betting
on a new bus
with
Top Ten Wealthy Manga Arti
SEEN THE NEWS? WAY TO GO!
SO I GUESS THEY LIKED OUR MARKETING IDEA?
LIKED IT? THEY LOVED IT!
It's Not About Shoe.
bsn
shoes that wear you.
I SHOWED IT TO THE CEO AND BSN.
AND BAM! THE DEAL WAS DONE.

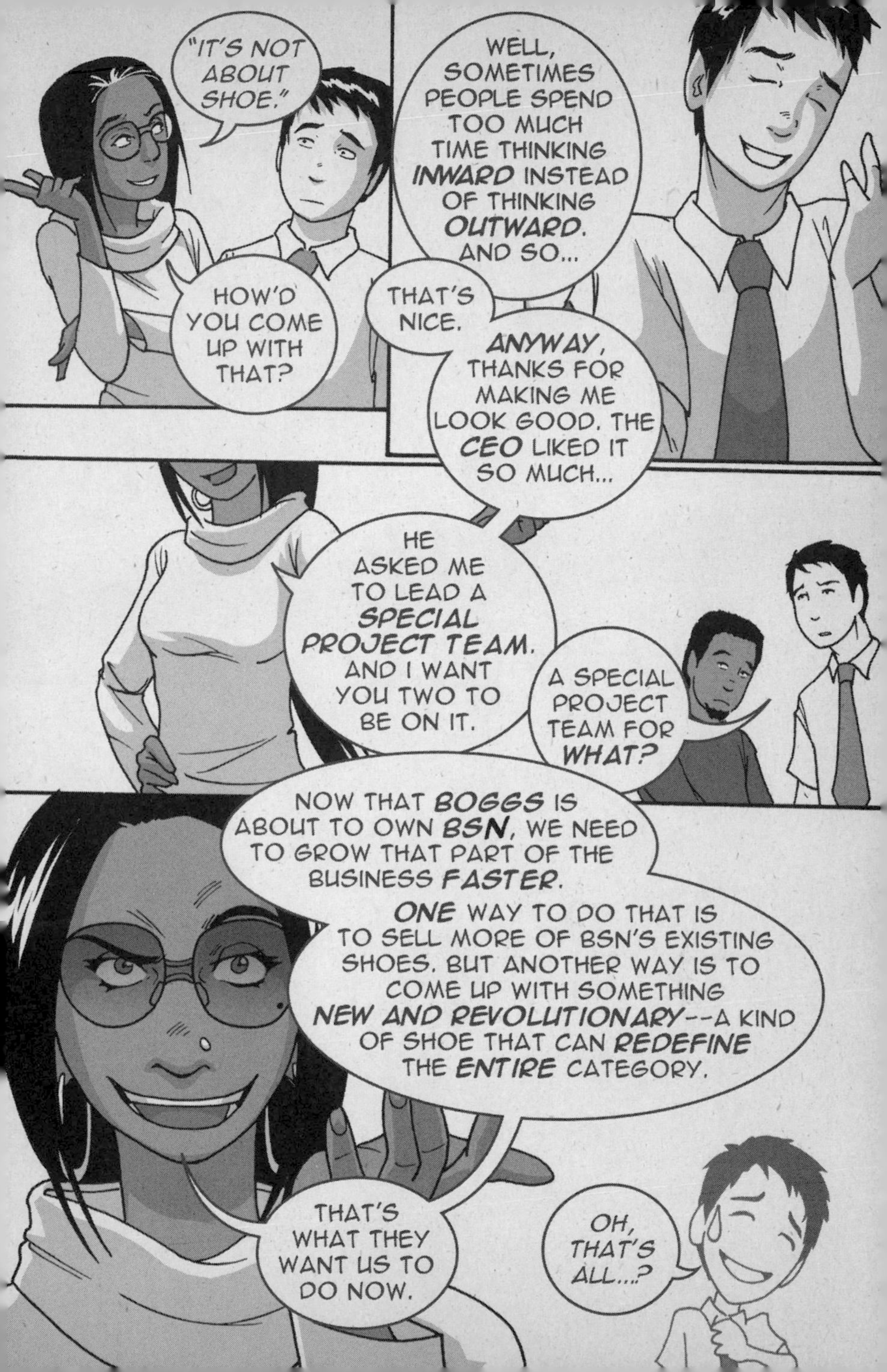
"IT'S NOT ABOUT SHOE."
HOW'D YOU COME UP WITH THAT?
WELL, SOMETIMES PEOPLE SPEND TOO MUCH TIME THINKING INWARD INSTEAD OF THINKING OUTWARD. AND SO...
THAT'S NICE.
ANYWAY, THANKS FOR MAKING ME LOOK GOOD. THE CEO LIKED IT SO MUCH...
HE ASKED ME TO LEAD A SPECIAL PROJECT TEAM. AND I WANT YOU TWO TO BE ON IT.
A SPECIAL PROJECT TEAM FOR WHAT?
NOW THAT BOGGS IS ABOUT TO OWN BSN, WE NEED TO GROW THAT PART OF THE BUSINESS FASTER.
ONE WAY TO DO THAT IS TO SELL MORE OF BSN'S EXISTING SHOES. BUT ANOTHER WAY IS TO COME UP WITH SOMETHING NEW AND REVOLUTIONARY--A KIND OF SHOE THAT CAN REDEFINE THE ENTIRE CATEGORY.
THAT'S WHAT THEY WANT US TO DO NOW.
OH, THAT'S ALL...?

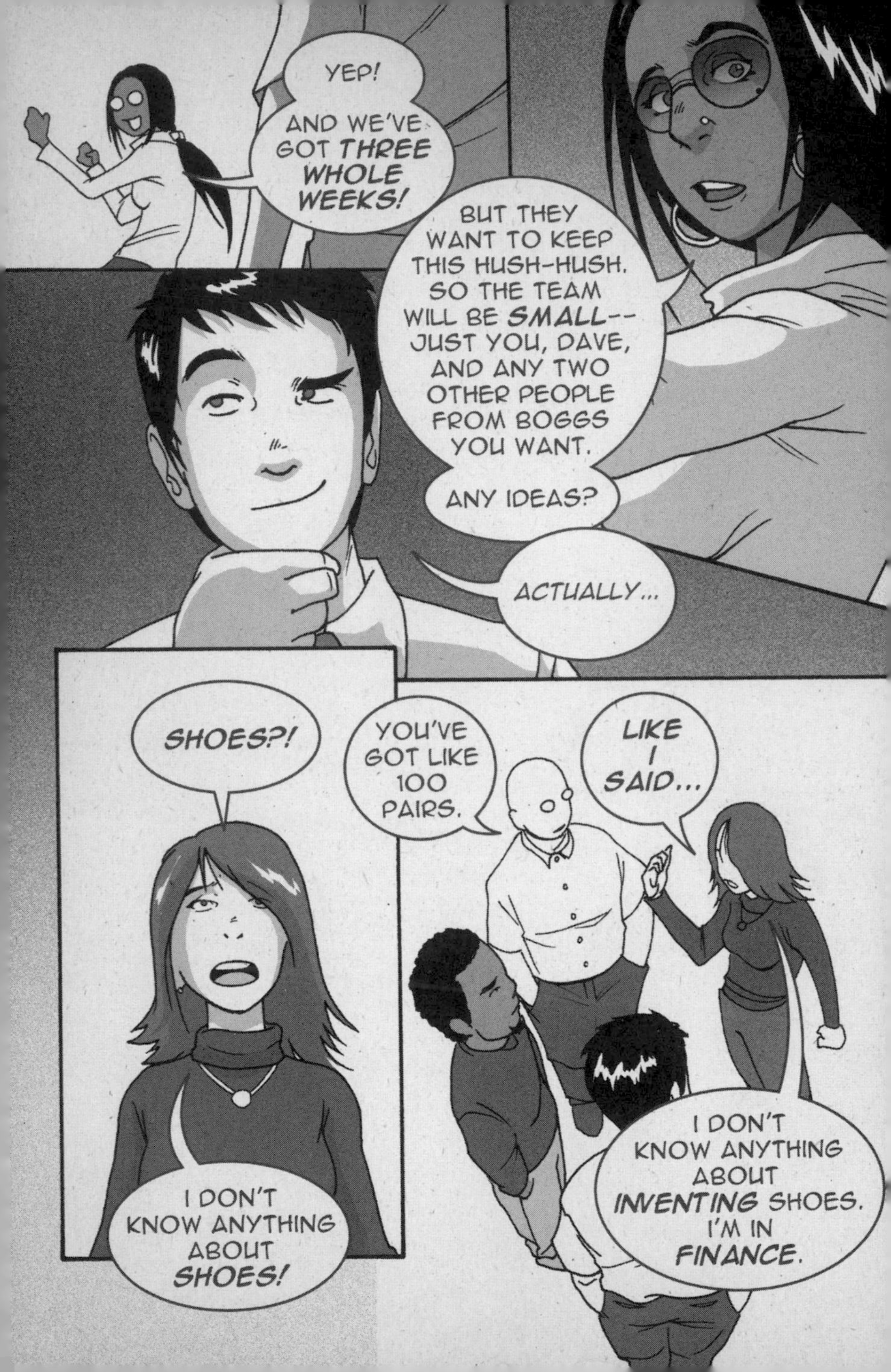
YEP!
AND WE'VE GOT THREE WHOLE WEEKS!
BUT THEY WANT TO KEEP THIS HUSH-HUSH. SO THE TEAM WILL BE SMALL-- JUST YOU, DAVE, AND ANY TWO OTHER PEOPLE FROM BOGGS YOU WANT.
ANY IDEAS?
ACTUALLY...
SHOES?!
I DON'T KNOW ANYTHING ABOUT SHOES!
YOU'VE GOT LIKE 100 PAIRS.
LIKE I SAID...
I DON'T KNOW ANYTHING ABOUT INVENTING SHOES. I'M IN FINANCE.

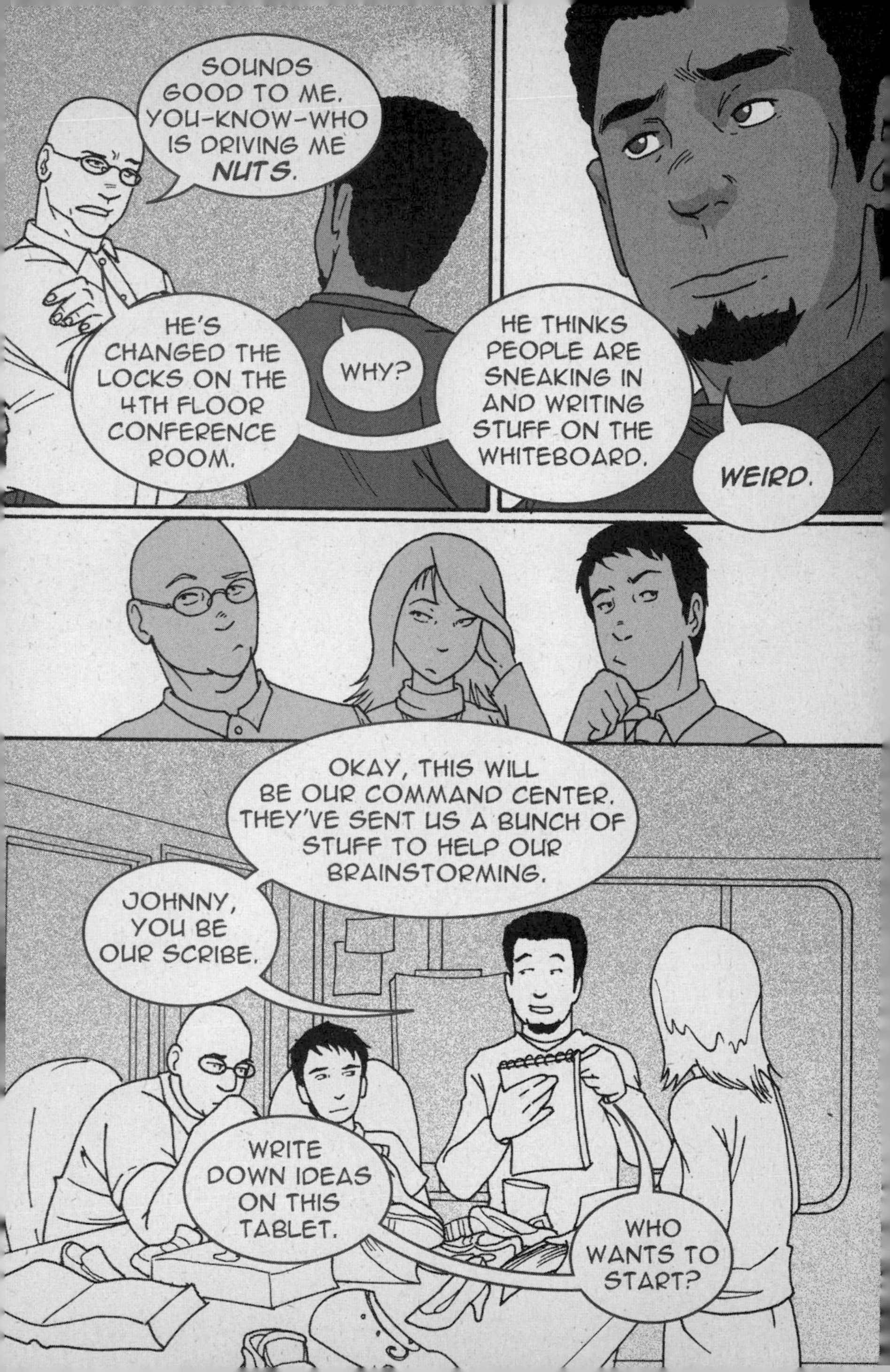
SOUNDS GOOD TO ME. YOU-KNOW-WHO IS DRIVING ME NUTS.
HE'S CHANGED THE LOCKS ON THE 4TH FLOOR CONFERENCE ROOM.
WHY?
HE THINKS PEOPLE ARE SNEAKING IN AND WRITING STUFF ON THE WHITEBOARD.
WEIRD.
OKAY, THIS WILL BE OUR COMMAND CENTER. THEY'VE SENT US A BUNCH OF STUFF TO HELP OUR BRAINSTORMING.
JOHNNY, YOU BE OUR SCRIBE.
WRITE DOWN IDEAS ON THIS TABLET.
WHO WANTS TO START?

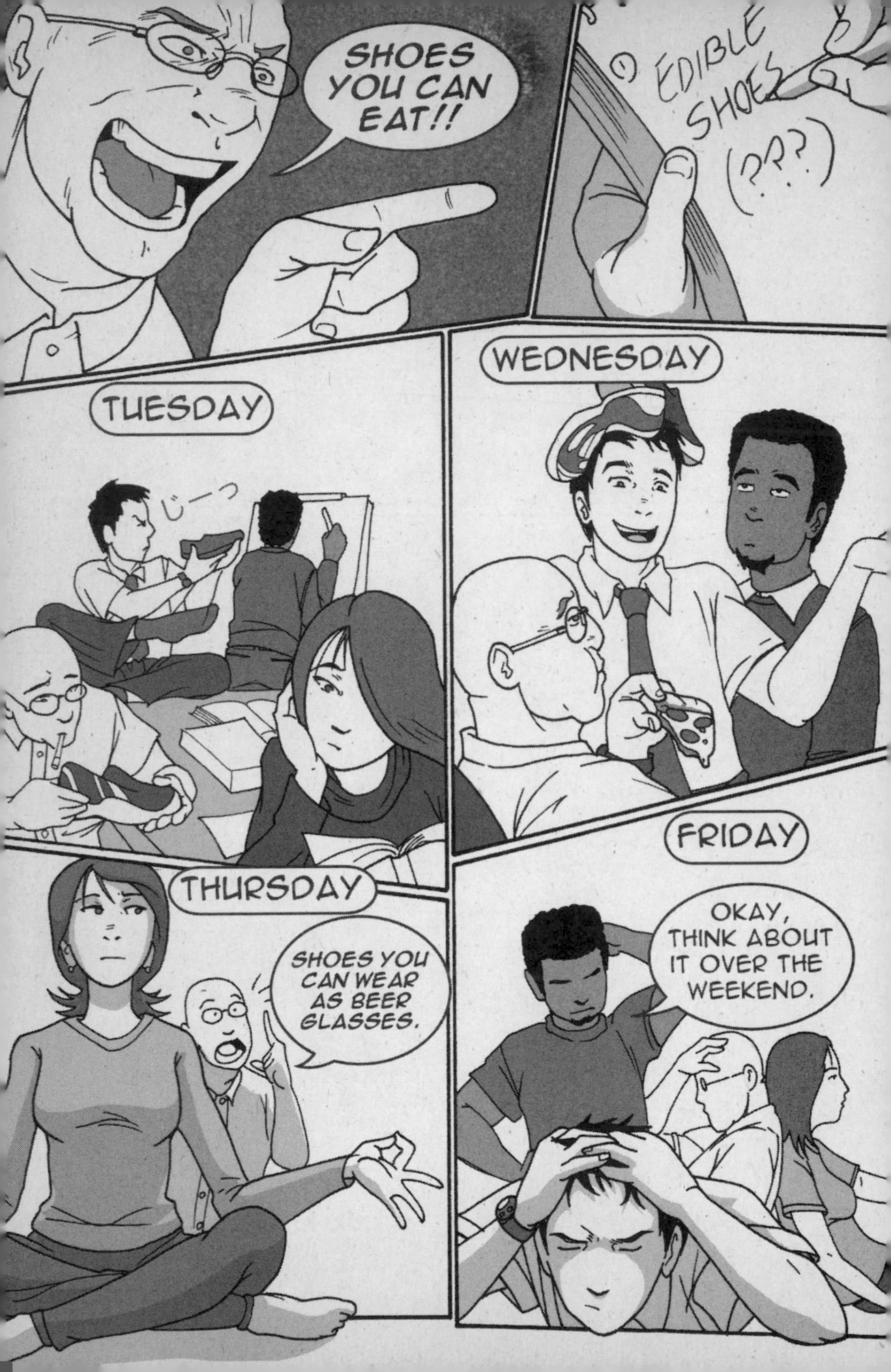
SHOES YOU CAN EAT!!
① EDIBLE SHOES (???)
TUESDAY
じーっ
WEDNESDAY
THURSDAY
SHOES YOU CAN WEAR AS BEER GLASSES.
FRIDAY
OKAY, THINK ABOUT IT OVER THE WEEKEND.

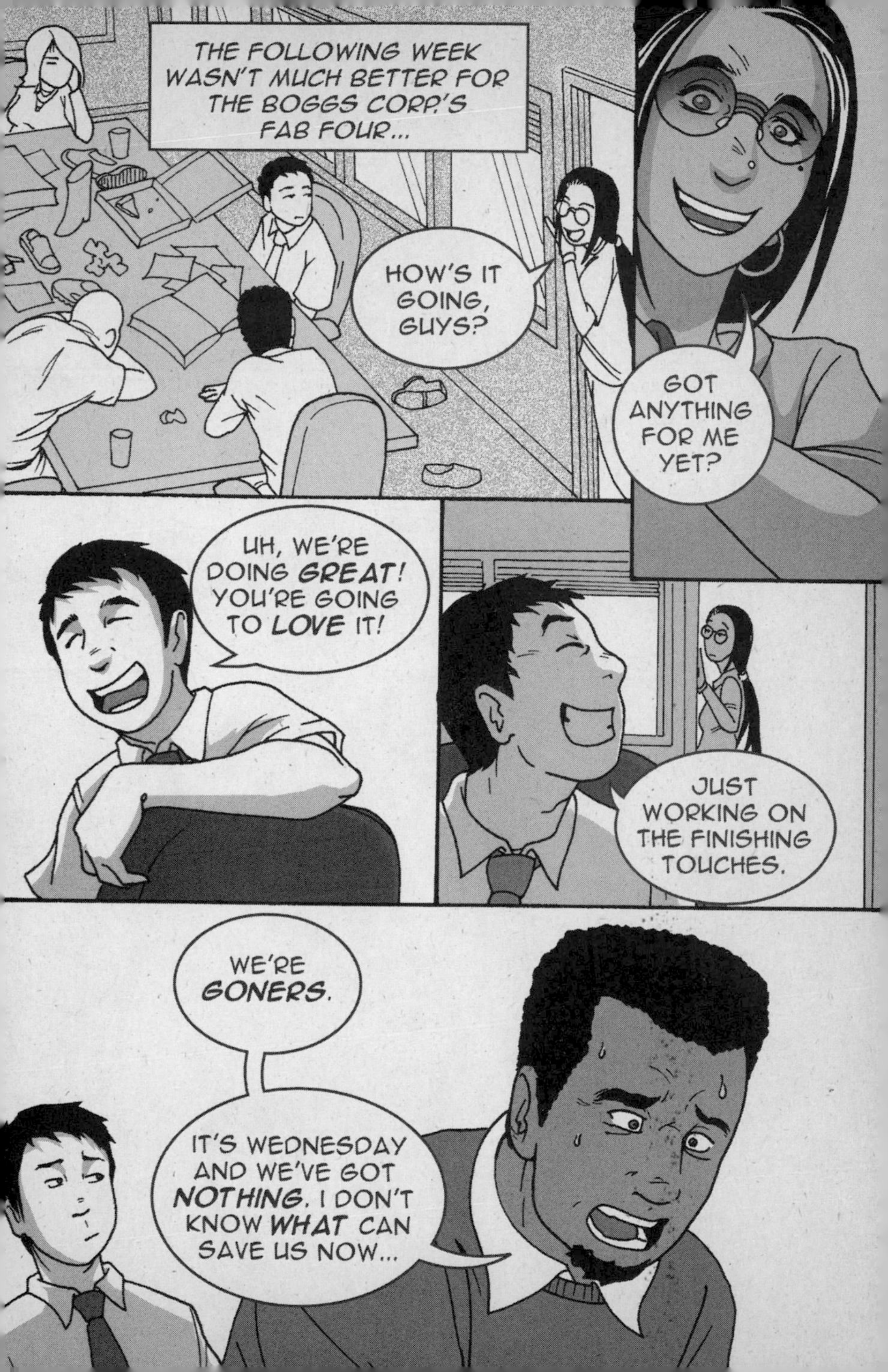
THE FOLLOWING WEEK WASN'T MUCH BETTER FOR THE BOGGS CORP.'S FAB FOUR...
HOW'S IT GOING, GUYS?
GOT ANYTHING FOR ME YET?
UH, WE'RE DOING GREAT! YOU'RE GOING TO LOVE IT!
JUST WORKING ON THE FINISHING TOUCHES.
WE'RE GONERS.
IT'S WEDNESDAY AND WE'VE GOT NOTHING. I DON'T KNOW WHAT CAN SAVE US NOW...

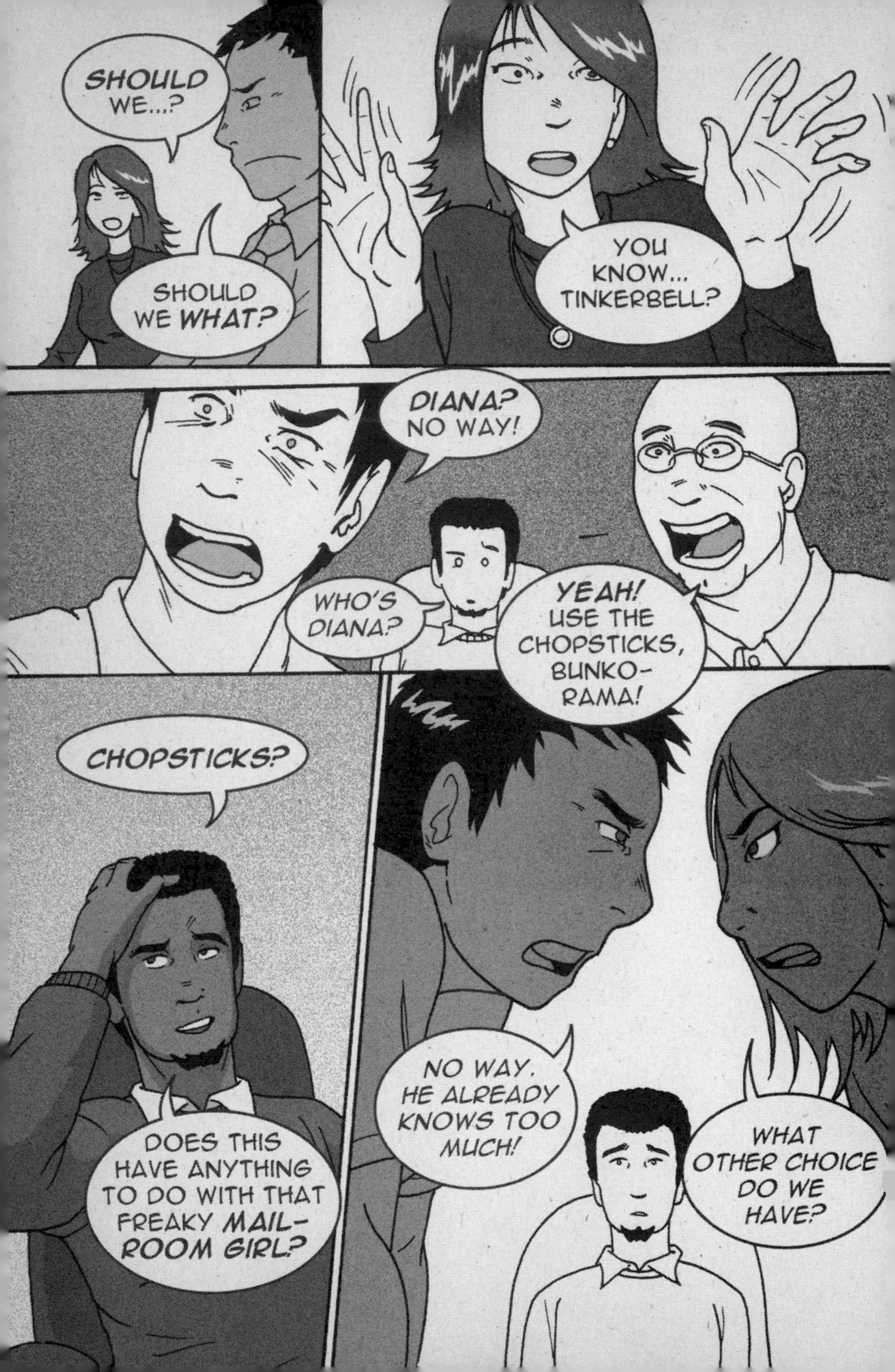
SHOULD WE...?
SHOULD WE WHAT?
YOU KNOW... TINKERBELL?
DIANA? NO WAY!
WHO'S DIANA?
YEAH! USE THE CHOPSTICKS, BUNKO-RAMA!
CHOPSTICKS?
DOES THIS HAVE ANYTHING TO DO WITH THAT FREAKY MAIL-ROOM GIRL?
NO WAY, HE ALREADY KNOWS TOO MUCH!
WHAT OTHER CHOICE DO WE HAVE?

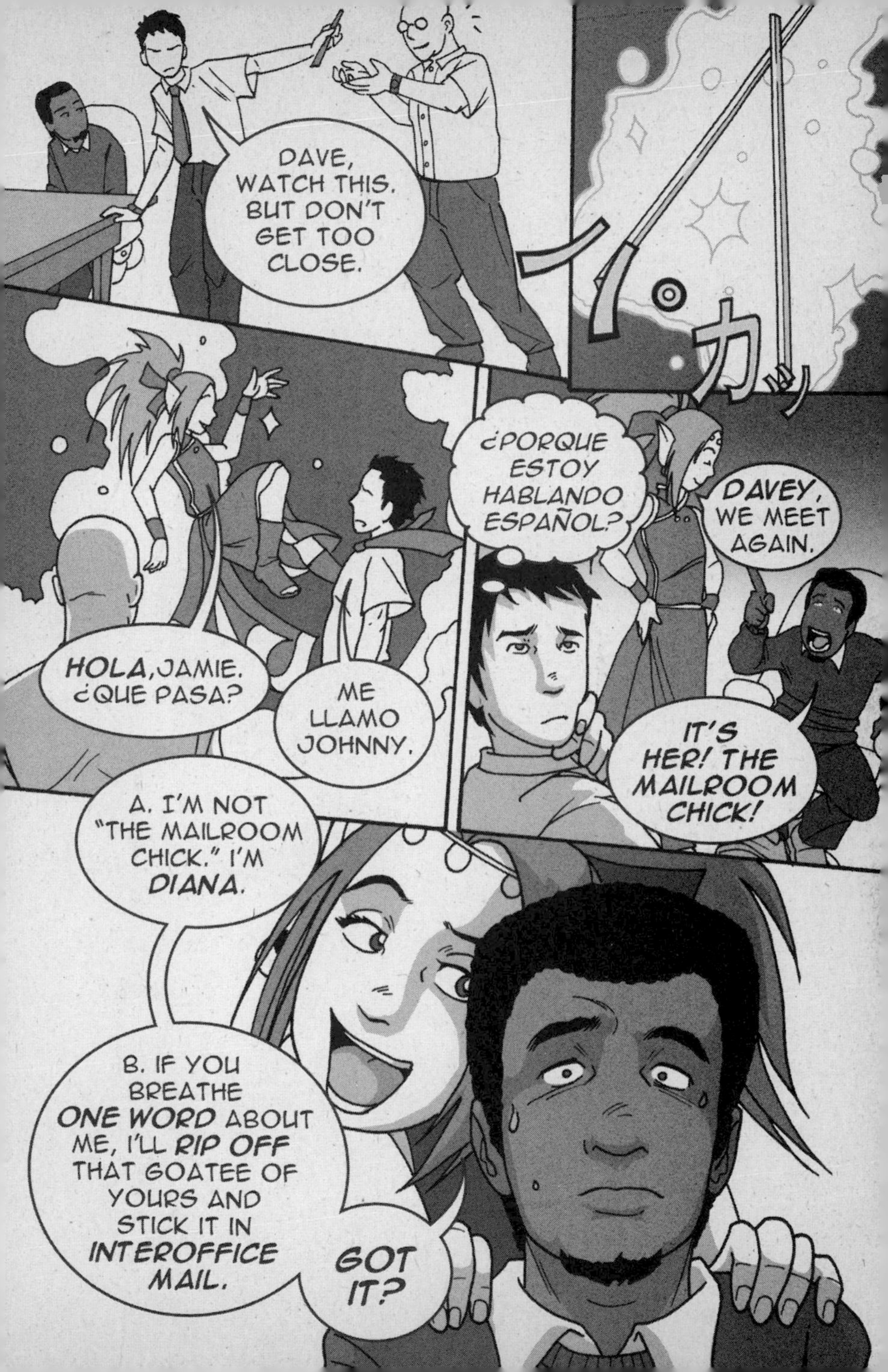
DAVE, WATCH THIS. BUT DON'T GET TOO CLOSE.
カッ
HOLA, JAMIE. ¿QUE PASA?
ME LLAMO JOHNNY.
¿PORQUE ESTOY HABLANDO ESPAÑOL?
DAVEY, WE MEET AGAIN.
IT'S HER! THE MAILROOM CHICK!
A. I'M NOT "THE MAILROOM CHICK." I'M DIANA.
B. IF YOU BREATHE ONE WORD ABOUT ME, I'LL RIP OFF THAT GOATEE OF YOURS AND STICK IT IN INTEROFFICE MAIL.
GOT IT?

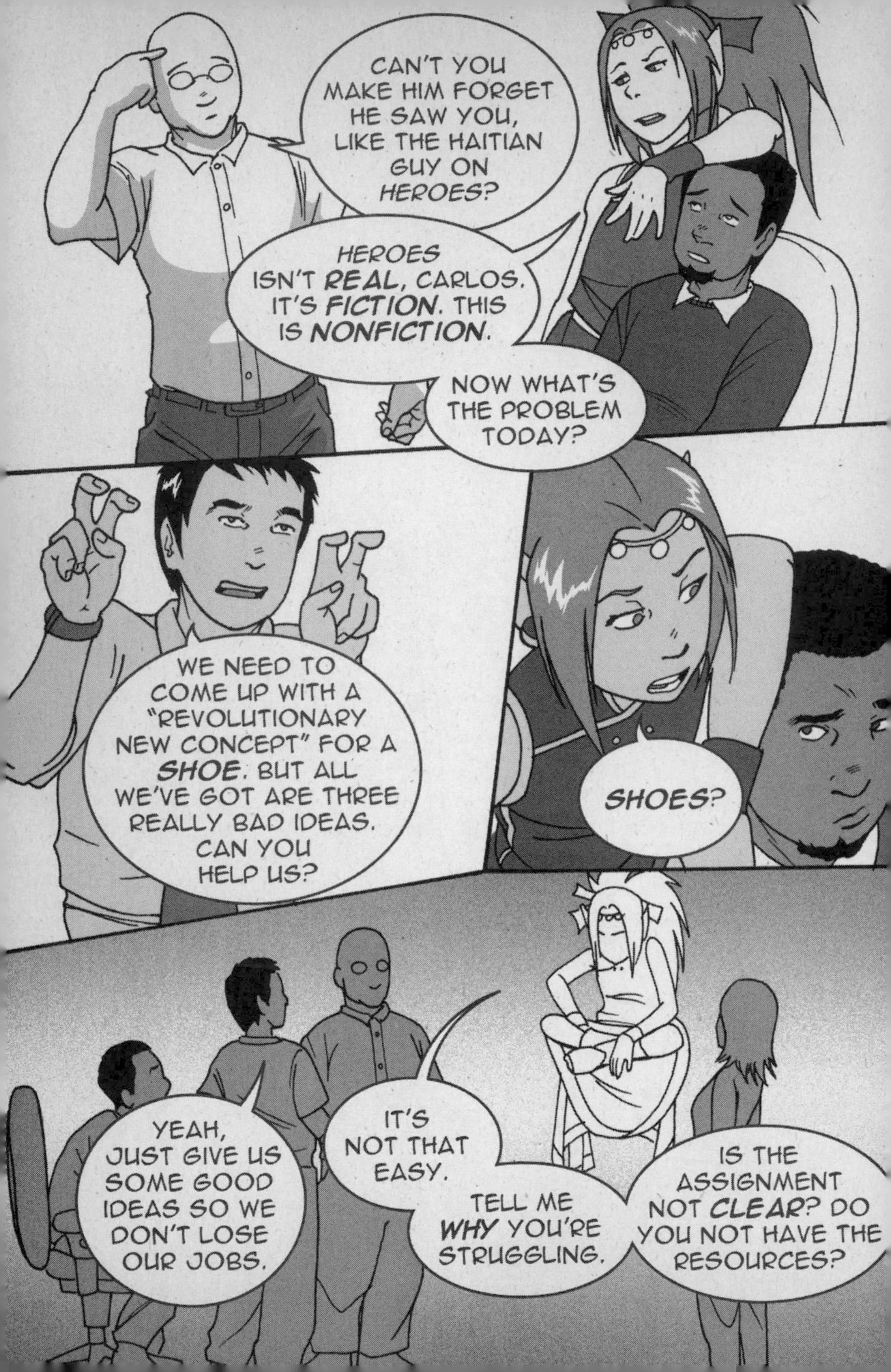
CAN'T YOU MAKE HIM FORGET HE SAW YOU, LIKE THE HAITIAN GUY ON HEROES?
HEROES ISN'T REAL, CARLOS. IT'S FICTION. THIS IS NONFICTION.
NOW WHAT'S THE PROBLEM TODAY?
WE NEED TO COME UP WITH A "REVOLUTIONARY NEW CONCEPT" FOR A SHOE. BUT ALL WE'VE GOT ARE THREE REALLY BAD IDEAS. CAN YOU HELP US?
SHOES?
YEAH, JUST GIVE US SOME GOOD IDEAS SO WE DON'T LOSE OUR JOBS.
IT'S NOT THAT EASY.
TELL ME WHY YOU'RE STRUGGLING.
IS THE ASSIGNMENT NOT CLEAR? DO YOU NOT HAVE THE RESOURCES?

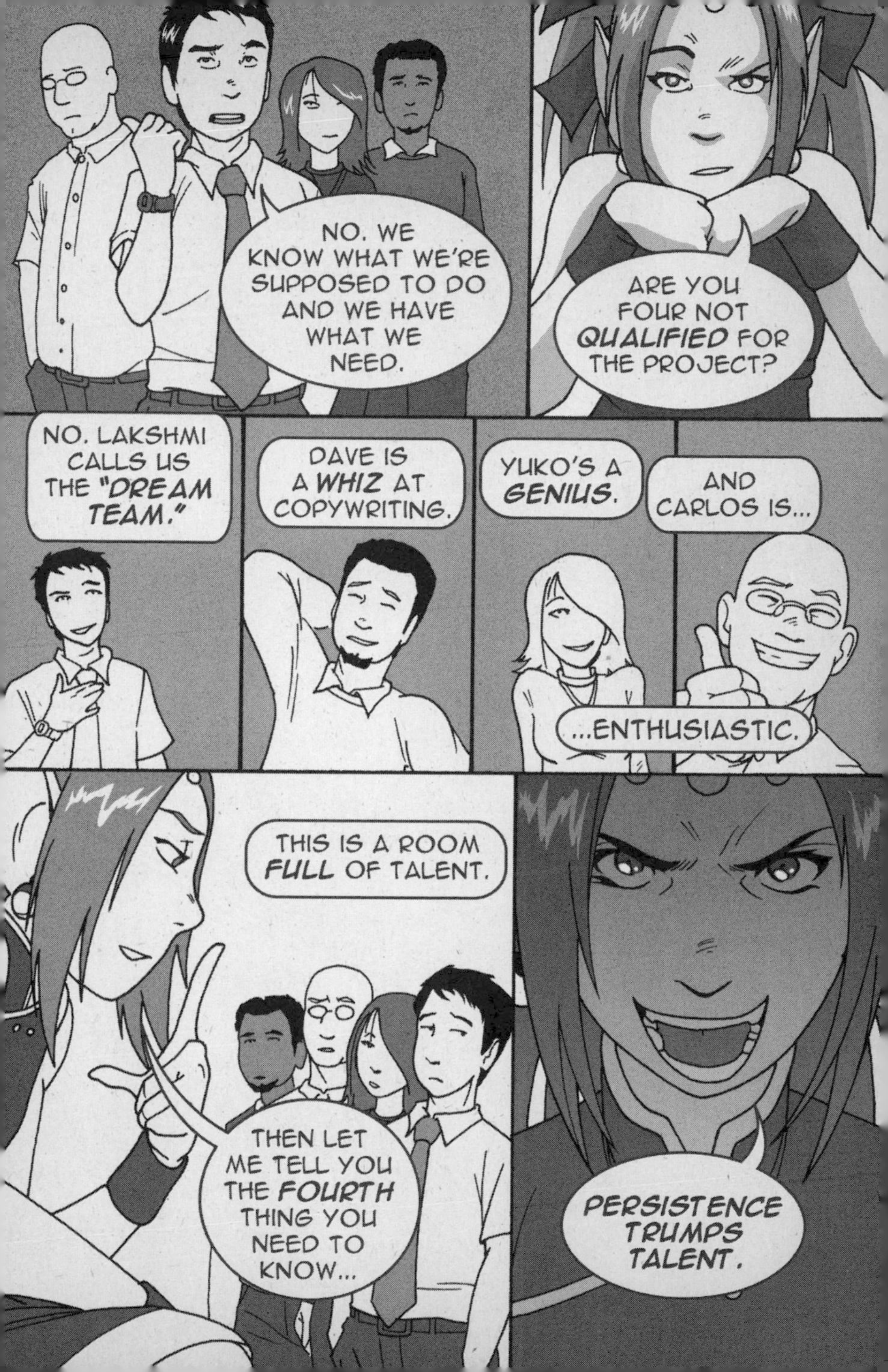
NO. WE KNOW WHAT WE'RE SUPPOSED TO DO AND WE HAVE WHAT WE NEED.
ARE YOU FOUR NOT QUALIFIED FOR THE PROJECT?
NO. LAKSHMI CALLS US THE "DREAM TEAM."
DAVE IS A WHIZ AT COPYWRITING.
YUKO'S A GENIUS.
AND CARLOS IS...
...ENTHUSIASTIC.
THIS IS A ROOM FULL OF TALENT.
THEN LET ME TELL YOU THE FOURTH THING YOU NEED TO KNOW...
PERSISTENCE TRUMPS TALENT.

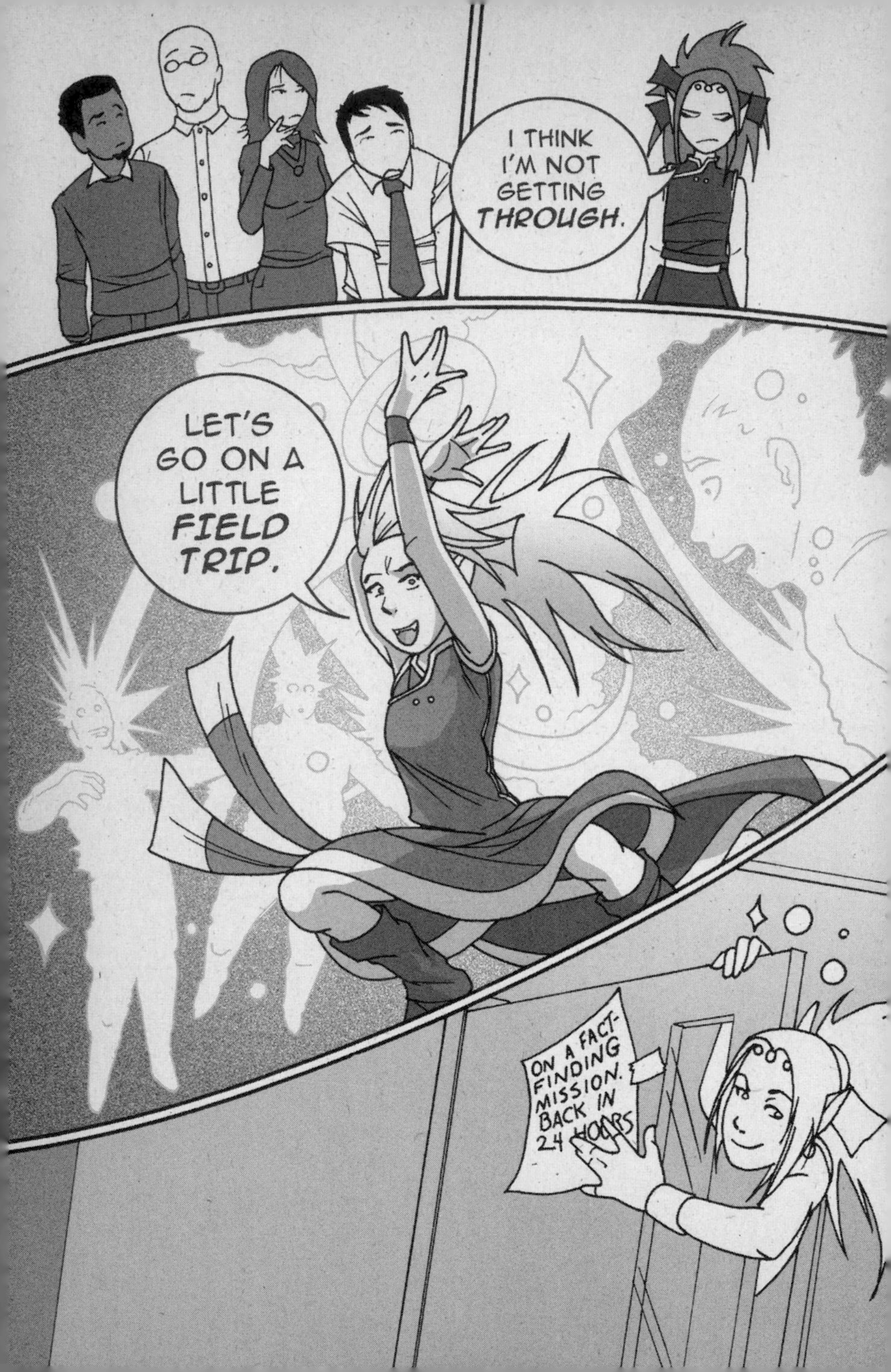
I THINK I'M NOT GETTING THROUGH.
LET'S GO ON A LITTLE FIELD TRIP.
ON A FACT-FINDING MISSION. BACK IN 24 HOURS

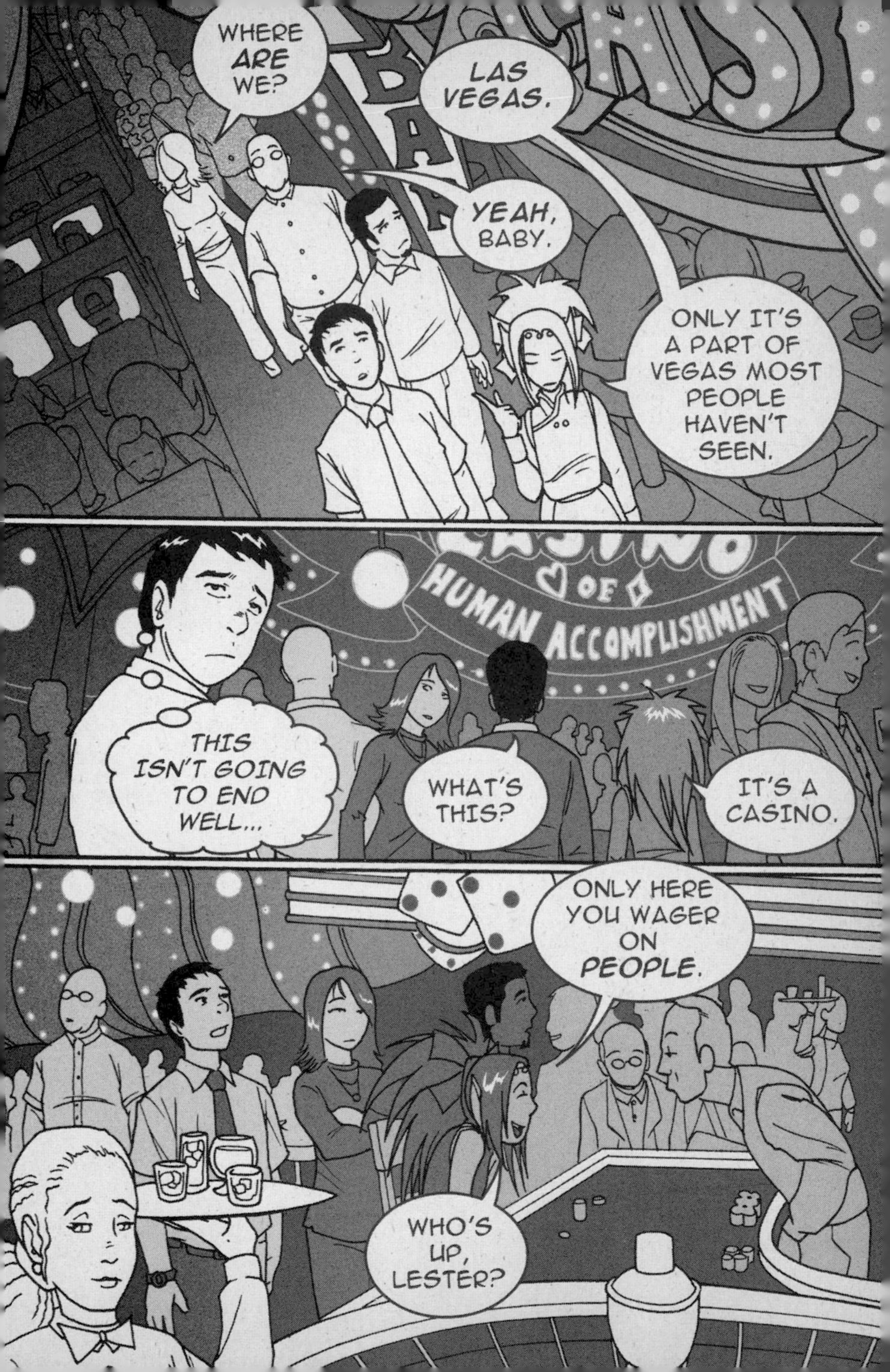
WHERE ARE WE?
LAS VEGAS.
YEAH, BABY.
ONLY IT'S A PART OF VEGAS MOST PEOPLE HAVEN'T SEEN.
CASINO OF HUMAN ACCOMPLISHMENT
THIS ISN'T GOING TO END WELL...
WHAT'S THIS?
IT'S A CASINO.
ONLY HERE YOU WAGER ON PEOPLE.
WHO'S UP, LESTER?

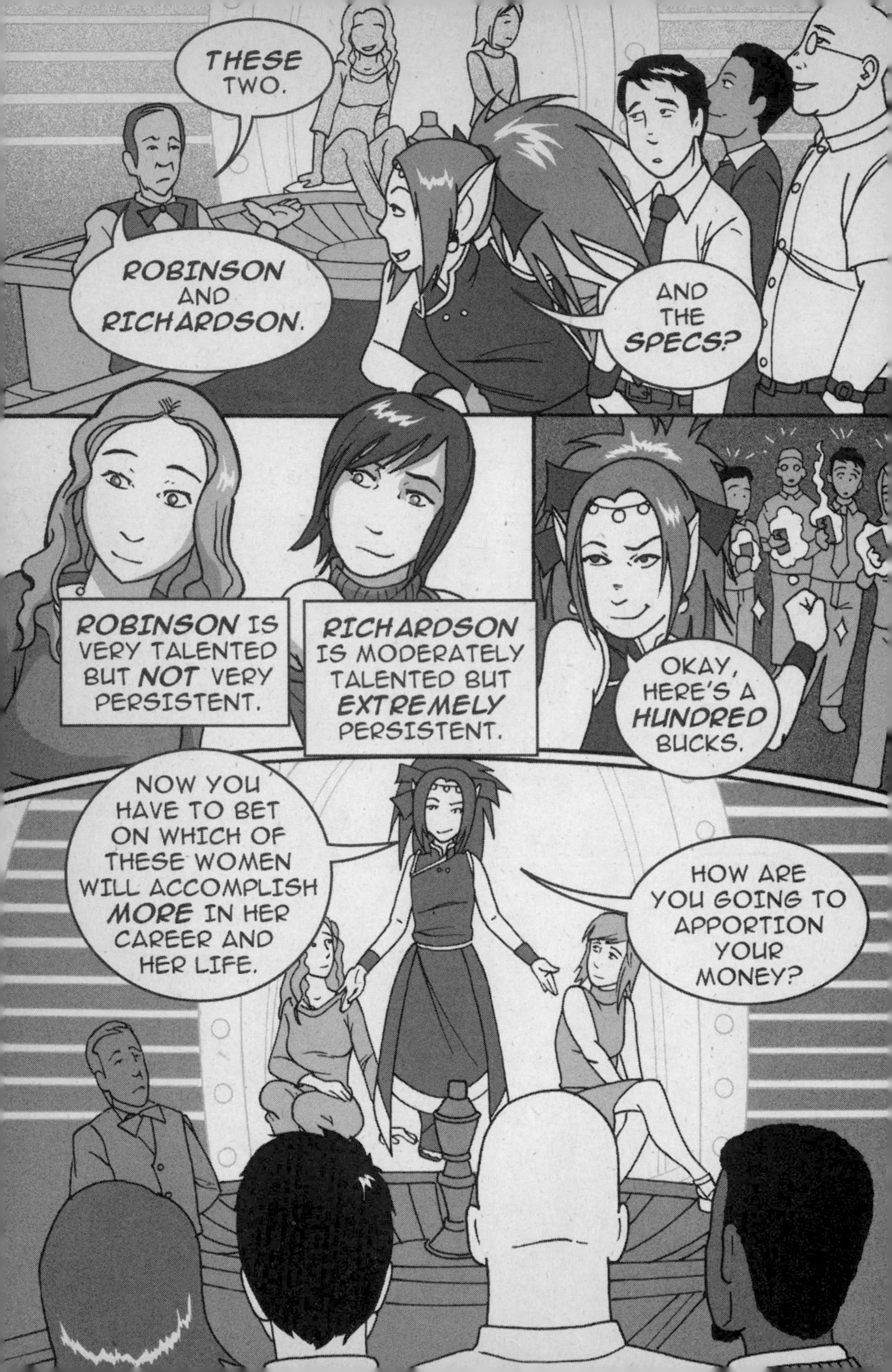
THESE TWO.
ROBINSON AND RICHARDSON.
AND THE SPECS?
ROBINSON IS VERY TALENTED BUT NOT VERY PERSISTENT.
RICHARDSON IS MODERATELY TALENTED BUT EXTREMELY PERSISTENT.
OKAY, HERE'S A HUNDRED BUCKS.
NOW YOU HAVE TO BET ON WHICH OF THESE WOMEN WILL ACCOMPLISH MORE IN HER CAREER AND HER LIFE.
HOW ARE YOU GOING TO APPORTION YOUR MONEY?

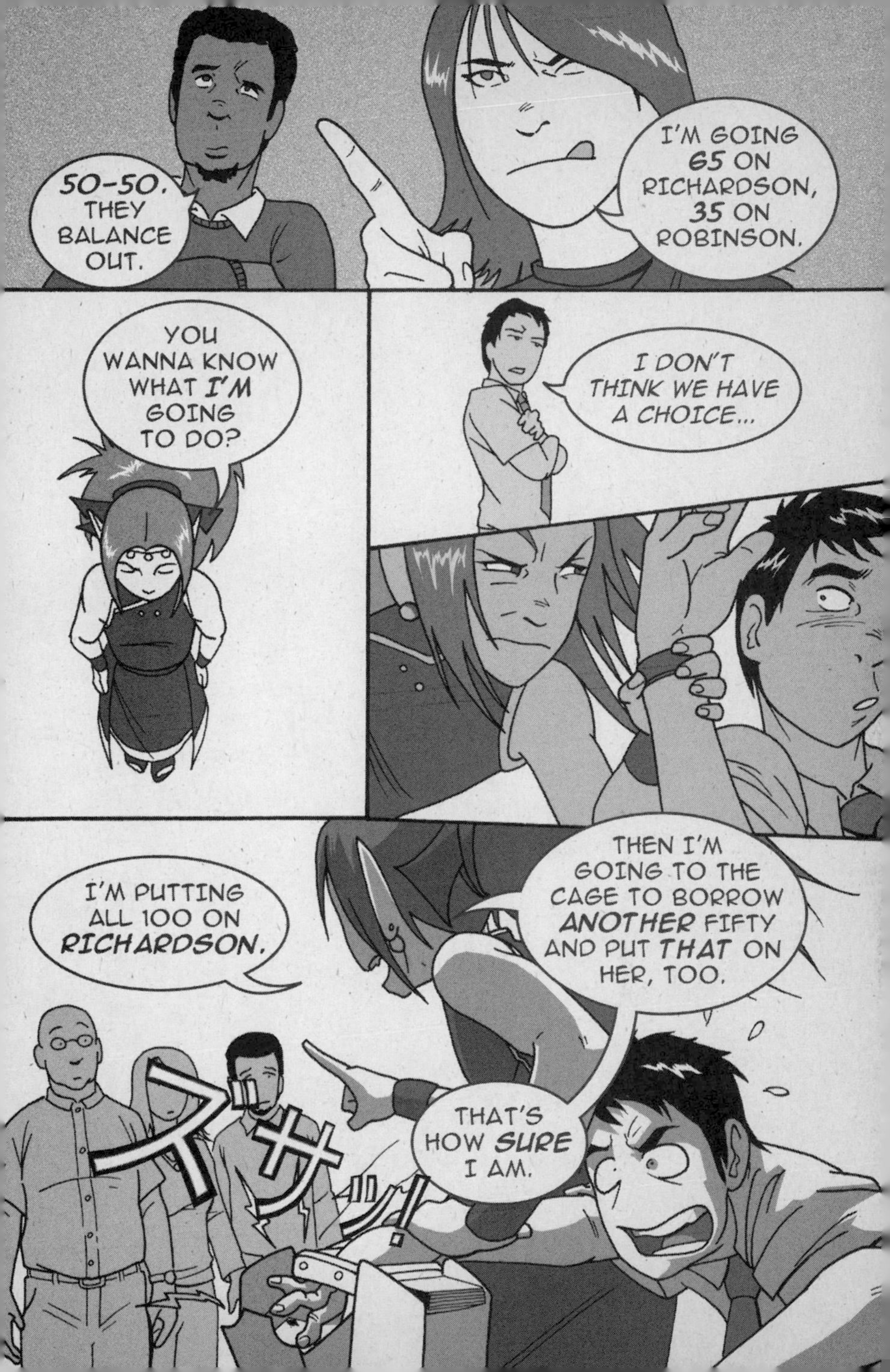
50-50. THEY BALANCE OUT.
I'M GOING 65 ON RICHARDSON, 35 ON ROBINSON.
YOU WANNA KNOW WHAT I'M GOING TO DO?
I DON'T THINK WE HAVE A CHOICE...
I'M PUTTING ALL 100 ON RICHARDSON.
THEN I'M GOING TO THE CAGE TO BORROW ANOTHER FIFTY AND PUT THAT ON HER, TOO.
THAT'S HOW SURE I AM.

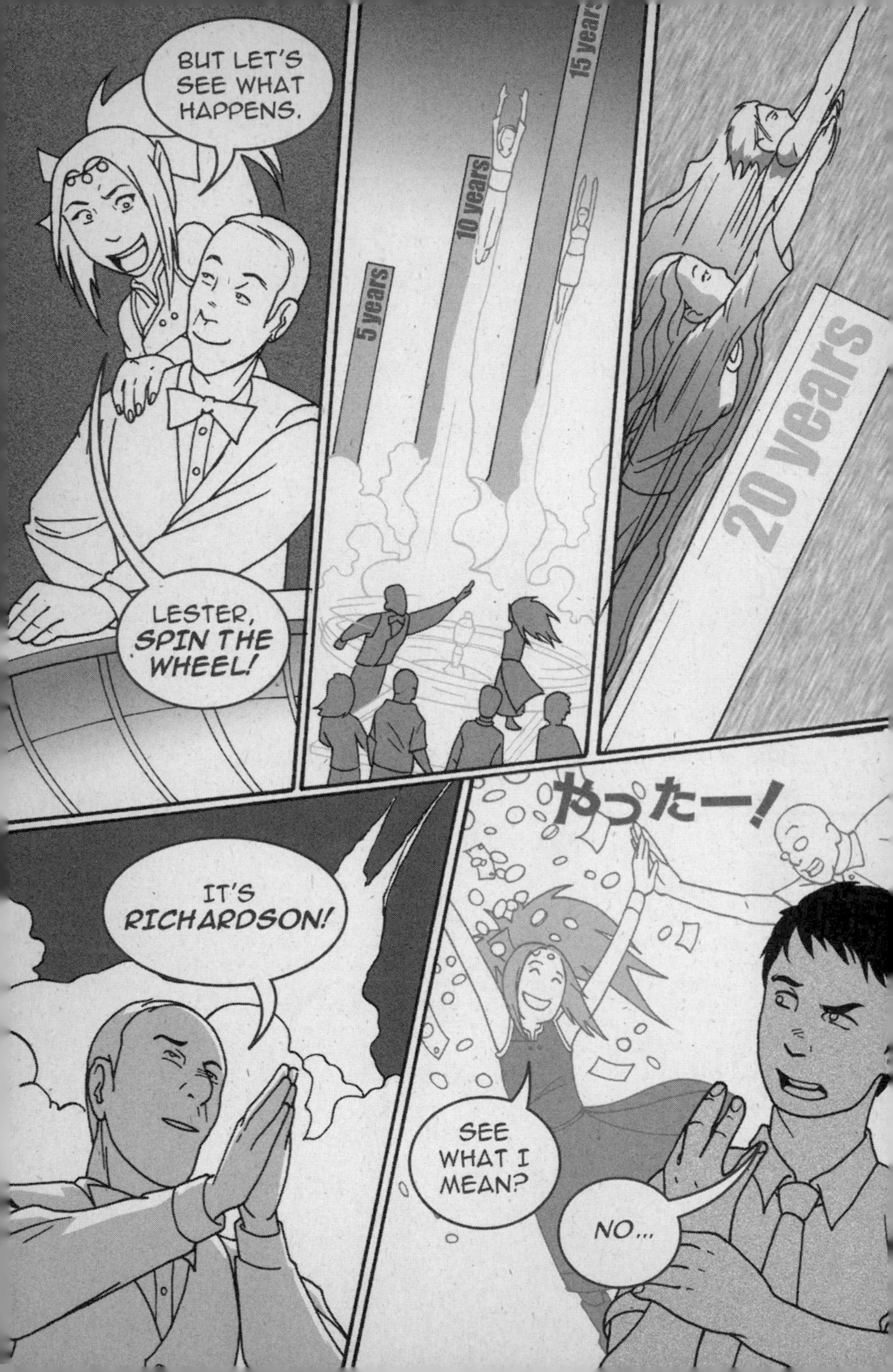
BUT LET'S SEE WHAT HAPPENS.
LESTER, SPIN THE WHEEL!
5 years
10 years
15 years
15 years
20 years
IT'S RICHARDSON!
やったー!
SEE WHAT I MEAN?
NO...

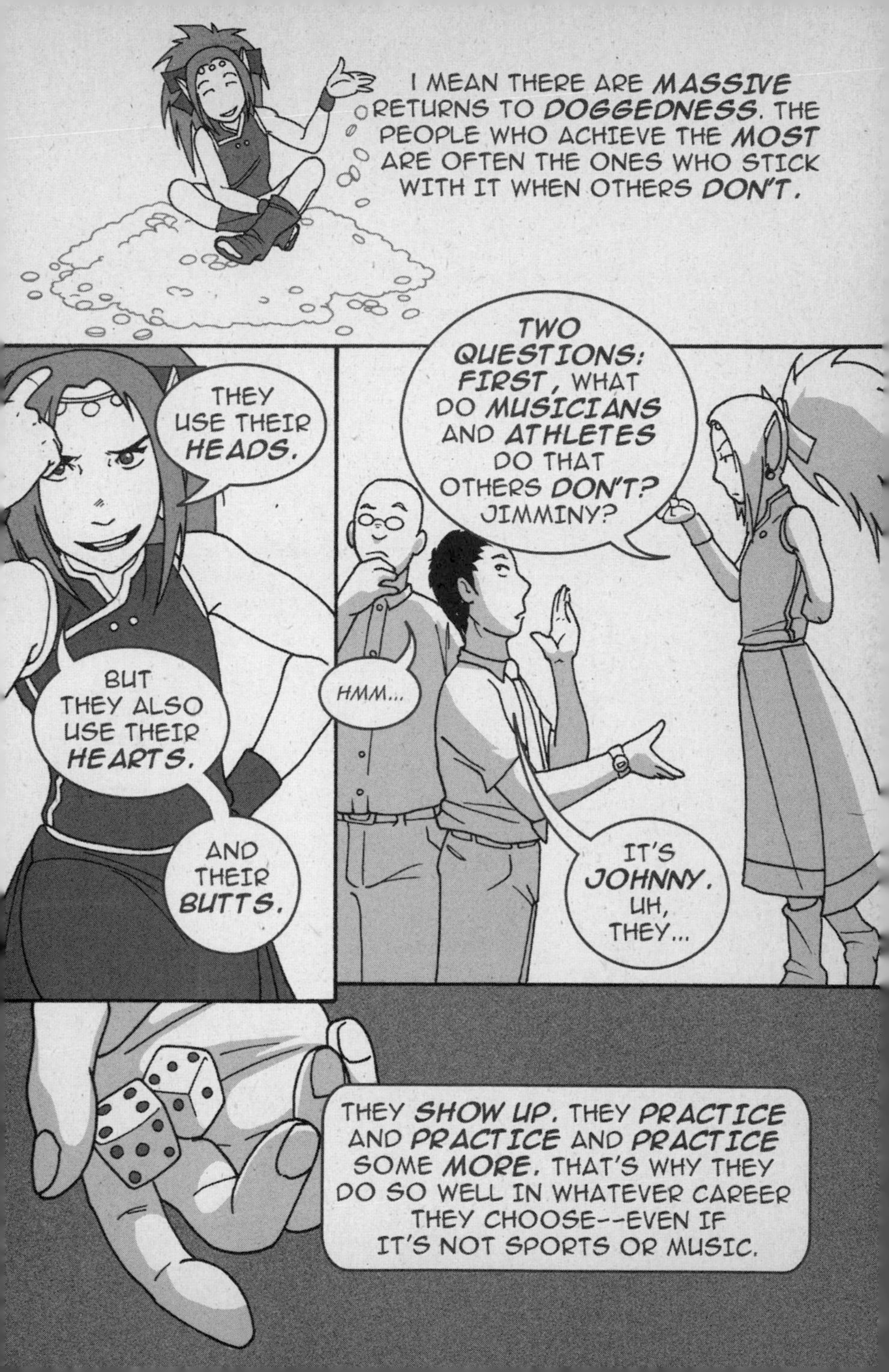
I MEAN THERE ARE MASSIVE RETURNS TO DOGGEDNESS. THE PEOPLE WHO ACHIEVE THE MOST ARE OFTEN THE ONES WHO STICK WITH IT WHEN OTHERS DON'T.
THEY USE THEIR HEADS.
BUT THEY ALSO USE THEIR HEARTS.
AND THEIR BUTTS.
TWO QUESTIONS: FIRST, WHAT DO MUSICIANS AND ATHLETES DO THAT OTHERS DON'T? JIMMINY?
HMM...
IT'S JOHNNY. UH, THEY...
THEY SHOW UP. THEY PRACTICE AND PRACTICE AND PRACTICE SOME MORE. THAT'S WHY THEY DO SO WELL IN WHATEVER CAREER THEY CHOOSE--EVEN IF IT'S NOT SPORTS OR MUSIC.

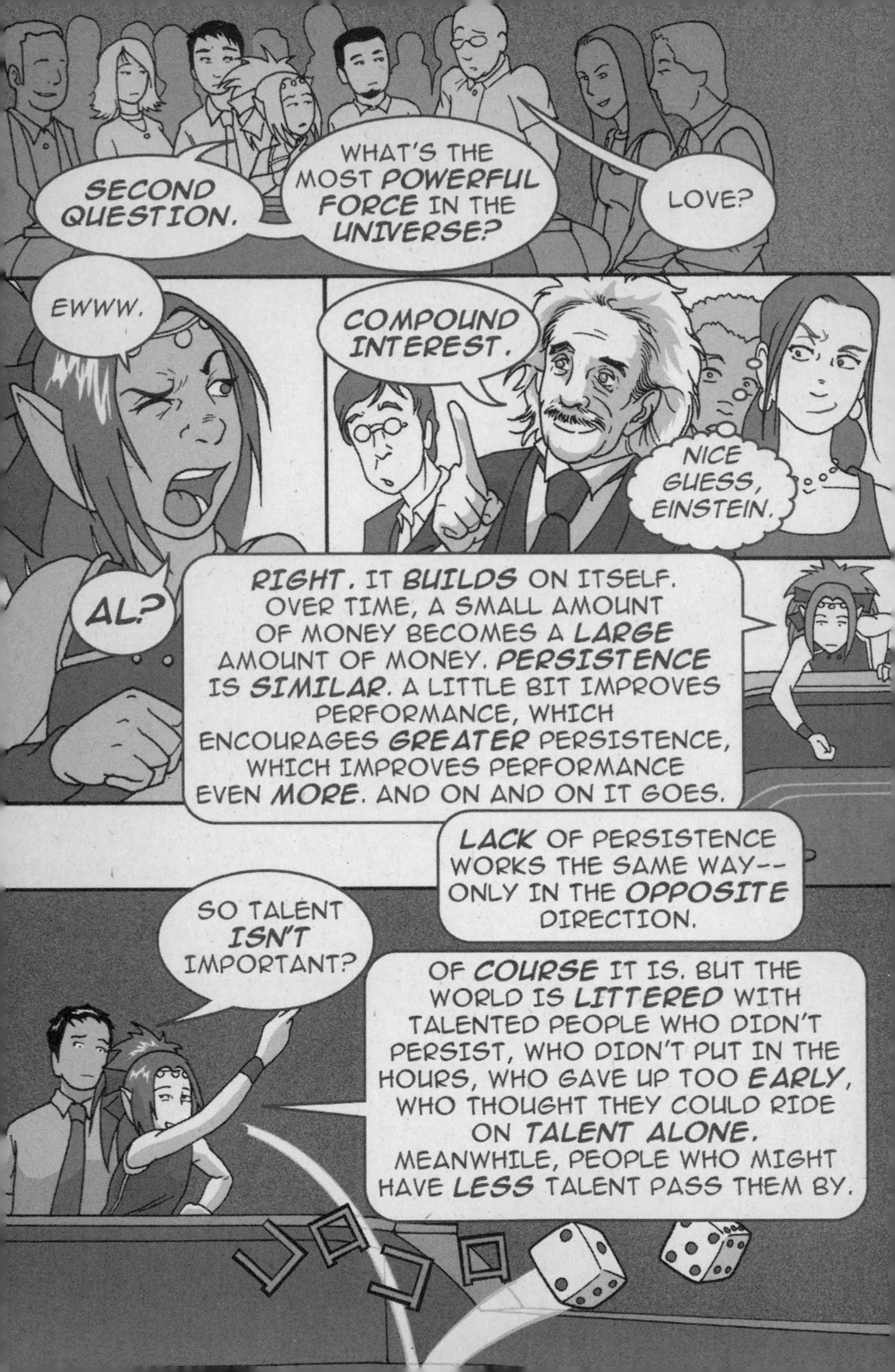
SECOND QUESTION.
WHAT'S THE MOST POWERFUL FORCE IN THE UNIVERSE?
LOVE?
EWWW.
COMPOUND INTEREST.
NICE GUESS, EINSTEIN.
AL?
RIGHT. IT BUILDS ON ITSELF. OVER TIME, A SMALL AMOUNT OF MONEY BECOMES A LARGE AMOUNT OF MONEY. PERSISTENCE IS SIMILAR. A LITTLE BIT IMPROVES PERFORMANCE, WHICH ENCOURAGES GREATER PERSISTENCE, WHICH IMPROVES PERFORMANCE EVEN MORE. AND ON AND ON IT GOES.
LACK OF PERSISTENCE WORKS THE SAME WAY-- ONLY IN THE OPPOSITE DIRECTION.
SO TALENT ISN'T IMPORTANT?
OF COURSE IT IS. BUT THE WORLD IS LITTERED WITH TALENTED PEOPLE WHO DIDN'T PERSIST, WHO DIDN'T PUT IN THE HOURS, WHO GAVE UP TOO EARLY, WHO THOUGHT THEY COULD RIDE ON TALENT ALONE. MEANWHILE, PEOPLE WHO MIGHT HAVE LESS TALENT PASS THEM BY.

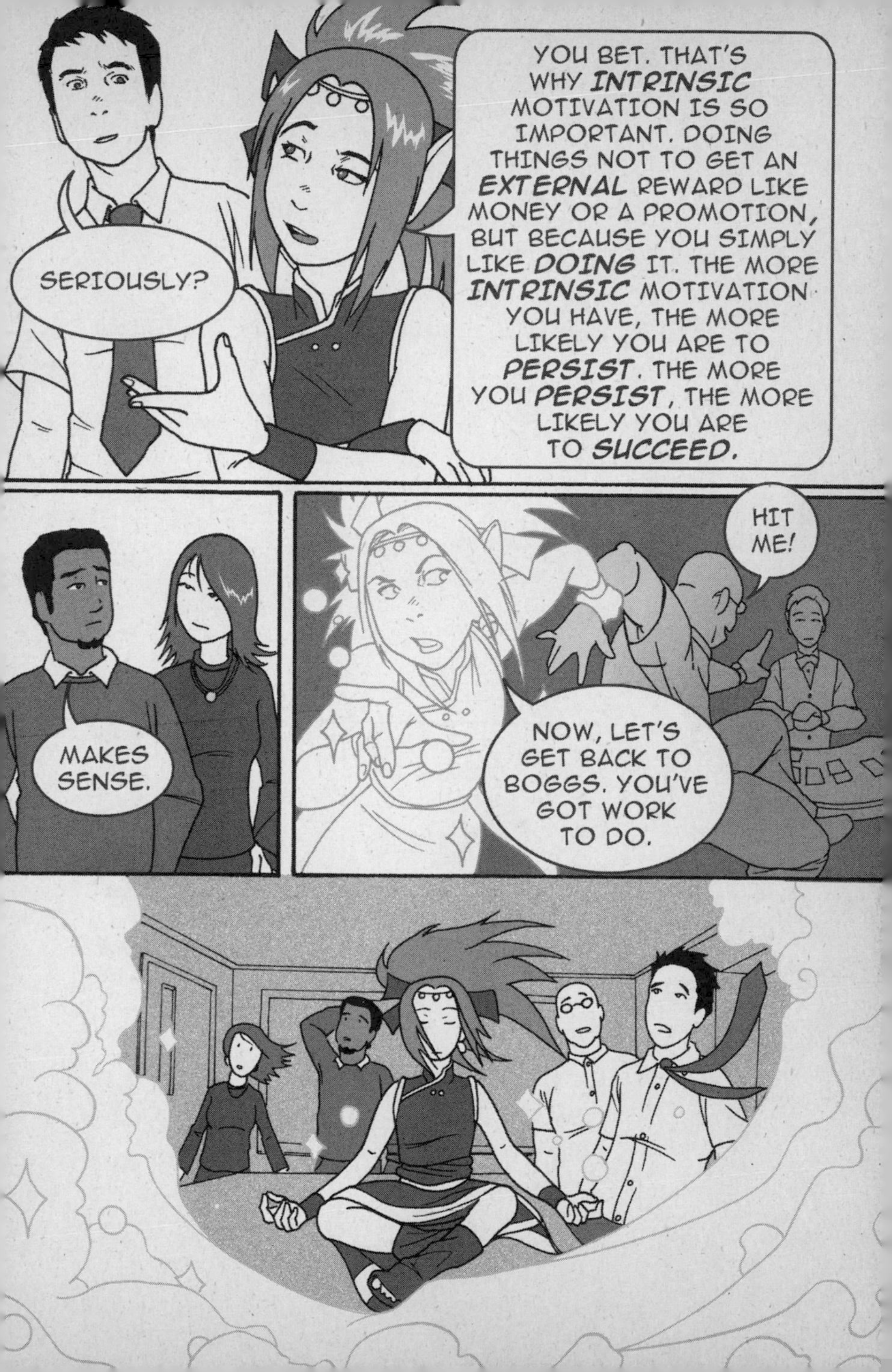
YOU BET. THAT'S WHY INTRINSIC MOTIVATION IS SO IMPORTANT. DOING THINGS NOT TO GET AN EXTERNAL REWARD LIKE MONEY OR A PROMOTION, BUT BECAUSE YOU SIMPLY LIKE DOING IT. THE MORE INTRINSIC MOTIVATION YOU HAVE, THE MORE LIKELY YOU ARE TO PERSIST. THE MORE YOU PERSIST, THE MORE LIKELY YOU ARE TO SUCCEED.
SERIOUSLY?
MAKES SENSE.
HIT ME!
NOW, LET'S GET BACK TO BOGGS. YOU'VE GOT WORK TO DO.

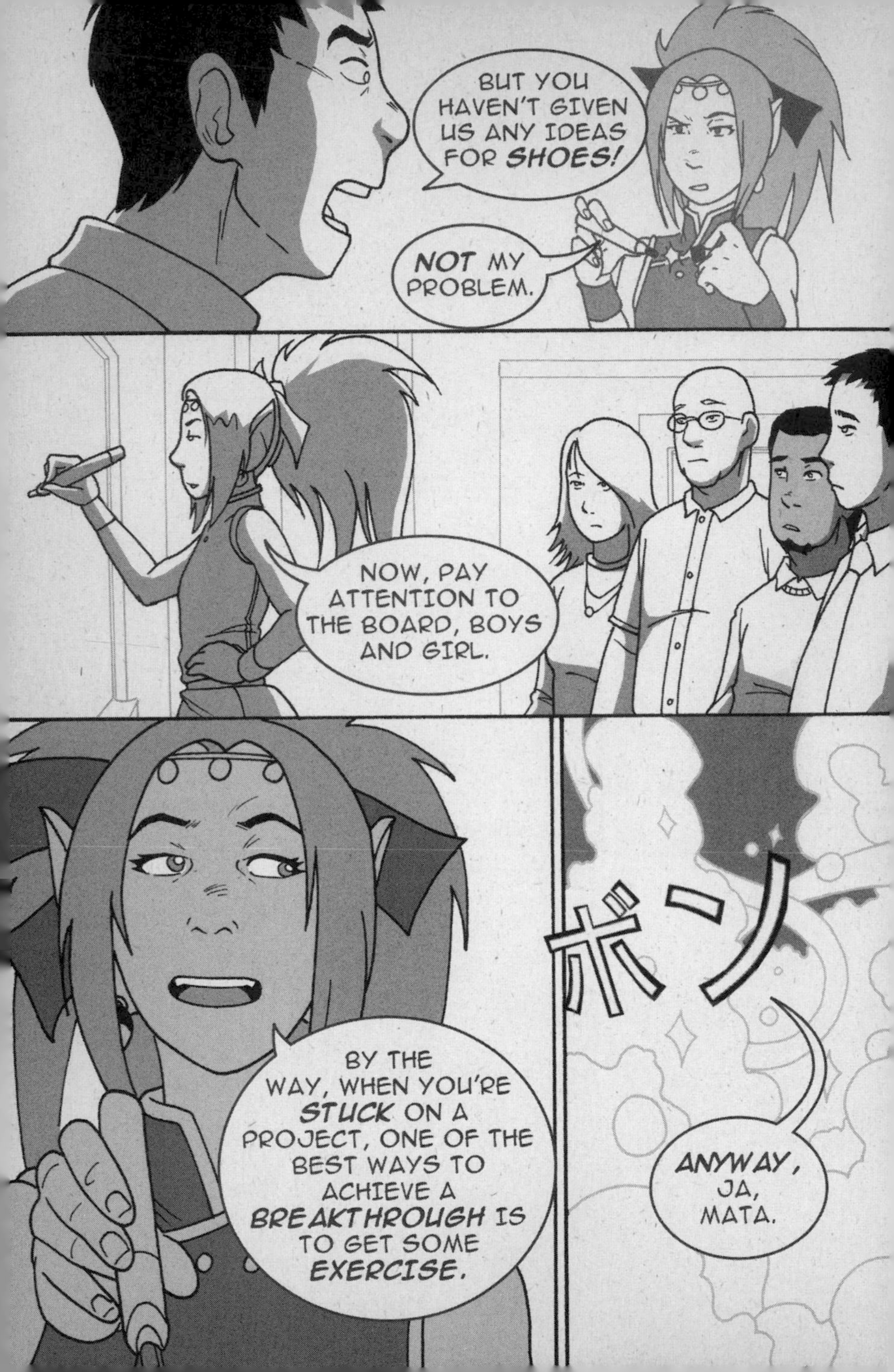
BUT YOU HAVEN'T GIVEN US ANY IDEAS FOR SHOES!
NOT MY PROBLEM.
NOW, PAY ATTENTION TO THE BOARD, BOYS AND GIRL.
BY THE WAY, WHEN YOU'RE STUCK ON A PROJECT, ONE OF THE BEST WAYS TO ACHIEVE A BREAKTHROUGH IS TO GET SOME EXERCISE.
ボーン
ANYWAY, JA, MATA.

. There is no plan.
2. Think strengths, not weakness
3. It's not about you.
4. Persistence trumps talent.

LESSON FIVE

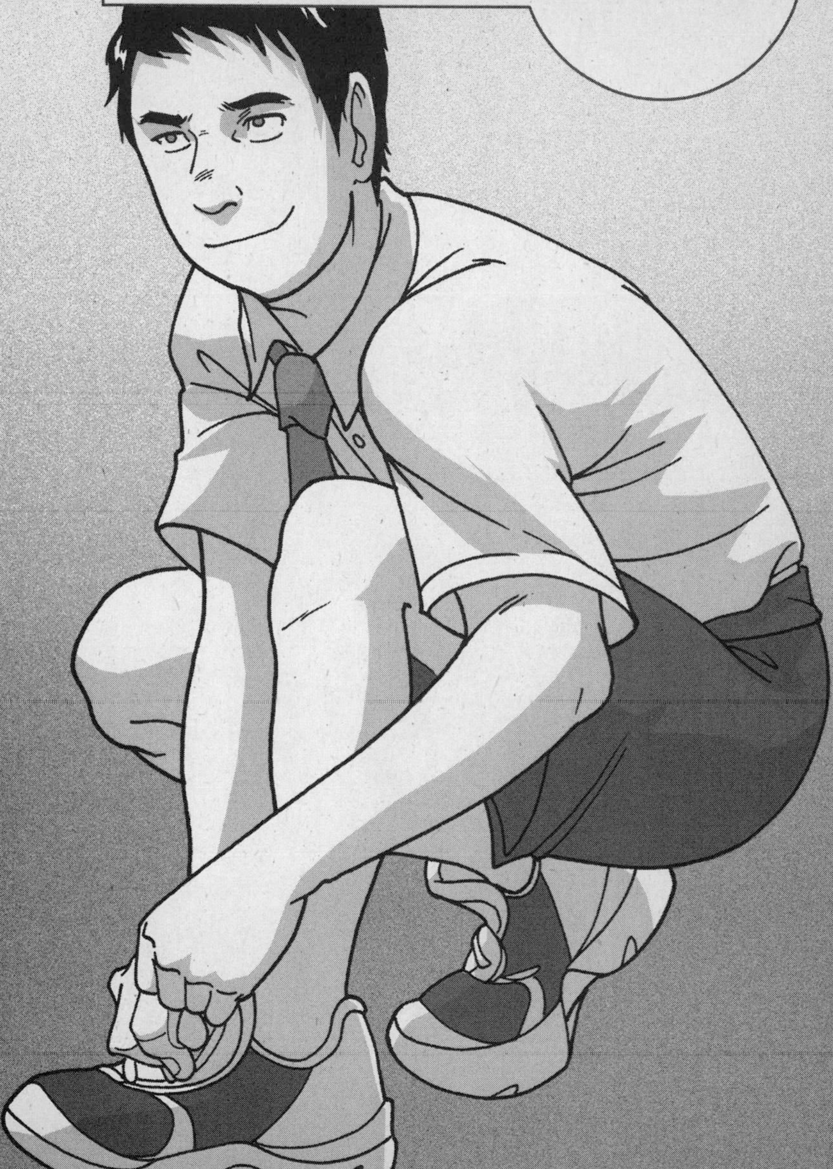

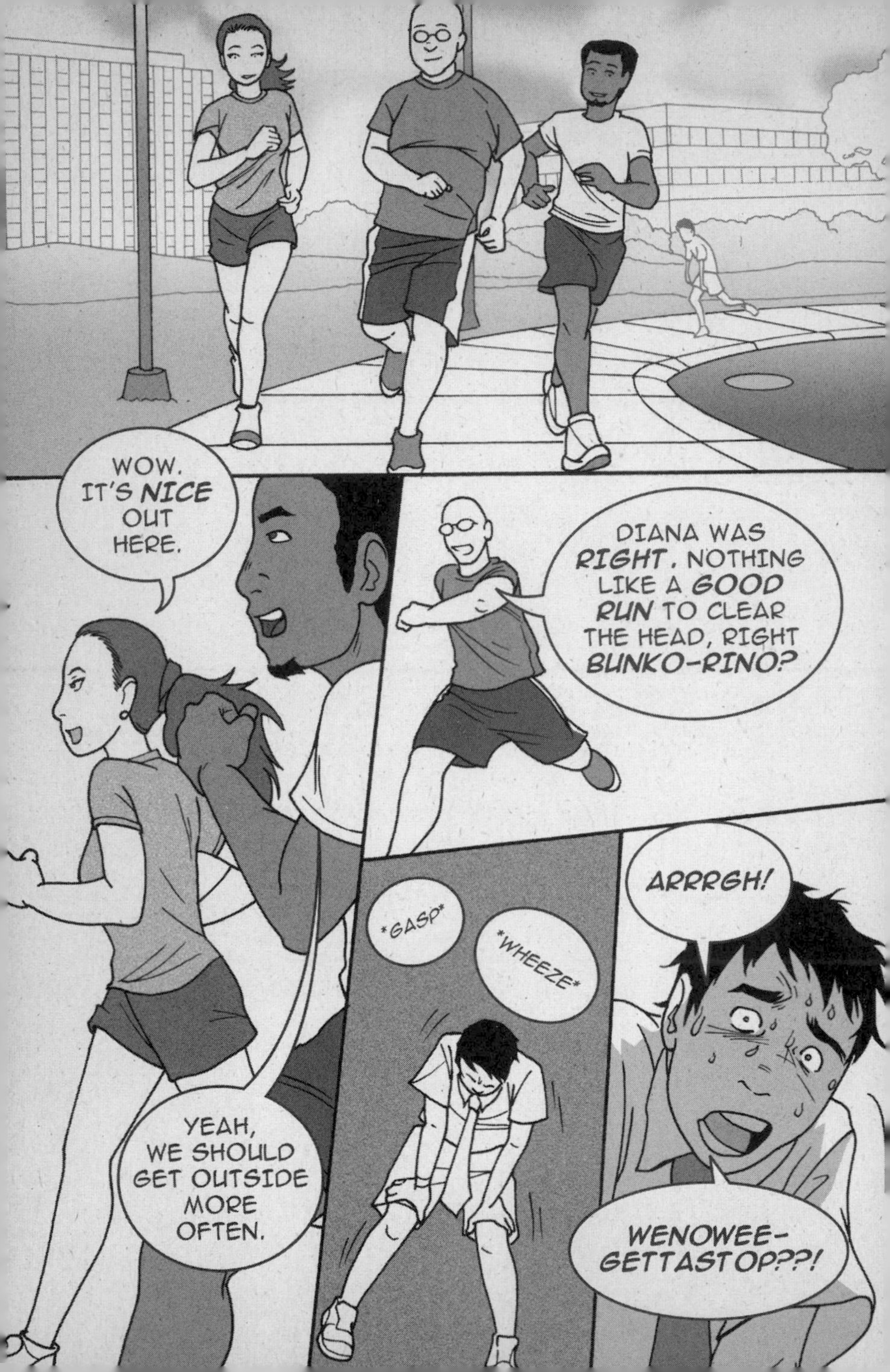
WOW. IT'S NICE OUT HERE.
DIANA WAS RIGHT. NOTHING LIKE A GOOD RUN TO CLEAR THE HEAD, RIGHT BUNKO-RINO?
YEAH, WE SHOULD GET OUTSIDE MORE OFTEN.
GASP
WHEEZE
ARRRGH!
WENOWEE-GETTASTOP??!

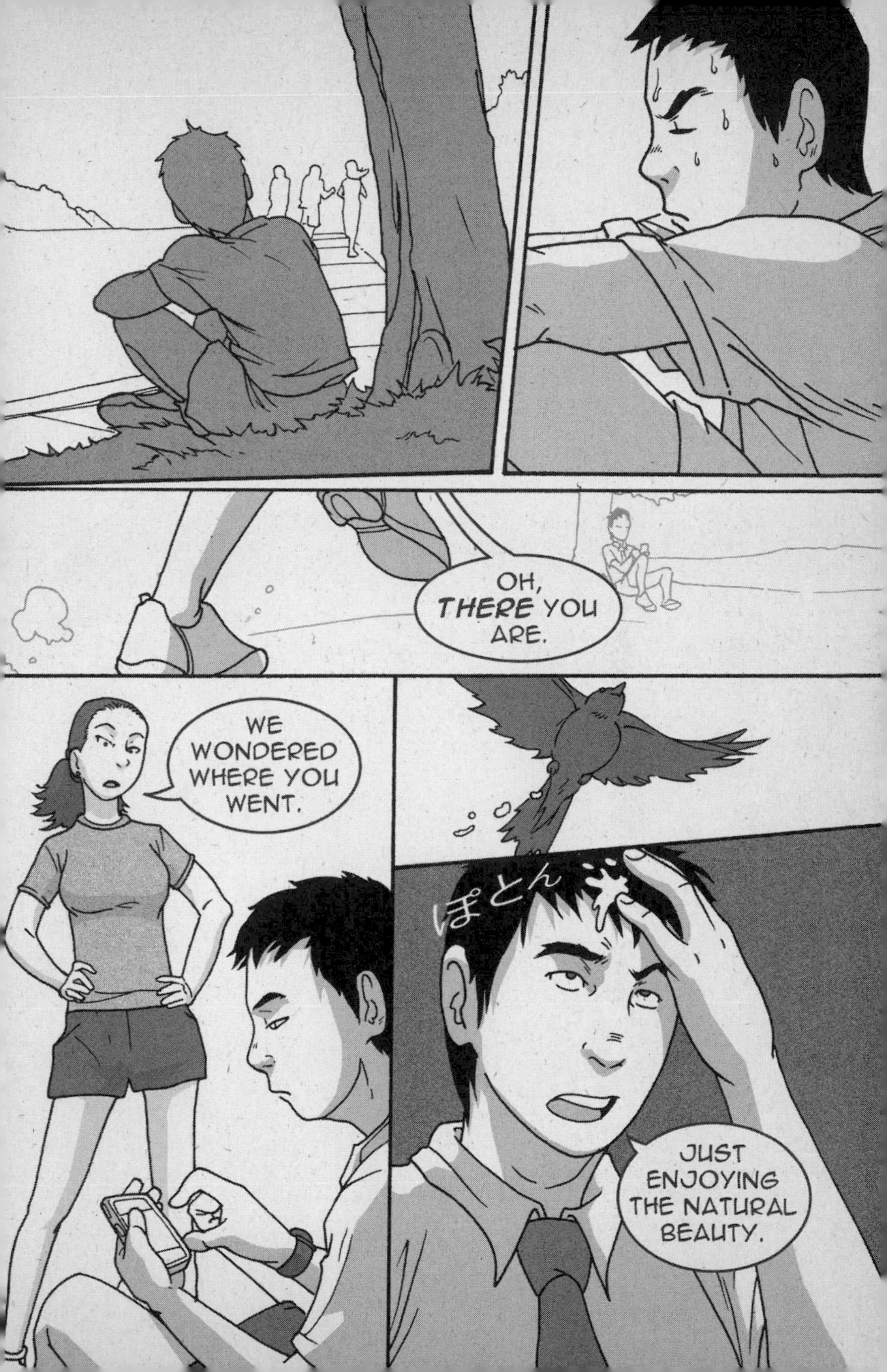
OH, *THERE* YOU ARE.
WE WONDERED WHERE YOU WENT.
ぽとん
JUST ENJOYING THE NATURAL BEAUTY.

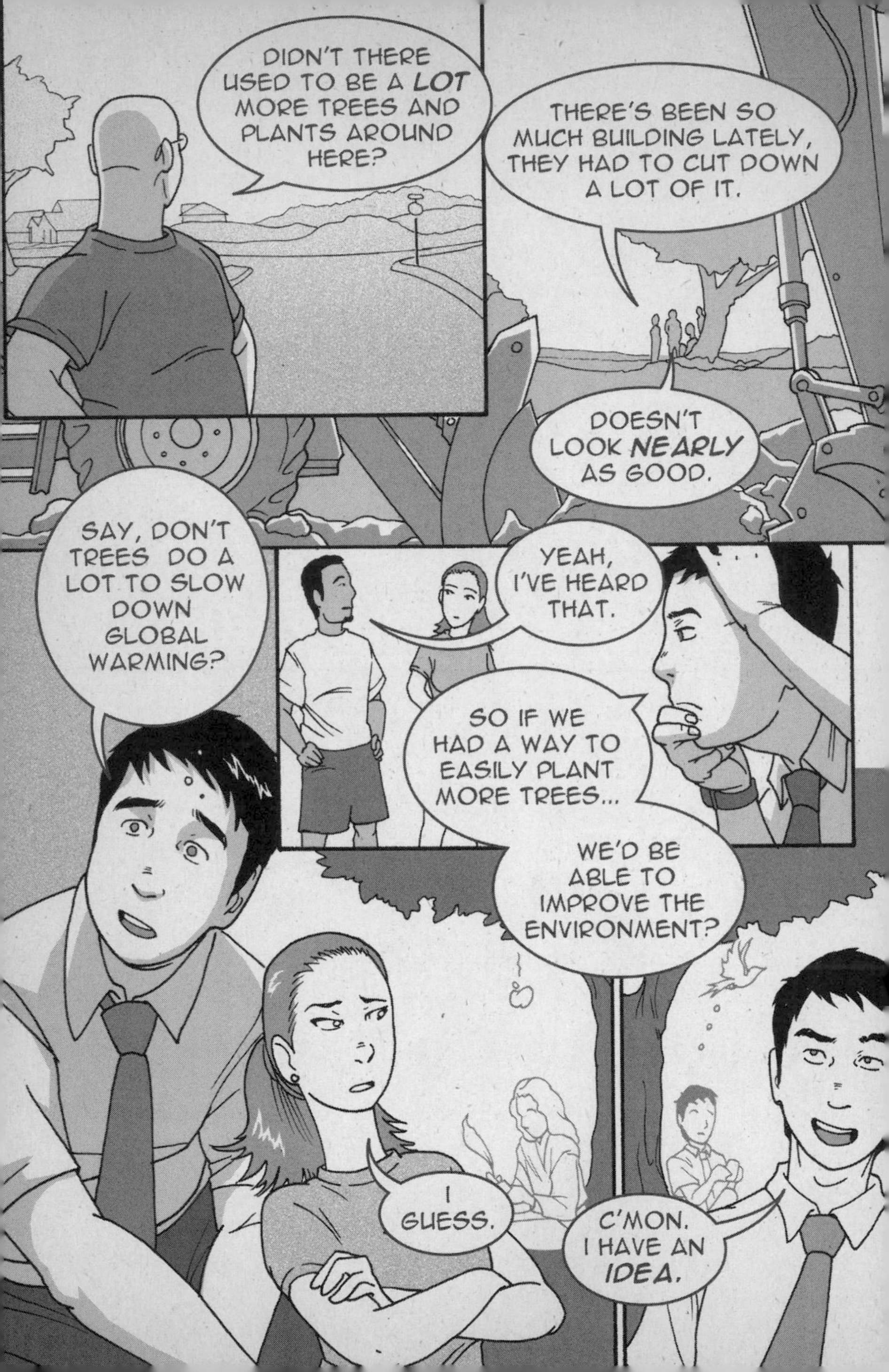

DIDN'T THERE USED TO BE A LOT MORE TREES AND PLANTS AROUND HERE?
THERE'S BEEN SO MUCH BUILDING LATELY, THEY HAD TO CUT DOWN A LOT OF IT.
DOESN'T LOOK NEARLY AS GOOD.
SAY, DON'T TREES DO A LOT TO SLOW DOWN GLOBAL WARMING?
YEAH, I'VE HEARD THAT.
SO IF WE HAD A WAY TO EASILY PLANT MORE TREES...
WE'D BE ABLE TO IMPROVE THE ENVIRONMENT?
I GUESS.
C'MON. I HAVE AN IDEA.

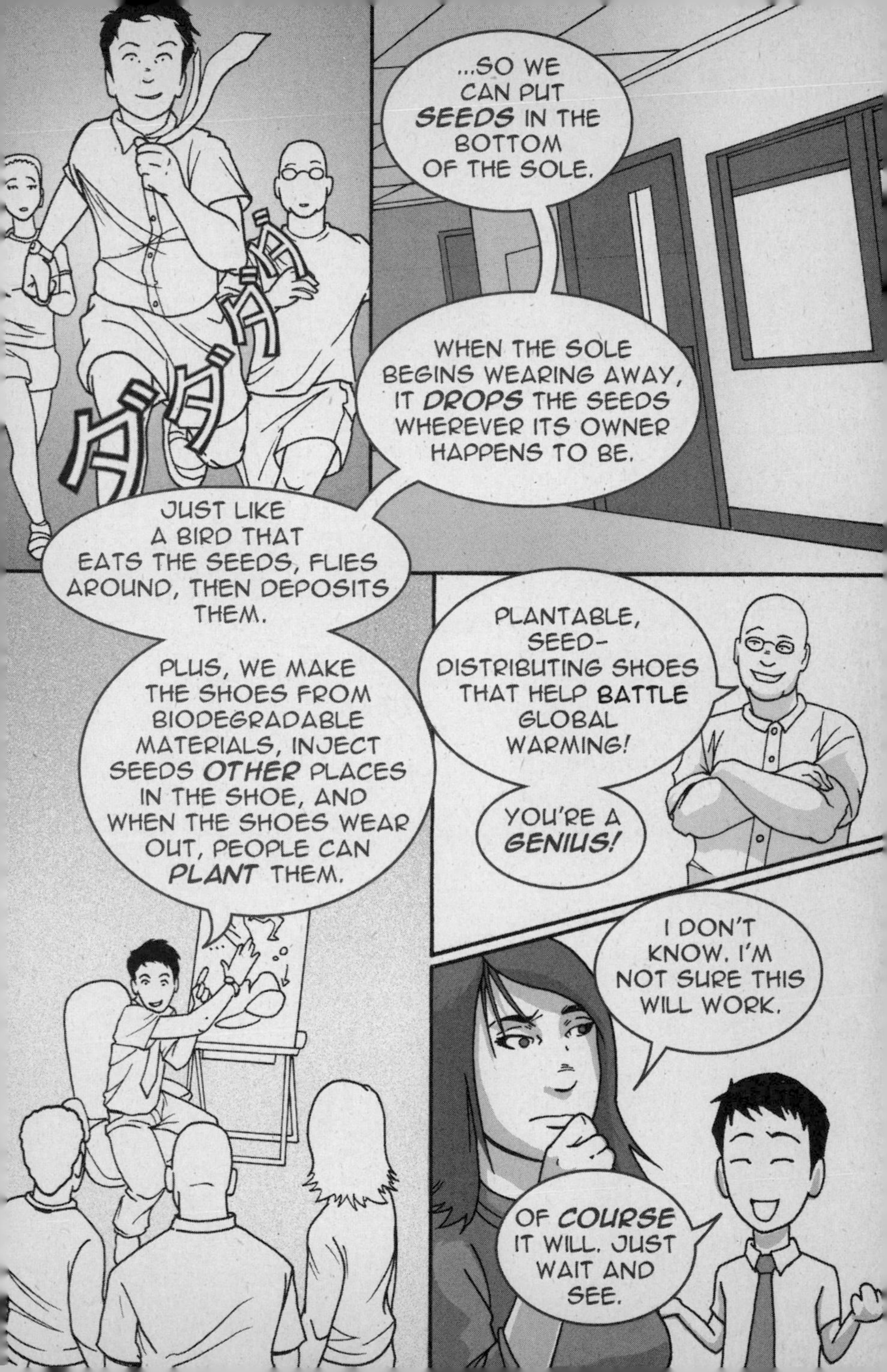
...SO WE CAN PUT SEEDS IN THE BOTTOM OF THE SOLE.
WHEN THE SOLE BEGINS WEARING AWAY, IT DROPS THE SEEDS WHEREVER ITS OWNER HAPPENS TO BE.
JUST LIKE A BIRD THAT EATS THE SEEDS, FLIES AROUND, THEN DEPOSITS THEM.
PLUS, WE MAKE THE SHOES FROM BIODEGRADABLE MATERIALS, INJECT SEEDS OTHER PLACES IN THE SHOE, AND WHEN THE SHOES WEAR OUT, PEOPLE CAN PLANT THEM.
PLANTABLE, SEED-DISTRIBUTING SHOES THAT HELP BATTLE GLOBAL WARMING!
YOU'RE A GENIUS!
I DON'T KNOW. I'M NOT SURE THIS WILL WORK.
OF COURSE IT WILL. JUST WAIT AND SEE.

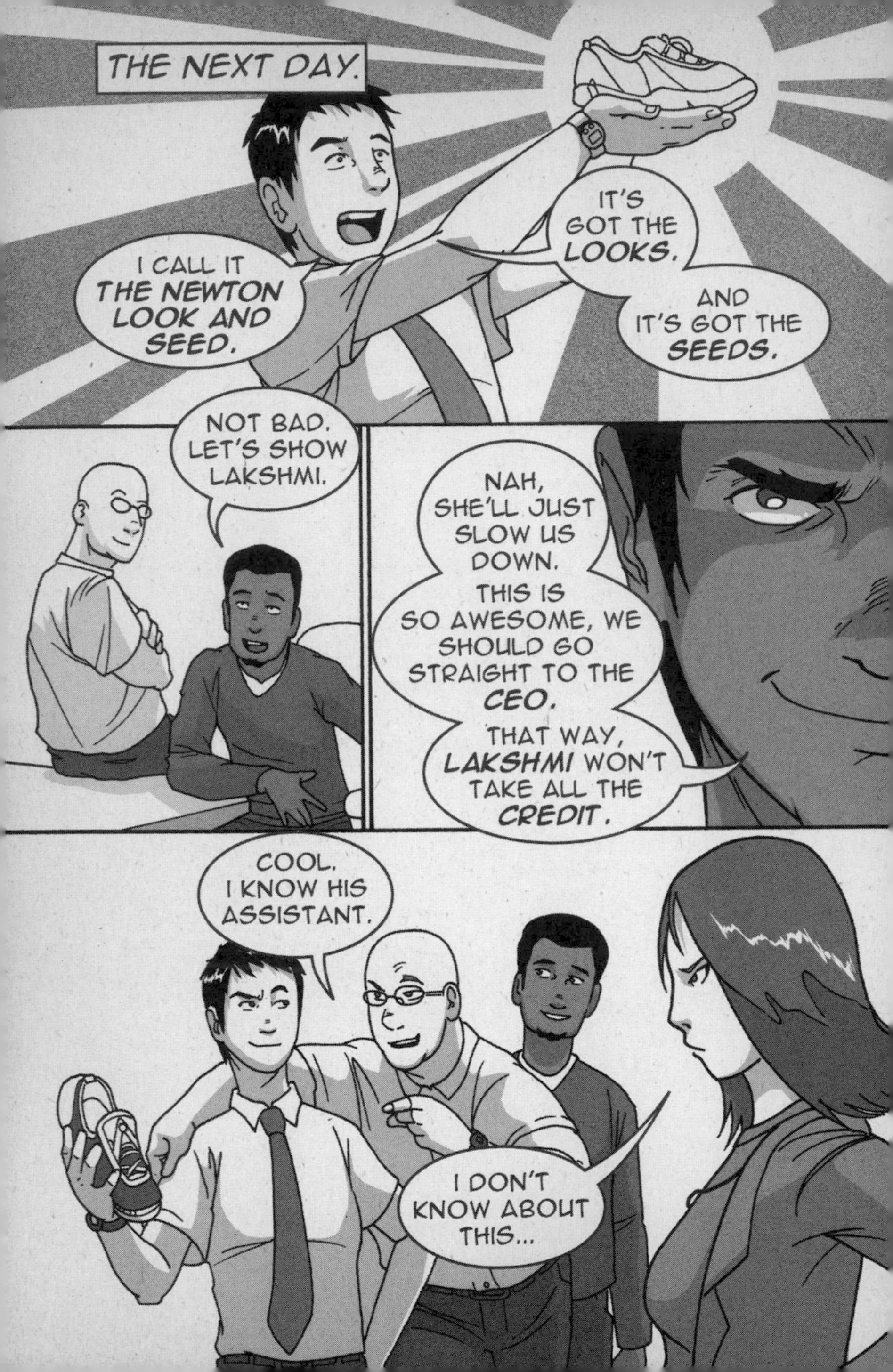
THE NEXT DAY.
I CALL IT THE NEWTON LOOK AND SEED.
IT'S GOT THE LOOKS.
AND IT'S GOT THE SEEDS.
NOT BAD. LET'S SHOW LAKSHMI.
NAH, SHE'LL JUST SLOW US DOWN.
THIS IS SO AWESOME, WE SHOULD GO STRAIGHT TO THE CEO.
THAT WAY, LAKSHMI WON'T TAKE ALL THE CREDIT.
COOL. I KNOW HIS ASSISTANT.
I DON'T KNOW ABOUT THIS...

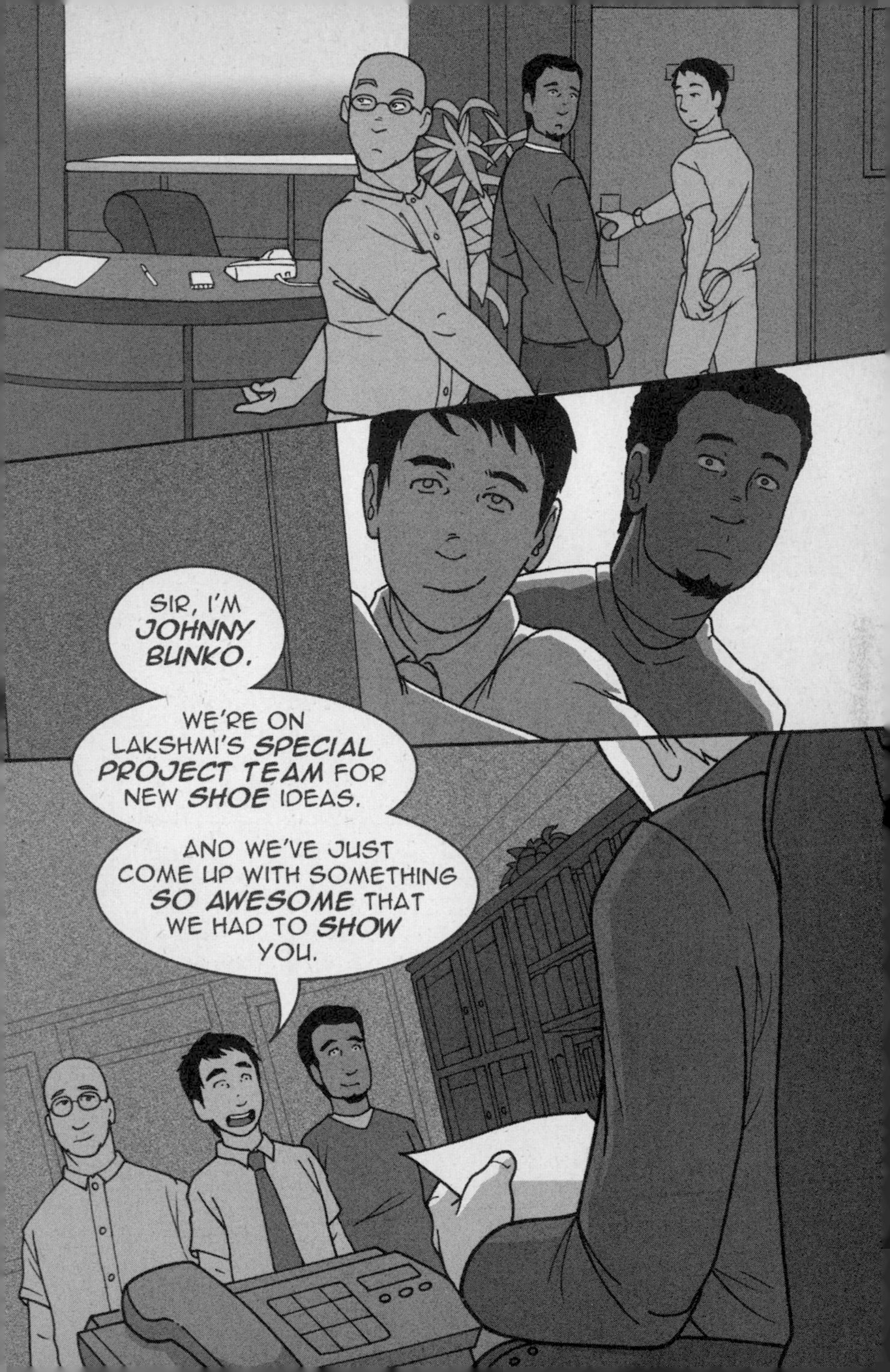
SIR, I'M JOHNNY BUNKO.
WE'RE ON LAKSHMI'S SPECIAL PROJECT TEAM FOR NEW SHOE IDEAS.
AND WE'VE JUST COME UP WITH SOMETHING SO AWESOME THAT WE HAD TO SHOW YOU.

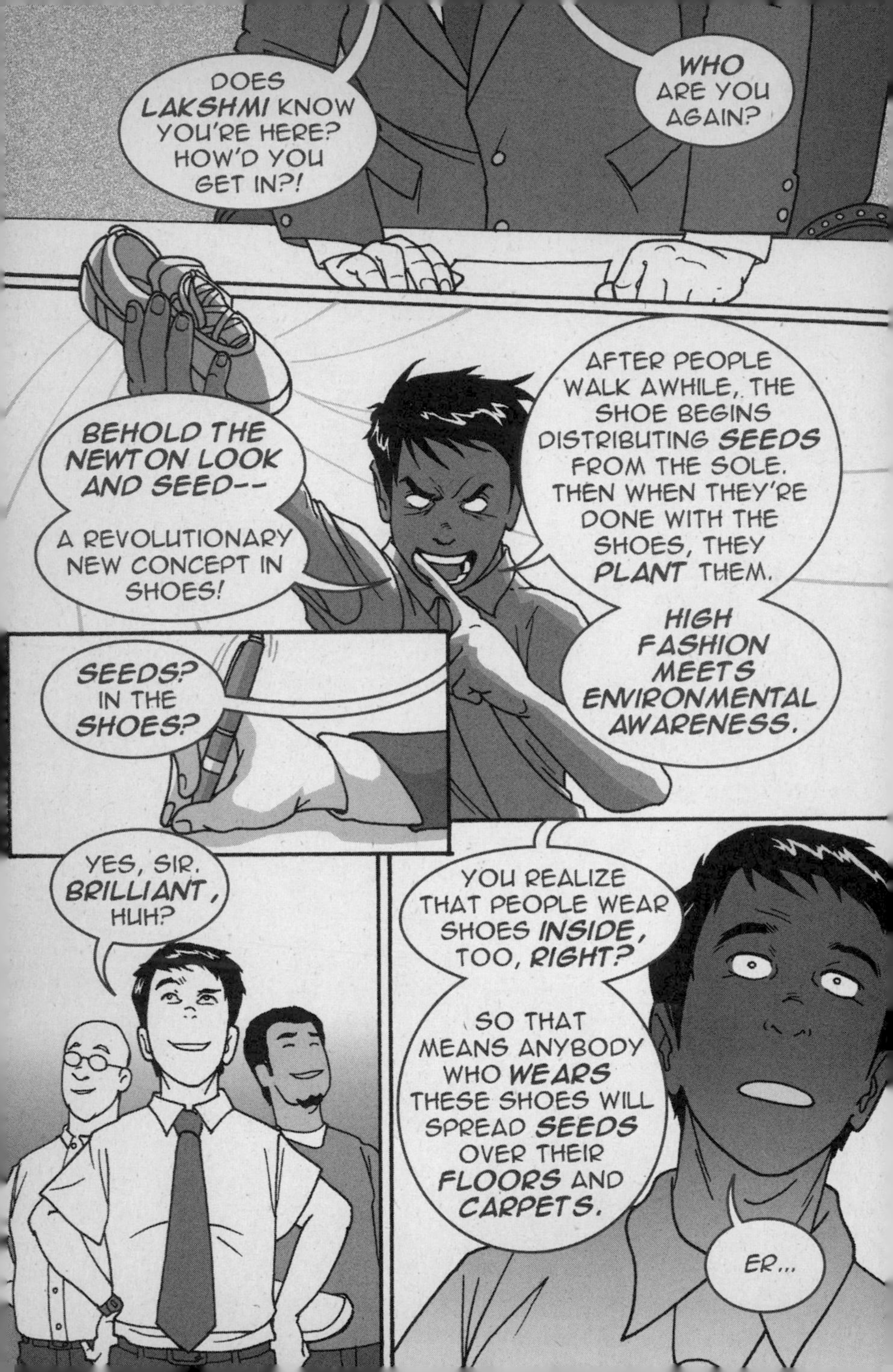
DOES LAKSHMI KNOW YOU'RE HERE? HOW'D YOU GET IN?!
WHO ARE YOU AGAIN?
BEHOLD THE NEWTON LOOK AND SEED--
A REVOLUTIONARY NEW CONCEPT IN SHOES!
AFTER PEOPLE WALK AWHILE, THE SHOE BEGINS DISTRIBUTING SEEDS FROM THE SOLE. THEN WHEN THEY'RE DONE WITH THE SHOES, THEY PLANT THEM.
HIGH FASHION MEETS ENVIRONMENTAL AWARENESS.
SEEDS? IN THE SHOES?
YES, SIR. BRILLIANT, HUH?
YOU REALIZE THAT PEOPLE WEAR SHOES INSIDE, TOO, RIGHT?
SO THAT MEANS ANYBODY WHO WEARS THESE SHOES WILL SPREAD SEEDS OVER THEIR FLOORS AND CARPETS.
ER...

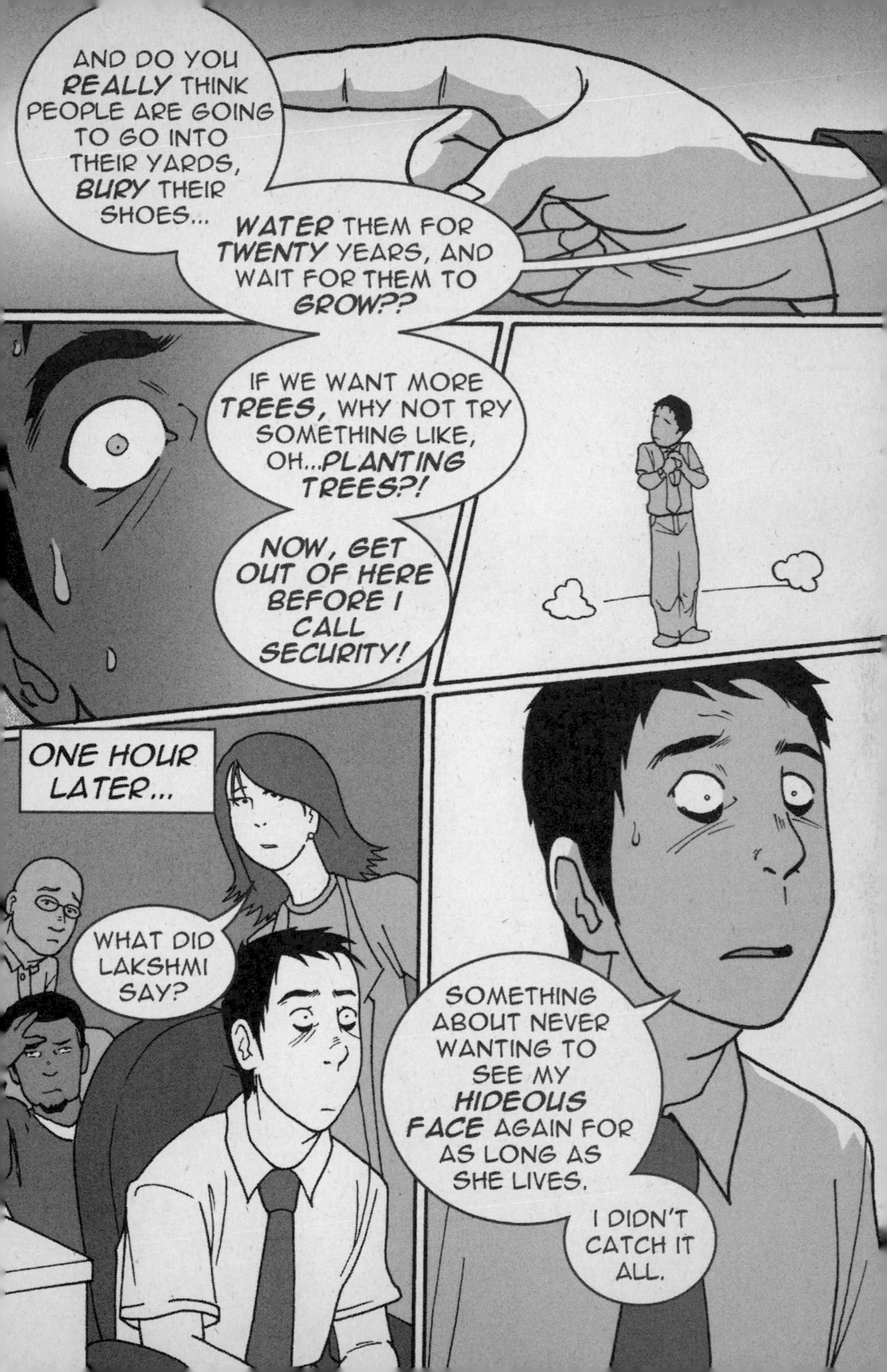
AND DO YOU REALLY THINK PEOPLE ARE GOING TO GO INTO THEIR YARDS, BURY THEIR SHOES...
WATER THEM FOR TWENTY YEARS, AND WAIT FOR THEM TO GROW??
IF WE WANT MORE TREES, WHY NOT TRY SOMETHING LIKE, OH...PLANTING TREES?!
NOW, GET OUT OF HERE BEFORE I CALL SECURITY!
ONE HOUR LATER...
WHAT DID LAKSHMI SAY?
SOMETHING ABOUT NEVER WANTING TO SEE MY HIDEOUS FACE AGAIN FOR AS LONG AS SHE LIVES.
I DIDN'T CATCH IT ALL.

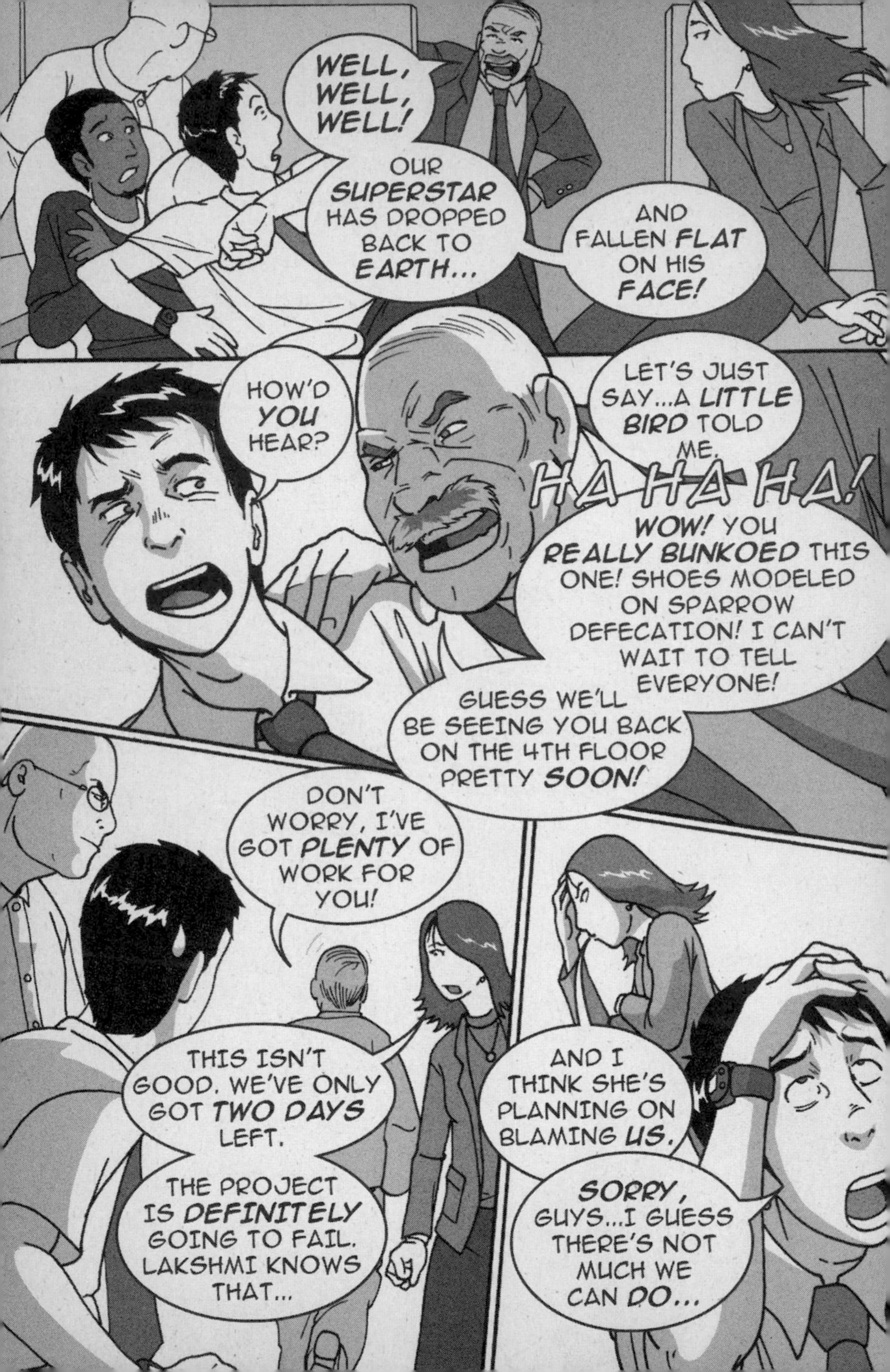
WELL, WELL, WELL!
OUR SUPERSTAR HAS DROPPED BACK TO EARTH...
AND FALLEN FLAT ON HIS FACE!
HOW'D YOU HEAR?
LET'S JUST SAY...A LITTLE BIRD TOLD ME.
HA HA HA HA!
WOW! YOU REALLY BUNKOED THIS ONE! SHOES MODELED ON SPARROW DEFECATION! I CAN'T WAIT TO TELL EVERYONE!
GUESS WE'LL BE SEEING YOU BACK ON THE 4TH FLOOR PRETTY SOON!
DON'T WORRY, I'VE GOT PLENTY OF WORK FOR YOU!
THIS ISN'T GOOD. WE'VE ONLY GOT TWO DAYS LEFT.
THE PROJECT IS DEFINITELY GOING TO FAIL. LAKSHMI KNOWS THAT...
AND I THINK SHE'S PLANNING ON BLAMING US.
SORRY, GUYS...I GUESS THERE'S NOT MUCH WE CAN DO...

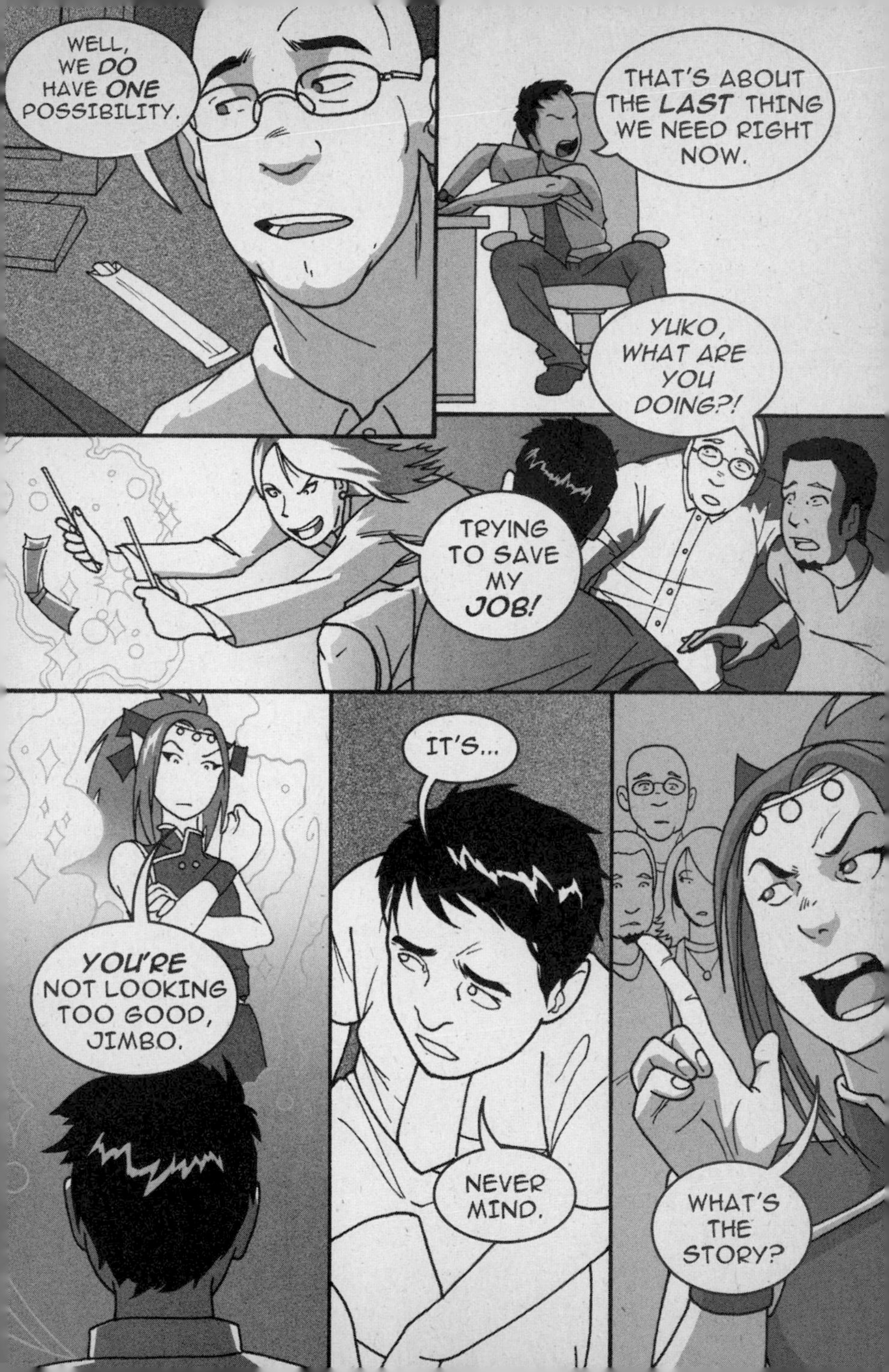
WELL, WE DO HAVE ONE POSSIBILITY.
THAT'S ABOUT THE LAST THING WE NEED RIGHT NOW.
YUKO, WHAT ARE YOU DOING?!
TRYING TO SAVE MY JOB!
YOU'RE NOT LOOKING TOO GOOD, JIMBO.
IT'S...
NEVER MIND.
WHAT'S THE STORY?

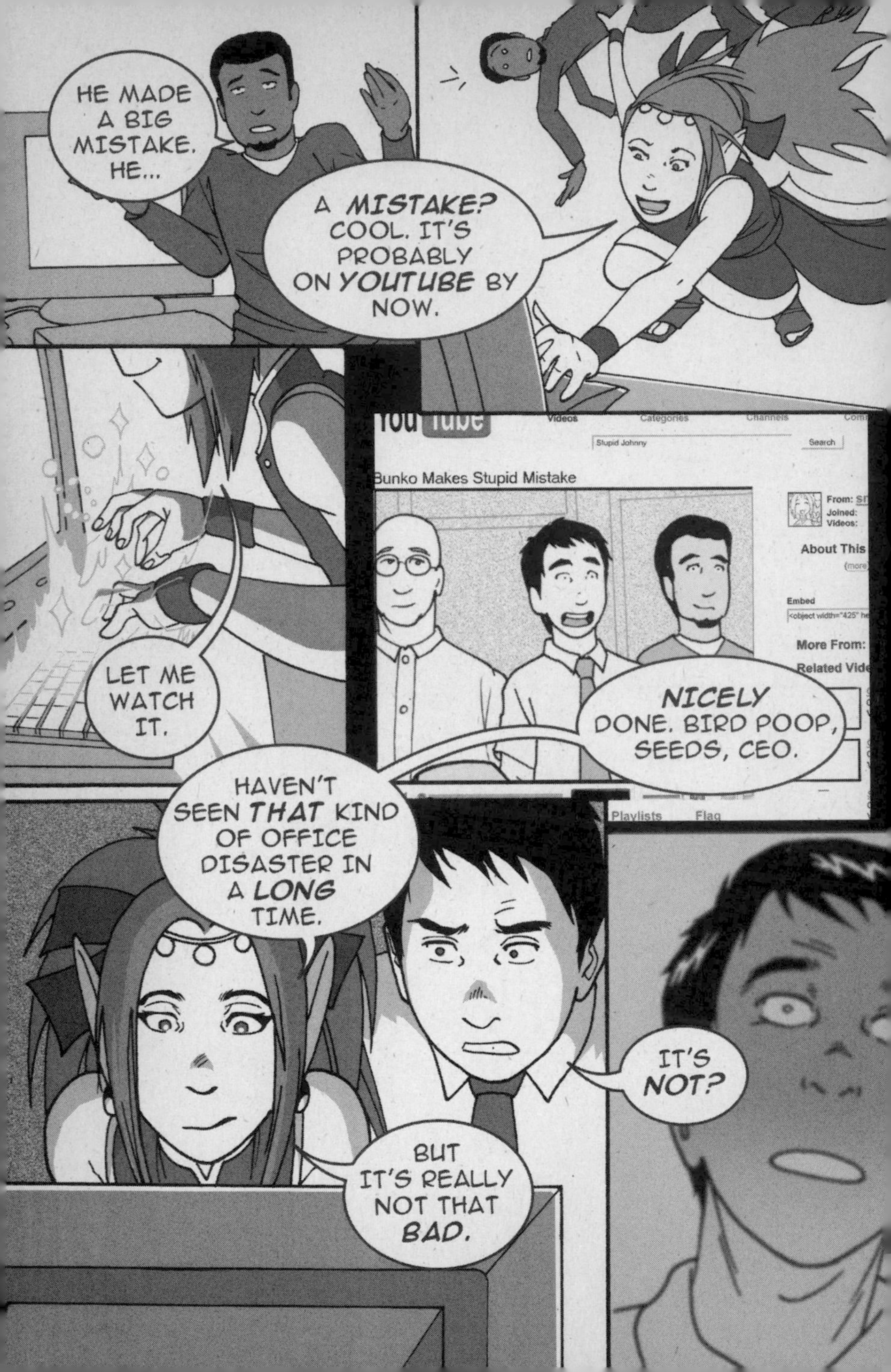

HE MADE A BIG MISTAKE. HE...
A *MISTAKE?* COOL. IT'S PROBABLY ON *YOUTUBE* BY NOW.
LET ME WATCH IT.
Videos
Categories
Channels
Stupid Johnny
Search
Bunko Makes Stupid Mistake
From:
Joined:
Videos:
(more)
Embed
More From:
NICELY DONE. BIRD POOP, SEEDS, CEO.
Playlists
Flag
HAVEN'T SEEN *THAT* KIND OF OFFICE DISASTER IN A *LONG* TIME.
BUT IT'S REALLY NOT THAT *BAD.*
IT'S *NOT?*

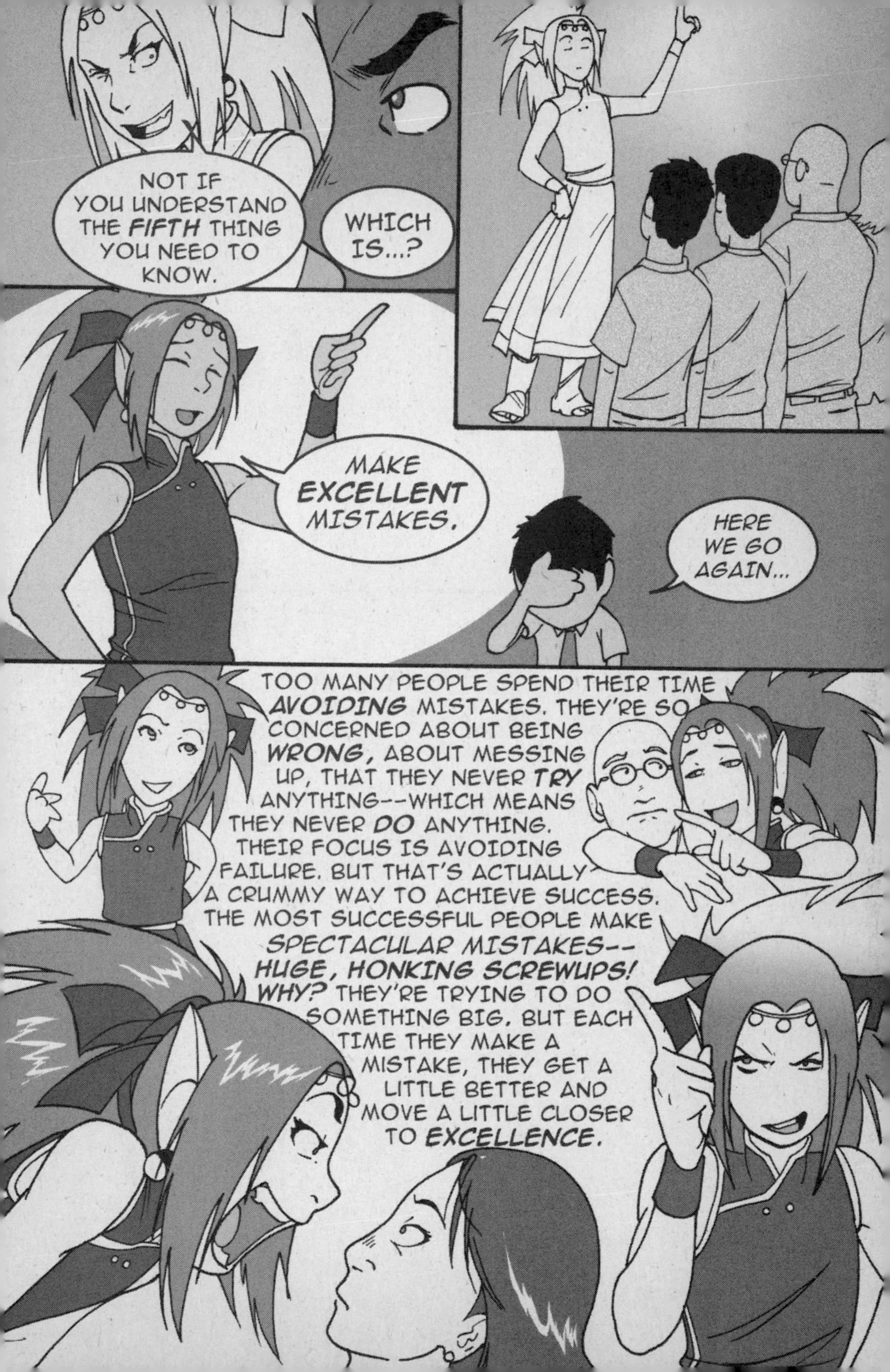
NOT IF YOU UNDERSTAND THE *FIFTH* THING YOU NEED TO KNOW.
WHICH IS...?
MAKE **EXCELLENT** MISTAKES.
HERE WE GO AGAIN...
TOO MANY PEOPLE SPEND THEIR TIME ***AVOIDING*** MISTAKES. THEY'RE SO CONCERNED ABOUT BEING ***WRONG***, ABOUT MESSING UP, THAT THEY NEVER ***TRY*** ANYTHING--WHICH MEANS THEY NEVER ***DO*** ANYTHING. THEIR FOCUS IS AVOIDING FAILURE. BUT THAT'S ACTUALLY A CRUMMY WAY TO ACHIEVE SUCCESS. THE MOST SUCCESSFUL PEOPLE MAKE *SPECTACULAR MISTAKES--* ***HUGE, HONKING SCREWUPS! WHY?*** THEY'RE TRYING TO DO SOMETHING BIG. BUT EACH TIME THEY MAKE A MISTAKE, THEY GET A LITTLE BETTER AND MOVE A LITTLE CLOSER TO ***EXCELLENCE***.

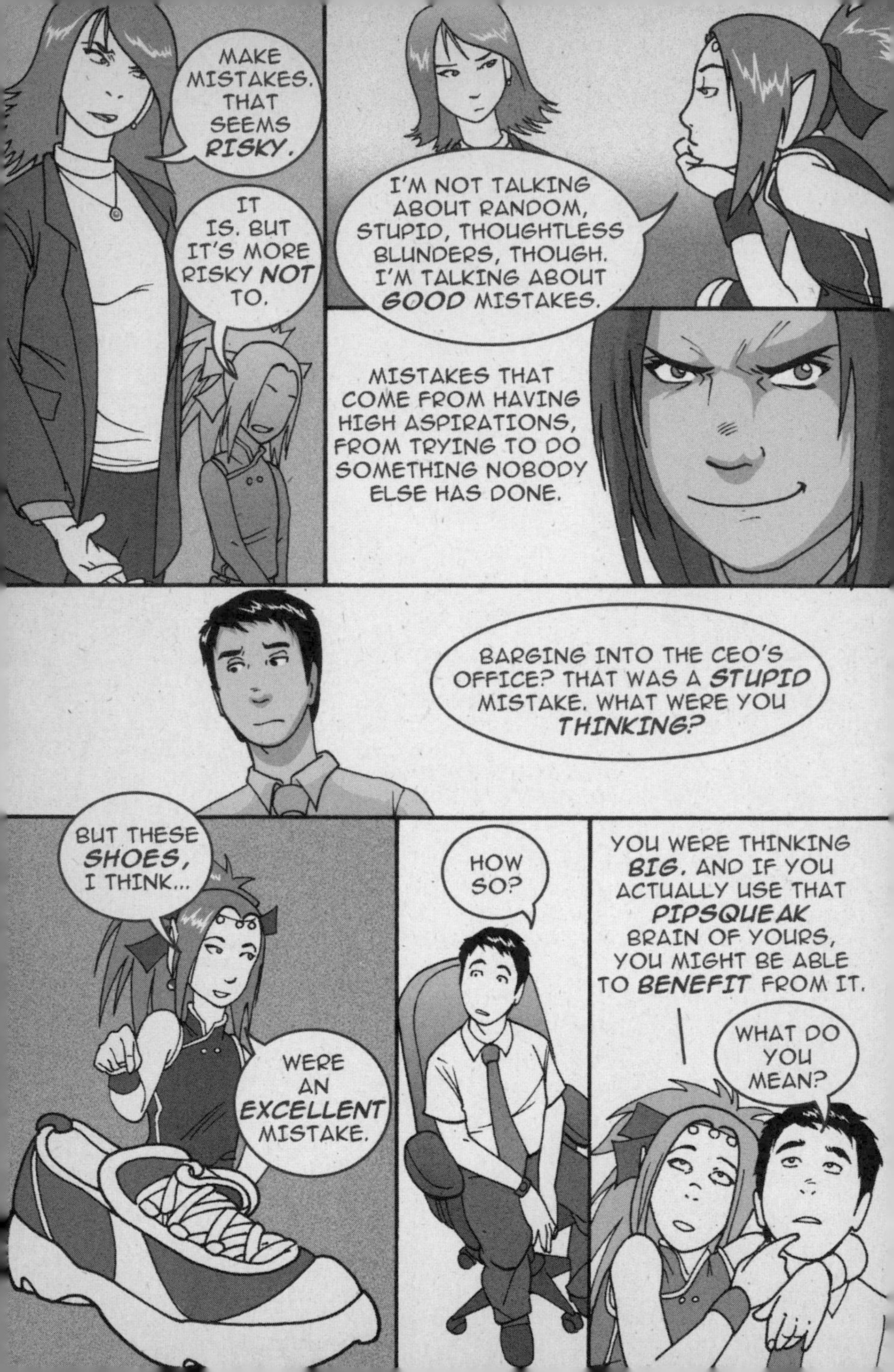
MAKE MISTAKES. THAT SEEMS RISKY.
IT IS. BUT IT'S MORE RISKY NOT TO.
I'M NOT TALKING ABOUT RANDOM, STUPID, THOUGHTLESS BLUNDERS, THOUGH. I'M TALKING ABOUT GOOD MISTAKES.
MISTAKES THAT COME FROM HAVING HIGH ASPIRATIONS, FROM TRYING TO DO SOMETHING NOBODY ELSE HAS DONE.
BARGING INTO THE CEO'S OFFICE? THAT WAS A STUPID MISTAKE. WHAT WERE YOU THINKING?
BUT THESE SHOES, I THINK...
WERE AN EXCELLENT MISTAKE.
HOW SO?
YOU WERE THINKING BIG. AND IF YOU ACTUALLY USE THAT PIPSQUEAK BRAIN OF YOURS, YOU MIGHT BE ABLE TO BENEFIT FROM IT.
WHAT DO YOU MEAN?

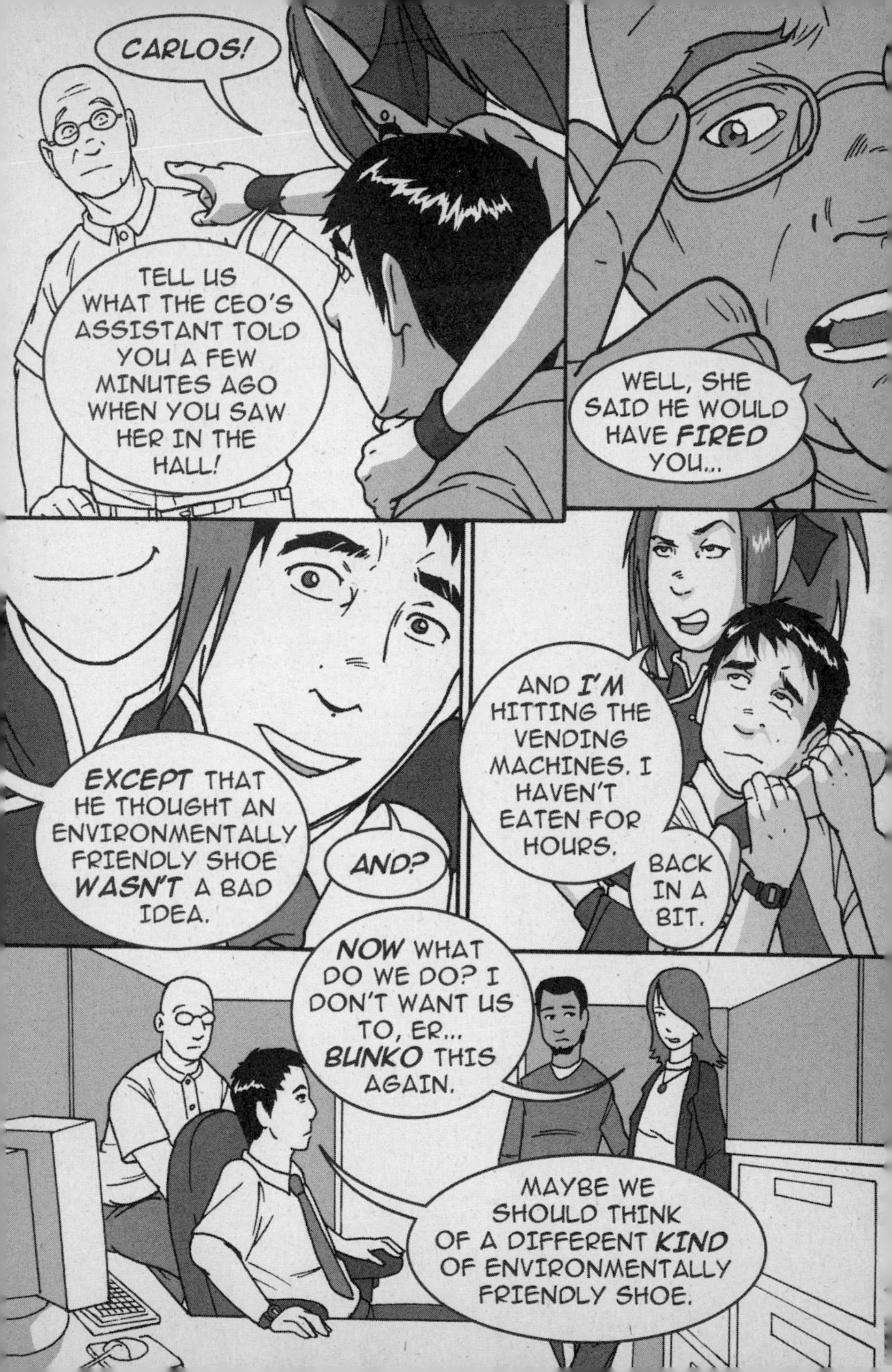
CARLOS!
TELL US WHAT THE CEO'S ASSISTANT TOLD YOU A FEW MINUTES AGO WHEN YOU SAW HER IN THE HALL!
WELL, SHE SAID HE WOULD HAVE FIRED YOU...
EXCEPT THAT HE THOUGHT AN ENVIRONMENTALLY FRIENDLY SHOE WASN'T A BAD IDEA.
AND?
AND I'M HITTING THE VENDING MACHINES. I HAVEN'T EATEN FOR HOURS.
BACK IN A BIT.
NOW WHAT DO WE DO? I DON'T WANT US TO, ER... BUNKO THIS AGAIN.
MAYBE WE SHOULD THINK OF A DIFFERENT KIND OF ENVIRONMENTALLY FRIENDLY SHOE.

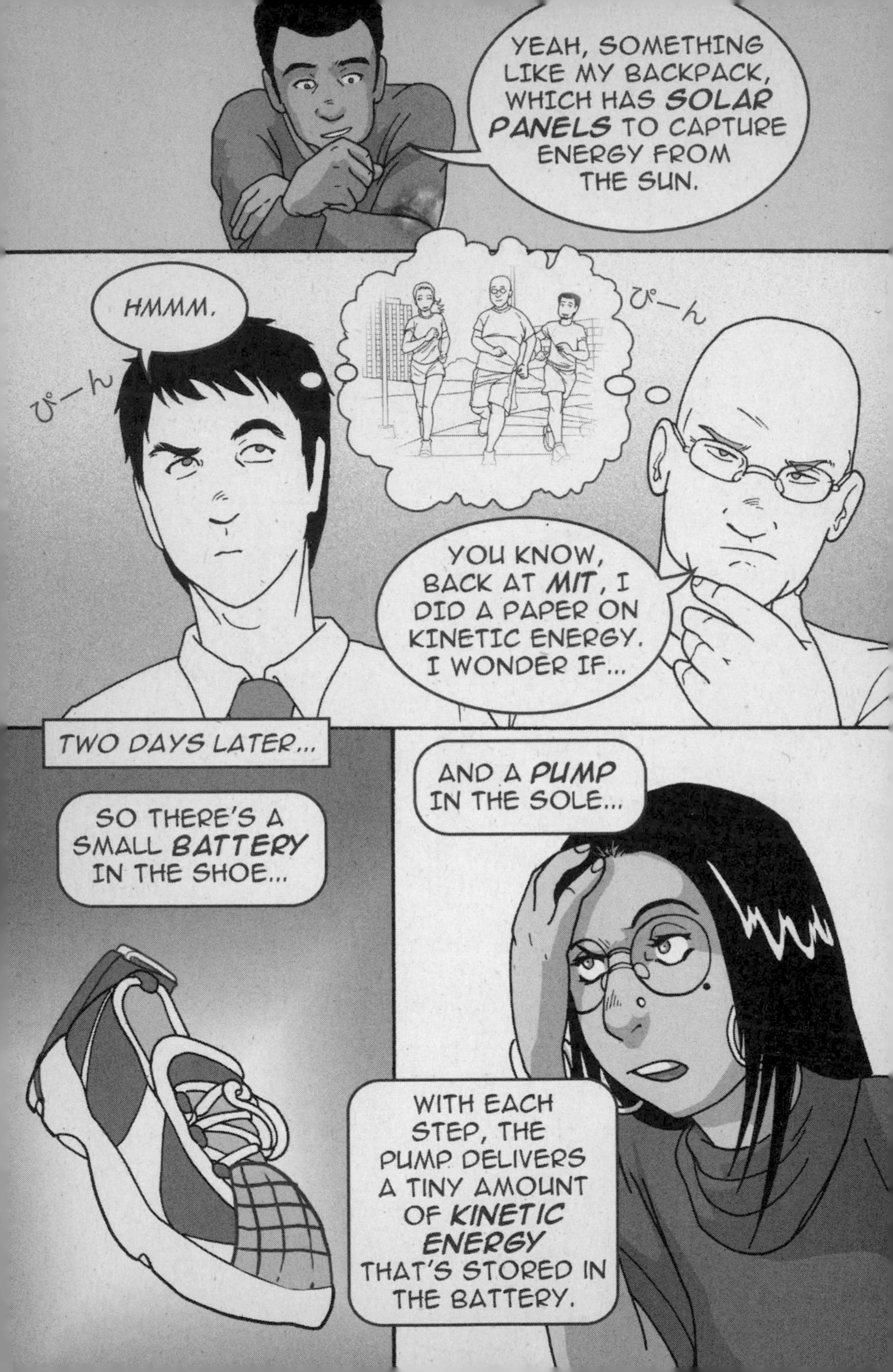
YEAH, SOMETHING LIKE MY BACKPACK, WHICH HAS SOLAR PANELS TO CAPTURE ENERGY FROM THE SUN.
HMMM.
ぴーん
ぴーん
YOU KNOW, BACK AT MIT, I DID A PAPER ON KINETIC ENERGY. I WONDER IF...
TWO DAYS LATER...
SO THERE'S A SMALL BATTERY IN THE SHOE...
AND A PUMP IN THE SOLE...
WITH EACH STEP, THE PUMP DELIVERS A TINY AMOUNT OF KINETIC ENERGY THAT'S STORED IN THE BATTERY.

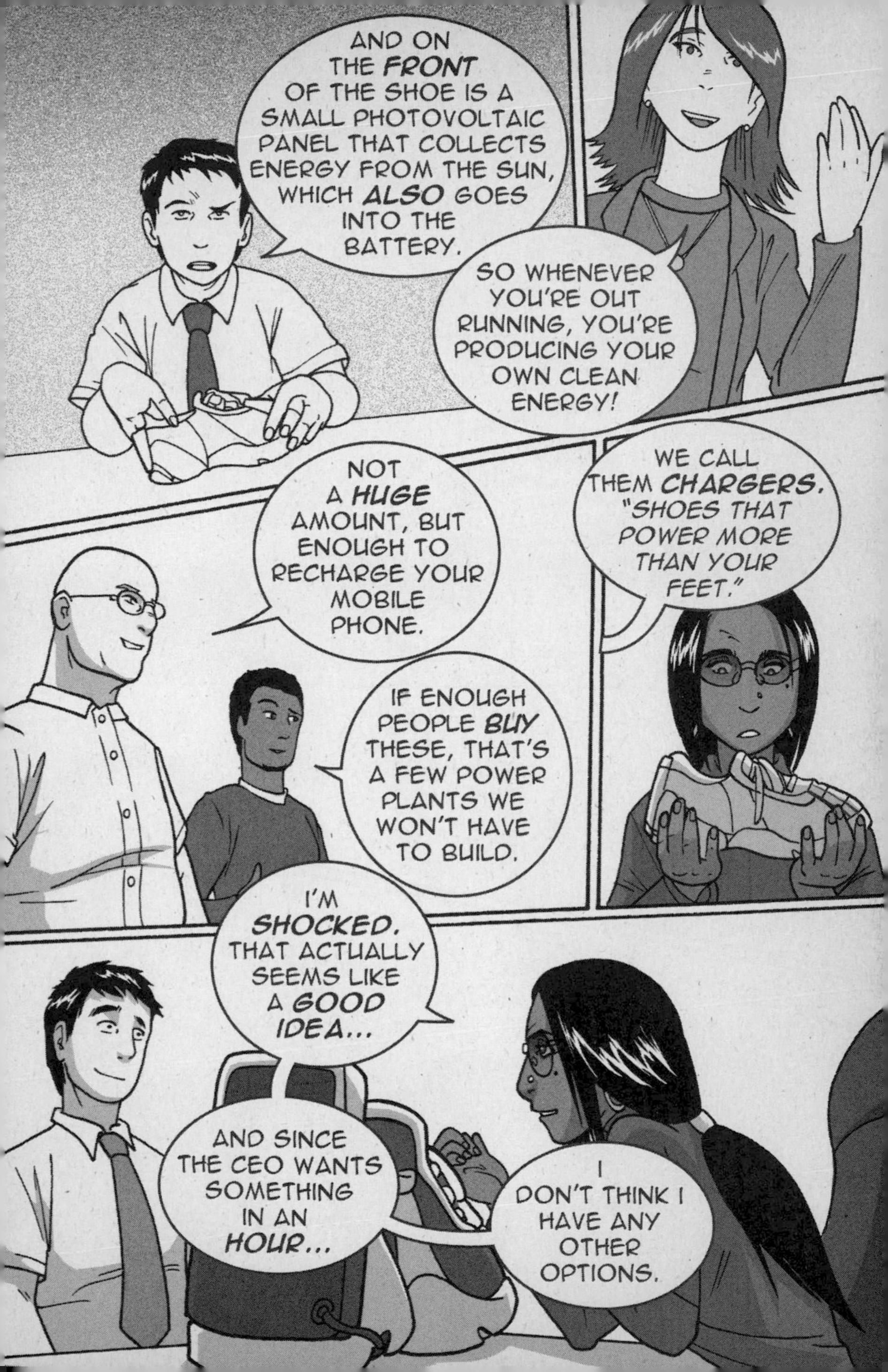
AND ON THE *FRONT* OF THE SHOE IS A SMALL PHOTOVOLTAIC PANEL THAT COLLECTS ENERGY FROM THE SUN, WHICH *ALSO* GOES INTO THE BATTERY.
SO WHENEVER YOU'RE OUT RUNNING, YOU'RE PRODUCING YOUR OWN CLEAN ENERGY!
NOT A *HUGE* AMOUNT, BUT ENOUGH TO RECHARGE YOUR MOBILE PHONE.
WE CALL THEM *CHARGERS.* "*SHOES THAT POWER MORE THAN YOUR FEET.*"
IF ENOUGH PEOPLE *BUY* THESE, THAT'S A FEW POWER PLANTS WE WON'T HAVE TO BUILD.
I'M *SHOCKED.* THAT ACTUALLY SEEMS LIKE A *GOOD IDEA...*
AND SINCE THE CEO WANTS SOMETHING IN AN *HOUR...*
I DON'T THINK I HAVE ANY OTHER OPTIONS.

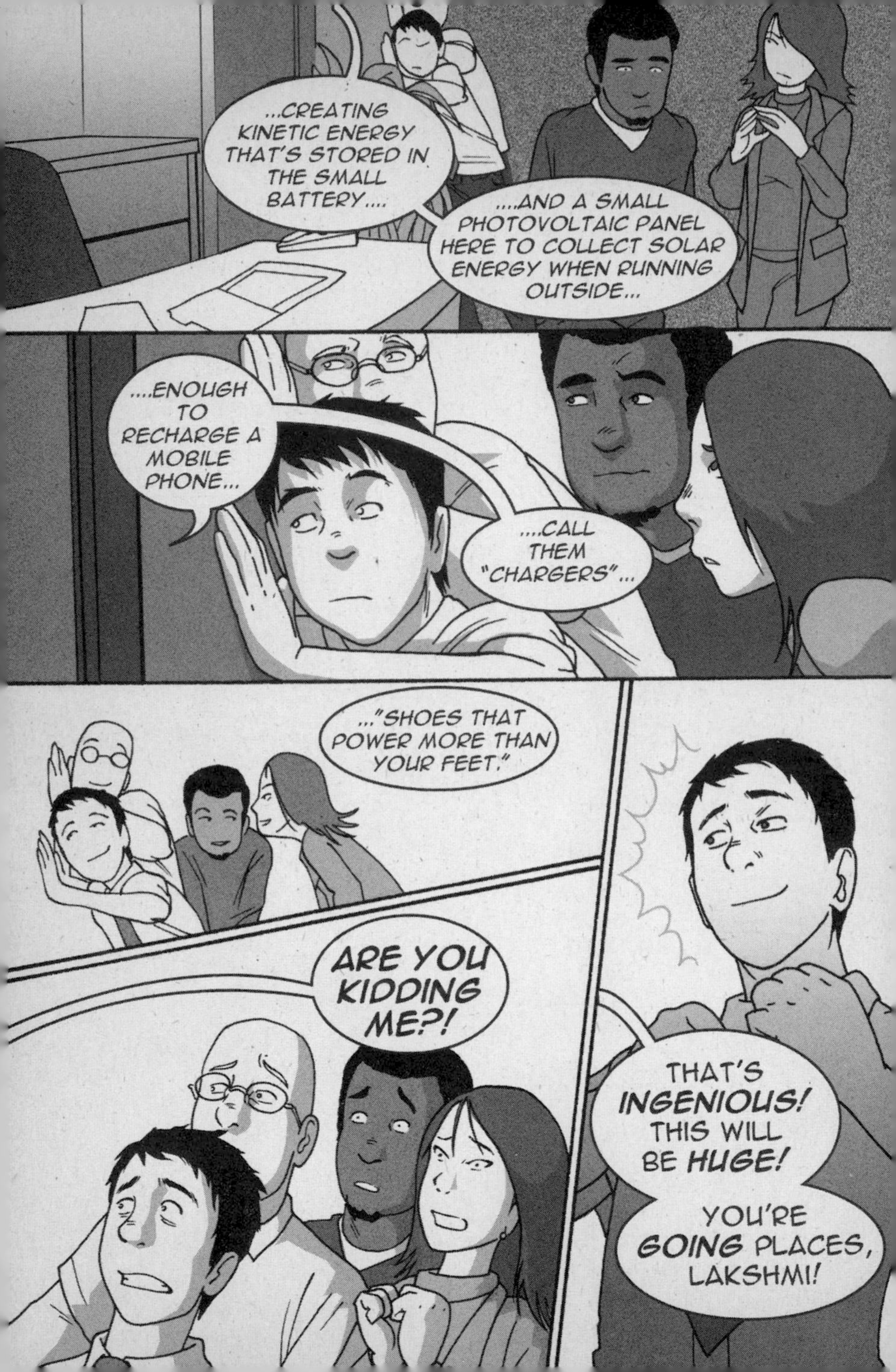
...CREATING KINETIC ENERGY THAT'S STORED IN THE SMALL BATTERY....
....AND A SMALL PHOTOVOLTAIC PANEL HERE TO COLLECT SOLAR ENERGY WHEN RUNNING OUTSIDE...
....ENOUGH TO RECHARGE A MOBILE PHONE...
....CALL THEM "CHARGERS"...
..."SHOES THAT POWER MORE THAN YOUR FEET."
ARE YOU KIDDING ME?!
THAT'S INGENIOUS! THIS WILL BE HUGE!
YOU'RE GOING PLACES, LAKSHMI!

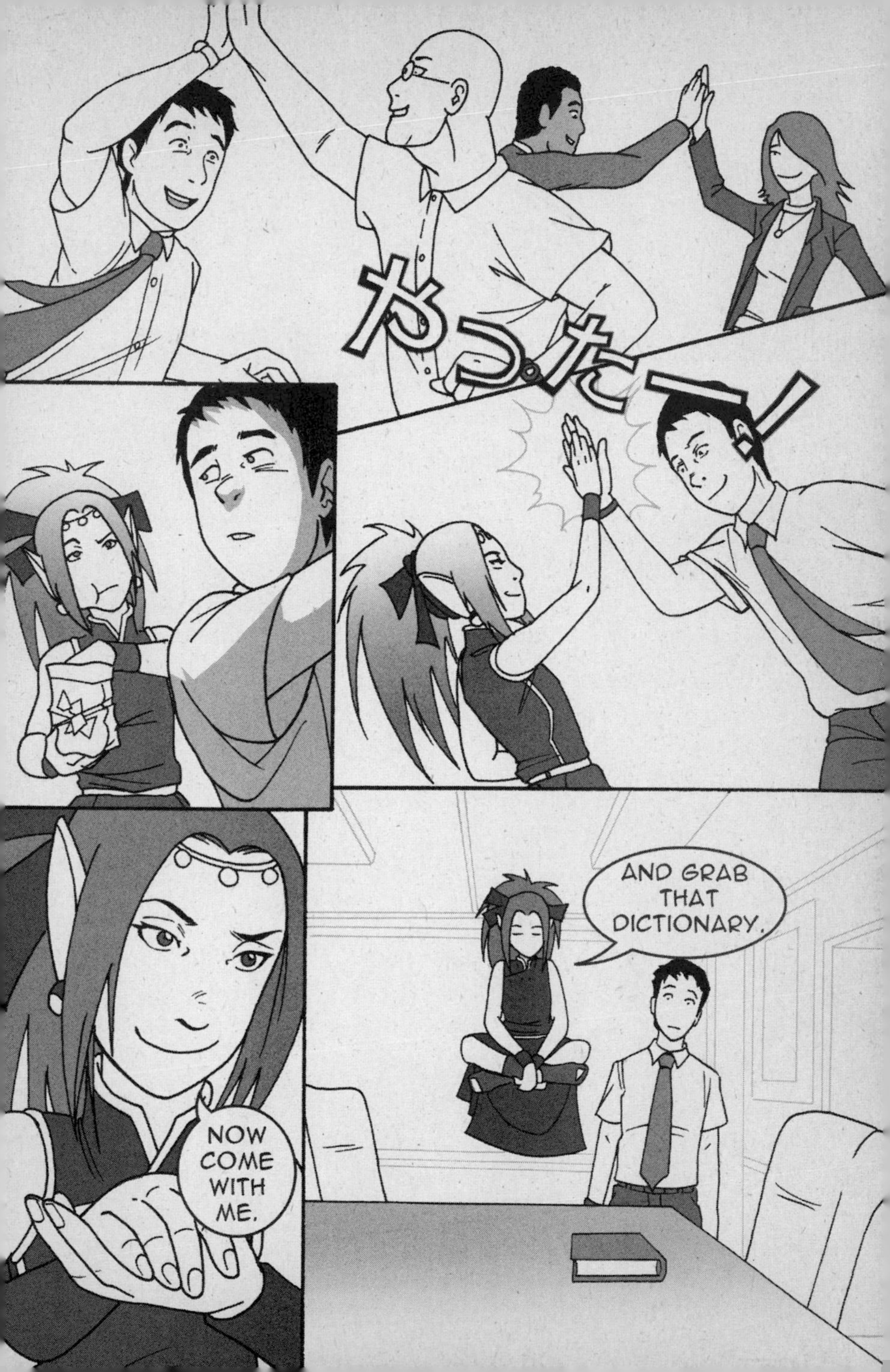
やったー!
AND GRAB THAT DICTIONARY.
NOW COME WITH ME.

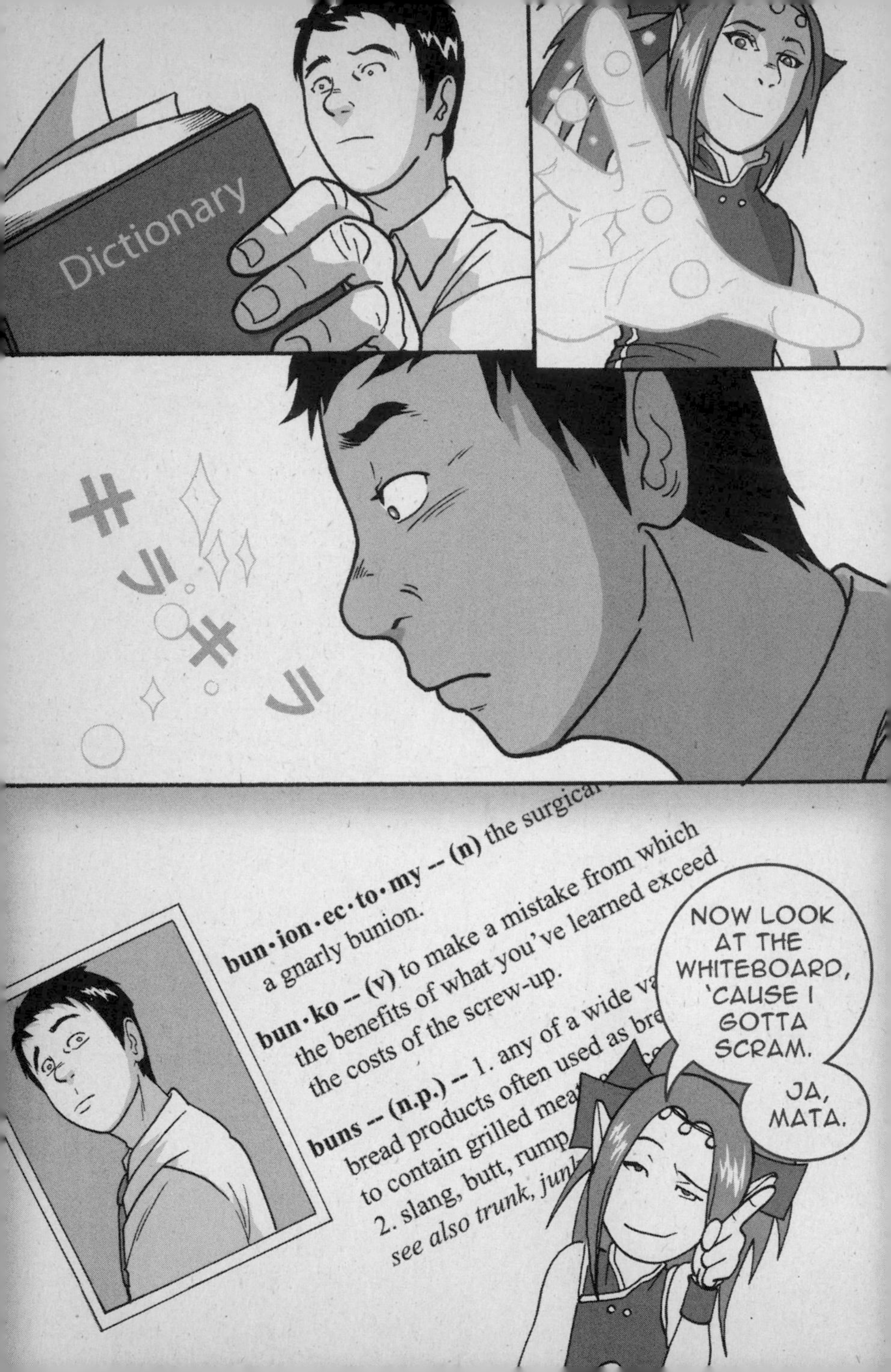
Dictionary
bun·ion·ec·to·my -- (n) the surgical
a gnarly bunion.
bun·ko -- (v) to make a mistake from which
the benefits of what you've learned exceed
the costs of the screw-up.
buns -- (n.p.) -- 1. any of a wide va
bread products often used as bre
to contain grilled meat
2. slang, butt, rump
see also trunk, jun
NOW LOOK AT THE WHITEBOARD, 'CAUSE I GOTTA SCRAM.
JA, MATA.

1. There is no plan.
2. Think strengths, not weaknesses.
3. It's not about you.
4. Persistence trumps talent.
5. Make excellent mistakes.

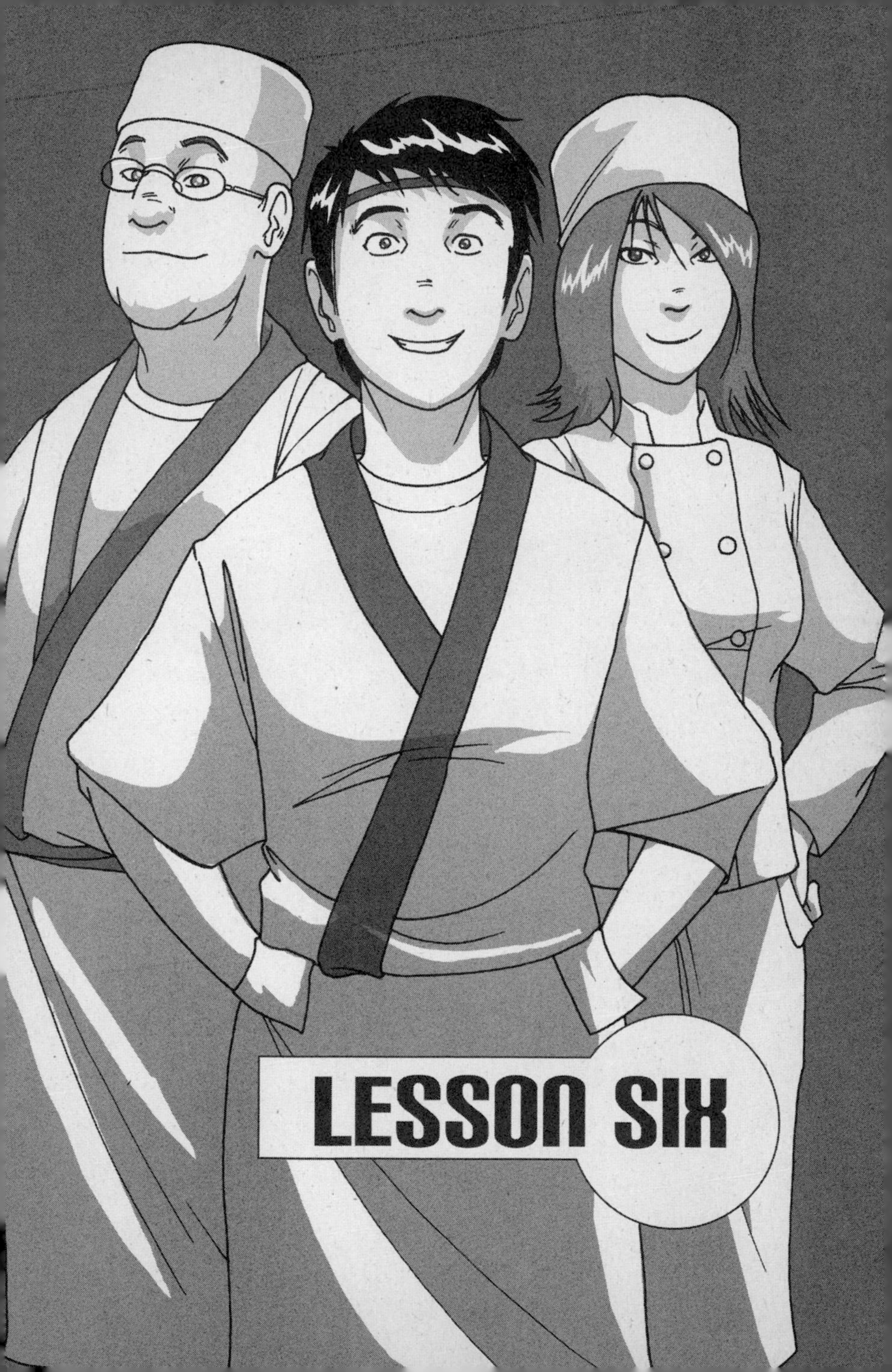
LESSON SIX

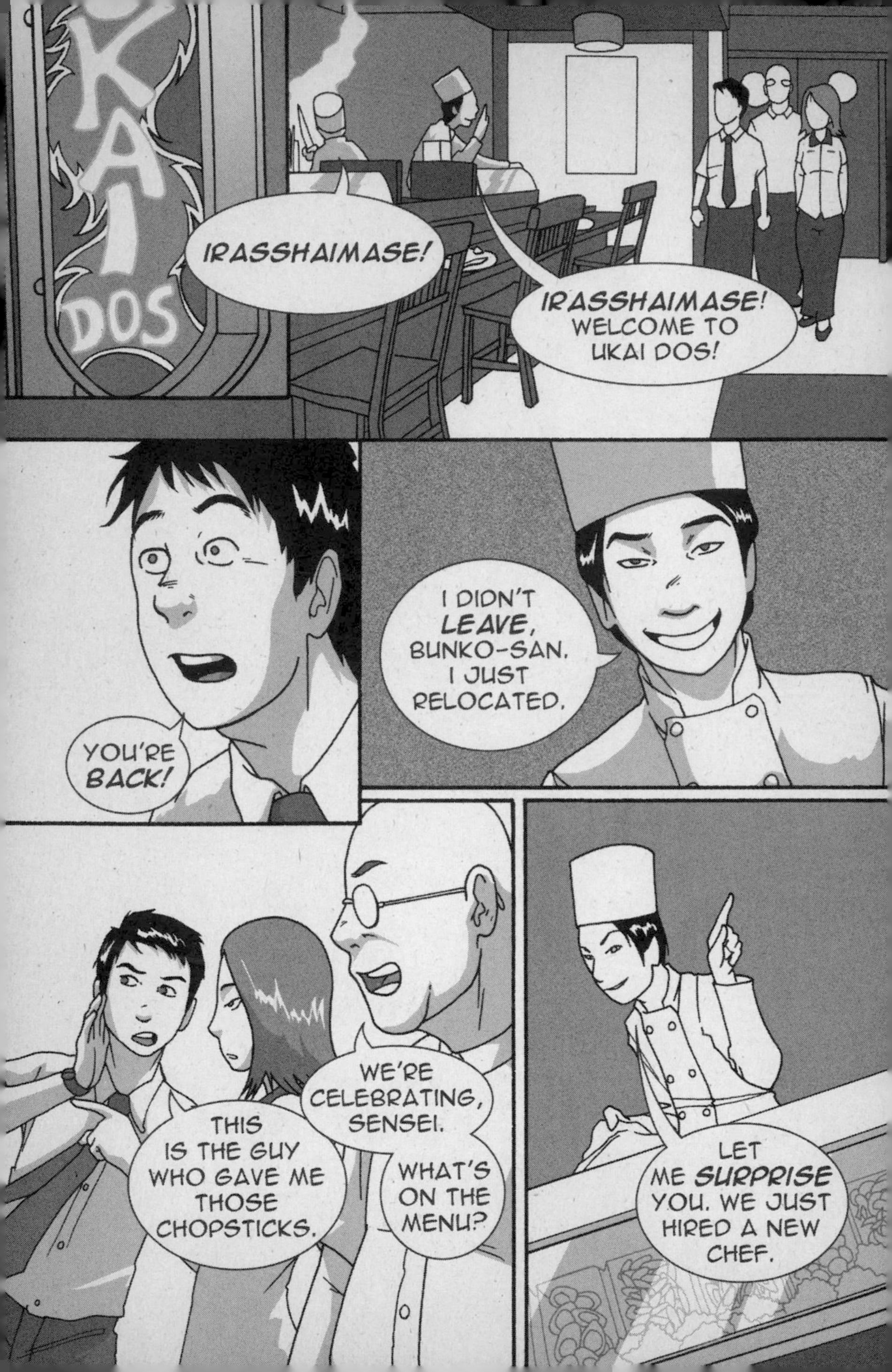

IRASSHAIMASE!
IRASSHAIMASE! WELCOME TO UKAI DOS!
YOU'RE BACK!
I DIDN'T LEAVE, BUNKO-SAN. I JUST RELOCATED.
THIS IS THE GUY WHO GAVE ME THOSE CHOPSTICKS.
WE'RE CELEBRATING, SENSEI.
WHAT'S ON THE MENU?
LET ME SURPRISE YOU. WE JUST HIRED A NEW CHEF.

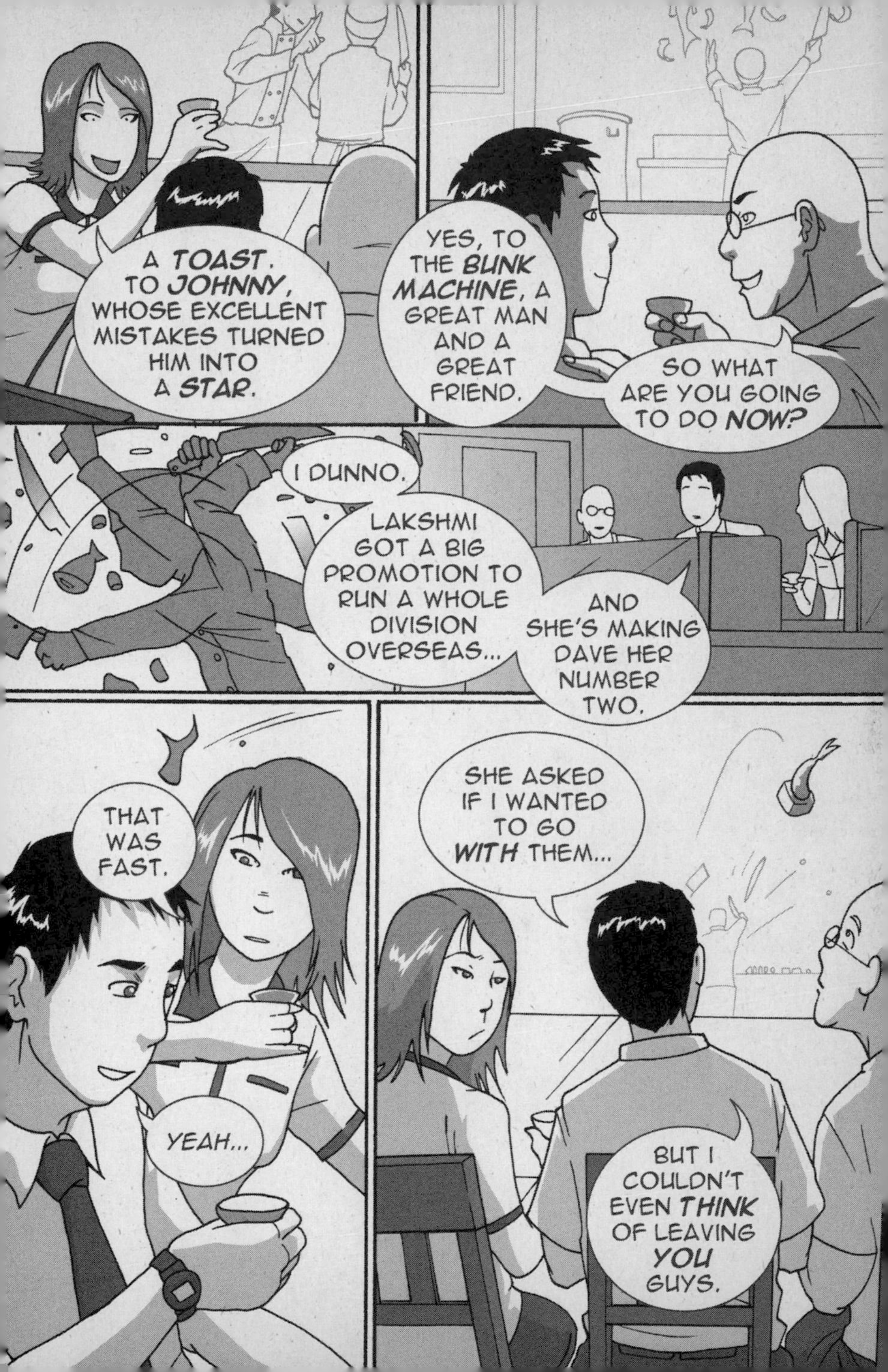
A TOAST. TO JOHNNY, WHOSE EXCELLENT MISTAKES TURNED HIM INTO A STAR.
YES, TO THE BUNK MACHINE, A GREAT MAN AND A GREAT FRIEND.
SO WHAT ARE YOU GOING TO DO NOW?
I DUNNO.
LAKSHMI GOT A BIG PROMOTION TO RUN A WHOLE DIVISION OVERSEAS...
AND SHE'S MAKING DAVE HER NUMBER TWO.
THAT WAS FAST.
YEAH...
SHE ASKED IF I WANTED TO GO WITH THEM...
BUT I COULDN'T EVEN THINK OF LEAVING YOU GUYS.

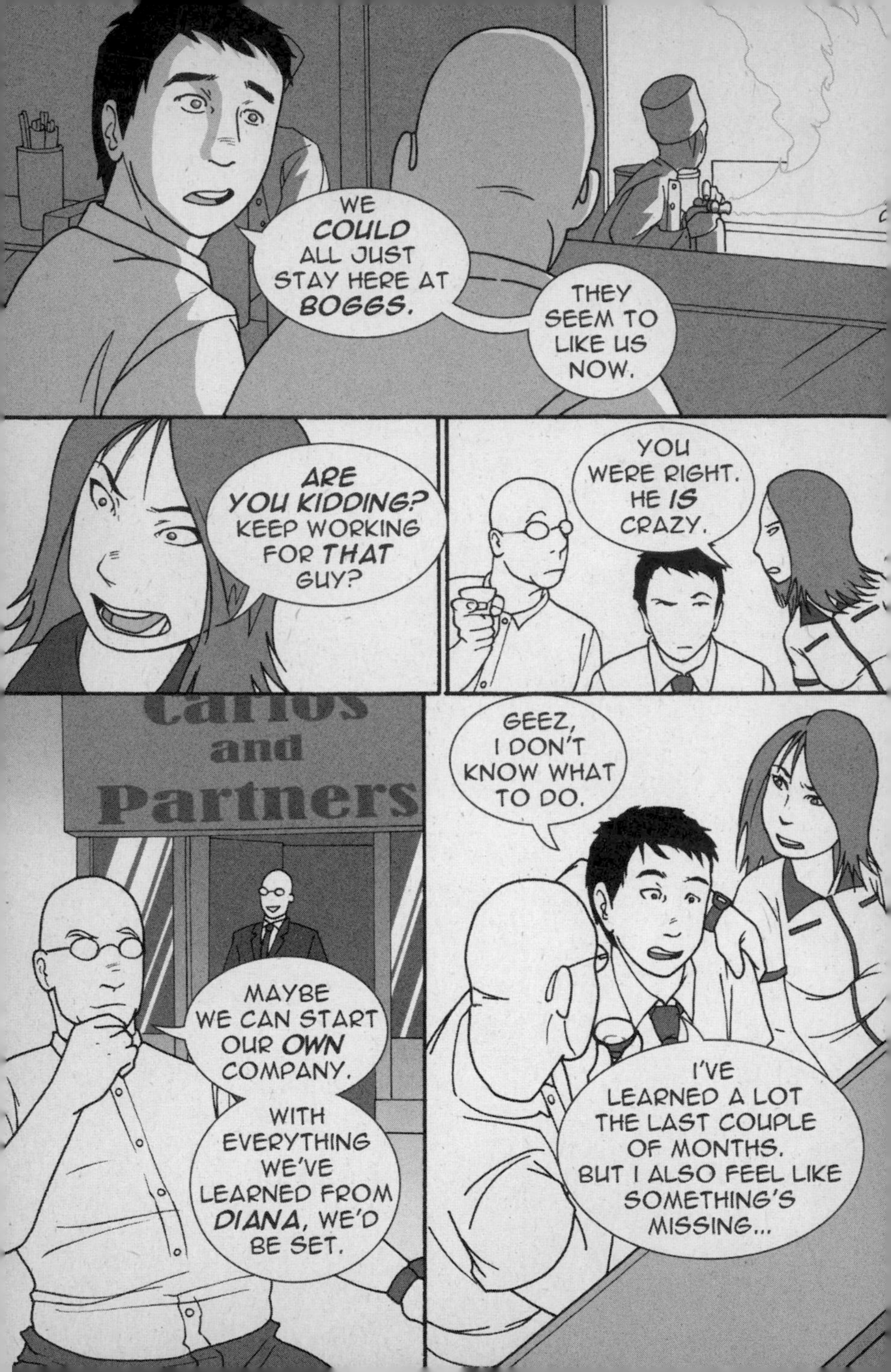
WE COULD ALL JUST STAY HERE AT BOGGS.
THEY SEEM TO LIKE US NOW.
ARE YOU KIDDING? KEEP WORKING FOR THAT GUY?
YOU WERE RIGHT. HE IS CRAZY.
Carlos and Partners
MAYBE WE CAN START OUR OWN COMPANY.
WITH EVERYTHING WE'VE LEARNED FROM DIANA, WE'D BE SET.
GEEZ, I DON'T KNOW WHAT TO DO.
I'VE LEARNED A LOT THE LAST COUPLE OF MONTHS. BUT I ALSO FEEL LIKE SOMETHING'S MISSING...

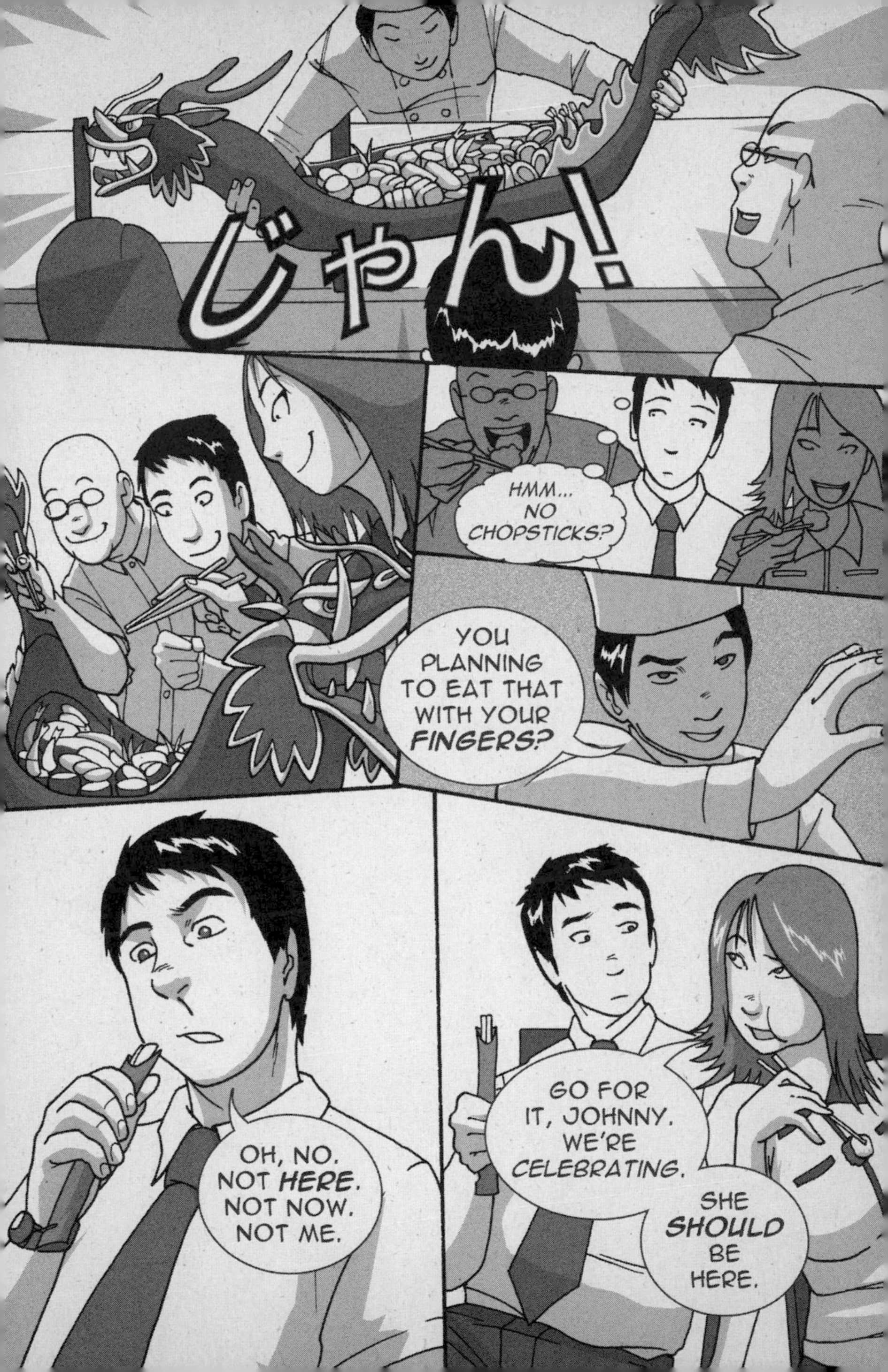
じゃん!
HMM... NO CHOPSTICKS?
YOU PLANNING TO EAT THAT WITH YOUR FINGERS?
OH, NO. NOT HERE. NOT NOW. NOT ME.
GO FOR IT, JOHNNY. WE'RE CELEBRATING.
SHE SHOULD BE HERE.

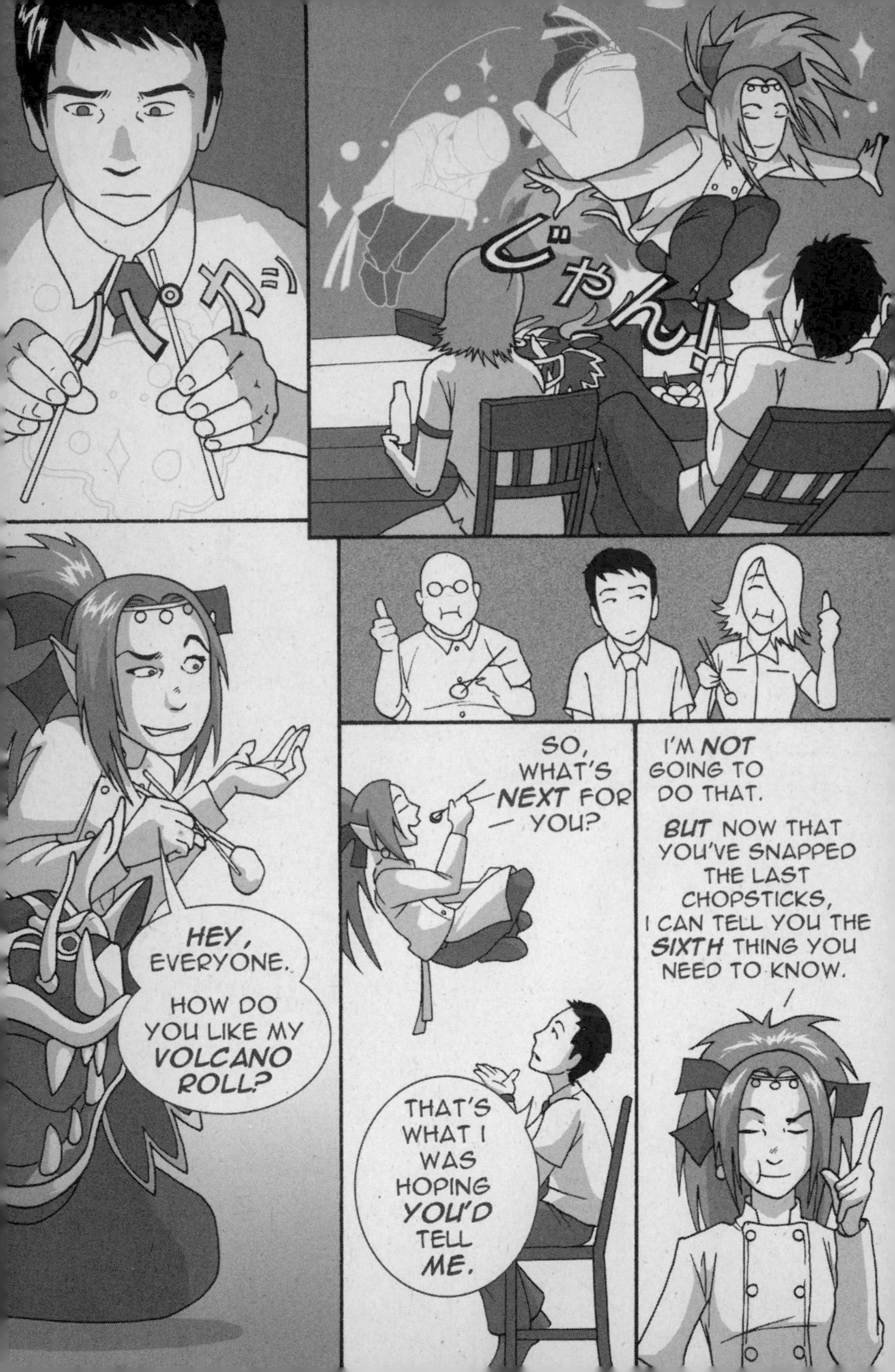

じゃん!
HEY, EVERYONE.
HOW DO YOU LIKE MY VOLCANO ROLL?
SO, WHAT'S NEXT FOR YOU?
THAT'S WHAT I WAS HOPING YOU'D TELL ME.
I'M NOT GOING TO DO THAT.
BUT NOW THAT YOU'VE SNAPPED THE LAST CHOPSTICKS, I CAN TELL YOU THE SIXTH THING YOU NEED TO KNOW.

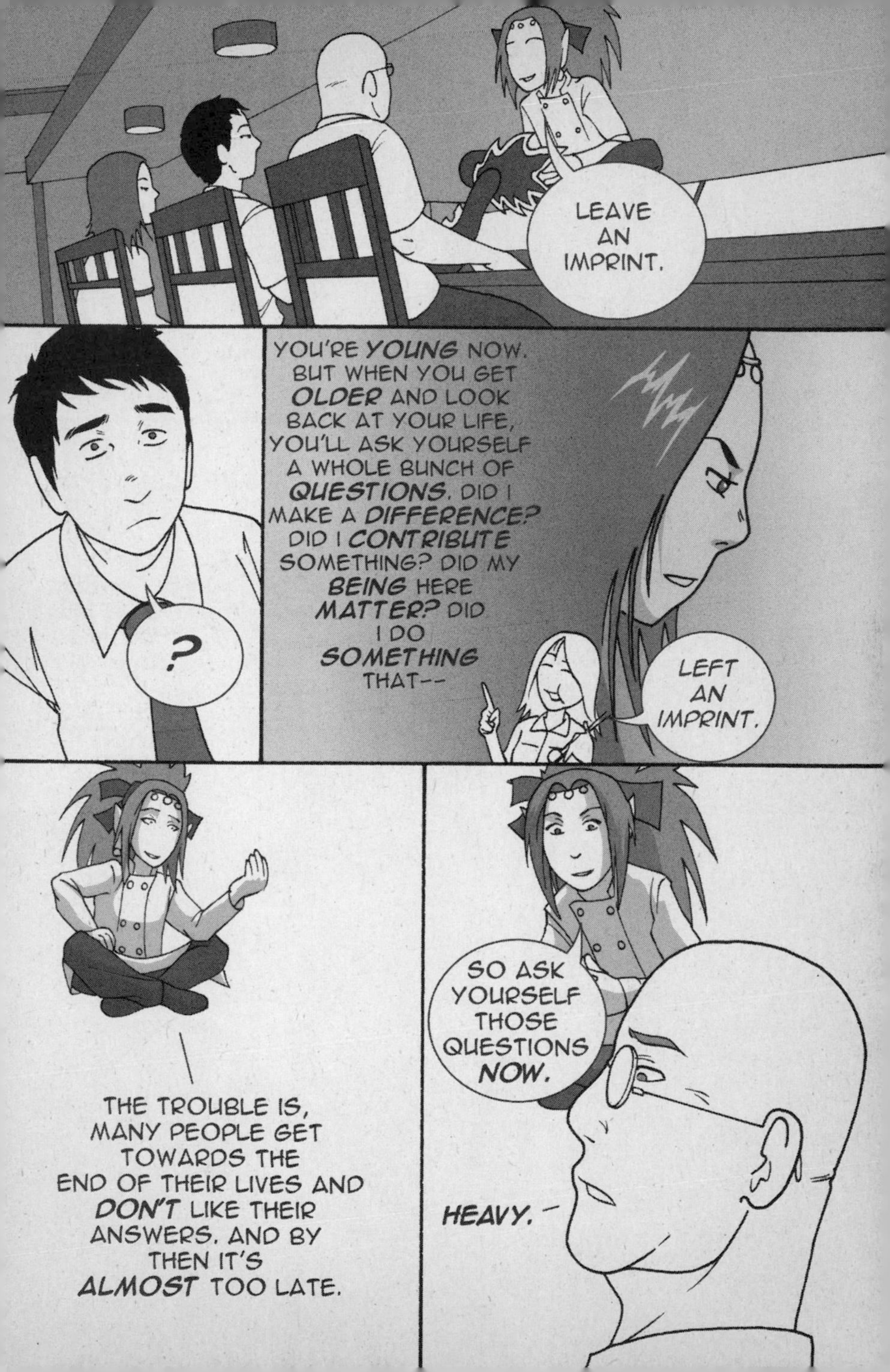
LEAVE AN IMPRINT.
YOU'RE YOUNG NOW. BUT WHEN YOU GET OLDER AND LOOK BACK AT YOUR LIFE, YOU'LL ASK YOURSELF A WHOLE BUNCH OF QUESTIONS. DID I MAKE A DIFFERENCE? DID I CONTRIBUTE SOMETHING? DID MY BEING HERE MATTER? DID I DO SOMETHING THAT--
?
LEFT AN IMPRINT.
THE TROUBLE IS, MANY PEOPLE GET TOWARDS THE END OF THEIR LIVES AND DON'T LIKE THEIR ANSWERS. AND BY THEN IT'S ALMOST TOO LATE.
SO ASK YOURSELF THOSE QUESTIONS NOW.
HEAVY.

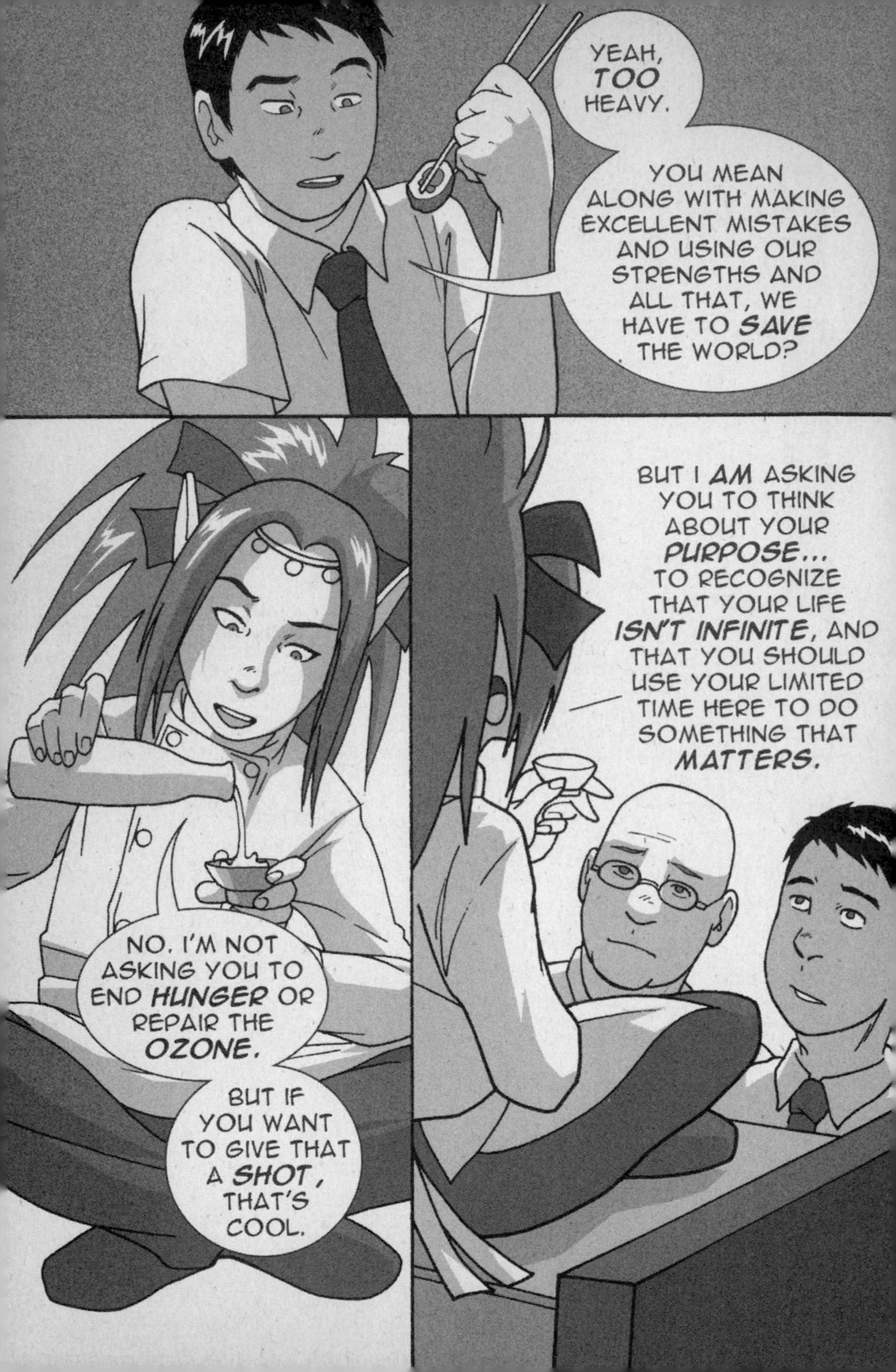
YEAH, TOO HEAVY.
YOU MEAN ALONG WITH MAKING EXCELLENT MISTAKES AND USING OUR STRENGTHS AND ALL THAT, WE HAVE TO SAVE THE WORLD?
NO. I'M NOT ASKING YOU TO END HUNGER OR REPAIR THE OZONE.
BUT IF YOU WANT TO GIVE THAT A SHOT, THAT'S COOL.
BUT I AM ASKING YOU TO THINK ABOUT YOUR PURPOSE... TO RECOGNIZE THAT YOUR LIFE ISN'T INFINITE, AND THAT YOU SHOULD USE YOUR LIMITED TIME HERE TO DO SOMETHING THAT MATTERS.

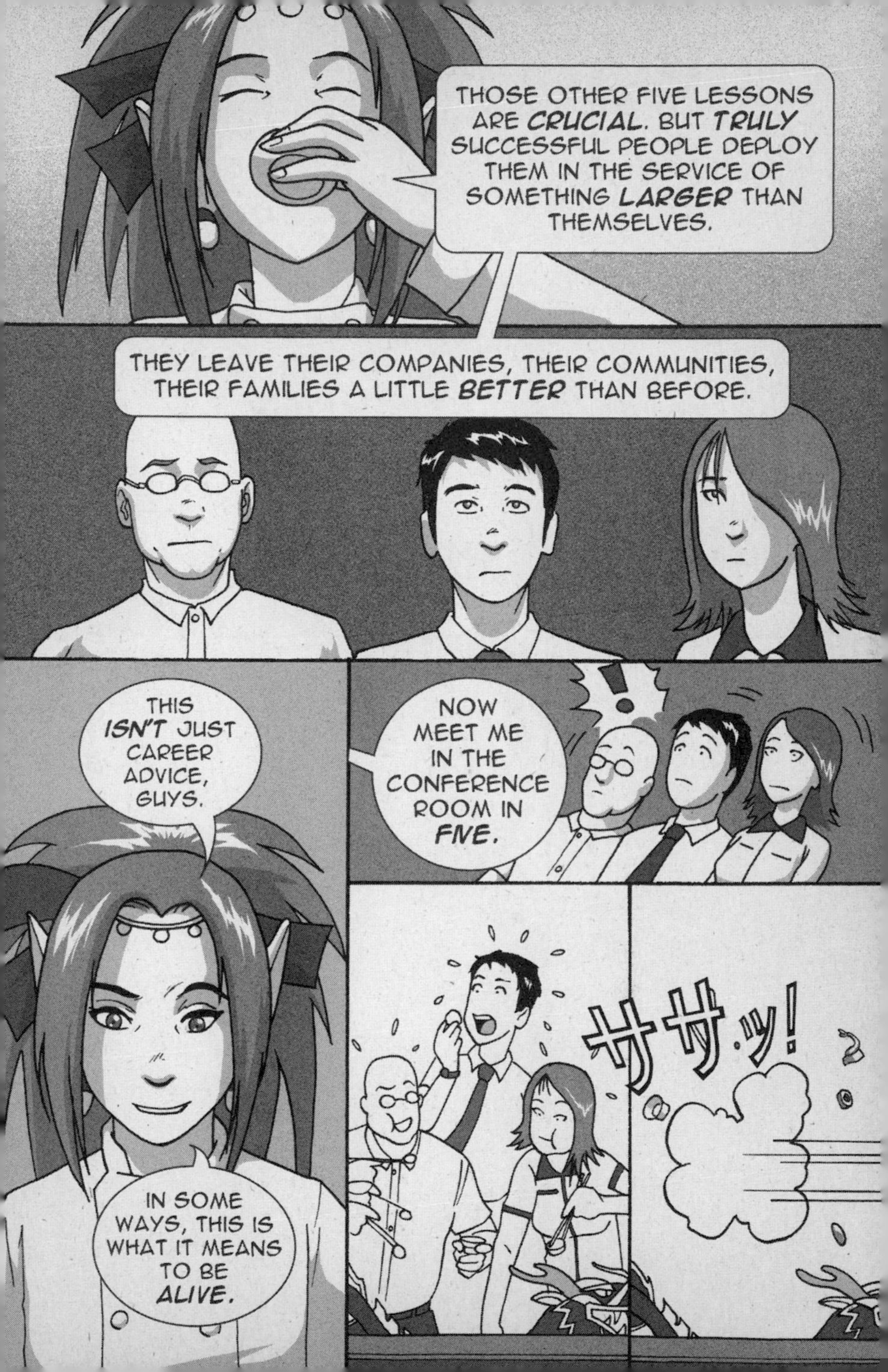
THOSE OTHER FIVE LESSONS ARE CRUCIAL. BUT TRULY SUCCESSFUL PEOPLE DEPLOY THEM IN THE SERVICE OF SOMETHING LARGER THAN THEMSELVES.
THEY LEAVE THEIR COMPANIES, THEIR COMMUNITIES, THEIR FAMILIES A LITTLE BETTER THAN BEFORE.
THIS ISN'T JUST CAREER ADVICE, GUYS.
IN SOME WAYS, THIS IS WHAT IT MEANS TO BE ALIVE.
!
NOW MEET ME IN THE CONFERENCE ROOM IN FIVE.
ササッ!

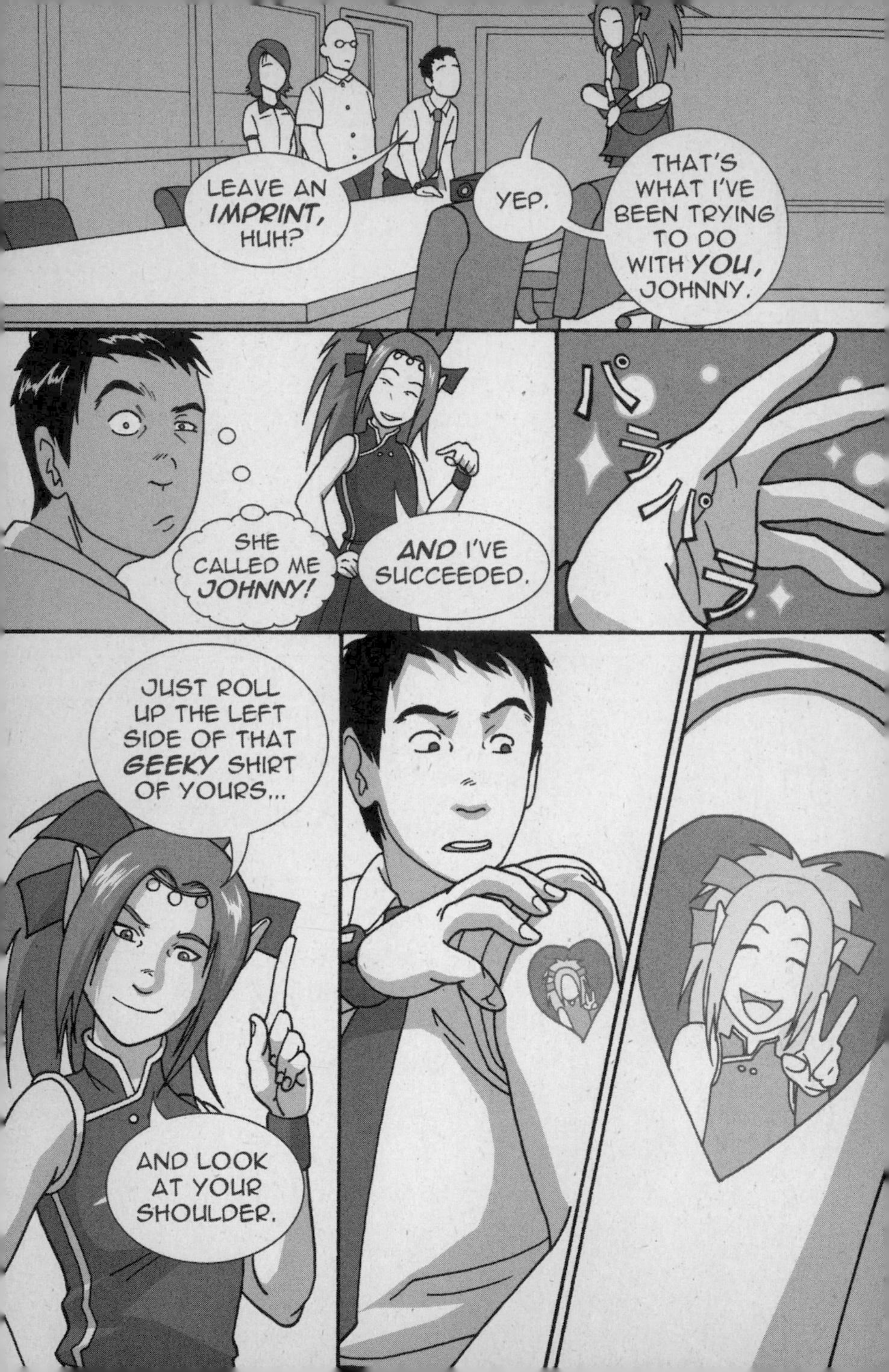
LEAVE AN IMPRINT, HUH?
YEP.
THAT'S WHAT I'VE BEEN TRYING TO DO WITH YOU, JOHNNY.
SHE CALLED ME JOHNNY!
AND I'VE SUCCEEDED.
パラパラ
JUST ROLL UP THE LEFT SIDE OF THAT GEEKY SHIRT OF YOURS...
AND LOOK AT YOUR SHOULDER.

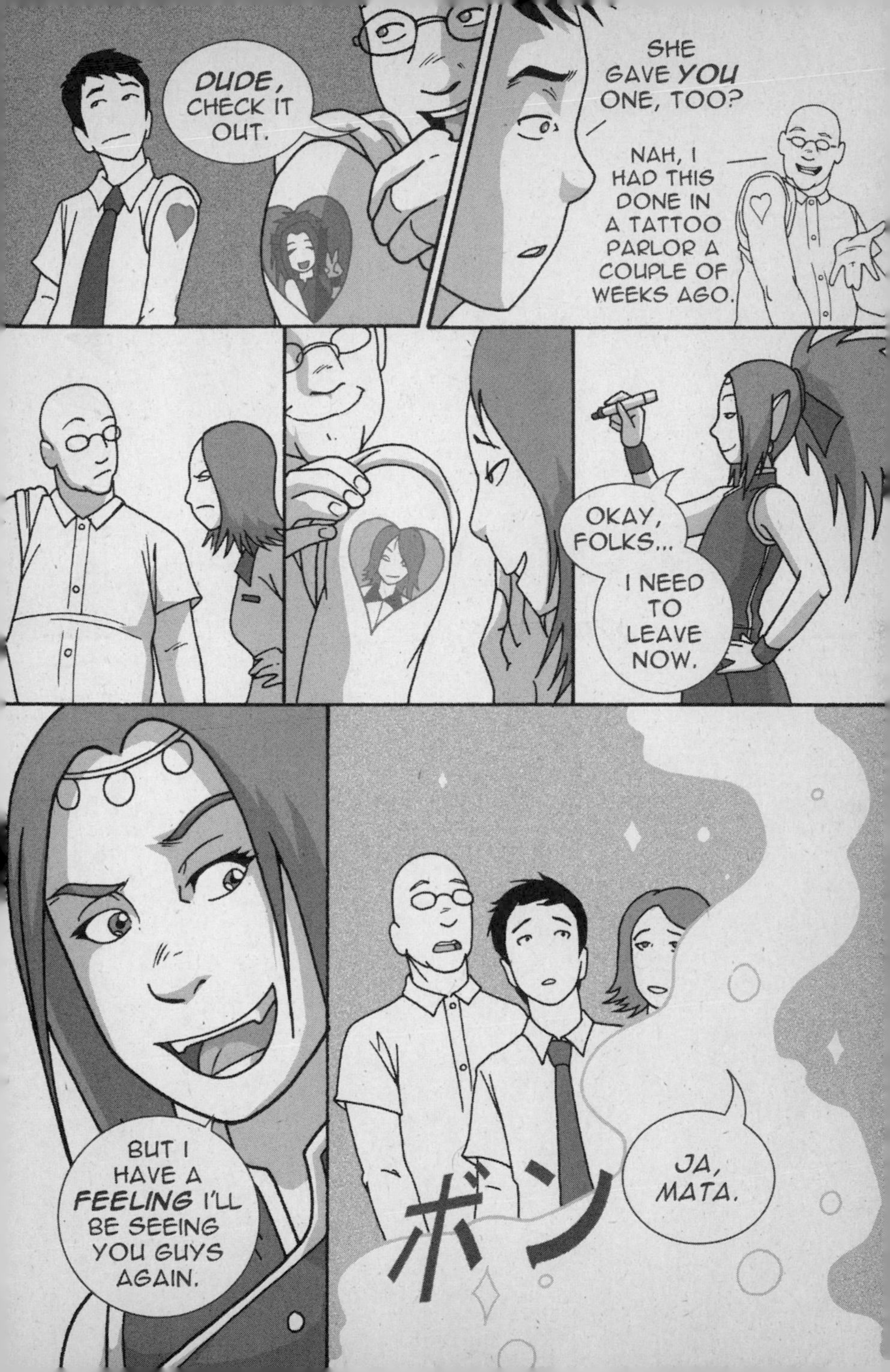
DUDE, CHECK IT OUT.
SHE GAVE YOU ONE, TOO?
NAH, I HAD THIS DONE IN A TATTOO PARLOR A COUPLE OF WEEKS AGO.
OKAY, FOLKS...
I NEED TO LEAVE NOW.
BUT I HAVE A FEELING I'LL BE SEEING YOU GUYS AGAIN.
JA, MATA.
ボン

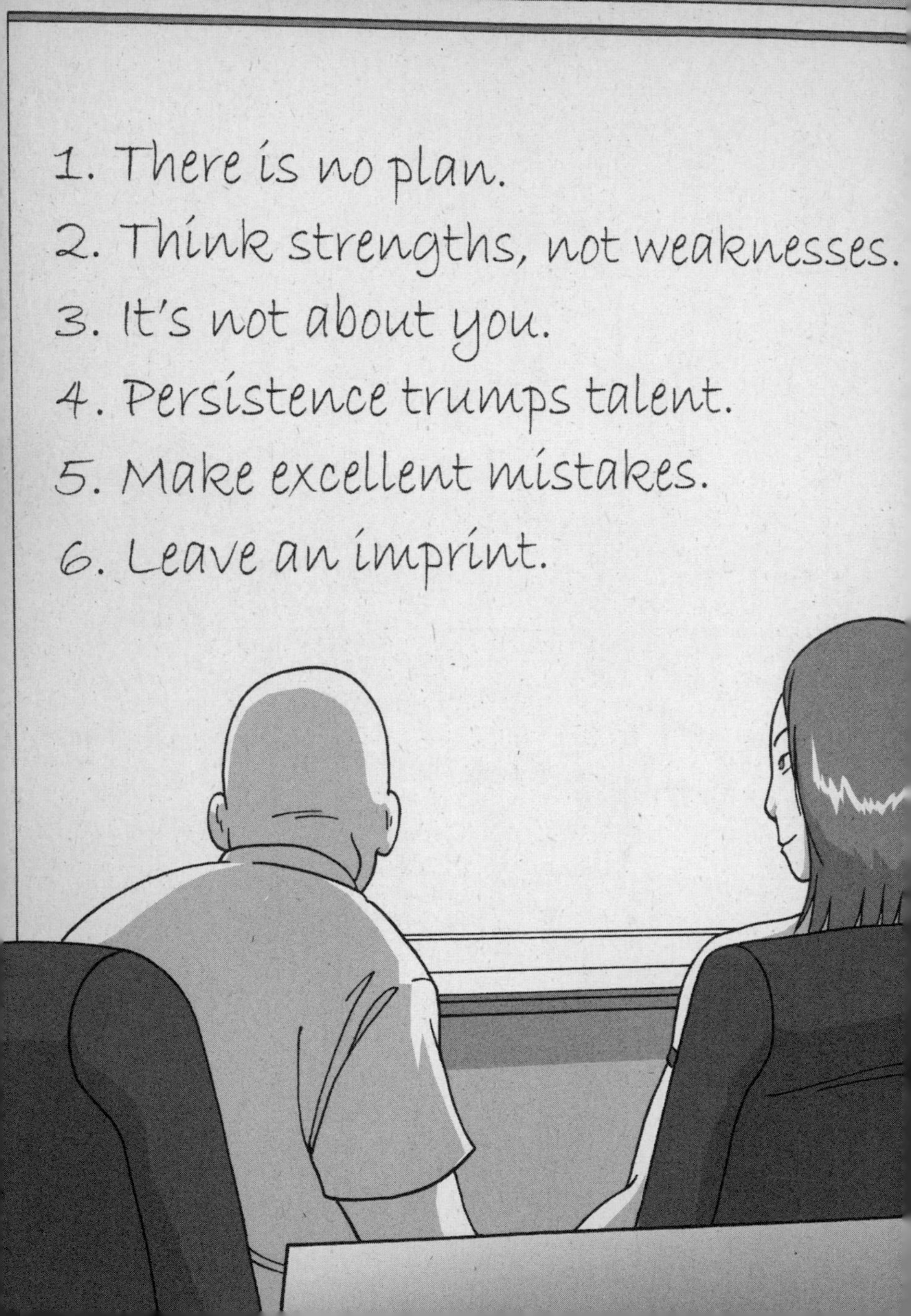
1. There is no plan.
2. Think strengths, not weaknesses.
3. It's not about you.
4. Persistence trumps talent.
5. Make excellent mistakes.
6. Leave an imprint.

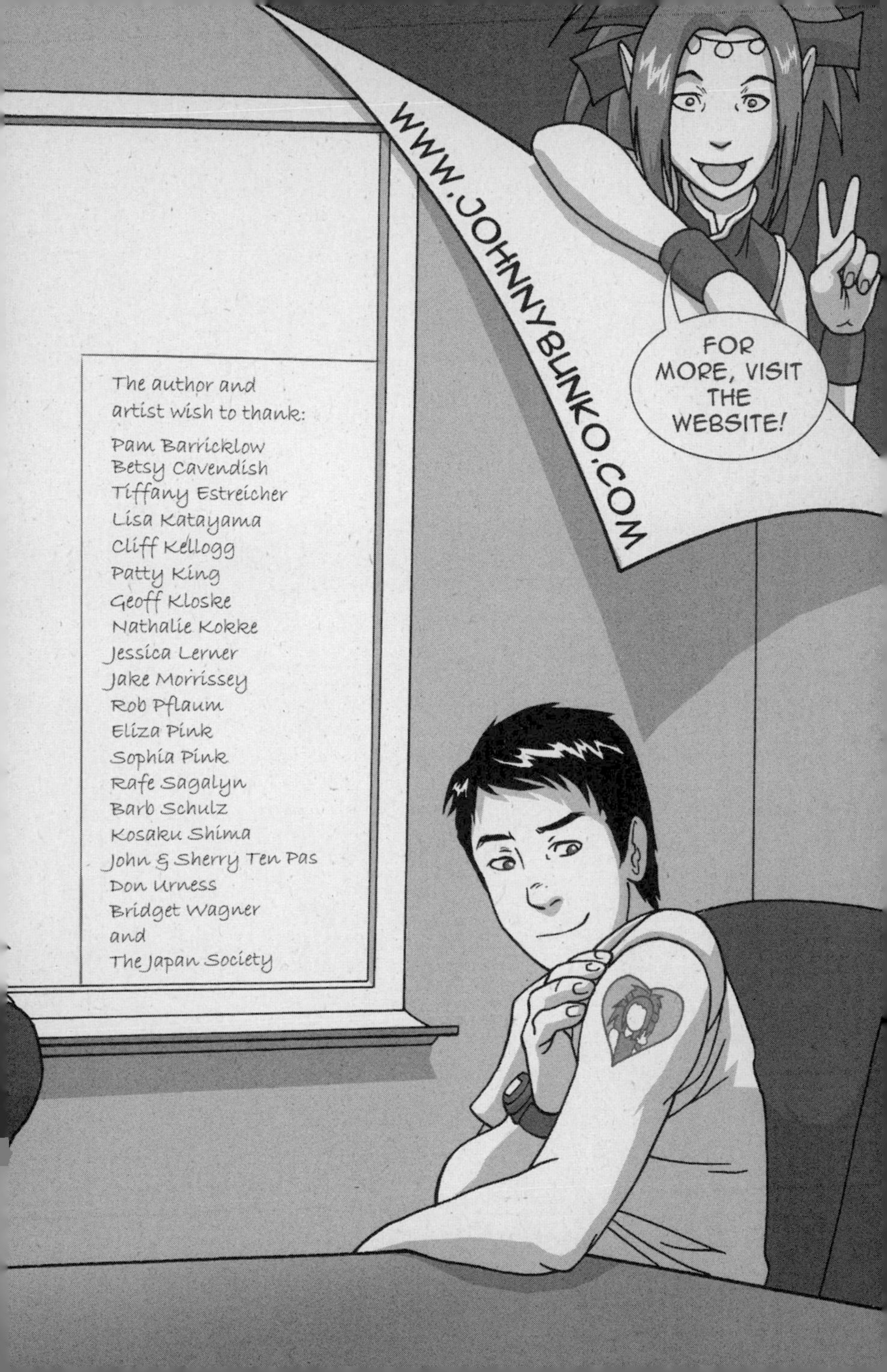
The author and artist wish to thank:
Pam Barricklow
Betsy Cavendish
Tiffany Estreicher
Lisa Katayama
Cliff Kellogg
Patty King
Geoff Kloske
Nathalie Kokke
Jessica Lerner
Jake Morrissey
Rob Pflaum
Eliza Pink
Sophia Pink
Rafe Sagalyn
Barb Schulz
Kosaku Shima
John & Sherry Ten Pas
Don Urness
Bridget Wagner
and
The Japan Society
WWW.JOHNNYBUNKO.COM
FOR MORE, VISIT THE WEBSITE!

RIVERHEAD BOOKS
PUBLISHED BY THE PENGUIN GROUP
PENGUIN GROUP (USA) INC.
375 HUDSON STREET, NEW YORK, NEW YORK 10014, USA
PENGUIN GROUP (CANADA), 90 EGLINTON AVENUE EAST, SUITE 700, TORONTO, ONTARIO M4P 2Y3, CANADA
(A DIVISION OF PEARSON PENGUIN CANADA INC.)
PENGUIN BOOKS LTD., 80 STRAND, LONDON WC2R ORL, ENGLAND
PENGUIN GROUP IRELAND, 25 ST. STEPHEN'S GREEN, DUBLIN 2, IRELAND
(A DIVISION OF PENGUIN BOOKS LTD.)
PENGUIN GROUP (AUSTRALIA), 250 CAMBERWELL ROAD, CAMBERWELL, VICTORIA 3124, AUSTRALIA
(A DIVISION OF PEARSON AUSTRALIA GROUP PTY. LTD.)
PENGUIN BOOKS INDIA PVT. LTD., 11 COMMUNITY CENTRE, PANCHSHEEL PARK, NEW DELHI -- 110 017, INDIA
PENGUIN GROUP (NZ), 67 APOLLO DRIVE, ROSEDALE, NORTH SHORE 0632, NEW ZEALAND
(A DIVISION OF PEARSON NEW ZEALAND LTD.)
PENGUIN BOOKS (SOUTH AFRICA) (PTY.) LTD., 24 STURDEE AVENUE, ROSEBANK, JOHANNESBURG 2196,
SOUTH AFRICA

PENGUIN BOOKS LTD., REGISTERED OFFICES: 80 STRAND, LONDON WC2R ORL, ENGLAND

THE PUBLISHER DOES NOT HAVE ANY CONTROL OVER AND DOES NOT
ASSUME ANY RESPONSIBILITY FOR AUTHOR OR THIRD-PARTY WEBSITES OR THEIR CONTENT.

THE ADVENTURES OF JOHNNY BUNKO

FIRST RIVERHEAD TRADE PAPERBACK EDITION: APRIL 2008

ISBN: 978-1-59448-291-5

AN APPLICATION TO REGISTER THIS BOOK FOR CATALOGING HAS
BEEN SUBMITTED TO THE LIBRARY OF CONGRESS.

PRINTED IN THE UNITED STATES OF AMERICA

10   9   8   7   6   5   4   3   2   1